COMPARING CULTURES

INTERNATIONAL STUDIES
IN
SOCIOLOGY AND SOCIAL ANTHROPOLOGY

EDITED BY

Tukumbi Lumumba-Kasongo,
Rubin Patterson and Masamichi Sasaki

VOLUME XCIII

COMPARING CULTURES

Dimensions of Culture in a Comparative Perspective

EDITED BY

HENK VINKEN, JOSEPH SOETERS AND PETER ESTER

BRILL

LEIDEN · BOSTON

2004

This book is printed on acid-free paper.

Library of Congress Cataloging-in-Publication Data

Comparing cultures : dimensions of culture in a comparative perspective / edited by Henk
Vinken, Joseph Soeters and Peter Ester.
    p. cm. — (International studies in sociology and social anthropology, ISSN 0074-8684 ;
v. 93)
    Includes bibliographical references and index.
    ISBN 90-04-13115-9 (pbk. : alk. paper)
    1. Cross-cultural studies. 2. Sociology—Research—Methodology. I. Vinken, Henk. II.
Soeters, J. III. Ester, P. IV. Series.

GN345.7.C66 2004
306—dc22

                                                                        2003065320

ISSN 0074-8684
ISBN 90 04 13115 9

PRINTED IN THE NETHERLANDS

CONTENTS

CONTRIBUTORS

Isabelle Albert (1975) is a doctoral student in developmental psychology and cross-cultural psychology at the University of Konstanz. She received her diploma in psychology from the University of Trier in 2001 and spent one year of studies in Bologna, Italy. Her primary research interests are in the areas of intergenerational relations and value transmission in cross-cultural comparison. She is specialized on European cultures like Italy and France and will focus on German-French comparisons for her dissertation.

Cecilia Benoit (1954) is a Professor in the Department of Sociology at the University of Victoria, Canada, and executive member of one of Canada's five national Centres of Women's Health. Her recent research projects have focused on the historical transformation of midwifery and maternity care, non-urban women's access to maternity care, and the health concerns of Aboriginal women in Vancouver's Downtown Eastside. Other projects have involved investigation of the working conditions, health status and access to health services of marginalized service workers. She has published over 50 books, journal articles, book chapters and scientific research reports.

Allan Bird (1953) is the Eiichi Shibusawa-Seigo Arai Professor of Japanese Studies in the College of Business Administration, University of Missouri-St. Louis, USA, and the Director of the International Business Institute. His current research focuses on the role of sense making in cross-cultural work settings. He also conducts research on Japanese companies and their senior executives. He co-edited, with Schon Beechler, *Japanese Multinationals Abroad: Individual and Organizational Learning*. His most recent volume is *The Encyclopedia of Japanese Business and Management*. He has served as a consultant to Japanese and American companies as well as to the Japanese several trade associations.

Raymond de Vries (1951) is Professor of Sociology at St. Olaf College in Northfield, Minnesota, USA, and visiting professor at the Center for Bioethics at the University of Minnesota. He has done a great deal of research on maternity care and midwifery and has just completed a book, *A Pleasing Birth* (Temple University Press), on the maternity care system of the Netherlands. He is the editor of *Birth By Design* (Routledge) and

Bioethics and Society (Prentice-Hall). He is currently at work on a sociological study of the emergence of the profession of bioethics.

Eugene Declercq (1949) is Professor of Maternal and Child Health and Assistant Dean for Doctoral Education at the Boston University School of Public Health, USA. He is President of the Association of Teachers of Maternal and Child Health and the lead author of the 2002 report Listening to Mothers. His current research is focused on issues relating to cesarean birth.

Pieter Drenth (1935) studied at the Vrije Universiteit, Amsterdam, the Netherlands, and New York University, New York, USA (PhD in 1960). He has been professor of psychology at the Vrije Universiteit, Amsterdam since 1967. He has published widely on intelligence theory, testtheory, organizational psychology and cross-cultural psychology. He received an honorary doctors degree from the Universities of Gent and Paris (V). From 1982-1987 he was Rector Magnificus of the Vrije Universiteit, and from 1990-1996 President of the Royal Netherlands Academy of Arts and Sciences. Since 2000 he is President of All European Academies (ALLEA).

Peter Ester (1953) is Professor of Sociology at Tilburg University, the Netherlands, Director of OSA, Institute for Labor Studies, and Program Director Civil Society at Globus, Institute for Globalization and Sustainable Development. He was visiting professor at the University of Michigan (Ann Arbor) and ZUMA, Center for Survey Methodology and Analysis (Mannheim) and authored over 160 publications. Ester is the former chairman of the Dutch Association of Social and Cultural Sciences.

Geert Hofstede (1928) is Professor Emeritus of Organizational Anthropology and International Management of Maastricht University, the Netherlands. Since his retirement in 1993 he has been a Fellow of IRIC, Institute for Research on Intercultural Cooperation, of which he was a co-founder, and of the CentER for Economic Research, at Tilburg University. He was a pioneer of comparative intercultural research; his ideas are used worldwide.

Ronald Inglehart (1934) is a Professor of Political Science and Program Director at the Institute for Social Research at the University of Michigan, USA. He helped found the Euro-Barometer surveys and directs the World Values Surveys. His research deals with changing belief systems and their impact on social and political change. His most recent books are Modernization and Postmodernization (1997), Human Values and Beliefs (1998), (with Pippa Norris) Rising Tide (2003), and Mass Values and Social Change (2003).

Author of over 170 publications, he has been a visiting scholar in Europe, Asia, South America and Africa, and has served as a consultant to the U.S. State Department and the European Union.

Wolfgang Jagodzinski (1943) is Professor of Sociology, Director of the Institute for Applied Social Research, and Director of the Central Archive for Empirical Social Research (ZA), all at the University of Cologne, Germany. He was a Visiting Professor in Tucson, Arizona, and Kwansei Gakuin University, Japan. He has published empirical research in political sociology and value change in national and international journals and books. Religion and moral values have become a more central focus in these publications. He has been and still is active in international research projects, such as the European Science Foundation (ESF) 'Beliefs in Government' Project, the ESF-project 'Religious and Moral Pluralism' (RAMP), the International Social Survey Programme (ISSP), and the European Values Study (EVS).

Antonios K. Klidas (1971) is a Research Fellow at IRIC, Institute for Research on Intercultural Cooperation, and Assistant Professor at the Department of Leisure Studies, at Tilburg University in the Netherlands. He holds a BSc degree in Management and Business Administration from the Athens University of Economics and Business in Greece and an MSc degree in International Hotel Management from the University of Surrey in England. He obtained his doctorate degree in 2001 from Tilburg University following a Marie Curie Fellowship from the European Commission.

Kazufumi Manabe (1942) is a Professor of Sociology and Research Methodology at Kwansei Gakuin University, Japan. His research interests include political culture, postmodern values and global communications. He has published more than 100 books, book chapters, and journal articles. He is a participant of the international comparative project called International Social Survey Programme. He is now exploring the possibilities of secondary analysis of large-scale multi-national survey data for the advancement of comparative research in sociology. He also has had research and teaching experiences in Israel, USA, Germany, France, and China.

Boris Mayer (1973) is a doctoral student in developmental psychology and cross-cultural psychology at the University of Konstanz. He received his diploma in psychology from the University of Konstanz in 2002 after studying one semester in Seoul, Korea. His primary research interests are in German-Korean comparisons of adolescent and family development as well as in cross-cultural methodology.

[x]

Lynn E. Metcalf (1956) is Professor of Marketing at California Polytechnic State University, USA. Her current research interests encompass university-industry alliances and cross-cultural negotiation. Her teaching specializations include international marketing, Internet marketing, high-tech marketing. From 1995-1999, Dr. Metcalf was on leave from Cal Poly. As Director of University Alliances for Royal Philips Electronics, her role was to build strategic alliances with world-class universities in the US — primarily Stanford, Berkeley, and MIT. Dr. Metcalf maintains currency in developments in the high-tech sectors of the US economy via consulting assignments.

Hans-Peter Müller (1942) is Professor of Social Anthropology at the University of Zürich, Switzerland. He spent nine years in West Africa and South Asia for UNHCR, for the Swiss Development Corporation, and for anthropological field research. In recent years, he developed national indicators of the socio-economic characteristics of pre-colonial societies for 95 African and Asian countries. His main publications deal with cross-cultural and cross-national analysis, rural sociology, and social movements.

Daphna Oyserman (1960), Ph.D. University of Michigan, USA, is an Associate Professor at the University of Michigan with joint appointments in the Department of Psychology and the School of Social Work, as well as the Institute for Social Research, where she is an Associate Research Scientist. Her research focuses on self-concept and self-regulation, one line of research focuses on racial identity and social cognition, particularly how social and cultural contexts influence self-concept, judgment, reasoning, attribution and important everyday behaviors (e.g. school persistence and academic attainment) and the effect of self-concept and racial identity on motivation, reasoning and behavior. A second line of research focuses on cultural and cross-cultural psychology and multiculturalism and their implications for how we think.

Karen Phalet (1963) is an Associate Professor of Cross-Cultural Psychology and a Permanent Research Fellow of ERCOMER (European Research Center On Migration and Ethnic Relations) and ICS (Inter-university Center for Social Science Theory and Methodology) at Utrecht University, the Netherlands. She has published extensively on issues of acculturation and multiculturalism in a comparative European perspective. The present paper was written during a 2000-2001 visiting fellowship at CISB (Center for the Interdisciplinary Study of Brussels), VU Brussels, Belgium.

Shalom H. Schwartz (1936), a social and cross-cultural psychologist, is the Sznajderman Professor of Psychology at the Hebrew University in

Jerusalem, Israel. He is President-elect of the International Association of Cross-Cultural Psychology. His present research focuses on the social and psychological antecedents and consequences of individual differences in value priorities and on the social structural and historical sources of national [xi] differences in cultural orientations and on their implications for social policy and individual behavior and welfare. He has published over 100 articles, books, and chapters.

Joseph Soeters (1954) is Professor of Social Sciences at the Royal Netherlands' Military Academy and Professor of Organizational Sociology at Tilburg University, the Netherlands. From 1999 to 2003 he was Dean of Studies at the Academy. His main research interests focus on international cooperation between organizations (mergers, joint ventures and temporary collaboration in emergency — for instance post-conflict-situations); in addition, he works on Human Resources and diversity management (both in a Western and non-Western context). He has published over 140 books, articles and chapters in Dutch and international publications.

Marc Swyngedouw (1956) is Professor of Political Sciences and Academic Director of IPSOM (Institute for Political Sociology and Methodology) and ISPO (Inter-university Center on Politics and Public Opinion Research) at the Universities of Leuven and Brussels, Belgium. His extensive publications are concerned mainly with electoral studies, social science methodology, political cleavages, extreme right parties and ethnic minorities.

Harry C. Triandis (1926) is Professor of Psychology Emeritus at the University of Illinois, Champaign-Urbana, USA. He was President of the International Association of Cross-Cultural Psychology, the Society for the Psychological Study of Social Issues, the Society for Personality and Social Psychology, the Interamerican Society of Psychology, the Society for Cross-Cultural Research, and the International Association of Applied Psychology. He has published more than 200 journal papers, chapters, and seven books and has edited two handbooks. Some have been translated into Japanese, German, and Spanish. He received an honorary degree from the University of Athens, Greece.

Gisela Trommsdorff (1941) is Professor and Chair of Developmental Psychology and Cross-Cultural Psychology in the Department of Psychology at the University of Konstanz, Germany. She is Vice-President of the German-Japanese Society for Social Sciences and has frequently been a Visiting Professor in Japan, e.g. at Keio University in Tokyo, Japan. She has functions in numerous international scientific committees and editorial boards of scientific journals in youth studies, psychology, and sociology. Her current research focuses at cross-cultural studies on intergenerational relations, child-parent relationships, and subjective parenting theories; at values of children, development of emotions, and pro-social behavior, control orientations, future time perspectives, and value change.

Edwin van Teijlingen (1960) is a medical sociologist, Senior Lecturer in the Department of Public Health and Researcher in the Dugald Baird Centre for Research on Women's Health, University of Aberdeen, UK. His present research focuses on organization of maternity care, health promotion and psychosocial aspects of the new genetics. He has published nearly 100 books, journal articles, book chapters and scientific research reports.

Henk Vinken (1962) is a sociologist, Director of IRIC, Institute for Research on Intercultural Cooperation, and Senior Fellow at Globus, Institute for Globalization and Sustainable Development, at Tilburg University, the Netherlands. His present research focuses on cultural change, citizenship, life courses, future orientations, and (young) generations in a cross-cultural perspective. He has published almost 100 books, journal articles, book chapters and scientific research reports.

Sirpa Wrede (1963) is a sociologist, Academy Research Fellow at Academy of Finland and Researcher at the Department of Sociology, Åbo Akademi University, Finland. She has published internationally on comparative research on maternity care and midwifery and on health care occupations. Her ongoing research deals with the recent reshaping of professional groups that provide welfare services. Wrede's work with the article was funded through the Academy of Finland project "Service Professions in Transition".

Patrick Ziltener (1967) is a sociologist, Ph.D. from the University of Zurich, Switzerland. Since 1995 he has conducted empirical research at the Sociological Institute of the University of Zurich, in areas of political and economic sociology and from 2000-2002 at the Max-Planck-Institute for the Study of Societies, Cologne, Germany. His present research focuses on the cultural and historical determinants of the rise of East Asia.

ACKNOWLEDGEMENTS

The editors of this book would like to thank IRIC, Institute for Research on Intercultural Cooperation, and Globus, Institute for Globalization and Sustainable Development, at Tilburg University, Tilburg, the Netherlands, for supporting this book. We especially like to thank Rianne Mutsaers, Ludo van Dun, Hans van Poppel, and Carlo Praet (all at IRIC) and Petra van der Ham and Paul van Seters (Globus) for their inspiring comments and continuing support, also in the more practical sides of an international book project like this. We are grateful to Amelia Román for helping us enhance our use of the English language.

We are grateful to Loek Halman and Fons van de Vijver, both of the Department of Social and Behavioral Sciences at Tilburg University, for their initial support at the very start of this book project following IRIC's international conference Comparing Culture, April 27, 2001. We also thank them for chairing sessions at this conference. With much gratitude for the very same reason we acknowledge the invaluable help of Paul Dekker (Globus, Tilburg University), Irena Guidikova (Council of Europe, France), Romi Littrel (Aalen University, Germany), Ad van Iterson (University of Maastricht, the Netherlands), and Arzu Wasti (Sabanci University, Turkey). We also thank the many participants of this conference that helped make it an academically productive and lively event. We convey our greatest gratitude to Lieke Jonker and Marijn van Vilsteren, graphic designers for supporting the conference with their graphical materials, to Wim Luyendijk, alderman of the City of Tilburg, for the warm welcome to the conference participants, to Lucia King, visual artist, for her impressive artistic performance during the conference, and to conference manager Hans van Poppel, conference secretaries Matthijs Visser and Rianne Mutsaers and IRIC staff Susanne Duffin, Ludo van Dun, Henk Dekkers, Ard van der Kruis, Toon van der Kwast, Mieke Lustenhouwer, Mihaela Muresan, and Jason Sanders for their enthusiastic assistance during the course of the conference. Without their input and help this book would never have been written.

Culture's consequences revisited

PIETER J.D. DRENTH

On April 27, 2001 an interesting conference took place at Tilburg University on the subject of recent developments in research on cross-cultural comparison of organizations and human behavior. Tilburg University is a pre-eminently suitable location for such a conference, being the domicile of IRIC, Institute for Research on Intercultural Cooperation, as well as accommodating the "nerve center" of the European Value Study EVS, a large-scale, cross-national, and longitudinal survey research program on basic human values in Europe.

The immediate cause for the conference was a momentous event: the publication of the second, revised edition of Geert Hofstede's book "Culture's Consequences". The first edition appeared in 1980 with the subtitle "international differences in work-related values". The study was based on a survey among employees of a multinational corporation in 1968 and 1972, producing over 115.000 questionnaires. Hofstede processed and analyzed these data in a both scholarly and imaginative fashion, and published his findings and interpretations in a tome of almost 500 pages. His book became a classic and is one of the most cited sources in the entire Social Science Citation Index at present. The second edition carries the subtitle "comparing values, behaviors, institutions, and organizations across nations", stressing the cross-disciplinary aspirations as well as the multi-level nature of his analyses. In the new edition the number of represented countries has raised from 40 to 50, a fifth dimension (long-term versus short- term orientation) has been added to the famous original four: power distance, uncertainty avoidance, individualism-collectivism, and masculinity-femininity, and more recent literature since the first edition, including the many references and criticisms, has been incorporated as far as possible. The result is a second monument. Surely it will be widely read and quoted again. No future cross-cultural researcher or student will be able to get round this book. Geert Hofstede will continue to be the most frequently cited Dutch social scientist for quite some time.

The present volume comprises in the first place the contributions of four other speakers at the Tilburg conference. These speakers were selected so as to represent a number of other major cross-national or cross-cultural studies.

[2]

In the first place Harry Triandis, whom many psychologists would consider as one of the true godfathers of cross-cultural psychology. In his numerous cross-cultural comparative studies, for instance on "collectivism versus individualism" which he considers as one of the essential cultural dimensions, Triandis has always shown an enlightening insight in both the compatibilities between cultures and the singularities of indigenous cultures. His chapter is another proof of this insight.

Secondly the originator and leader of another major international study on individual values Shalom Schwartz. He shares with Hofstede the view that the prevailing emphases in a society may be the most central feature of culture, since they shape individual beliefs, actions and goals, and express shared conceptions of what is good and desirable in culture. He collected data in a great many countries in the world, comprising over 75% of the world population, and used these data to develop an interesting and comprehensive typology of cultural dimensions. In his chapter he describes this typology and discusses possible causes and consequences.

The third speaker, Ronald Inglehart, originally joined the EVS team, contributing to the study data and background information on the 'new' (European) world, the US and Canada. Later he extended the study to other non-European countries, resulting in a separate research endeavor, called the World Value Survey. Cooperation with the European Value Study has resulted in a global research program, that studies national similarities and differences in values over time (so far data has been gathered from 1981 through 2002) and worldwide (covering 80 societies containing some 85% of the world's population). Inglehart may be best known for his book on "modernization and postmodernization", which analyzes the cultural, economic, and political change in a large number of societies in the world, making use of the data from EVS and WVS. In his article he emphasizes again that economic development produces pervasive social and cultural consequences.

The fourth speaker was Wolfgang Jagodzinski, a German sociologist, director of the Central Archive ZA-EUROLAB in Köln, which is specialized in building data bases for comparative research and for training in advanced social science research methods and data management and archiving. Jagodzinski is member of the EVS-team, and responsible for the preservation and accessibility of the EVS-data. In his presentation he shed light on the too often unrecognized difficulties and pitfalls in cross-national comparative studies.

At the end of the conference the floor was given to Geert Hofstede, who used the occasion to unfold again the stages of development of the first edition of "Culture's Consequences", and the subsequent efforts to produce the second edition, and, further, to dwell on the different presentations of the afternoon. Many of these concluding observations can be found in the Epilogue of the present volume. [3]

This book encompasses more than just the five contributions of the intellectual leaders of major cross-cultural research programs or 'schools'. It further contains an interesting selection of empirical studies or theoretical elaborations of the themes discussed in the foregoing contributions. It is encouraging to see that a next generation of social scientists is eagerly picking up the challenges left by the 'patriarchs'. The subjects vary from nationalism to immigration, and from maternity care to empowerment and negotiating strategies in organizations. It is a small selection from a rapidly growing supply of cross-cultural studies. After a long time of reluctance researchers in psychology and social sciences are now increasingly turning their interest to the importance of cultural factors in understanding differences or (sometimes) similarities in behavior of people being raised and living in different cultural environments.

And in point of fact, such an increasing scientific interest is not needless. Quite a number of conceptual and methodological questions in cross-cultural research have remained unanswered as yet and need further theoretical consideration or empirical testing. To give a few random examples:

The prevalence of etic (universal) or emic (cultural-specific) cultural elements. It may be that emic concepts are really necessary for understanding a culture, and for proper communication within that culture. However, if one wants to make cross-cultural comparisons, or to develop generalizations about relationships between variables over cultures, one has to adopt a universalistic position and to rely on etics. But, as some will ask, do we then do those cultures justice? And how far can we allow for emic dimensions in regions or clusters of countries (the Chinese connection)?

The breadth or narrowness of the cultural dimensions. Do we have to address ourselves to broad, "second order" factorial, dimensions, such as the four Hofstede-factors or the two Inglehart polarities, or can we better understand differences and similarities in cultural behavior if we use more and more narrow dimensions?

Should culture be seen as a static external phenomenon, being responsible for differences between individuals or social groups, or should cultural differences be seen as emerging from social processes, and, therefore, as being dynamic and changing? If the latter is the proper view, how does this affect the required research design?

[4]
How does culture have influence on organizations: directly through legal, political or social forces shaping the nature and structure of the organization, or indirectly through affecting the attitudes, beliefs and values, and, consequently, the behavior of the people in organizations, which then may influence organizational processes and structures?

Is there empirical evidence for the 'convergence' hypothesis, which assumes that for the functioning of organizations cultural factors are becoming of dwindling importance and that technological and economic factors become more dominant, and that, as a consequence, organizations are increasingly coming to resemble one another, since these technological and economic factors (industrialization, automation, standards of living, globalized economies) all converge?

How can we avoid the risk of circular reasoning in our not unusual attempts to explain differences in people's values, attitudes and opinions by means of 'culture' if culture, as a rule, is defined itself in terms of values, norms, opinions and attitudes? At least a choice should be made of which values, attitudes and norms (for instance more stable and more comprehensive) are to be considered as 'culture' and which are not. But the danger of arbitrariness and circularity of the argument remains.

How can we properly defy the many methodological problems and difficulties in cross-cultural research, including language effects, cultural differences in response sets and faking, equivalence requirements for the instruments to be used, differences and bias in the selection of samples of respondents or organizations, and the incomparability caused by the use of varying levels of aggregation in much of the cross-cultural research (individuals, groups, organizations, regions, population layers, etc.).

This list of open questions and issues can be extended considerably. But it is probably enough to demonstrate that the development of a complete and conclusive cross-cultural discipline is an endeavor that has not been carried through by a long way, not to mention the opportunity to address 'real' problems, for which such a development is essential. Think of questions like: why is there still racism, how does acculturation take place, what causes ethnocentrism and xenophobia, what does integration mean for immigrants, what causes tensions between cultures, how can we further détente in intercultural conflicts, and many others.

Let us hope that the cross-cultural perspective in the behavioral and social sciences will continue to receive attention, and that many more studies like the present one will contribute to the further augmentation of solid learning on the for us often still enigmatic interface between culture and human behavior.

CHAPTER ONE

Cultures and dimensions

Classic perspectives and new opportunities in 'dimensionalist' cross-cultural studies

HENK VINKEN, JOSEPH SOETERS, AND PETER ESTER

In social sciences the empirical study of global cultural diversity has gained impetus. Especially since the early 1970s, as large-scale cross-national survey data collections first became available, the study of cultural similarities and dissimilarities across the globe started to flourish. The increasing interest in studies on global cultural diversity not only depends on the availability of robust cross-cultural empirical data. As social scientists, politicians, policy makers, the media and the lay public as well as managers of internationally operating firms recognized that the globalization process might well be the key driving force of cultural change, the need for thorough studies assessing causes and consequences of this process became more pressing. Furthermore, for politicians, the public, and corporate business representatives alike it has become increasingly clear that cultural diversity plays a crucial role in social tensions and conflicts, either in the public sphere within a nation or in doing business between nations (e.g., Berger & Huntington, 2002; Holden, 2002; Van Nimwegen, 2002).

Social science studies that addressed issues of either persisting cultural differentiations, of increasing cultural disparities, or of declining cultural distinctions worldwide could and can count on a wide audience. These social science studies each derive from today's broad range of social science disciplines, each with its own tradition of theoretical perspectives, paradigmatic assumptions, intellectual roots, particular set of methods of analysis, and styles of framing and prioritizing specific subjects related to culture. The social science reading of cultural diversity and cultural change seems almost as rich as the number of social scientists involved. In this introductory chapter we aim to provide some insight in the existing social science models of comparing cultures. We start with reviewing the basic alignments in cross-cultural studies and will address the main differences in perspectives that govern these cultural studies today. In that paragraph we will focus on the

[6]

four key concepts of comparing cultures represented by the seminal works of Geert Hofstede, Harry Triandis, Shalom Schwartz, and Ronald Inglehart. The focus of the following paragraph will be put on the similarities and dis-similarities in these scholarly works as well as on some lessons that can be drawn from this analysis for future cross-cultural studies. The final paragraph will present the further outline of this book, in which, first of all, the authors mentioned above will systematically present their own view on the similarities and dissimilarities of their own work and that of the other key authors. It is unique that these leading scholars of cross-cultural diversity reflect on each other's work in one publication. These presentations make this book a source of cross-references of key authors in cross-cultural studies. Next, in this book a variety of scholars, all from different countries and different social science disciplines, will present their findings on the impact of cultural dimensions on a wide range of contemporary topical issues that presently are in the forefront of public and social science discussions. In doing so they provide an eloquent overview of the state-of-the-art in contemporary social science studies comparing cultures.

The separate worlds of cross-cultural studies

Cultural studies are gaining front positions in contemporary social science. The resurgence of the interest in culture in social science is, however, both remarkable and discomforting. After a long period of emphases on under-standing social life from the perspective of structures, systems, life chances, social stratification, socio-economic factors, and the like, there now seems to be a growing recognition and appreciation of the role of the cultural factor as well as an increasing sense for cultural diversity (Featherstone & Lash, 1999). In the continuing battle of paradigms it now seems the 'structuralists', to whom culture is but epiphenomenal, lag a serious number of game points behind on the 'culturalists' who see culture as ultimately constraining.[1] The discomfort with the pro-culturalist result of this struggle lies in the ambiguity of the concept of culture that has gained popularity particularly among post-modern culturalists. Culture is conceptualized as a phenomenon lacking coherence, full of complexities, something that is dynamic, continuously changeable, fundamentally fluid, and endlessly multiplicit.[2] Culture has become everything in this perspective, defining culture as "the complex

---

[1] See for a critical overview and stance in the old structuralist and culturalist debate: Hannertz, 1992: 15-18.

[2] See for similar positions related to the hybridization of institutions, particularization of worldviews, fragmentations of moral frames of references, etc.: De Ruijter, 2002

everyday world we all encounter and through which we all move" (Edgar & Sedgwick, 2002: 102). Social scientists seem to agree that culture on the conceptual level includes almost everything and excludes almost nothing known to human life (see Hannertz, 1996). Perceived this way culture lacks ground. It freely floats in isolation in a non-human space without relevant linkages to social structure or people's actions. [7]

In this respect, at least three dominant perspectives are to be distinguished in cross-cultural studies: a postmodernist perspective, a 'particularist' one, and a 'dimensionalist' one.

The postmodernist view stresses the role and importance of the productive, playful individual, an individual who is producing, instead of reproducing, culture in his or her own particular way and for his or her own means (if at all for any means). Of course, there is much sense in emphasizing the role of the individual if this leads to an analysis addressing patterns of regularity and continuity and does not stop at claiming that culture today has entered an 'everyone can be anyone' phase of hyper-individualization. In this type of analysis we are witnessing a cultural 'Big Bang' on a truly global scale in which culture loses both its traditional bedrocks and basic guiding capacities and in which individuals become solipsists devoted to a continuous personal re-invention of culture. This is also the stream that even goes as far as stating that 'cultures do not exist' (Van Binsbergen, 1999). Still, the awareness that individuals play with culture and stretch cultural concepts, and hence create hybrid and ambivalent instead of one-dimensional entities, is important because it prevents theoretical oversimplifications. That is the main contribution of this postmodernist perspective. Considering this, for postmodernists the whole idea of culture as a well-defined unifying pattern with a strong internal homogeneity and as a uniformly shared entity that has an uni-interpretable direct power to shape people's identities is most likely to be a somewhat grotesque overestimation, if not a fiction (see e.g., Rosaldo, 1993; Soeters, 2000). In this perspective 'culture' is a reification and a too deterministic concept that might lead to an overstatement of cultural differences, and hence to academically based stereotypes and moral judgments (Moss Kanter & Cron, 1994; see Soeters, 2000).

A 'particularist' view upholds the belief in structures and patterns, but is associated to cultural studies in which particular subjects of analysis are stressed, either being work values, religious beliefs, political convictions or other types of domain specific cultural values, beliefs and attitudes (e.g., Ester et al., 1994; Arts et al., 2003). Emphases in theory and empirical work are not put on addressing an overarching system, a cultural canopy, which connects the various cultural domains. The core business of this type of

analyses is focused on the assessment of states of and developments in particular, seemingly mutually unrelated domains.[3] In this perspective, the individual, or better still, social groups of individuals, is not playing an important
constitutive role in culture, but it neither emphasizes culture as a unifying
pattern.

[8]

This latter emphasis is more likely to be found among the 'dimensionalists' of cultural studies. They, by contrast, are on a quest for a systemic whole
that crosses life domains and groups of individuals. The dimensionalist study
aims at finding the ultimate, most frugal, and yet most meaningful basic set
of axes with which to explain the broad range of attitudes, beliefs, life styles
and the diversity of practices among large populations and/or organizations
across societies. The very focus is on empirically validating the existence of
a unifying, universal (etic; see also Triandis in this volume) pattern, that
regardless of social differentiation, displays homogeneity, is broadly shared,
and has the power to shape people's identities, attitudes, and all other aspects
of their culture. The individual playing a directing role in producing culture
is, almost by definition, least present in the dimensionalist view. Says, for
instance, Triandis (1995: 6): "Culture is superorganic (does not depend on
the presence of particular individuals)...". The importance of behavior by
groups of individuals for the production of culture seems underestimated.
Culture in this respect is a mindset, a mental software that is only but weakly
dependent on culturally productive social behavior.

In this book the dimensionalist's perspective gets most of the attention. As
we will display below, starting with this most widely adopted type of analysis allows us to frame some important questions on how individuals, or better
still, groups of individuals, play a productive role in cultural diversity and
cultural change. Before doing so, we will depict the core elements of thought
of the four leading figures among the 'dimensionalists', being Geert Hofstede, Harry Triandis, Shalom Schwartz, and Ronald Inglehart.

Culture is multi-layered in the perspective of *Geert Hofstede* (1980a, 2001),
a Dutch scholar active in a broad range of social science disciplines. For Hofstede (2001: 9-10) the core elements of culture are values. Values, Hofstede
explains following classic anthropological thought on the matter, are fundamental tendencies to prefer certain states of affairs over others, and are held
by individuals and collectivities. Culture always presupposes a collectivity

---

[3] See e.g., the Globe-project on work values and leadership (e.g., Javidan & House,
2002a+b). See also one of the large-scale Human Resources Management projects focusing
on cultural impacts by Aycan et al., 2000.

and culture, in Hofstede's view, determines the very uniqueness of a group, be it groups within the framework of nation-states, regions or ethnicities within or across nations (Hofstede, 2001: 5, 10). Cultures consist of values, rituals, heroes and symbols, according to Hofstede. Values are seen as relatively fundamental compared to rituals, heroes and symbols. Hofstede places the latter three in the world of practices to separate them from the basics of culture. [9]

Hofstede is, of course, highly associated with the tradition of cross-cultural research at the nation-state level, comparing the values of numerous nations. Hofstede's fame in this tradition is, at the same time, his vulnerability. Though he leaves room for cultural distinctions at other levels, he is seen and stays seen as an old-school, i.e. modernist scholar who still believes in the supremacy of *national* culture, culture which is well-defined and relatively stable across nations and on which nations take up distinct positions. Much of Hofstede's later efforts (e.g. Hofstede, 2001) have been put in searching for meaningful correlations between contemporary national-level indicators and his famous five dimensions of national culture. These five dimensions are (Hofstede, 2001: 98, 161, 225, 297, 359):

1. *Power distance:* the extent to which the less powerful members of institutions and organizations within a country expect and accept that power is distributed unequally.
2. *Uncertainty avoidance:* the extent to which members of a culture feel threatened by uncertain or unknown situations.
3. *Individualism:* Individualism stands for a society in which the ties between individuals are loose: everyone is expected to look after him/herself and her/his immediate family only. Collectivism stands for a society in which people from birth onwards are integrated into strong cohesive in-groups, which throughout people's lifetime continue to protect them in exchange for unquestioning loyalty.
4. *Masculinity:* Masculinity stands for a society in which social gender roles are clearly distinct: men are supposed to be assertive, tough, and focused on material success; women are supposed to be more modest, tender, and concerned with the quality of life. Femininity stands for a society in which social gender roles overlap: Both men and women are supposed to be modest, tender, and concerned with the quality of life.
5. *Long-term orientation*: Long-term orientation stands for the fostering of virtues oriented towards future rewards, in particular, perseverance and thrift. Its opposite pole, short-term orientation, stands for the fostering of virtues related to the past and present, in particular, respect for tradition, preservation of 'face' and fulfilling social obligations.

[10]

Hofstede demonstrated the existence of these dimensions empirically by analyzing large-scale survey data gathered in the late 1960's and early 1970's among more than 115,000 IBM-employees across more than 50 countries in the world.[4] Hofstede's work received worldwide attention, among others from Harry Triandis, another influential 'dimensionalist'.

Harry Triandis, an American cross-cultural psychologist, has devoted much work to develop an alternative view on comparing cultures by emphasizing the individualism/collectivism construct (e.g., Triandis, 1988, 1994b, 1995). The contrast of individualism versus collectivism dwells on the basic issue in social sciences of independent versus interdependent selves, a theme that is at the very core of both classic (modernization) sociology (e.g., with Durkheim's distinction between organic and mechanics solidarity, with Tönnies' Gemeinschaft versus Gesellschaft, or with Weber's modern forms of rationality) and contemporary (cross-cultural) psychology.[5] Collectivism for Triandis (1995: 6) includes an emphasis on views, needs, and goals of the in-group (rather than on the self), on behavior determined by social norms and duties (rather than pleasure or personal advantage), on common beliefs shared with the in-group, and a willingness to cooperate with in-group members. Individualism taps the mirror image of these views, needs, goals, beliefs, and behaviors. Whether or not cultures are more individualistic or more collectivistic depends on two specific cultural syndromes, according to Triandis (1995: 52), being: cultural tightness versus looseness, and cultural complexity versus simplicity. The tighter and simpler a culture, the more collectivist it is.

In tight cultures people tend to have consensus about what correct action is, to behave according to cultural norms, and to be confronted with severe countermeasures if they deviate from these norms. Japan is the most commonly cited example of a tight culture, as are more Eastern countries.[6] Immigrant cultures in Western societies are other much provided examples. Complex cultures are cultures where functional differentiation in various life domains is large. These heterogeneous societies have a higher openness of group membership with a shorter time perspective (and an accelerated rate of change of membership) and less reciprocity, are high-density and thus have

---

[4] See Hofstede's 2001 *Culture's Consequences* for more data. In this book he provides international data on his five dimensions for about 70 countries based on recent replication studies.

[5] This theme is again one of the ultimate issues in contemporary social science. See the fierce debates on the rise and the pro's and con's of a 'self-ideology' in governing socialization and education strategies in the Western world (Vinken, 2003).

[6] See e.g., Wasti (1998) on Turkey.

high numbers of in-groups as well as many behavioral rules (and institutions to control and sanction rules) aimed at avoiding conflict, and have a large number of choices for action leading to higher number of different decisions. These decisions are seen as individually motivated, deriving from purely personal motives. Complex cultures are to be found all around the globe, especially in the developed world and more so in the larger city areas in the developed societies. The examples of simple culture that Triandis provide (e.g., 1995: 59-61) include classic hunter and gatherer societies and inten-tionally isolated and sect-like groups within developed societies such as the Mennonites and Amish in the US.

[11]

In more tight and simple cultures, collectivism is maximal. In loose and complex ones, individualism is. Collectivism and individualism, however, are not uni-dimensional with Triandis. Based on the mutual dependency of individuals he distinguishes between horizontal and vertical individualism and collectivism. Horizontal individualism, found in Sweden for instance, signifies that people are independent but stress sameness and de-emphasize inequality. In horizontal, collectivist cultures people are interdependent but also emphasize social cohesion and oneness with in-group members. One example of a horizontal collectivist culture is traditional Confucian China. In vertical individualist cultures — Triandis (1995: 45) mentions France and Germany among others as exemplary societies — independent individuals value distinction, being conspicuous, reflecting their 'different self', on 'being the best' and having particular privileges. In vertical collectivist coun-tries people expect and accept difference, have a strong sense of duty, a ten-dency to serve their in-group, even of sacrifice for group benefit. Again, Japan is thé prime example of a society with a vertical collectivist culture.

Of course, combinations of individualism-collectivism and horizontal versus vertical traits clearly remind us of Hofstede's dimensions. It seems to com-bine his collectivism-individualism and his power distance dimension, sug-gesting that individualism aligns with horizontalism (low power distance) and collectivist countries with verticalism (high power distance). For instance, in highly individualist and low power distance societies, such as Sweden and also the Netherlands, people do value individualism (indepen-dency, autonomy, etc.) highly, but do not like to 'stick out', to be unique or distinctive. Although Triandis does not suggest a one-on-one relationship between collectivism-individualism and horizontalism-verticalism, he argues that individualist cultures, relative to collectivists, are more probable to be horizontal. Much more, the combinations of individualism-collec-tivism and horzontalism-verticalism are regarded 'situation'-specific, depending on the domain at hand, either being work relationships, family

[12]

life, community life, etc. In every society, Triandis hypothesizes, there will be proportions of people 'sampling' all four-combination types, depending on their self-perception, being an achievement oriented (vertical individualist), cooperative (horizontal collectivism), dutiful (vertical collectivism) or unique self (horizontal individualism). Before going into more similarities and dissimilarities of Hofstede's and Triandis' set of basic cultural dimensions, we first introduce yet another classic-status author in the field of 'dimensionalist' cross-cultural studies: Shalom Schwartz.

Shalom Schwartz is an Israeli social and cross-cultural psychologist who gained his fame with an international value study among various samples of students and teachers in the late 1980's and early 1990's in about 40 nations around the world, including samples of respondents from specific cultural groups (Christian, Jewish, Druze, and Arab respondents from Israel, e.g.) within these nations. Culture with Schwartz is a complex, multidimensional structure that can be arrayed along a limited set of dimensions, both at the individual level and at the culture- or 'ecological' level (Schwartz, 1992, 1994a+b). The latter level is referring to a society's mean or average cultural characteristics, the level at which Hofstede's work can be located as well. Both Hofstede and Schwartz place values at the core of culture, being in Schwartz' terms: "criteria people use to select and justify actions and to evaluate people (including the self) and events" (Schwartz, 1992: 1). Like Hofstede, Schwartz discerns culture-level value emphases prevailing in societies. Before doing so, Schwartz starts with identifying distinct types of value constructs at the individual level, being value constructs that, according to Schwartz, *all* individuals across cultures recognize (Schwartz, 1994b: 88-89):

Power: social status and prestige, control or dominance over people and resources;
Achievement: personal success through demonstrating competence according to social standards;
Hedonism: pleasure and sensuous gratification for oneself;
Stimulation: excitement, novelty, and challenge in life;
Self-direction: independent thought and action — choosing, creating, exploring;
Universalism: understanding, appreciation, tolerance, and protection for the welfare of all people and nature;
Benevolence: preservation and enhancement of the welfare of people with whom one is in frequent personal contact;
Tradition: respect for, commitment to, and acceptance of the customs and ideas that traditional culture or religion impose on the self;

Conformity: restraint of actions, inclinations, and impulses likely to upset or harm others and to violate social expectations or norms;
Security: safety, harmony, and stability of society, of relationships, and of self.

[13]

Schwartz regards these ten value types as being universal and exhaustive.[7] With specific types of analyses (smallest space analyses) Schwartz places all values both adjacent and opposite to one another. The values form a circle with closely related values at adjoining positions in the circle and with incompatible values at the opposing side in the circle. Within that circle one can draw two axes, one from top to bottom and one from left to right, partitioning the circle into four quadrants. The axes represent two dimensions, each with two different poles, being:

1. *Openness to change* versus *conservation*: Openness to change includes the value types of self-direction, stimulation, and hedonism; Conservation includes conformity, tradition, and security.
2. *Self-enhancement* versus *self-transcendence*: Self-enhancement includes hedonism (as well), achievement, and power; Self-transcendence taps into universalism and benevolence.

Doing the same analyses with the ten values at the level of the different societies and regions included in his study, Schwartz identified seven higher order or culture-level value types:

Conservatism: values emphasizing the status quo, propriety, avoidance of actions or inclinations of individuals that might disturb the order (see security, conformity, and tradition);
Intellectual and *affective autonomy*: the opposite of conservatism, viewing the person as an autonomous whole pursuing his or her own goals; the intellectual variant emphasizes self-direction; the affective one stimulation and hedonism;
Hierarchy: Adjacent to conservatism, opposing intellectual autonomy, this value type stresses the legitimacy of hierarchical roles and resource allocations; it refers to the self-enhancement pole with emphases on achievement and power, together with;
Mastery: the emphasis is on active mastery of the social environment through self-assertion (mastery is related to active social behavior, intellec-

---

[7] In an earlier version Schwartz (1992: 10-110) identified 11 value types, now also including spirituality.

tual autonomy, by contrast, stresses flexibility of thought regardless of action)

[14] *Egalitarian commitment*: a value type exhorting voluntary commitment to promoting welfare to other people, opposing hierarchy and mastery and referring to the individual level benevolence and universalism types.

Harmony: from the broad self-transcendent region of value this value type emphasizes harmony with nature and social harmony (helping others, social justice), thus placed between conservatism and egalitarian commitment.

These seven culture-level value types are the result of positions on four basic societal issues:

1. The independent versus interdependent individual: an individual entering relationships voluntarily versus he or she who lacks autonomy and feels part of a collectivity (i.e. the two types of Autonomy and Egalitarian Commitment versus Conservatism)
2. Equality versus inequality: treatment of people and resources in an equal or hierarchical way (Egalitarian Commitment versus Hierarchy and Mastery)
3. Change versus preservation and fitting in: change or holding on to the social and material environment (Mastery, Affective Autonomy versus Harmony and Conservatism)
4. Self- or generalized-other-directedness: acceptance of selfish pursuits of individuals or groups versus favoring goals that transcend the self or in-group interests.

The Openness to change versus Conservatism dimension at the individual level, according to Schwartz (1994b: 98) is closest to the idea of individualism-collectivism, as formulated by Hofstede and Triandis. The dimension tapped in the above mentioned first core societal issue (the independent or interdependent individual) seems to do so too. Of course, looking at the other dimension of Self-enhancement and Self-transcendence — or Hierarchy and Mastery versus Egalitarian Commitment and Harmony — and at the other three issues mentioned above one can conceive many other, more or less overlapping relationships with the constructs of Hofstede and Triandis. The equality versus inequality issue, for instance, seems compatible with Hofstede's power distance and the vertical versus horizontal types of individualism and collectivism of Triandis. In this volume Shalom Schwartz will fortunately go extensively into the relationships between his work and that of Hofstede and others. We will address only a few similarities and dissimilarities among the 'dimensionalists' in the next paragraph. Before doing that, we introduce the last of the four influential 'dimensionalists': Ronald Inglehart.

Political scientist *Ronald Inglehart* is a fourth key author in empirical cross-cultural analysis. Inglehart's culture shift studies (1990, 1997) have received massive response in the social sciences, including criticism, particularly from outside the US. He has induced a true tradition of political values studies working with his instruments, especially with the materialism-postmaterialism index. Inglehart forecasting a 'silent revolution' in Western democracies hardly needs any further elucidation. An abundance of studies, articles, papers and even media debates have followed in response to Inglehart's assumption of the growing hegemony of postmaterialist over materialist outlooks. The contrast between young and older generations in this case is seen as a major antecedent for the assumed reshaping of political culture in Western societies. Two key hypotheses underlie the presence of materialist and postmaterialist values: 1 the *scarcity hypothesis* stating that one's priorities reflect one's socio-economic environment and that one places greatest subjective value on those things that are in relatively short supply, and; 2 a *socialization hypothesis* posing that one's basic values reflect the conditions that prevailed during one's pre-adult years (Inglehart, 1990: 56). Together the hypotheses imply that during times of prosperity and absence of insecurities accompanying war or other severe political turmoil, younger cohorts place less interest on economic and physical security than do older groups who did experience these events. Conversely, young people give higher priority to nonmaterial goals. Inglehart's theory in fact predicts that postwar historical events in western society, which can be characterized by unprecedented stability in socioeconomic and political terms, have generated a gradual but pervasive shift towards postmaterialism. The socialization thesis is supposed to complement simplistic views on how scarcity, in line with the need hierarchy thinking of Maslow (1954) and the principle of diminishing marginal utility in economic theory, affects overt behavior and covert value orientations.[8] Inglehart (1990: 69) acknowledges that after the preadult years people may undergo behavioral and attitudinal shifts, but in his perception pre-adulthood is the period in which change is most rapid and most lasting. This generates a silent revolution in western democracies; revolutionary because changes are so pervasive and silent because changes take place via

[15]

---

[8] Inglehart's theory clearly refers to Maslow's theory of developmental stages and the affiliated hierarchy of needs and values (Maslow, 1954). Maslow's theory was highly criticized for it's a-historic, culturally insensitive, deterministic, and subjective assumption that one can satisfy 'higher' needs only after satisfying 'lower' ones (cf. Möller, 1983).

[16]

replacement of generations. The values of individuals hardly change, Inglehart suggests, after the pre-adult years and the gradual process of generational replacement, in which older cohorts with materialist views die and young cohorts with postmaterialist views take their place, changes the average value pattern of society as a whole, in this case towards more postmaterialism. This implies that life cycle effects or influences of growing older, attaining a partner, having children, gaining more wealth, etc., are limited and that socialization or cohort effects are more important for the change from materialism to postmaterialism.[9] In his 1997-book Inglehart has broadened the analyses of his large-scale international value data by discerning two main dimensions according to which cultures, in his view, differentiate worldwide: survival versus well-being values and traditional versus secular-rational authority values. In the *survival/well-being* dimension the key dichotomy materialism-postmaterialism is prominently present, but the dimension now also includes attitudes such as life satisfaction and generalized social trust (Inglehart & Baker, 2000: 24).[10] The global modernization project, however, is two-dimensional according to Inglehart. There is not only a shift from survival to well-being values but also a transformation from *traditional* to *secular-rational orientations* toward *authority*. Societies in which social and political life is dominated by religious or hierarchical bureaucratic institutions, where male dominance and parental authority is defended, and where authoritarian attitudes prevail are regarded traditional; societies in which opposite characteristics are found and where individual freedom is going hand in hand with the rejection of the previously mentioned institutions and with opposition to centralization and 'bigness' of government are typified as secular-rational (Inglehart, 1997: 78-81).

In the dimensionalist tradition of cross-cultural studies at least five (Hofstede), one (Triandis), seven (Schwartz), or two (Inglehart) basic culture-level dimensions to compare cultures come to the fore. At first glance, these different sets of axes to compare cultures seem to have a lot in common. For instance, Hofstede's power distance values in Triandis' view might well be a part of his overarching individualism-collectivism dimension, might seem to overlap with Schwartz' hierarchy values and to have a relationship with Inglehart's dimension of traditional versus secular-rational authority values.

---

[9] See Vinken (1997) for an overview of studies that build further on this assumption, e.g., De Graaf (1988) and De Graaf & De Graaf (1988).

[10] See for an international and generational analysis of the relationship of Inglehart's as well as Hofstede's dimensions with generalized social trust and political involvement Dekker et *al.*, 2003.

In some of the following chapters of this book Triandis, Schwartz, and Ingle-hart themselves will assess some of the most important relationships of their own work with that of others, including Hofstede's. In the following para-graph we will address some of the basic similarities and dissimilarities [17] between the different culture-level approaches and focus on a core issue for the future of cross-cultural studies at this level: cultural change.

Similarities and dissimilarities in cultural dimensions

There are some core similarities and dissimilarities in the work of the key-four authors in the 'dimensionalist' tradition. In this paragraph we will only touch upon a few of these similarities and dissimilarities. The 'dimensional-ists' themselves take up the challenge to fully address the overlap of their work in the remainder of this book.

One of the main similarities of the work of Hofstede, Triandis, Schwartz, and Hofstede is the focus on the 'etic' instead of the 'emic' in cultural compar-isons. Etic refers to what is general in cultures; emic to what is specific in one or more cultures (see Hofstede, 2001, Schwartz, 1994b, and also Triandis in this volume). Of course, doing cross-cultural research presupposes that there is a common ground to compare cultures, that there are shared polycultural classification schemes, or as Hofstede (2001: 24) puts it "that each culture is not so unique that any parallel with another culture is meaningless". For some classic anthropologists and contemporary postmodernists alike, the etic approach might be a severe challenge to their perspective, often regard-ing this approach an enterprise of comparing incomparables (see Hofstede, 2001, for an overview).

  Furthermore, the authors mentioned here share the perspective of values being at the core of culture. Although one may debate about what values belong to this core, or even about whether or not some of the characteristics single authors discern are values at all, the common ground is the presuppo-sition that values are the most important fundaments of culture, more impor-tant than the rituals, heroes, symbols, and artifacts that also make up a cul-ture. There are some serious differentiations in the authors' perception of val-ues, as will be shown below, but the key element is that they all attribute val-ues the most important position in cross-cultural analyses. This is not that striking of course, if one considers the widely shared conceptualization of values as being the most enduring and hardest to change element of culture from which in the end all other afore mentioned elements of culture arise.

  The third similarity is the predisposition towards socialization. More or less explicitly all authors argue that values, and especially values, are inter-

[18]

nalized by individuals in the early years of their human life after which change over the life course of these individuals is highly improbable. One possible debate is on the exact timing of these crucial formative experiences: in childhood in the secured world of family life socialization (as Hofstede seems to argue) or in early adolescence when young people come to experience a broader world and experience socialization from a wider range of socialization agents and agencies (as theories in generation and youth studies suggest; see Diepstraten et *al.*, 1999a+b).

This debate is not without consequence. In the former position family members, especially parents, are the crucial significant others. Family socialization of values is then the logical key focus of analysis. In the second case, family socialization, i.e. value socialization taking place in the encounter of parents and children, might well be least important, and the socialization processes taking place with peers, colleagues, authority figures in school or media, etc., might well be much more crucial. Perhaps an even more important discussion can be held on the stability of value internalization over the life course. Many studies argue that change also on value adherence can be found after (post-)adolescence. People growing older can change in the value priorities they adhere to and emphasize different values than they did in their teen years (life course effects). Furthermore, generations can be discerned in terms of their value support indicating that socialization of values — in terms of structure and content — is not similar for every generation within a given society (generation effects).

There are of course other obvious similarities, such as the use of quantitative survey methods or a notion of culture located within national boundaries — very disturbing to some believers in globalization cutting back the importance of nations, similarities that we will not discuss further here. To do cross-cultural studies of the 'dimensionalist' type quantitative survey methods are just plainly indispensable and the studies themselves seem to prove sufficiently that national boundaries are far from historic reminiscences.[11]

One of the more important dissimilarities in the work of the four 'dimensionalists' is related to the order and structure of the dimensions presented. Another dissimilarity has to do with the nature of the values used by the authors to arrive at these dimensions. Looking at the order and structure of the dimensions, we find a clear difference. Hofstede uses dimensions that are not hierarchically ordered and dimensions with two poles (e.g., a pole of individualism versus a pole of collectivism). Moreover, Hofstede's dimensions are mean-

---

[11] See Harkness et *al.* (2003) for a broad and thorough discussion on cross-cultural survey methods.

ingful at the culture-level only.[12] Triandis' dimension of individualism versus collectivism (I/C) seems to be an overarching construct that incorporates different other constructs, constructs that can be regarded, again, as dimensions (e.g. horizontalism versus verticalism). Triandis seems to suggest a one-on-one relationship between the culture-level dimension of I/C and similar phenomena at the individual level. Schwartz makes a clear distinction between individual and culture-level dimensions, dimensions however that have clearcut and theoretically substantiated relationships at both levels. His dimensions at both of these levels, furthermore, are complex. Each dimension has relationships with more or less adjacent other dimensions and even with opposite dimensions. Behind the sets of dimensions lies a two-dimensional pattern that, however, seems to be two-poled (e.g., self-enhancement versus self-transcendence). Inglehart system of two cultural axes is more straightforward. These two dimensions each with two contrasting poles (e.g. survival versus well-being) are derived from individual-level data. It is less clear how the two dimensions hold after analyses at the aggregated level of cultures.[13]

[19]

Another issue of dissimilarity is related to the nature of values used in the studies of Hofstede, Triandis, Schwartz, and Inglehart. Hofstede devoted much of his work to theoretically specifying the values that are most probable to arrive at his five dimensions of culture at the culture-level. A prominent distinction Hofstede (2001: 6) makes in doing so, is the distinction between the 'desired' and the 'desirable', being the differentiation between what people actually want and what they think they should want. Hofstede has directed his values studies at the first category of the 'desired'. Triandis (1995: 1989-217), in line with this thought, provides a wide range of psychological instruments to measure I/C at the individual level. It is less clear which of these instruments are the key instruments that make up the I/C-construct at the culture-level. Schwartz, however, builds much more on the 'desirable' by asking people in his surveys to address his large set of values on the basis of their functioning as 'guiding principles in your life'. Furthermore, his values seen in this perspective seem to address personal goals, despite the attention given to values that assess more 'holistic' perspectives, e.g., being in harmony with or inseparable from nature. Inglehart, by contrast, in one of his key constructs — postmaterialism — within his survival-well-being dimension directly asks for people's concept of their most desirable future emphases in society. In doing so Inglehart's approach is different from the more personal value concept of Schwartz (values as a guiding principle in one's live) and from the one of Hofstede (emphasizing the 'desired' and not the 'desirable').

---

[12] See for a more extensive discussion on this issue Hofstede, 2001 and Schwartz, 1994b.

[13] Using country means. See Hofstede, 2001, for more details.

[20]

These are only a few of the similarities and dissimilarities that can be found when comparing the work of the 'grand-old four' in 'dimensionalist' cross-cultural studies. In the following chapters, these authors themselves will address many more analogies and differentiations. A key issue in cross-cultural studies is, however, that most of them pay little attention to the issue of cultural change. The four authors seem to suggest that the structure of the different dimensions is independent of historical developments. The pattern with which to compare culture seems — referring to already mentioned quote of Triandis — itself 'superorganic' and independent of the presence of particular individuals. Still, the cultural change debate, at least at the macro level of comparing cultures, is frequently dealing with the question of growing global uniformity of values or persisting diversity of values. Cross-cultural research of one kind shows that value priorities of different segments of the globe's population rank highest or lowest on the order of self-actualization and self-expression. Cultural change in this perspective is the adoption of these values in an ever-growing circle of populations. Another line of cross-cultural research aims to show that a population's cultural heritage, despite for example the increasing worldwide spread of single origin cultural artifacts (ranging from jeans to McDonald's restaurants), is extremely enduring and will continue to shape a society's 'turnover' on its basic social, political and economic parameters. Continuation of cultural diversity is the stability of value differences. Let us shortly take a look at the four authors' position on cultural change.

Hofstede's divisions of national culture are regarded and, more so, worked with as if they are stable across time. Especially in times of strong debates on the effects of globalization, including the cultural effects, this claim is confronting (see Vinken et al., 2002). Globalists and anti-globalists alike, either welcoming or opposing the process of globalization, are troubled by a message that despite the massive acceleration in the worldwide exchange of capital, products and people and thus of ideas, beliefs and modes of action, global culture remains in an equilibrium without the basic structure of cultural variety being affected.[14] Hofstede himself has contributed to the stability-change debate by showing how correlations between his divisions of nation-

---

[14] See Berger and Huntington (2002) for a subtle position on the effects of globalization on cultural diversity. Contributors to their edited volume clearly show for different nations around the world how, especially at metropolitan levels, culturally 'foreign' and 'native' traits not only coexist but are synthesized leading to a revitalization of 'native' culture as well as diffusion of this culture across national borders thus inspiring other cultures to creatively rearrange their cultural makeup. See also Soeters (2000) and Vinken et al. (2002) for more on cultural change and the interaction between traditional cultural uniqueness and modern global culture.

al cultures and an almost endless range of other contemporary macro characteristics of nations (economic, political, social, etc.) remain stable over time
(see esp. Hofstede, 2001).[15] Hofstede (2001: 36) suggests that national cultures, if at all affected by globalization or other forces of change, all transform in the same direction leaving the relative cultural distances between
nations as good as untouched. This theoretical claim might be called the 'relative cultural stability' hypothesis and is in urgent need of a forceful and convincing empirical test, especially by re-addressing the Hofstede concepts of
cultural dimensions in a large-scale multi-country empirical study of similar
magnitude as his monumental IBM-study.[16]

Triandis (e.g., 1995, 2001) assumes that individuals can take up their own
particular position within collectivist or individualist culture and even that
seemingly homogeneous collectivist cultures include traditions (symbols,
sayings, etc.) that dwell not only on collectivist, but also on individualist
themes. Still, he argues that humans in the different types of cultures 'sample' themes that, overall, are in line with the broad characteristic of that culture (e.g., Triandis, 1995: 61). More precisely: in collectivist cultures,
humans are more probable to 'pick up', cultivate and thus reproduce collectivist themes. For instance, collectivist sayings in collectivist cultures outnumber individualist ones. In individualist cultures it is the same for individualist themes: these themes are much more emphasized. Cultural change as a
concept is not included in this 'modal pattern' perception of culture. In the fit
between individuals and cultures, the emphasis seems to be put on *adaptation* and assimilation of individuals in cultures varying in tightness, complexity and mutual dependency of individuals ('horizontalism' and 'verticalism'). In this volume (see next chapter) Triandis does reflect further on ways

---

[15] Of course, full proof of the stability of the structure of global cultural variety, the structure
of originally four, later five dimensions of culture on which nations vary almost worldwide
according to Hofstede, can be provided only when a full range cultural study would be set up
among a large number of nations that includes cultural indicators building on the tradition of
Hofstede.

[16] Of course, Hofstede in his new edition of *Culture's consequences* (2001) shows the relevance of his dimensions for explaining international diversity in a wide range of current phenomena, thus indicating that his dimensions have a strong present-day importance and thus
that cultures still differentiate on the basis of his dimensions. Still, it is worthwhile if one aims
to fully address the hypothesis of relative cultural stability to again empirically measure the
cultural dimensions themselves and assess eventual changes in prevalence and adherence.
Rightly so, finally, one can argue that competing hypotheses of rapid cultural convergence, of
cultures growing together to form one super-culture, are neither thoroughly put to the empirical test.

to perceive cultural change and the role of individuals within the framework of his cultural theory.

[22]   In his quest for a universal structure and content of worldwide cultures, Schwartz (e.g., 1992, 1994a+b) is, almost by definition, less sensitive for the possibilities, correlates and consequences of cultural change. The universals identified by Schwartz at the individual and cultural level seem to influence people on a profoundly durable way. The issue of interacting people reshaping culture and/or producing new forms of culture is not a part of his theory. The assumption is prominent that individuals in their socialization process internalize the existing values that are set by institutional priorities in a society in order to function effectively in such a society, which, in turn, leads them to promote the interests and conform to the requirements of cultural institutions (Schwartz, 1994b: 93). Given this line of reasoning, Schwartz, much more than Hofstede, expects individual level value pursuits to overlap with culture-level value emphases. Pursuits and social actions that are psychologically and socially compatible with overall culture are those that are reinforced, and vice versa, societies fostering specific values are likely to "run more smoothly if citizens give high priority..." to the same values (Schwartz, 1994b: 93). In other words, the relationship between individuals and cultures is perceived from a classic functionalist perspective.

Inglehart (1990, 1997) is the only 'dimensionalist' most explicitly incorporating the issue of cultural change in his work. However, how cultural change shapes and is shaped by individuals is less vivid also in his studies. People themselves are, however, usually not included in the explanation of cultural change. Explanations fall back on processes — the boost in information technology, the growth of economic affluence, the rise of educational levels — that coincide with the depicted shifts at hand.[17] The very vehicle of change, the individual — or better still groups of individuals, is hardly ever included in the analyses.

---

[17] A general issue that needs further reflection would be the reliance on correlation analysis in many of the large-scale cross-cultural survey studies. The mere fact that certain developments in time or differentiations at a given time across societies correlate with cultural distinctions across the same societies is, of course, not sufficient to prove that there is a self-evident substantive, let alone causal relationship between the two. More theoretical and empirical efforts to make the relationships — e.g., between climate data and cultural dimensions, between cultural data series and political (e.g., corruption) data, between the same cultural dimension data series and data on intimate relationships (e.g., family size) — under investigation more plausible is called for.

In Karl Mannheim's classic generation theory (1928/1929) the true vehicles of change are *generation units*, socially well-defined groups of individuals who function as core advocates of change for generations as a whole (e.g., Diepstraten et *al.*, 1999a+b). The theoretical and empirical sensitivity of [23] contemporary modernization studies for the role these generation units play in creating change is, however, almost non-existent. A focus on the impact of avant-gardes, on their recruiting power both for the generations they are born in and for succeeding generations would 'bring man back in' and correct a major hiatus in modernization studies. Of course, in a more subtle manner of perceiving the role of avant-gardes and their devotee circles one would have to emphasize that there is likely to be no such thing as a single group that conveys the messages of cultural change and/or a mass of individuals that solely serve as a seismograph of the 'messageries generationelles'. Generational avant-gardes and the network from which they emerge, what Mannheim perceives of as generations as an actuality ('Generationszusammenhang'), are engaged in a constant interplay on what the culture is that shapes them and the culture will be that they shape. Cultural pathfinders will emerge and submerge from this condition without an ending.

Although the relationship between generational renewal as an abstract mechanism and cultural change is a widely studied subject there still is a wide gap between pinpointing the effects of generational replacement and understanding the process of intergenerational cultural production.[18] This gap has a straightforward cause. Generations are not mere statistical birth cohorts. To begin with, a generation refers to individuals who are born in the same historical period, who live in the same socio-cultural space, and according to Mannheim (1928/1929) are aware of sharing similar youth experiences in their formative years. This conceptualization presupposes that generation members subjectively identify with their generation, are linked by a common biography, have an elementary sense of a joint destiny and of being different from other generations. Generation membership

---

[18] See also the work of Inglehart (e.g., 1997) for the notion of generational replacement. More elementary than Inglehart's work is that of the main author of today's popular notion on the decay of civic virtues, Robert Putnam (2000). Putnam points at generational replacement as the single most important cause (50% of the cause; Putnam, 2000: 283) of this decay. What Putnam fails to indicate are the basic commonly shared features of his different generations that make these generations more or less engaged in civil society. An answer to the straightforward question *why* younger, postwar generations, including the sixties generation, are less involved in their community or have less social capital than older generation is simply missing (see for further comments Ester & Vinken, 2003).

[24]

assumes generation *consciousness* and a cognizance that one's generation is *distinct* from other generations. Generation membership thus depends on the subjective views of people in a particular social and historical setting. Analytically this implies that objective and subjective aspects should both be taken into account in empirical generation research. Much of the generation research aims at assessing the objective intergenerational differences by only examining differences between birth cohorts. All things considered, this means that from a sociological point of view, birth cohorts are at best generation locations (Mannheim's 'Generationslagerung'), but by implication do not represent an actual generation. By merely measuring objective differences between statistical birth cohorts, generational accountancy has floated a long way from its sociological heritage.

It is in the end unclear how cultural change constructs and is constructed by (younger) generations or by other socially defined 'categories' of individuals for that matter. The question how groups of individuals make sense of culture, the extent to which they are bearers and followers of the worlds of 'tradition' or of 'modernity', to put it in popular binary terms, and how they engage in the process framed as 'cultural change', the process in which both the worlds of tradition and modernity meet, is yet to be answered.[19]

One of the major lessons that can be learned from this book is that in order to take cross-cultural studies some steps further we need to address the issue of worldwide cultural change. A pressing issue is to assess the structure, causes, correlates, and consequences of cultural change, as well as to identify the bearers of this cultural change, either younger generations, business elites or other social groupings. Thorough empirical and sociologically imaginative cross-cultural research should concentrate on the bearers of cultural change and explicitly focus on the productive impact of what binds generations (or other groupings) whose members (wittingly or unwittingly) change culture. In the same fashion cross-cultural research should address the impact of the undoubtedly accelerated number of interactions between the local, national and the global (or supranational) and see what this means for the future of culture confined to nation-state boundaries. New studies should incorporate a focus on the status and the dynamics of cultural profiles of regions within nations, of nations, and of regions of nations. Of course, this ambition starts with developing a robust value theory firmly based in

---

[19] See for a first attempt to assess the international impact of cultural dimensions on basic political values related to civil society along the lines of generational cleavages: Dekker et *al.*, 2003.

existing models to compare cultures.[20] What is needed first of all, of course, is the insight in the connectivity, the similarities and dissimilarities of the different classic models of comparing cultures. This insight is what this book intends to provide.

[25]

Outline of this book

This book is, in other words, devoted to the comparison of key worldwide dimensions of culture. The book includes the almost classic-status authors mentioned above, who, especially for the occasion of this book, all do their utmost to reflect on the cultural dimensions known from the key literature of their comrade 'dimensionalists'. Harry Triandis kicks off in Chapter 2 with a thorough theoretical analysis of what he considers the key cultural dimension in cross-cultural studies: the dimension of collectivism versus individualism. Triandis explicitly relates his thought on this dimension with overlapping concepts, especially those of Geert Hofstede. Hofstede's work, discerning five basic cultural dimensions, among which the dimension of collectivism versus individualism, has inspired all authors of this book, as will be shown. Hofstede himself evaluates the comparisons with his work in the Epilogue of this book. Following Triandis in Chapter 3 is Shalom Schwartz who unfolds a system of seven both mutually contrasting and adjacent value dimensions, including dimensions that not only theoretically but also empirically seem associated with Hofstede's cultural dimensions. Schwartz also relates his value systems to the work of another influential 'dimensionalist' in cross-cultural studies, Ronald Inglehart. In Chapter 4, Inglehart and his co-author Daphna Oyserman depict their view on comparing cultures with Inglehart's two cultural dimensions of survival versus well-being and traditional versus secular-rational authority values. They especially focus on the relationship of these dimensions with the collectivism-individualism concept found with Triandis, Schwartz and Hofstede. The cultural dimensions conceptualized and empirically studied by Triandis, Schwartz, Hofstede and Inglehart on a truly vast global scale, in some cases covering more than 80% of the world's population, have not only gained much public attention and adoption in social science research, but have also triggered fierce method-

---

[20] See the volume of Berger & Huntington (2002) providing a variety of examples from different nations building on Berger's idea of the existence of different distinct global cultures that co-exist with national (or other level) cultures, e.g., a McWorld culture of young people sharing similar values, symbols, and life styles worldwide or a Davos culture of economic and science elites doing much the same on a global scale. See for a thorough empirical counterbalance as far as the rise of a global consumer culture goes: De Mooij, 2003.

ological critique and empirical replications aimed at providing counter-balancing perspectives. In Chapter 5, Wolfgang Jagodzinski, a German sociologist, shows what the basic pitfalls in methodological terms are when comparing cultures with the help of cultural dimensions.

[26]

Of course, not only the debate among the founders of the variety of cultural dimensions (and one of their most profound criticasters) yields insights in the value of comparing cultures with basic cultural dimensions. Also the work of younger generation scholars who implement the work of these 'founding fathers' in contemporary social science studies provides vital insights. From different nations and from various social science disciplines, a selection of teams of authors was invited to present their findings when working with cultural dimensions. This way a unique state-of-the-art overview of contemporary social science perspectives on comparing cultures comes to the fore. In Chapter 6 Hans-Peter Müller and Patrick Ziltener, working as anthropologists in Switzerland, analyze the relationship of cultural dimensions, especially those of Geert Hofstede, with deep historically grown, pre-colonial structural differentiations in a number of non-Western societies. In Chapter 7 the Japanese sociologist Kazufumi Manabe and two of the editors of this book give deeper insight in Japans basic feeling of cultural uniqueness, captured in the concept of Nihonjinron, a fine example of existing cultural nationalism that seriously counterbalances the idea of worldwide cultural homogenization on the waves of globalization. In Chapter 8, German psychologist Gisela Trommsdorff and her co-authors Boris Mayer and Isabelle Albert show that within Germany, due to divergent socialization effects in the East and West regions, cultural distinctions do exist, but have blurred among young generations. Chapter 9 presents a study of Belgian cross-cultural psychologist Karen Phalet and sociologist Marc Swyngedouw on the impact of cultural differences, aligning with Schwartz' value theory, on the acculturation processes of immigrants in the Belgian capital city of Brussels. Chapter 10 is by the American social scientist Raymond de Vries and his (multinational) author team focusing on the cultural explanation, especially by referring to Hofstede's work, of cross-national variations in concepts and routines of maternity care. Chapter 11 is authored by Greek management scientist Antonios Klidas, who has conducted a cross-national study in the hospitality industry aimed at assessing the adoption of the US-origin notion of employee empowerment. Again, Hofstede's concepts proved useful for explaining success and failure of this adoption process. Chapter 12, finally, is by US marketing scientist Lynn Metcalf and business administration scientist Allan Bird, who provide a framework for analyzing cross-cultural negotiation behavior from the perspective of Hofstede's cultural dimensions.

As mentioned, at the close of this book, Geert Hofstede evaluates the comparisons of cultural dimensions provided by his fellow classic-status authors and dwells on the extent to which the subsequent chapters further the understanding of comparing cultures. Hofstede does so in what he calls an [27] Epi-dialogue of this book.

CHAPTER TWO

Dimensions of culture beyond Hofstede[1]

HARRY C. TRIANDIS

Students of culture have often focused on particular dimensions of cultural variation. For example, there have been emphases on cultural complexity (Carneiro, 1970; Chick, 1997), tightness (Pelto, 1968), structural complexity and structural tightness (Boldt & Roberts, 1979), differentiation and integration (Lomax & Berkowitz, 1972), need for achievement (McClelland, 1961), various dimensions of value orientation (Kluckhohn, 1954; Kluckhohn & Strodtbeck, 1961), emphasis on social axioms (Leung & Bond, 2003; Leung et al., 2002), emphasis on community sharing, authority ranking, equality matching or market pricing (Fiske, 1990), linear versus holistic reasoning (Fiske et al., 2001; Nisbett, 2003), guilt and shame (Creighton, 1990), Apolonian versus Dionysian cultures (Benedict, 1934), and on other contrasts.

Georgas & Berry (1995) reported clusters of countries reflecting different ecology, education, mass communication, population, and religion. The well-known work of Inglehart (1997; this volume) and Schwartz (1992; this volume) has also produced dimensions of cultural variation. Hofstede (1980a, 1991, 2001) provided a systematic argument concerning five dimensions of cultural variation.

In addition to the universal (etic) dimensions of cultural variation mentioned above, there are probably innumerable culture specific (emic) dimensions. For example, Cheung et al., (2001) identified an emic Chinese dimension they called Ren Qing. It is likely that each culture uses emic dimensions, but this discussion is beyond the scope of this chapter.

Given the large number of dimensions one feels the need for some sort of theory that will place them into a single framework. This is what is attempted here.

In this chapter I propose to present a theory of cultural variations that has relevance for psychological processes. I will start with a definition of culture,

---

[1] I thank Dov Cohen, for very useful comments on an earlier draft of this paper.

and examine culture in terms of its antecedents and consequences. Then I will argue that the major antecedents of cultural differences are differences in the ecology, history, and influences through cultural diffusion. I will describe some of the major ways ecologies differ, but will not have enough space to deal with the other factors. From differences in ecology I will derive differences in culture.

[29]

For each of the dimensions of cultural variation again I will focus on its antecedents and consequents, so as to clarify what this dimension is and its importance in understanding psychological phenomena that include culture as the major factor. In doing this I will argue that some dimensions of cultural variation, such as *cultural complexity, differences in power, collectivism, individualism* and *tightness* (or uncertainty avoidance) are the primary dimensions of cultural variation from which several secondary dimensions evolved.

The secondary dimensions evolved when a primary dimension was used with great frequency. Then one of the aspects of the primary dimension became independent of it.

The idea has parallels in biology. If there are very few members of a species, random variation and selective retention, which are the basic processes of evolution, cannot generate another species. But if there are many members of a species, the probability is high that random variation will generate some new varieties of that species. Then some of these varieties will be more successful in a particular environment, and eventually will become a species independent and distinguishable from the species that generated them. In addition random events can result in cultural drift (Ehrlich, 2000: 66) where diversification of a culture or language can result in a new culture or language that may have only minor relationships to the previous culture or language.

The secondary dimensions of cultural variation, as I see it, are *masculinity, pragmatic induction* versus *ideological authoritarianism, long term time perspective*, focus on the *past, present* or *future, planning* versus *spontaneity, universalism, specificity*; and emphases on *achievement, instrumental behaviors, suppression of negative emotion*, and on *process* rather than *outcome*.

Definition of culture

Culture is to society what memory is to individuals (Kluckhohn, 1954). It includes what has worked in the history of the society — tools, concepts, ideologies, norms, values, prejudices, standard operating procedures, unstated assumptions, patterns of sampling information from the environment — that

[30]

most members of the society teach to the next generation. This teaching is done by example or explicitly. What has worked is perceived as having helped the society to adjust to its environment. Elements of culture are shared among those who speak a particular dialect, and can communicate with each other because they live in the same time period and geographic region.

Cultural psychologists think of culture 'in' the person. In fact, they state that culture and psychology make each other up (Markus & Kitayama, 1991). In short, there is no psychological process that is not shaped, to some extent, by culture. Cross-cultural psychologists tend to think of culture 'outside' the person, like an experimental treatment. Recent thinking has emphasized that both positions are defensible (Triandis, 2000). There are aspects of culture that change rapidly, such as the meaning of words. In that case, the conception of cultural psychologists is valid. There are also aspects of culture that do not change, e.g., driving to the right or left. In that case the conception of cross-cultural psychologists is valid. But most aspects of culture are somewhere in-between. We need to think of reciprocal causation. An antecedent of culture when examining one phenomenon may be a consequence of culture when we examine another phenomenon. For instance, the availability of a good educational system is outside the person, but the person can shape the educational system and change the culture. Thus, we should not be too rigid in thinking about the antecedents and consequences of culture.

Evolution of cultures

Cultures evolved much the same way, as did living organisms. Sperber (1996) used the analogy of an epidemic. A useful idea (e.g., how to make a tool) is adopted by more and more people and becomes an element of culture. Barkow, Cosmides, and Tooby (1992) distinguished three kinds of culture: metaculture, evoked, and epidemiological. They argue that "psychology underlies culture and society, and biological evolution underlies psychology" (Barkow et al., 1992: 635). The biology that has been common to all humans as a species distinguishable from other species results in a 'metaculture' that corresponds to panhuman mental contents and organization. Biology in different ecologies results in 'evoked culture' (e.g., hot climate leads to light clothing), which reflects domain-specific mechanisms that are triggered by local circumstances, and leads to within group similarities and between group differences. What Sperber described they called 'epidemiological culture.'

Differentiation is important in culture change. A tool that works well may be replaced by a tool that works slightly better, but frequently the culture retains both tools. Random variation and selective retention result in different species of tools, just as they also result in different dimensions of cultural variation. Campbell (1965) argued that random variation provided the bases of cultural evolution. It is followed by selective retention, and propagation of the positively selected variants. The more a dimension of culture is being used, the greater is the probability that variations will appear. Some of these variations are retained, and propagated, resulting in new dimensions of culture that are derivatives of the previous dimension of culture. In short, each culture through differentiation can become a new culture. [31]

Each dimension of cultural variation can be conceived as an entity that is very broad or very narrow. Broad dimensions are 'cultural syndromes' (Triandis, 1996), i.e., shared patters of attitudes, beliefs, categorizations, self-definitions, norms, role definitions, values, standard operating procedures, unstated assumptions, etc. organized around a theme. Cultural syndromes require communication and sharing of perspectives. Thus, they can be identified among those who speak a language dialect, during a specific historic period, and a definable geographic region. Examples of narrow dimensions are a special pattern of selecting information from the environment or an emphasis on achievement or on suppression of negative information in interpersonal relationships.

Kluckhohn (1954) did the most extensive review of the literature on dimensions of cultural variation, which he called value orientations. Kluckhohn & Strodtbeck (1961) operationalized five basic value orientations. Many of the empirical findings of the past 40 years specify more precisely what these orientations imply. For example, the Hofstede (1980a) individualism-collectivism dimension was in the Kluckhohn individualist versus collateral value orientation; power distance was in the lineal social relationships of the Kluckhohn typology.

Over the past twenty thousand years, as cultures evolved their complexity increased (Chick, 1997). Hunters and food gatherers later engaged in slush and burn agriculture. Nomads moved their cattle from one pasture to another, as the pastures became exhausted. This life style does not provide a steady source or food, so people learned to domesticate wild plants and became permanent farmers. Later they started producing artifacts that they sold in local markets, then they mass produced more complicated objects that sold in international markets, then information became the main source of income and so on. Of course, many contemporary nations, such as Brazil, have some members who are at all those stages of cultural evolution right now. Nations consist of thousands of cultures and subcultures.

Ecology and culture

[32] Cultures are shaped by many factors (see above). Here only ecologies as shapers of cultures will be discussed. But even the link between ecology and culture is complex (Cohen, 2001) and thus my discussion is necessarily over-simplified.

Ecologies differ in many ways (Berry, 1979; Diamond, 1999). Diamond (1999: 58) mentioned climate, geological type, marine resources, area, terrain fragmentation, and geographical isolation. He provided a detailed examination of the way such factors influence the size of the population, social structure, culture, and history. It is not possible to consider each of these factors separately here, so I selected some factors that I think are especially relevant:

(a) resource availability or abundance (oil rich versus barren countries), especially how do people make a living in an environment;
(b) resource mobility;
(c) homogeneity-heterogeneity in beliefs, attitudes, norms and values (e.g., Japan is more homogeneous than the USA). Strictly patrilinear societies are more homogeneous than bilateral societies, where when children are socialized the norms of both the father's and the mother's family are present, creating a pattern of partially conflicting norms;
(d) activity interdependence (to make a living in some environments people have to cooperate more than in others; for example, a person can not dig a canal alone);
(e) there is a range of the degree to which one needs to engage in dangerous activities in order to get food (e.g., to make a living in some ecologies one must engage in dangerous activities such as fishing in the high sea while in other ecologies one can simply get food from tropical gardens without much personal risk);
(f) population density, e.g., the difference between the Netherlands (390 persons per square kilometer) and Montana (2.1 persons per sq. km) has implications for the probability that people will be observed if they break an important norm;
(g) migrations that separate individuals from in-groups (some are forced by wars, some by differences in the standard of living, some by environmental deterioration);
(h) climate.

Each of these differences in ecology maps into differences in culture. For example, (a) abundance of resources and dependable availability of resources are likely to result in a more positive view of the way the world is than shortage of resources or random availability of resources. Extreme shortages, as in the work of Turnbull (1972) with the Ik, may result in parents abandoning their children, triage of children, and extreme social disorganization. Random availability of resources, as occurs among unemployed individuals without resources, who survive by means of petty crimes, results in distrust of both people and events (Triandis, 1976). Such individuals have been found to have a culture characterized by 'ecosystem distrust.' Where there are shortages, there is emphasis on survival. When there is affluence there is emphasis on well-being. This is a major dimension of cultural variation discussed by Inglehart (1997).

[33]

(b) Another ecological variable is whether the resources required for survival have high (e.g., cattle) or low (e.g., trees) mobility. Cultures where wealth is easily moveable develop a 'culture of honor,' in which people are socialized to be fierce and to react aggressively to insults, so that strangers will be discouraged from stealing their moveable goods. Nisbett and Cohen (1996) showed that a culture of honor is more common in the Southern than in the Northern parts of the USA, because migrations to these regions from Europe involved different kinds of cultures. Cohen, Nisbett, Bowdle, and Schwarz (1996) showed that, compared to students from the North, students from the South of the USA were more easily provoked and became more aggressive when they were verbally insulted.

(c) The homogeneity of cultures results in *tightness* (cultures where there are many norms that are strictly observed; people are very likely to be punished when they deviate from these norms; see Triandis 1994a: 159-164, for details). Extreme examples of tight cultures include the Taliban, where people were killed because they broke trivial norms, such as wearing an 'incorrect' attire, or listening to music. In that culture a woman walking in the street without a male relative was punished severely. Executions were so common that one of the Ministers of the Taliban considered them an essential business of the state (interview with the BBC). An other example is North Korea, where people march in unison according to the instructions of 'the dear Leader'.

Heterogeneity can lead to *looseness*, that is, few norms, since most people do not agree on many norms, and then norms are enforced with laxity. Thailand is a loose culture. It is heterogeneous because both India and China influenced its culture. When norms are not observed, people simply smile and say: "it does not matter". Looseness results in a perspective that Inglehart (1997) calls 'post-modern'. It is characterized by general tolerance, and acceptance of divorce, homosexuality, abortion, and so on.

(d) Activity interdependence, as is required for instance for major public works, such as irrigation canals, is likely to result in collectivism. Cooperation within the in-group is an important value in collectivist cultures (Triandis, 1995).

[34]   (e) Dangerous activities are likely to result in status differentiations, e.g., between men and women, or between soldiers and civilians. To induce some people to engage in dangerous activities the society has to reward them. Thus high power distance or vertical societies must have had, at some time in the past, people in dangerous occupations, such as warriors. These people acquired both status and power. When resources are available those who have access to the resources have more power and status than those who do not have access to the resources do. Thus, simple societies (e.g., hunters and gatherers), tend to have few resources, and have no way to accumulate resources (no banks, refrigerators, storage bins), so they do not have much hierarchy (Diamond, 1999). Agricultural societies have considerable hierarchy. Inequality becomes greater as societies become more complex, but most power distance is found in cultures with relatively low levels of economic development. High levels of economic development are associated with other factors, such as democracy, populism, social security systems and the like that decrease inequality. Additional factors, such as high literacy in some groups and illiteracy in other groups, many resources owned by one group and few resources by other groups, and so on, will also result in high power distance.

(f) Diamond (1999: 87) links the availability of suitable wild species that can be domesticated, to increases in food supplies, and thus to greater population density. Large population increases the probability of much hierarchy (Diamond, 1999), superior technology, and thus the ability to prevail in war. But the domestication of animals and high density result in epidemic diseases. Those who survive these diseases are especially able to transmit diseases to populations that have not developed immunities, and thus again prevail in war (e.g., the Europeans decimated Native Americans).

In addition, population density is probably curvilinearly related to tightness. As density increases there is more tightness since people in dense ecologies are more likely to note and punish those who do not obey the in-group's rules. However, extreme density may make conformity to others unbearably intrusive, and thus might result in less tightness. Other things being equal, population density should be related to collectivism, because tightness is related to collectivism (Carpenter, 2000). In fact, states like Montana are more individualist than states that are higher in density, such as the South East of the USA (Vandello & Cohen, 1999).

(g) Migrations that remove individuals from their in-groups should be related to looseness, because one moves away from the in-group and no longer has to follow in-group norms (Gerganov et al., 1996).

(h) Cold climates are related to individualism (Hofstede, 1980a, 2001).

Rationale for the distinction between primary and secondary dimensions of cultural variation

The link between ecology and culture is sometimes direct (e.g., cultural iso- [35]
lation related to agreement about norms, and hence to tightness) and sometimes remote. The more direct the link, the more likely it is that the dimension of cultural variation will be primary. Secondary dimensions emerge
over time, from primary dimensions. Primary and secondary dimensions are
related, for instance, the way recent human forms, such as *homo sapiens* are
related to previous forms, such as *homo habilis* (Ehrlich, 2000: 83). If we
describe cultures by examining only the primary dimensions we have a good
first approximation of cultural differences but miss details and distinctions
that can be very important under some conditions. For example, the secondary dimension of emphasis on achievement is important if we are discussing economic development, but not so important if we are discussing
population trends.

Dimensions of cultural variation

We do not know how many cultural syndromes there are. A first approximation is that complexity, tightness, individualism-collectivism, and power distance are broad enough to be called cultural syndromes. They are also directly linked to the ecology that produces the culture (see above for examples).
The organizing themes are complexity, importance of norms, importance of
the individual or the collective, and the importance of power. The dimensions of cultural variation identified by Hofstede (1980a) correspond to at
least three of these dimensions.

The dimensions can be examined in terms of content, antecedents and
consequences. Hofstede (1980a) has provided associations for his dimensions, which I will use as bases for this exercise.

Power distance. The central content of this dimension is emphasis on hierarchy — seeing the people at the top of the hierarchy as very different from
those at the bottom of the hierarchy. The antecedents include tropical climate, emphasis on agriculture, large differences in education across the
social structure, low social mobility, low affluence; wealth and power in the
hands of a few elite, large size of the population, colonial experience, centralized power, static society, children depend on their parents. The consequences are low mastery over nature, teachers are omniscient, and authori-
ties are not questioned.

We can speculate why the particular antecedents seem important. Obvi-

[36]

ously, if historical factors, such as wars and colonialism, have created centralization of power in the hands of a few elite, people will see a big difference between the people at the top and bottom of the society. The history of colonialism shows links between tropical climates and domination by one nation over another. Diamond (1999) has described how high concentrations of population resulted in inventions, thus in the development of guns and steel. He also discussed how domestication of animals resulted in germs. The combination of guns, germs, and steel has resulted in the domination of the world by the European powers, which had superior arms and were able to infect populations that had not developed immunities to European germs. Approximately 90 percent of the population of the Americas died after contact with Europeans.

The countries that had colonies in the 19th century were generally individualist, and individualism is related to climate — the most individualist nations were found in cold climates (Hofstede, 2001: 254). In addition, as pointed out above, dangerous occupations carried out by a segment of the society will also contribute to power differentials, so that in cultures that were shaped by warriors there is a relatively high likelihood of hierarchy.

Uncertainty avoidance. In my view this is very similar to *tightness.* The antecedents, according to my analysis (Triandis, 1994a), are at least three:
(1) cultural homogeneity (so that people can agree on the norms that are to be used);
(2) activity interdependence (so that it is important for people to do what is expected of them, otherwise tasks do not get done), and;
(3) high population density (so that there is a high probability that deviations from norms will be detected and punished), though extreme density may result in less tightness.

The consequences are anxiety, worries, and stress, all reported by Hofstede (1980a) as correlates. It follows from the concept of tightness that people in such cultures will be afraid that they will be criticized, and this may reduce their subjective well-being. Since tightness and collectivism are related (Carpenter 2000), we can expect well-being to be related to individualism (Diener et al., 1995; Diener & Suh, 2000).

Individualism and collectivism. There is more research on this dimension than on any of the others. Greenfield (2000) saw it as the 'deep structure' of cultural differences, from which all other differences evolved. Triandis (1994a) saw cultural complexity and tightness as the more basic dimensions. Collectivism evolved in tight and simple cultures; individualism in loose and complex cultures. Carpenter (2000), using data from the Human Relations Area Files, found support for the link between collectivism and tightness.

Ehrlich (2000: 300) suggests that biological evolution 'designed' humans to be collectivists. But cultural evolution is much faster than biological evolution, and has resulted in individualism in some cultures. He further indicates that the impact of humans on the environment threatens to create an environment that will no longer support life. Impact, he argues, is a function of (1) size of the population times (2) affluence times (3) level of technology. Clearly, individualist societies have the most impact on the environment, and thus threaten human survival more than collectivist societies. But he injects an optimistic note. Cultural evolution can be reversed, if people understand what they are doing. He gives as an example the understanding of how nuclear weapons may result in nuclear winter, which has prevented so far their use.

[37]

Triandis (1995, 2001) summarized some of the research on this dimension, so it needs to be mentioned here only briefly. The essence of this dimension is the definition of the self as independent or interdependent (Markus & Kitayama, 1991) with some in-group (family, tribe, coworkers, nation, co-religionists, etc.). People in individualist cultures see the self as stable and the environment as changeable (e.g., if I do not like my job I change jobs). Conversely, people in collectivist cultures see the environment as stable and themselves as changeable, ready to 'fit in' (Chiu et al., 1997; Chiu & Hong, 1999; Hong et al., 1999; Su et al., 1999).

In individualist cultures people are most likely to sample cues about events 'inside' persons (beliefs, attitudes, values), while in collectivist cultures they are most likely to sample cues about external events and social entities (norms, roles, situations, social structures, agreements, intergroup conflict).

Norenzayan, Choi, and Nisbett (1999) reviewed evidence that when East Asians make dispositional attributions they see traits as quite malleable, while Western individualist samples see them as fixed. They reviewed a wide range of information, from laboratory studies to ethnographies, and concluded that probably all cultures make dispositional attributions, but cultural differences occur because samples from East Asia make situational attributions much more frequently, and to a greater extent, than samples from the West.

When people communicate, in individualist cultures they sample the content and in collectivist cultures they sample the context (level of voice, eye contact, gestures, emotional expression) of the communication (Gudykunst & Kim, 1997; Gudykunst et al., 1996).

People in individualist cultures give priority to personal norms and goals. People from collectivist cultures emphasize ingroup norms and goals. In individualist cultures behavior is shaped primarily by attitudes; in collectivist cultures it is also shaped substantially by duties, expectations, roles and other social influences. In individualist cultures interpersonal relations are calculative (do I get more out of this relationship than it costs me?). In collectivist cultures interpersonal relations tend to be communal (all share in the available resources) (Triandis, 1995).

[38]

Triandis (1989) argued that people in individualist cultures, such as those of North and Western Europe and North America, sample with high probability elements of the personal self (e.g., "I am busy, I am kind"). People from collectivist cultures, such as those of Asia, Africa and South America, tend to sample mostly elements of the collective self (e.g., "my family thinks I am too busy, my co-workers think I am kind"). Empirical evidence supports this hypothesis (Triandis et al., 1990; Trafimow et al., 1991).

Antecedents of individualism include affluence, migration (leaving the in-group), leadership roles, education, living in heterogeneous environments, such as in a large city. Antecedents of collectivism include poverty (survival depends on the help of the in-group), stable residence, low social class roles, and living in homogeneous environments such as in rural, simpler environments (Triandis, 1995). Age and religious adherence are also related to collectivism.

Inglehart's (1997) secular-rational authority, with its emphasis on achievement and acceptance of abortion has some common elements with both individualism and looseness (the two are correlated, of course, see Carpenter, 2000). His well-being axis is also related to individualism, because tolerance is linked to looseness, which is linked to individualism. His survival pole, with its strong rejection of out-groups, has common elements with collectivism. The traditional authority pole, with its link to religiosity, has that common element with collectivism (Triandis & Singelis, 1998). In my opinion the individualism-collectivism axis is located in-between (perhaps at 45 degrees) to the two axes of Inglehart.

De Luque & Sommer (2000) identified four dimensions of cultural variation. (1) Specific — holistic has much in common with the emphasis on content versus context, and psychological differentiation (Witkin & Berry, 1975). I list it below as a secondary dimension of cultural variation. (2) Tolerance for ambiguity, has much in common with the tight-loose dimension. (3) Individualism and collectivism, and (4) Status identity, has much in common with power distance.

The fact that many reviews of the literature on dimensions of cultural converge in identifying similar dimensions of cultural variation, encourages us to think that we do have identified the most useful set of dimensions.

Kinds of individualism and collectivism. These cultural patterns take different forms in different cultures. Specifically, there are horizontal and vertical individualist and collectivist cultures (Triandis, 1995). Horizontal individualist cultures, such as Sweden, emphasize that the individual is independent from groups, and self-reliant, but people do not wish to 'stick out.' Modesty is a virtue.

[39]

People wanting to be 'the best' characterize vertical individualist cultures, such as the corporate and academic cultures in the US. Competition is high in such cultures and modesty is not a virtue.

Horizontal collectivist cultures, such as the Israeli kibbutz, emphasize interdependence of the individual and the group, but there is no hierarchy. In theory, every member does all the jobs, whether they are prestigious or not.

In vertical collectivist cultures, such as in China and India, sacrifice for the group is virtuous. The individual is not that important; the group is all-important.

Another variety of collectivism is the one that stresses the relationship of children to all the women of the extended family, as happens in India, where there is no particular emphasis on the child-mother relationship. This pattern contrasts with the Japanese pattern, where the mother-child relationship is all-important, and the relationship of the child to the women of the extended family is not important.

It is likely that further research will identify many more kinds of individualism and collectivism.

Secondary dimensions of cultural variation

I am now going to argue that the cultural syndromes of cultural complexity, power differences, tightness, and individualism are the *basic* dimensions of cultural variations. These dimensions evolved into additional dimensions, through differentiation, as occurs in all kinds of evolution.

The power distance dimension can become differentiated into a dimension that stresses the ideology and authority of the person at the top of the hierarchy. This *ideological authoritarianism* view is usually associated with arguments that use deduction, where the position of the authority is presented first and 'facts' are presented *only* if they fit the ideology (Glenn, 1981). The contrasting perspective is associated with *pragmatism* and uses induction. One starts an argument by presenting the 'facts' and from those one induces generalizations. The pragmatic perspective favors experimentation and doing what the 'law of the situation' (Follett, 1941) requires.

The Uncertainty Avoidance or the tightness dimension can become differentiated into a *planning* versus *spontaneity* dimension. Tightness and

[40] planning are logically linked, as are looseness and spontaneity. There is some basis for thinking that in many economically less developed societies people do not have many skills for planning and prefer to do things spontaneously (Jones, 1999). This tendency may emerge also when political instability makes planning impractical (Triandis, 1972).

The individualism dimension got differentiated into masculinity, universalism, modern use of time, emphasis on what the individual has achieved (earnings, recognition, advancement, leadership position) versus ascription (family position, hereditary titles), and self-realization, all elements listed by Hofstede (1980a) as associations. In addition, emphasis on guilt is likely to be especially high in some societies, and that would have evolved from individualism.

Masculine cultures, according to Hofstede (1980a), emphasize independence, achievement, work centrality, low benevolence, little interest in serving others, and much sex role differentiation. Feminine societies are classic post-modern cultures in Inglehart's (1997) studies.

Another evolution through differentiation from individualism and collectivism is the emphasis on the analytic, linear cognitive style found in the West and the holistic, dialectical style often found in the East (Nisbett et *al.*, 2001; Nisbett, 2003). Recall that, during communications, in collectivist cultures people depend on the context (how something was said, history of the issue) more than on the content (what was said) of the communication. The person who says something is part of the context of the message, so the source of a communication is more likely to be used as a clue for making judgments about the meaning of the communication in collectivist than in individualist cultures. This results in emphasis on *diffusion* (little differentiation of the source and content of the communication) rather than *specificity* (clear differentiation of source and context and on paying attention only to the content). This was the first dimension of cultural variation identified by De Luque & Sommer (2000).

Individualism, through differentiation, became an emphasis on *achievement* rather than *ascription* in social perception.

Collectivism, through further differentiation becomes a *long time perspective*. People in collectivist cultures feel linked to ancestors and descendents in ways that are not typical among people in individualist cultures.

Levine (1997) found relationships between the use of time and individualism, with people using time as a precious commodity in individualist cultures, while people in collectivist cultures waste time easily. Thus, for instance, people walk faster and do simple transactions more quickly in individualist cultures. In collectivist cultures they walk more slowly and take much time for their transactions. However, Japan's use of time is similar to the use of time in individualist cultures, and there are a number of confounds. For instance, people move slowly in hot climates, and collectivist cultures are more frequent in hot climates.

A more elaborate discussion of time perception was provided by Mosakowski & Earley (2000) who distinguished five kinds of patterns of the use of time. They contrasted (1) 'real' with 'epiphenomenal' time, (2) objective vs. subjective, (3) novel, cyclical or punctuated, (4) discrete, continuous or epochal,(5) emphasis on the past, present or future. Most of these distinctions came from anthropological work with cultures that do not participate in the world economy, so that they are of little interest to organizational psychologists, but nevertheless these authors suggest how researchers and practitioners might benefit by considering these distinctions.

More useful, perhaps, is the work of Levine (1997) who suggested that people who travel to other cultures ought to pay attention to differences in the use of time. Especially important are:

(1) monochronic (e.g., one conversation at a time) vs. polychonic (e.g., holding several conversations with different people at the same time) time;
(2) work (time to work and not socialize) vs. social time;
(3) doing (one is supposed to do things during that time) vs. not doing time, and;
(4) clock (e.g., meetings end at a certain time) vs. event time (e.g., meetings end when the purpose of the meeting has been accomplished).

Levine points out that one of the most difficult cultural differences one must learn to adjust to in other cultures is the way people deal with appointments. In some cases high status people schedule several appointments for the same time and plan to be late for all of them!

Furthermore, collectivism through further differentiation may develop a dimension of emphasis on *process* rather than *outcome*. People in collectivist cultures are especially concerned about not hurting the feelings of in-group members, not imposing on such persons, and avoiding negative evaluations by such persons. On the other hand, people in individualist cultures are most concerned with getting things done and with the clarity of communications and their effectiveness (Kim et al., 1996). The other-oriented concerns are focusing on the *process* while the outcome–oriented concerns focus on the *outcome* of communications.

This dimension can generalize to focus on *how* things are done as opposed to *whether* the things were done. Social control is likely to emphasize shame in collectivist cultures, and that can become an independent dimension. Also, in some collectivist cultures (Stephan et al., 1996) people

[41]

suppress their negative emotions toward in-group members, so as to keep the relationships intact. The *suppression of negative emotions* can be a way to distinguish different kinds of collectivist cultures. The Israeli kibbutz is not as concerned with the suppression of negative feelings as is common in East Asian collectivist cultures. However, it is also possible for this dimension to become independent of collectivism, and require separate measurement.

[42]

Secondary dimensions become independent of the primary dimensions

The important point about the secondary dimensions of cultural variation is that once they become established they can act independently of the dimensions that generated them in the first place. When this happens one can observe contradictory patterns, such as collectivists who do not worry much about suppressing their negative emotions (e.g., the Israeli kibbutz) as well as collectivists who are very strict about not expressing negative emotions (e.g., Japan). Similarly, the other secondary dimensions can become independent of the primary dimensions of cultural variation, thus resulting in very much more complexity in the analysis of the way the dimensions of cultural variation operate.

Conclusion

In this chapter I outlined a theoretical framework that integrates the dimensions of cultural variation that have been discussed in the literature. While the literature includes very many dimensions, my emphasis has been primarily on the work of Hofstede, who has identified three of the primary dimensions and two of the secondary dimensions of my analysis. The two dimensions of Inglehart appear to be related to both individualism-collectivism and looseness-tightness. The ten value types identified by Schwartz are detailed reflections of Individualism (self-direction, stimulation, hedonism, achievement) and Collectivism (security, conformity, tradition), and the Vertical (Power) and Horizontal (benevolence, universalism) emphases of the vertical and horizontal kinds of individualism and collectivism discussed above.

I am proposing that in addition to the dimensions identified by Hofstede, some additional dimensions need to be considered because in some cases they may provide additional, and more subtle, details about the way culture influences a phenomenon.

When we analyze a psychological phenomenon it may not be necessary to consider all the dimensions that I mentioned. Probably the primary ones will be most useful, and some of the secondary dimensions may prove useful when we examine specific psychological phenomena.

CHAPTER THREE

Mapping and interpreting cultural differences around the world[1]

SHALOM H. SCHWARTZ

Most of us have notions about how the cultures of particular nations differ from one another. For theory and practice to progress, however, we need reliable ways to describe and compare cultures. This chapter presents an empirically validated typology of value orientations, developed in recent years to describe, map, and give insight into cultural differences (Schwartz, 1994a, 1999). This approach is distinctive in its use of a priori theorizing to derive cultural dimensions and to specify how they form a coherent, integrated system. The chapter explicates this typology, compares it with others, and applies it to characterize the broad cultural orientations in the countries where over 75% of the world's population lives. It also discusses a selection of possible causes and consequences of national differences on these cultural orientations.

Cultural orientations: A values approach

I view culture as the rich complex of meanings, beliefs, practices, symbols, norms, and values prevalent among people in a society. The prevailing value emphases in a society may be the most central feature of culture (Hofstede, 1980a; Schwartz, 1999; Weber, 1958; Williams, 1968). These value emphases express shared conceptions of what is good and desirable in the culture, the cultural ideals.

Cultural value emphases shape and justify individual and group beliefs, actions, and goals. Institutional arrangements and policies, norms, and everyday practices express underlying cultural value emphases in societies. For example, a cultural value emphasis on success and ambition may be reflected in and promote highly competitive economic systems, confronta-

[1] My thanks to Anat Bardi, Moshe Berger, Ariel Knafo, Yuval Piurko, Tammy Rubel and Lilach Sagiv for comments on an earlier version of this chapter. This research was supported by Israel Science Foundation Grant No. 921/02-1.rch.

[44]

tional legal systems, and child-rearing practices that pressure children to achieve. A cultural emphasis on success and ambition may also justify the prevalence of symbols of status (e.g., a Porsche) and of norms that encourage assertiveness (e.g., Don't stop 'til you reach the top!).

The preference element in cultural value orientations — values as ideals — promotes coherence among the various aspects of culture. Because prevailing cultural value orientations represent ideals, aspects of culture that are incompatible with them are likely to generate tension and to elicit criticism and pressure to change. Consider a society whose cultural value orientations emphasize collective responsibility. Firing long-term employees in the interests of profitability is likely to elicit widespread criticism and efforts to force policy change. Of course, cultures are not fully coherent. In addition to a dominant culture, subgroups within societies espouse conflicting value emphases. The dominant cultural orientation changes in response to shifting power relations among these subgroups.

But change is slow. Another important feature of cultural value orientations is that they are relatively stable (Hofstede, 2001; Schwartz et al., 2000). Some researchers argue that elements of culture persist over hundreds of years. For example, Kohn and Schooler (1983) identified the lingering impact of feudalism in present-day national variation in the importance of autonomy vs. conformity. Putnam (1993) traced the success of democracy in different regions of Italy to cultural roots beginning in the 12th century. Yet, cultural value orientations do change gradually. Societal adaptation to epidemics, technological advances, increasing wealth, contact with other cultures, and other exogenous factors leads to changes in cultural value emphases.

Culture joins with social structure, history, demography, and ecology in complex reciprocal relations that influence every aspect of how we live. But culture is difficult to measure. To reveal the cultural orientations in a society, we could look at the themes of children's stories, at the systems of law, at the ways economic exchange is organized, or at socialization practices. These indirect indexes of underlying orientations in the prevailing culture each describe a narrow aspect of the culture. When researchers try to identify culture by studying the literature of a society or its legal, economic, family, or governance systems, what they seek, implicitly or explicitly, are underlying value emphases (Weber, 1958; Williams, 1968). Therefore, studying value emphases directly is an especially efficient way to capture and characterize cultures (cf. Hofstede, 1980a; Inglehart, 1997; Schwartz, 1999).

A theory of cultural value orientations

Cultural value orientations evolve as societies confront basic issues or prob- [45]
lems in regulating human activity (Hofstede, 1980a; Schwartz, 1994b). People must recognize these problems, plan responses to them, and motivate one
another to cope with them. The ways that societies respond to these basic
issues or problems can be used to identify dimensions on which cultures may
differ from one another. The cultural value orientations at the end-points of
these dimensions are Weberian ideal-types. I derived value dimensions for
comparing cultures by considering three of the critical issues that confront all
societies.

The first issue is the nature of the relation or the boundaries between the
person and the group: To what extent are people autonomous vs. embedded
in their groups? I label the polar locations on this cultural dimension *autonomy* versus *embeddedness*. In autonomy cultures, people are viewed as
autonomous, bounded entities. They should cultivate and express their own
preferences, feelings, ideas, and abilities, and find meaning in their own
uniqueness. There are two types of autonomy: *Intellectual autonomy* encourages individuals to pursue their own ideas and intellectual directions independently. Examples of important values in such cultures include broad-
mindedness, curiosity, and creativity. *Affective autonomy* encourages individuals to pursue affectively positive experience for themselves. Important
values include pleasure, exciting life, and varied life.

In cultures with an emphasis on *embeddedness*, people are viewed as
entities embedded in the collectivity. Meaning in life comes largely through
social relationships, through identifying with the group, participating in its
shared way of life, and striving toward its shared goals. Embedded cultures
emphasize maintaining the status quo and restraining actions that might dis-
rupt in-group solidarity or the traditional order. Important values in such cultures are social order, respect for tradition, security, obedience, and wisdom.

The second societal problem is to guarantee responsible behavior that
preserves the social fabric. People must be induced to consider the welfare of
others, to coordinate with them, and thereby manage their unavoidable inter-
dependencies. The polar solution labeled cultural *egalitarianism* seeks to
induce people to recognize one another as moral equals who share basic
interests as human beings. People are socialized to internalize a commitment
to cooperate and to feel concern for everyone's welfare. They are expected to
act for the benefit of others as a matter of choice. Important values in such
cultures include equality, social justice, responsibility, help, and honesty.

The polar alternative labeled cultural *hierarchy* relies on hierarchical
systems of ascribed roles to insure responsible behavior. It defines the

unequal distribution of power, roles, and resources as legitimate. People are socialized to take the hierarchical distribution of roles for granted and to comply with the obligations and rules attached to their roles. Values like social power, authority, humility, and wealth are highly important in hierarchical cultures.

[46]

The third societal problem is to regulate how people manage their relations to the natural and social world. The cultural response to this problem labeled *harmony* emphasizes fitting into the world as it is, trying to understand and appreciate rather than to change, direct, or to exploit. Important values in harmony cultures include world at peace, unity with nature, and protecting the environment. *Mastery* is the polar cultural response to this problem. It encourages active self-assertion in order to master, direct, and change the natural and social environment to attain group or personal goals. Values such as ambition, success, daring, and competence are especially important in mastery cultures.

If a cultural value orientation is emphasized in the extreme, it reveals a dark side. Problems arise due to the virtual absence of the opposing value emphasis. An extreme emphasis on embeddedness, for example, stifles individuality, and an extreme emphasis on autonomy breaks down vital social bonds. Overemphasis on mastery promotes exploitation of people and nature, and overemphasis on harmony discourages initiative and productivity. Too strong a stress on hierarchy encourages large disparities in social power and consumption, and an excessive stress on egalitarianism undermines acceptance of the unequal role obligations and rewards inherent in most social institutions.

In sum, the theory specifies three bipolar dimensions of culture that represent alternative resolutions to each of three problems that confront all societies: *embeddedness* versus *autonomy*, *hierarchy* versus *egalitarianism*, and *mastery* versus *harmony* (see Figure 1). A societal emphasis on the cultural type at one pole of a dimension typically accompanies a de-emphasis on the polar type, with which it tends to conflict. Thus, as I show below, American culture tends to emphasize mastery and affective autonomy and to give little emphasis to harmony. And the culture in Singapore emphasizes hierarchy but not egalitarianism and intellectual autonomy.

The cultural value orientations are also interrelated on the basis of compatibility among them. That is, because certain orientations share assumptions, it is easier for them to be emphasized simultaneously in a culture. For example, egalitarianism and intellectual autonomy share the assumption that people can and should take individual responsibility for their actions and make decisions based on their own personal understanding of situations. And

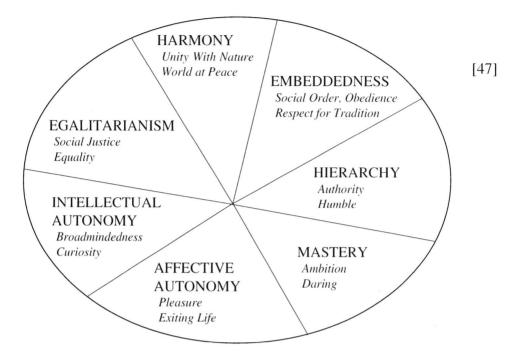

Figure 1: *Cultural dimensions: Prototypical Structure*

high egalitarianism and intellectual autonomy are both usually found together, as in Western Europe. Embeddedness and hierarchy share the assumption that a person's roles in and obligations to collectivities are more important than her unique ideas and aspirations. And embeddedness and hierarchy are both high in the Southeast Asian cultures I have studied.

The shared and opposing assumptions inherent in cultural values yield a coherent circular structure of relations among them. The structure reflects the cultural orientations that are compatible (adjacent in the circle) or incompatible (distant around the circle). This conception of cultural dimensions as forming an integrated system, derived from a priori theorizing, distinguishes my approach from others. Hofstede (1980a, 2001) conceptualized his dimensions as independent. He assessed them as orthogonal factors. Inglehart (1997) derived his two broad cultural syndromes empirically. He identified and labeled two orthogonal factors obtained in analyses of nation level correlations among numerous attitudes and beliefs.

Measuring cultural value orientations

[48] I assume that the value priorities of societal members point to the underlying cultural emphases. Is this justified? Recall that cultural value orientations find expression in the norms, practices, and institutions of a society. The cultural value orientations help to shape the contingencies to which people must adapt in their daily lives. They help to determine the individual behaviors, attitudes, and value preferences that are likely to be viewed as more legitimate in common social contexts or less, to be encouraged or discouraged. As a result, members of the dominant group in a society share many value-relevant experiences and they are socialized to accept and even to take for granted shared social values.

Of course, each individual has unique experiences and a unique genetic makeup and personality that give rise to individual differences in personal values within societies. Critically, however, these individual differences affect the variance in importance that dominant group members attribute to different values but not the *average* importance. The average reflects the impact of exposure to the same culture. Hence average value priorities in the dominant societal group point to the prevalent cultural value orientations. These cultural orientations are implicit. Individuals may not be aware of them, so they cannot serve as good informants about the culture. But the cultural orientations in a society can be discerned from their effects on the values that societal members have adopted.

Like Hofstede (2001) and Inglehart (1997), I infer the cultural value orientations that characterize societies by averaging the value priorities of individuals in matched samples from each society. The theory of cultural value orientations has been validated with data from close to 200 samples from 67 nations and 3 sub-national ethnic groups.

To operationalize the value priorities of individuals, I used a value survey intended to include all the motivationally distinct values likely to be recognized across cultures (Schwartz, 1992). The survey includes 56 or 57 single value items (e.g., social justice, humility, creativity, social order, pleasure, ambition). Respondents rate the importance of each 'as a guiding principle in MY life'. Respondents from cultural groups on every inhabited continent have completed the survey, anonymously, in their native language (N > 75,000).[2]

Values whose meanings differ across cultures should not be used in cross-cultural comparison. Otherwise, group differences might reflect the fact that different concepts are measured in each group. Separate multidi-

---

[2] I am indebted to over 100 collaborators for their aid in gathering the data.

mensional scaling analyses of the value items within each of 66 nations established that 45 of the items had reasonably equivalent meanings in each nation (Schwartz, 1994a; 1999). A nested multigroup confirmatory factor analysis in 21 nations affirmed this conclusion (Spini, 2003). I included only these 45 value items in the analyses to validate the cultural dimensions.[3] I specified in advance a set of three to eight value items expected to indicate an emphasis on each of the seven cultural orientations.

Empirical evaluation of the theory of cultural value orientations

I assessed the validity of the seven cultural value orientations and the relations among them with data gathered in 1988-2000. Participants were 80 samples of school teachers (k-12) from 58 national groups and 115 samples of college students from 64 national groups, together constituting 67 nations and 70 different cultural groups. The samples in ethnically heterogeneous nations came from the dominant, majority group. However, separate samples were drawn of French and English Canadians, Israeli Arabs and Jews, and Black and white South Africans. Most samples included between 180 and 280 respondents.

For each sample, the mean ratings of the 45 value items were computed. The sample was then treated as the unit of analysis. Correlations between items were computed across samples, using the sample means for each item. These correlations are independent of those across individuals within any sample. So the analyses are at the sample (nation) or culture level, not the individual level. Correlations between the sample means across samples were used in a multidimensional scaling analysis (SSA; Borg & Lingoes, 1987; Guttman, 1968).

The 2-dimensional projection in Figure 2 portrays the pattern of intercorrelations among values, based on the sample means. Each value item is represented by a point such that the more positive the correlation between any pair of value items the closer they are in the space, and the less positive their correlation the more distant. Comparing Figure 2 with Figure 1 reveals that the observed content and structure of cultural value orientations fully supports the theorized content and structure. This analysis clearly discriminates the seven orientations: The value items selected a priori to represent each value orienta-

---

[3] In contrast, the items used by Hofstede and Inglehart have not been subjected to analyses within each society to assess the cross-society equivalence of their meanings.

[4] One item, 'accepting my portion in life,' emerged in the egalitarianism region rather than in the expected harmony region, which is adjacent. Its correlations with other items also failed to support an interpretation as a harmony value. We therefore dropped it from the analyses.

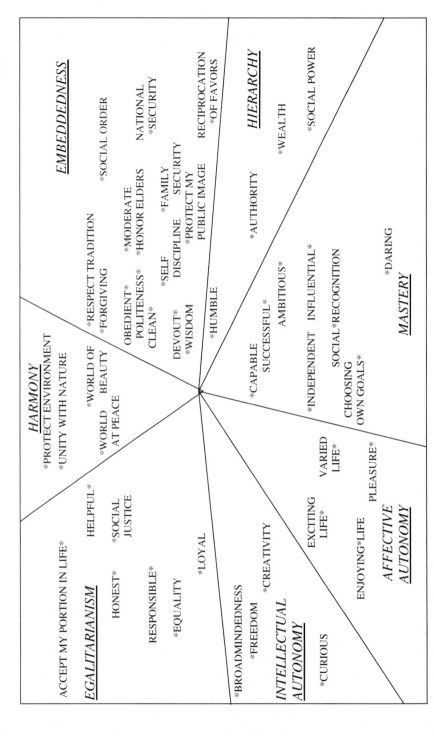

Figure 2: *Cultural level SSA-195 samples, 70 cultural groups (coefficient alienation .18)*

tion are located within a unique wedge-shaped region of the space.[4] Equally important, the regions representing each orientation form the integrated cultural system postulated by the theory: They emanate from the center of the circle, follow the expected order around the circle, and form the poles of the three broad cultural dimensions.

[51]

Contrasting the Hofstede and Schwartz dimensions

Given the empirical support for these cultural orientations, it is interesting to consider how they compare with the widely used dimensions of national work culture that Hofstede (1980a, 2001) proposed. I briefly discuss some of the conceptual similarities and differences and note empirical associations between the sets of dimensions (cf. Sagiv & Schwartz, 2000).

In order to increase reliability for my dimensions, I combined the teacher and student sample means in each of the 52 nations for which both types of samples were available. For 18 nations where either a teacher or student sample was missing, I estimated the missing means using regression coefficients derived from regressing the available 52 student and teacher samples on one another. This yielded scores for 70 nations or groups. Of these, it was possible to find scores on the Hofstede dimensions for 57, either in his original IBM data, in his reanalyses of national subcultures, or in his estimates for nations not in the IBM set (Hofstede, 2001: 500-502). Correlations between dimensions are based on these 57.

My autonomy/embeddedness dimension and Hofstede's individualism/collectivism overlap conceptually to some degree. Both concern relations between the individual and the collective and both contrast an autonomous with an interdependent view of people. However, the dimensions also differ. Autonomy/embeddedness contrasts openness to change with maintaining the status quo; individualism/collectivism does not. More important, many theorists associate individualism with the self-interested pursuit of personal goals (Kağitçibâşi, 1997; Triandis, 1995). Selfishness is not a characteristic of cultural autonomy. Indeed, it is welfare states that show the strongest emphasis on intellectual autonomy. In my view, no cultural emphasis could encourage individual selfishness among group members who interact regularly. This would be detrimental to the smooth running of families and of most societal institutions.

The correlations between the scores of nations on Hofstede's cultural dimensions and my cultural orientations indicate their degree of overlap. National scores on individualism correlated with national scores on embeddedness -.59, affective autonomy .63, and intellectual autonomy .49. They correlated .61 with an index of the broad autonomy/embeddedness dimension

[52]

formed by subtracting the embeddedness score from the mean of the affective and intellectual autonomy scores. This suggests considerable empirical overlap between individualism/collectivism and autonomy/embeddedness. But with 63% of their cross-national variance *not* shared ($1.00-.61^2$), they still order nations quite differently. For example, whereas the USA is first and Venezuela last among the 57 nations on individualism, the USA is 30th on the autonomy/embeddedness dimension and Venezuela is 33rd.

The hierarchy pole of the egalitarianism/hierarchy dimension has some conceptual overlap with Hofstede's power distance. Both concern legitimizing social inequality. Power distance refers to the acceptance of inequality by less powerful people. It also expresses their fear of authority. Hofstede sees it as a response to the inevitability of social inequality. The egalitarian/hierarchy dimension addresses a different issue — assuring responsible, cooperative behavior that will get societal tasks done. Hierarchical systems of ascribed roles obtain their legitimacy from their capacity to assure responsible behavior. Hierarchy does not necessary entail fear of authority by ordinary people. Egalitarianism emphasizes the moral equality of individuals, their capacity to internalize commitments to the welfare of others and to cooperate voluntarily with them. These key elements of egalitarianism are absent from low power distance.

Empirically, across 57 nations, power distance correlated .30 with hierarchy, -.46 with egalitarianism, and -.40 with the egalitarianism/hierarchy dimension. Thus, the dimensions are related as expected, but still distinct. For example, China is very high on power distance (9th) and very low on egalitarianism/hierarchy (last). But Slovakia differs across the dimensions, very high on power distance (tied for 1st) and moderate on egalitarianism/hierarchy (27th).

The mastery pole of harmony/mastery has some conceptual overlap with masculinity. Both emphasize assertiveness and ambition. Hofstede contrasts masculinity to femininity (tenderness, care, and concern for others). This implies that masculinity neglects or rejects the interests of others. I contrast mastery to harmony (being in tune with others and the environment). Mastery calls for an active, even disruptive stance, but it does not imply selfishness. Empirically, mastery and masculinity correlated only .15 implying independence.

Harmony might seem to overlap conceptually with uncertainty avoidance, since both idealize a harmonious order. However, harmony stresses that people and nature should exist comfortably together without assertion of control. In contrast, uncertainty avoidance emphasizes controlling ambiguity and unpredictability through institutions and beliefs that provide certainty. An empirical correlation of only .24 suggests little overlap.

There were three additional correlations greater than .30 between the two sets of dimensions.[5] Individualism correlated .52 with egalitarianism/hierarchy and .32 with harmony/mastery. Thus, individualism correlated significantly with all three of my dimensions. This implies that individualism includes elements from autonomy, egalitarianism, and harmony. Theorists rarely associate concepts such as egalitarianism and harmony with individualism, though they may see them as opposed (Kağitçibâşi, 1997; Triandis, 1995). I discuss problems and contradictions due to the catchall nature of individualism/collectivism as a cultural dimension below, in the section on culture in the 'West'.

[53]

Power distance correlated -.57 with autonomy/embeddedness. Conceptually, this makes good sense. Hofstede (2001) describes the power distance societal norm as dealing with the need for dependence versus interdependence in society. Where power distance is high, most people should be dependent, with everyone in his/her rightful place and protected by the social order in which they are embedded. Individuals are expected to conform their behavior and aspirations to their ascribed roles and to view limits on their autonomy as legitimate. Hence, power distance correlates negatively with autonomy and positively with embeddedness.

In sum, several conceptual similarities among the Hofstede and Schwartz dimensions are supported by correlations between the arraying of nations on the dimensions. However, even the most closely related dimensions differ conceptually and empirically in significant ways.

Contrasting the Inglehart and Schwartz dimensions

Inglehart (e.g., Inglehart & Baker, 2000) has extended his earlier work on materialism and post-materialism to propose two value dimensions on which to compare national cultures. His chapter in this volume explicates these two dimensions, tradition vs. secular-rational and survival vs. self-expression. Inglehart derived scores on these two dimensions for 72 nations, 57 of which overlap with the nations I have studied. I next consider conceptual and empirical relations between the two Inglehart dimensions and the cultural orientations I have presented.

The tradition/secular-rational dimension centrally concerns orientations

---

[5] The measured ordering of nations on cultural dimensions is not entirely reliable, of course. So the reported associations may underestimate empirical overlap between them. As the split-sample correlations in the next section show, however, the orderings of my cultural dimensions are quite reliable. This is probably true for Hofstede's and Inglehart's dimensions too, so the underestimation is not great.

toward authority. It contrasts societies in which religion, nation, and family are highly important with those in which they are not so important. In traditional societies, children's first duty is to their parents and parents are expected to sacrifice themselves for their children. Male dominance is the norm, absolute standards of morality prevail, and national pride is high. "Societies with secular-rational values have the opposite preferences on all of these topics" (Inglehart & Baker, 2000, p. 25). The five-item index used to measure this dimension correlates highly with these beliefs and attitudes. The two items that load most strongly on the factor, however, both concern religious belief.

[54]

This dimension overlaps conceptually with my autonomy/embeddedness dimension. Both concern the degree to which the individual is submerged in all-encompassing structures of tight mutual obligations. Inglehart's description implies that, in traditional societies, peoples' ties to their religious, national, and family groups are the source of meaning in their lives — a core aspect of embeddedness. The weakening of encompassing structures and of absolute standards in secular-rational societies frees individuals to think, do, and feel more independently — a core aspect of autonomy. Empirically, the tradition/secular-rational dimension correlates .55 with intellectual autonomy, .42 with affective autonomy, -.51 with embeddedness, and .52 with the autonomy/embeddedness dimension.

These two dimensions share considerable variance (27%), but they array nations somewhat differently. For example, East Germany ranks in the top 10% of nations on both dimensions and Zimbabwe in the bottom 15%. But Bulgaria, China, and Estonia rank in the top 10% on tradition/secular-rational but the bottom third on autonomy/embeddedness. The centrality of religion in the Inglehart index may explain this. The high secular-rational rankings may reflect the breakdown of religious faith and absolute standards of traditional morality during decades of communist rule. However, the culture in Bulgaria, China, and Estonia may still stress finding meaning through ties to the in-group. The autonomy/embeddedness dimension gives less weight to religious faith. It focuses more on how legitimate it is for individuals to cultivate unique ways of thinking, acting, and feeling vs. submerging the self in an encompassing collectivity.

The tradition/secular-rational dimension also has some conceptual overlap with the egalitarianism/hierarchy dimension. Both concern deference to authority. The emphasis on national pride in traditional societies also expresses a hierarchical orientation, and the preference for male dominance is compatible with hierarchy and opposed to egalitarianism. The overlap is limited, however, because the Inglehart dimension does not relate to the primary focus of egalitarianism/hierarchy. Both egalitarianism and hierarchy seek to preserve the social fabric by promoting responsible behavior that considers the welfare of others. They differ in grounding such behavior in voluntary choice based on internalized commitments (egalitarianism) or in conformity to the obligations and expectations of ascribed roles (hierarchy). The empirical associations reflect very little overlap. The tradition/secular-rational dimension correlated .05 with egalitarianism, -.25 with hierarchy, and .20 with the egalitarianism/hierarchy dimension. [55]

Unexpectedly, given no apparent conceptual overlap, the tradition/secular-rational dimension correlated positively with harmony (.48), though not with mastery (-.15). Thus, more secular-rational societies are also societies that tend to emphasize fitting into the natural and social world as it is, trying to understand and appreciate rather than to change, direct, or to exploit. The nations with cultures especially high on both harmony and secular-rational orientations are all in Western Europe. These nations have well-to-do, educated, and involved publics that have enabled them to respond to two devastating wars and to severe ecological crises by developing rationally based relations of harmony among themselves and with the environment.

Inglehart's second dimension, survival/self-expression, contrasts societies in which people primarily focus on economic and physical security (survival) with societies in which security is high and quality-of-life issues are central (self-expression). In the latter, many people are well educated and work in the services. This demands of them more freedom of judgment, innovation, and autonomous decision-making and equips them with relevant communication and information-processing skills. Trust, tolerance, subjective well-being, political activism, and concern for the environment are high. At the survival pole, people feel threatened by and are intolerant of those who are different (e.g., ethnically, in sexual preference) or seek cultural change (e.g., women's movements). At the self-expression pole, difference and change are accepted and even seen as enriching, and out-groups are increasingly seen as meriting equal rights.

This dimension also overlaps with the autonomy/embeddedness dimension. They both concern the degree to which individuals should be encouraged to express their uniqueness and independence in thought, action, and feelings. Empirically, they are substantially associated. Survival/self-expression correlated -.71 with embeddedness, .61 with affective autonomy, .58 with intellectual autonomy, and .69 with the autonomy/embeddedness dimension, with which it shares 48% of its variance. These two dimensions array nations quite similarly. For example, Sweden and Denmark rank very high on both dimensions and Uganda and Zimbabwe rank very low. But there are differences. Both Ghana and West Germany are moderate on survival/self-expression, but Ghana is very low on autonomy/embeddedness and West Germany very high.

[56]

The egalitarianism/hierarchy dimension also overlaps conceptually with survival/self-expression. The latter pits trust, tolerance, and support for the equal rights of out-groups against low trust, intolerance, and rejection of out-groups as threatening. This closely parallels some aspects of high vs. low egalitarianism. Political activism and opposition to change in accepted roles differences also conflict with hierarchy, though these elements are less critical. The empirical correlations support these inferences. Survival/self-expression correlated .73 with egalitarianism, -.41 with hierarchy, and .61 with the egalitarianism/hierarchy dimension with which it shares 37% of its variance. Sweden and Norway are very high on both dimensions and Bulgaria is very low on both. But many nations do not exhibit consistent ranks on the two cultural dimensions. Japan is very low on egalitarianism/hierarchy and moderately high on survival/self-expression, and Australia is moderate on the former and very high on the latter.

The contrasting feelings of interpersonal threat vs. trust and the focus on material security vs. environmental protection of the survival/self-expression dimension parallel a low vs. high harmony orientation. Empirically, however, there is no association either with harmony or with the harmony/mastery dimension. Harmony emphasizes fitting into and accepting the social and natural environments rather than changing or using them. Self-expression implies a more activist orientation to people and nature. This may explain the lack of association.

In the conclusions to this chapter, I will note aspects of the Hofstede, Inglehart, and Schwartz cultural dimensions that can be integrated. Next, however, I turn to a critical question about the meaningfulness of the unit used in the studies that validate all these dimensions.

Nations as a cultural unit

Almost all large, comparative, cross-cultural studies treat nations as their cultural unit. Is the nation a legitimate unit of cultural analysis? Nations are rarely homogeneous societies with a unified culture. Still, as Hofstede (1980a) argued, forces towards integration in established nations may produce substantial sharing of culture (e.g., the common dominant language, political and educational systems, shared mass media, markets, and national symbols). But inferences about national culture may depend on which subgroups are studied. Available data make it possible to address this issue empirically for my dimensions.

If there is substantial cultural unity within nations, the order of nations on cultural dimensions should be quite similar when culture is measured using one type of subsample from the dominant group as when using another. For example, the same nations should score higher and the same nations lower on each cultural orientation whether the set of samples is composed of older or of younger respondents. I assessed consistency in the relative scores of nations on the seven cultural orientations, using three types of subsamples. [57]

I first assessed whether younger and older subcultures yield similar relative national scores. In 42 nations with substantial age ranges among teachers, I split the samples at age 37. The relative national scores, based on these two subgroups, were very similar. Correlations ranged from .96 for embeddedness to .80 for affective autonomy (mean .90). I also compared national scores using male vs. female student subgroups across 44 nations. This yielded similar results: Correlations ranged from .96 for embeddedness and intellectual autonomy to .84 for harmony (mean .90). Finally, I compared national scores based on the teacher vs. the student samples across 52 nations. Correlations ranged from .88 for egalitarianism to .51 for harmony (mean .79). The weaker correlations in this last comparison reflect the fact that the samples differed both in age and occupation. This suggests that closely matching the characteristics of the samples from each nation is critical when comparing national cultural orientations.

Another way to assess cultural unity within nations is to compare the cultural distance between samples within countries to the cultural distance between samples from different countries. Samples from dominant groups in different regions were available in seven countries: student samples in France (2), Germany (2), Russia (2), Turkey (2), Japan (3) and the USA (5), and teacher samples in China (3), Russia (2), and the USA (2). I computed cultural distances between every pair of student samples or of teacher samples both within the same country and across countries. The cultural distance between two samples is the squared difference between the scores of the samples on each cultural orientation, summed across the seven orientations. The cultural distance between samples from different countries was almost always greater than the distance between samples from the same country. Between country distances were greater in 183 of 187 comparisons.

These data demonstrate that the similarity of cultural value orientations within nations, when viewed against the background of cultural distance between nations, is considerable. Taken together, the findings support the view that nations are meaningful cultural units. If the samples from different nations are matched, national cultures can be compared.

Cultural distinctiveness of world regions

Are there culturally distinct world regions? The combined teacher and student samples provide scores on the seven cultural value orientations for 67

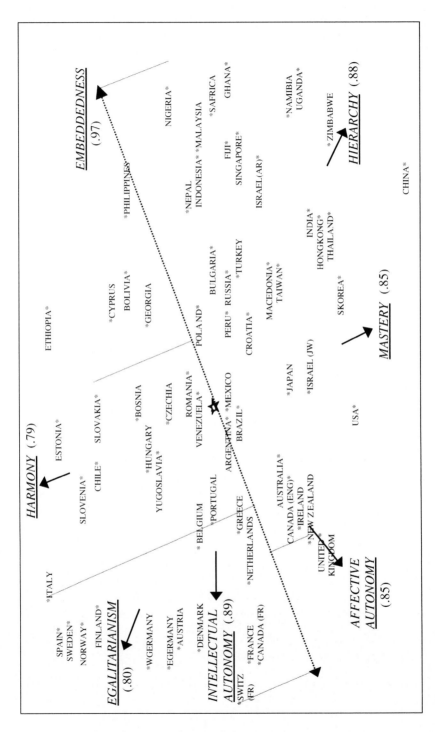

Figure 3: *Coplot map of 67 national groups of seven cultural orientations*

national groups. For cross-national comparisons of culture, I first standard-ized the mean importance of all seven orientations within each nation. Each national profile therefore reflects the relative importance of each cultural ori-entation within a nation. I then mapped the cultural distances between nations with the 'co-plot' multidimensional scaling technique (Goldreich & Raveh, 1993). It constructed a matrix of profile differences between all pairs of nations by summing the absolute differences between the ratings of each of the seven value dimensions in the two nations. From this matrix it generat-ed a two-dimensional spatial representation of the similarities and differ-ences among the nations (see Figure 3).

[59]

Finally, the 'co-plot' placed vectors in the space that indicate the direc-tion in which scores on each of the seven orientations increase. The full vec-tor is drawn for embeddedness from lower left to upper right. The vectors for the other orientations extend back from their labeled arrow through the cen-ter of the two-dimensional space. The vector for each cultural orientation is the regression line that optimally represents the scores of the nations on that orientation.

The co-plot summarizes locations of nations on seven different cultural ori-entations in only two spatial dimensions. Hence, the graphic representation cannot be perfect. Coefficients beside each label are the correlation between the observed scores and the scores represented by the vector. Their substan-tial magnitude indicates that the locations of the vast majority of samples do provide quite an accurate picture. This is because nations usually exhibit a profile that reflects the coherence of the theoretical structure of cultural dimensions. In nations whose culture emphasizes one polar value orienta-tion, the opposing polar orientation is typically not emphasized. Moreover, adjacent cultural orientations usually have similar levels of importance rela-tive to other nations. For example, Italian culture, relative to all others, is very high in harmony and the adjacent egalitarianism and very low in the opposing hierarchy and mastery. Chinese culture shows the reverse profile.[6]

Locations of nations along these vectors relative to one another reveal, graphically, the specific ways in which national cultures resemble or differ from one another. For example, the farther a nation toward the upper right,

---

[6] Japan presents a striking exception. Seven samples from around Japan reveal strong cultur-al emphases on hierarchy and harmony but not on embeddedness, which is adjacent to them, and a strong emphasis on intellectual autonomy but not on the adjacent egalitarianism. Thus, the location of Japan in the co-plot is necessarily misleading. The findings suggest that Japan-ese culture has evolved in a manner different from most others and/or that it is in a period of transition.

[60]

the greater the cultural emphasis on embeddedness relative to other nations; the farther toward the lower left, the less the cultural emphasis on embeddedness. To locate a nation on a cultural orientation, draw a perpendicular line from the position of the nation to the vector for that orientation. The perpendiculars drawn to the embeddedness vector show that this orientation is especially emphasized in Nigeria, less so in Slovakia, then Italy, New Zealand, and, finally, Switzerland (French).

Consider two examples of how Figure 3 represents the cultural profile of a nation on all seven cultural orientations. In Sweden (upper left), harmony, intellectual autonomy, and egalitarianism are strongly emphasized and affective autonomy is moderately emphasized. The cultural emphasis on embeddedness is low, and it is very low for mastery and hierarchy. In contrast, in Zimbabwe (lower right), mastery, embeddedness, and hierarchy are highly emphasized, affective autonomy moderately emphasized, and egalitarianism, intellectual autonomy, and harmony receive little cultural emphasis.

With few exceptions, the spatial map of the 67 nations reveals seven transnational cultural groupings: West European nations to the far left, East European nations in the upper center, English-speaking nations in the lower left center, Latin American nations in the center, South Asian nations in a band to the right of center, Confucian influenced nations below them to the right, and sub-Saharan African nations to the far right.[7] Most of these groupings are related to geographical proximity. Hence, some of the cultural similarity within regions is doubtless due to diffusion of values, norms, practices, and institutions across national borders (Naroll, 1973).

But shared histories, religion, level of development, and other factors also play a part.

The regions show striking parallels with the groupings suggested by Huntington (1993) and those found by Hofstede (1980a) and by Inglehart and Baker (2000). To augment these quantitative cultural profiles and explain them, it is necessary to carry out social and historical analyses of specific nations and transnational regions. Schwartz and Ros (1995) and Schwartz and Bardi (1997) provide initial explanations for the emergence of the English-speaking, West European, and East European cultural profiles.

Now let us examine the cultural orientations that characterize each of these distinct cultural regions. To quantify cultural emphases in addition to the visual presentation, I ran correlational analyses. I simplified by collapsing the seven cultural value orientations into the three cultural dimensions. Table 1 reports

---

[7] Absent from the set of 67 nations are Arab and Central American nations. They might yield additional regions.

Table 1: *Cultural distinctiveness of world regions: Correlations of tegion with cultural dimensions, controlling GNP per capita 1990, across 67 nations*

Region	N^a	Autonomy vs. Embeddedness	Egalitarianism vs. Hierarchy	Harmony vs. Mastery
West Europe	16/51	.37**	.54**	.38*
English-Speaking	6/61	.00	-.07	-.38**
Confucian	6/61	-.16+	-.44**	-.30*
Sub-Saharan Africa	6/61	-.24**	-.16	-.29*
South Asia	9/58	-.21*	-.33**	.04
East Europe	15/52	.23*	.09	.35**
Latin America	7/60	.11	.18	.03

Note: Positive correlations signify that the region is higher on autonomy, egalitarianism or harmony; negative correlations signify that the region is higher on embeddedness, hierarchy or mastery; ^aN = number of nations in this region/number of nations in other regions to which compared; **$p<.01$, *$p<.05$, +$p<.10$, 2-tailed

point-biserial correlations of each cultural dimension with each region (nations scored 1) compared to all others (nations scored 0).[8] These correlations are partialed on national wealth (GNP per capita, 1990). Hence they reflect cultural differences over and above any socioeconomic differences. Regions differ substantially in socioeconomic level both as a cause and a consequence of culture. Because socioeconomic development is inextricably bound up with culture, the partial correlations may underestimate cultural differences.

Positive correlations in column 1 of Table 1 indicate that autonomy is emphasized more in the culture of a region than of other regions and embeddedness less. Negative correlations indicate that embeddedness is emphasized more and autonomy less. Positive correlations in column 2 indicate a relatively strong emphases on egalitarianism in a region and negative correlations a relatively strong emphasis on hierarchy. Positive correlations in column 3 indicate a relatively strong emphases on harmony in a region and negative correlations a relatively strong emphasis on mastery. The correlations in Table 1 and the locations of regions in the world cultural map in Figure 3 tell the same story.

---

[8] The maximum possible magnitude of point-biserial correlations declines with increasing inequality in the relative sizes of the two groups compared. All the correlations in Table 1 are based on very unequal sized groups. The maximum possible correlations are therefore considerably less than 1.00. Hence, the reported correlations convey conservative estimates of group distinctiveness.

West Europe. Corresponding to its location on the upper left of Figure 3, the correlations show that West European culture emphasizes egalitarianism, autonomy, and harmony more than any other region. It is very low on hierarchy, mastery, and embeddedness. Its high socioeconomic level does not account for this, since national wealth has been controlled. This is the appropriate cultural profile for a region of democratic, welfare states where concern for the environment is especially high (cf. Ester et al., 1994). West European nations share a broad culture when compared with other world regions. Still, within Western Europe there is substantial variation on the affective autonomy orientation.

[62]

English-speaking. Contrary to the prevailing view that Western Europe and the United States share an individualist culture, the cultures of the West European and English-speaking regions are very different. The culture of the English-speaking region is especially high in mastery compared with the rest of the world. It is average in intellectual autonomy and egalitarianism. American samples emphasize mastery even more and autonomy and egalitarianism even less than the other English-speaking samples. This profile points to a cultural orientation that encourages an assertive, pragmatic, entrepreneurial, and even exploitative orientation to the social and natural environment. This region is particularly homogeneous. Within-region differences are largest on intellectual autonomy and harmony, but even these are small.

Cultural differences in the 'West'. A view of Western culture as individualist is central to applications of Hofstede's work. Hence, the striking differences within the West that our more complex conception of cultural orientations reveals deserve more detailed explication. Comparisons of 22 West European samples with six United States samples show large and significant differences on six of the seven culture orientations (Schwartz & Ros, 1995). Egalitarianism, intellectual autonomy, and harmony are higher in Western Europe; mastery, hierarchy and embeddedness are higher in the United States. Using the term 'individualist' to describe either of these cultures distorts the picture these analyses reveal.

Cultural orientations in Western Europe are individualist in one sense: They emphasize intellectual and affective autonomy and de-emphasize hierarchy and embeddedness relative to other cultures in most of the world. But West European priorities contradict conventional views of individualism in another sense: They emphasize egalitarianism and harmony and de-emphasize mastery. That is, this culture calls for selfless concern for the welfare of others and fitting into the natural and social world rather than striving to change it through assertive action. This runs directly counter to what individualism is usually understood to mean.

Cultural emphases in the United States show a different but equally complex pattern: The individualistic aspect of American value orientations is the [63] emphasis on affective autonomy and mastery at the expense of harmony. This combination may be the source of the stereotypical view of American culture as justifying and encouraging egotistic self-advancement. But this is not prototypical individualism because intellectual autonomy is relatively unimportant. Moreover, both hierarchy and embeddedness, the orientations central to collectivism, are high compared with Western Europe.[9] This profile recalls recent in depth analyses of American culture (Bellah et *al.*, 1986; Etzioni, 1993).

Confucian. The Confucian-influenced region also exhibits a pragmatic, entrepreneurial orientation, as the negative correlation in the last column of Table 1 shows. However, this orientation combines with a heavy emphasis on hierarchy and rejection of egalitarianism. This region emphasizes embeddedness more than all but the African and South Asian regions. This cultural profile is consonant with many analyses of Confucian culture (e.g., Bond, 1996). Within-region differences are largest on intellectual autonomy. Japan and Singapore are most dissimilar.

Sub-Saharan Africa. The culture in the sub-Saharan African region also emphasizes mastery rather than harmony. This may seem surprising. I think it reflects the current struggle to overcome poverty in these nations. This struggle encourages and legitimizes changing and even exploiting the environment. The culture in this region also emphasizes embeddedness — that is, finding meaning in life largely through social relationships and protecting

---

[9] For detailed explication, see Schwartz and Ros (1995). They also note that the contrast between Western Europe and the United States finds expression in core cultural ideals. The motto of the French Revolution — liberté, égalité, et fraternité — symbolizes West European orientations. 'Liberté' signifies the centrality of individual independence, a commitment to autonomy. But 'egalité et fraternité' emphasize the voluntary social responsibility of the autonomous individual, a commitment to egalitarianism and harmony. The Declaration of Independence expresses the parallel American ideal. It speaks of the inalienable rights of life, liberty, and the pursuit of happiness. Again, 'liberty' reflects the importance of individual autonomy. But the flavor of this autonomy is best understood in conjunction with 'the pursuit of happiness'. The American cultural ideal legitimates the pursuit of individual pleasure and success. These, of course, are the focus of affective autonomy and mastery, orientations unusually important in the United States. Inclusion of 'life' as an ideal implies concern for security and order. This concern is expressed in the fact that American culture does not reject embeddedness and hierarchy, orientations that foster security and order but oppose autonomy.

group solidarity and the traditional order. This fits well with the conclusions of anthropological studies in sub-Saharan Africa (e.g., Gyekye, 1997). Differences within the region are small, with the largest on affective autonomy.

[64]

South Asia. The culture in the South Asian region is particularly high in hierarchy and embeddedness. This points to an emphasis on fulfilling one's obligations in a hierarchical system — obeying expectations from those in roles of greater status or authority and expecting humility and obedience from those in inferior roles. As in Africa, here social relationships rather than autonomous pursuits are expected to give meaning to life. Within South Asia, mastery and harmony differences are relatively large.

East Europe. The East European cultural profile stands out in emphasizing harmony and de-emphasizing mastery. In detailed discussions of culture in East-Central Europe, my colleagues and I have argued that the culture reflects the impact of adapting to life under totalitarian communist regimes (Bardi & Schwartz, 1996; Schwartz & Bardi, 1997; Schwartz et al., 2000). We interpret the emphasis on harmony and the de-emphasis on mastery in East-Central Europe as an adaptive orientation that recognized the importance of avoiding trouble and refraining from taking initiatives. Not evident from the correlations with the bipolar dimensions in the table, the cultural orientations in this region disclaimed both egalitarianism ($r = -.27$) and hierarchy (-.29), but emphasized intellectual autonomy (.36). This may suggest that people in East-Central Europe rejected both the rhetoric and the social organization of communist regimes, while insisting on their intellectual independence (see similar arguments and further evidence in Schwartz & Bardi, 1997 and Schwartz et al., 2001). The largest variation within this region is on hierarchy.

According to the theory of cultural orientations, the East European profile in 1989-95 is not a coherent cultural profile. Cultures are expected to show relatively similar emphases on mastery and on hierarchy, not opposing emphases as here. And a de-emphasis on hierarchy should accompany an emphasis on egalitarianism, but both are de-emphasized here. Perhaps, the foreign ideology and social organization imposed on this region over 40 years, combined with the resistance to it, created cultural contradictions. I therefore expect cultural change over the coming decades, as indigenous modes of social organization reemerge.

Latin America. Finally, the Latin American region is distinctive by being average on all three dimensions. Within the region, the largest differences are on mastery and harmony. Latin American culture has been described as collectivist (e.g., Triandis, 1995). Compared with Western Europe, this seems to be so. Latin America is higher in hierarchy and embeddedness, the main components of what is often seen as collectivism. This is not the case, however, when we compare Latin America to Africa, South Asia, and Confucian-influenced cultures. This example highlights the importance of the frame of comparison. The culture of a group may look different when viewed in a worldwide perspective than when inferred from narrower comparisons.

[65]

Relations of culture to socioeconomic, political, and population characteristics

Having demonstrated that nations and regions of the world differ systematically on my cultural dimensions, two critical questions arise. Do these cultural differences matter? And where do they come from? Without answers to these questions, one might argue that national scores on these cultural orientations are mere artifacts, proxies for the social, structural, and demographic variables that actually influence what goes on in society. A significant strength of Hofstede's (1980a, 2001) contribution is precisely his reasoning and supportive data regarding antecedents and consequences of national differences on his cultural dimensions. As a start toward addressing these questions, I now discuss some relations of culture to development, political institutions, gender and income inequality, and population and family characteristics.

Some theorists see culture as a major determinant of socioeconomic success. Others see national wealth as a determinant of culture. My own position is that socioeconomic and cultural variables powerfully influence one another. Most interestingly, culture may sometimes mediate the effects of socioeconomic variables on individual behavior. The first three rows of Table 2 present correlations of the cultural dimensions with indicators of socioeconomic development.

High levels of education, long life expectancies, and high levels of average individual income all correlate positively and strongly with cultural autonomy and, by implication, negatively with cultural embeddedness. These indicators of development also correlate positively with cultural egalitarianism and negatively with hierarchy. Harmony/mastery has weaker links to development. Many other indicators of development (e.g., energy use, telephones, literacy) exhibit very similar associations with the cultural orientations.[10]

---

[10] The question arises whether correlations between variables across nations reflect causal relations among the variables or merely the fact that they have diffused together, the so-called 'Galton's problem'. Treating regions rather than nations as the unit of analysis would mitigate this problem but raise others, because regions are far from completely homogeneous (see conclusions section).

Table 2: *Relations of culture to socioeconomic, political, and demographic characteristics: Zero-order correlations and regressions including culture and national wealth variables*

Characteristic	N	Autonomy-Embeddedness		Egalitarianism-Hierarchy		Harmony-Mastery		GDP per capita 1985		
		r	β	r	β	β	r	β	r	β
Socioeconomic Development										
% Cohort Secondary Education 1984	64	.66**	.	.48**	.	.	26*	.	.70**	
Life Expectancy 1990	67	.74**	.	.48**	.	.	22	.	.75**	
GDP per capita 1985	67	.74**		.51**			23		1.00	
Political Institutions										
Democratization 1983, 1990 Mean	65	.60**	.31*	.50**		.33*	.08	-.28*	.60**	.27
Level of Law and Order	53	.68**	.31*	.58**		.31*	.18	.31*	.77**	.27*
Gender Equality	58	.51**	.34*	.41**		-.04	.41**	.29*	.40**	.17
Population Characteristics										
Ethnic Heterogeneity 1990	67	-.53**	-.49**	-.33*		.14	-.43**	-.32*	-.37*	-.00
Mean Family Size 1970, 1980, 1985	66	-.74**	-.38**	-.62**		-.22*	-.40**	-.08	-.65**	-.28*

Note: **p<.01, *p<.05, 2-tailed

Explications of the likely reciprocal relations among culture and development are available elsewhere (e.g., Hofstede, 2001; Inglehart, 1997; Triandis, 1995). They apply here as well. I therefore focus on other topics, but control the effects of country wealth in all analyses. Where the data suggest that culture mediates socioeconomic effects, I comment in more detail.

[67]

Political institutions are another aspect of the social structure that reciprocally influences culture. Rows 4 and 5 of the table present associations of cultural orientations with two aspects of the regulation of power in societies. Row 4 correlates cultural orientations with the mean level of democratization in 1983 and 1990 in 65 nations. Democratization refers to civil liberties and political rights (Gastil, 1987). Democratization correlates significantly with two of the cultural dimensions and with national wealth. To clarify the unique associations of each cultural dimension with democratization, net of the effects of national wealth and the other dimensions, I also present the standardized regression coefficients when all four variables are included.

Autonomy and democracy go together, regardless of national wealth, as shown by the significant beta (.31). Nations high in democracy are nations with cultures that emphasize that it is legitimate and desirable for individuals to pursue and express their own ideas and feelings. There is also a positive reciprocal relation between democracy and egalitarianism. A culture that encourages people to treat others as moral equals and to contribute voluntarily to maintaining the social fabric is conducive to and supportive of a democratic political system. And democratic institutions promote the emergence of such an egalitarian culture.

Less expected is the negative beta for harmony/mastery. Democracy is greater in cultures that emphasize mastery, when the other dimensions and national wealth are held constant. Perhaps an emphasis on mastery promotes democracy by encouraging citizens to try to influence the way the institutions of society run. At the same time, democratic institutions may foster cultural mastery, because they demand more active participation by individuals and groups and make it worthwhile.

Next, consider relations of culture to the level of graft and corruption in societies. This index gauges corruption among public and government officials (Kaufmann et al., 1999). The beta coefficients reveal that autonomy, egalitarianism, and harmony relate uniquely and substantially to the absence of corruption, regardless of national wealth. Now think about the reverse side of these dimensions — embeddedness, hierarchy, and mastery. The more cultural orientations emphasize identifying with the in-group in which one is embedded and fulfilling one's role obligations in a hierarchical social order, the less law and order in a nation. Both embeddedness and hierarchy put allegiances to one's family, in-group, or superiors ahead of rational, bureaucratic considerations.[11] Mastery gives legitimacy to and encourages assertive action to achieve goals, even at the expense of others, if necessary. Thus cultural mastery may justify using non-legal means to advance personal or group interests. These are probably the key paths through which these cultural orientations influence corruption.

[68]

The extent of gender equality is another important aspect of the social structure that culture may affect. The measure of gender equality is a composite of women's social, health, and employment equality in 1988 (Women's social equality, 1988). Row 6 of the table presents the relevant correlations and betas. Not surprisingly, gender equality is greater in nations whose culture emphasizes egalitarianism, autonomy, and harmony. Culture and practice are consistent. Equality is also greater in wealthier nations.

Only the betas for autonomy/embeddedness and harmony/mastery are significant. National wealth has no unique influence on gender equality. The data suggest that national wealth affects gender equality, if at all, largely through its influence on culture. Gender equality has changed fairly rapidly over the past 25 years, while culture change, as noted, is slow. It is therefore likely that culture causally facilitated or hampered change in gender equality. The absence of a significant beta for egalitarianism/hierarchy is apparently because much of its influence on gender equality is shared with autonomy/embeddedness.[12] Both egalitarianism and autonomy orientations encourage a view of people as autonomous decision-makers who are able to undertake social responsibilities voluntarily. This common emphasis fosters gender equality.

How can we explain the unique, positive association of harmony/mastery with gender equality? A cultural emphasis on mastery is expressed in a societal preference for assertive behavior. Such behavior is seen as stereotypically male (Williams & Best, 1990). I speculate that women would therefore be seen as meriting more equal employment and social opportunities the less the emphasis on mastery in the culture. This explanation is relevant to social and employment equality but not to health equality. And, indeed, harmony/mastery does not correlate with a separate health equality index.

Finally, let's examine reciprocal relations between cultural value orientations and two demographic variables. Row 7 of the table presents relations of

---

[11] In many of the most corrupt nations, external powers imposed state boundaries on diverse and conflicting ethnic groups (e.g., the French in Africa). In these nations, the need to preserve the in-group enhanced cultural embeddedness and further weakened allegiance to the state and its legal system.

[12] Removing autonomy/embeddedness from the regression yields a significant positive beta for egalitarianism/hierarchy.

culture with ethnic heterogeneity. This refers to the number of different ethnic groups that constitute 5% or more of the population. Consider only the unique associations indicated by the betas. The larger the number of ethnic groups in a nation, the stronger the cultural emphasis on embeddedness (beta -.49) and on mastery (beta -.32). The primary causal influence here is probably from heterogeneity to culture. As the number and size of ethnic groups in a nation increases, ethnic identity becomes more salient. This is the case in Western Europe and the USA today. This leads people to identify themselves and to relate to others more in terms of their ethnicity. Leaders evoke ethnicity to mobilize support and institutions may be organized along ethnic lines. This heightens the importance of group membership at the expense of individual uniqueness. It increases identification with in-group goals, symbols, and traditions and promotes a sense of shared fate. This underlies the cultural emphasis on embeddedness rather than autonomy. [69]

The emphasis on mastery rather than harmony may derive from competition among multiple ethnic groups. When there are two or three groups, a relatively stable dominance order may be maintained. When there are many groups, however, the dominance order is likely to be more ambiguous and less stable. Groups compete to move up the social ladder and to gain control over resources. A cultural emphasis on mastery — encouraging active assertion in order to change and exploit the physical and social environment to attain group goals — would be a natural outgrowth of such group competition.

GDP/cap correlates significantly with ethnic heterogeneity. Wealthy nations attract immigrants and thereby become more heterogeneous, and immigration contributes to economic success. However, when GDP/pc is entered into the regression with culture, its relation with ethnic heterogeneity disappears. This suggests that culture mediates the association of national wealth with ethnic heterogeneity. A partial interpretation is that it is the egalitarian and autonomous culture of wealthy nations that attracts immigrants rather than the wealth itself.

My last topic concerns the family, probably the most powerful link in the reciprocal influences of culture and social structure. The larger the average family, the greater the cultural emphasis on embeddedness and hierarchy. The final row of the table reports especially strong correlations of autonomy/embeddedness and of egalitarianism/hierarchy with average family size (-.74 and -.62). At the aggregate level, cultural value orientations relate strongly to family size. Surprisingly, however, the size of people's own family does not relate to their own personal values. How can this be? The key is societal norms for managing family relations. Societal norms reflect what is required and possible in order for the *typical* family to function smoothly.

These norms reflect the prototypical composition of households. They specify how families should be organized, how children should be raised, and how family members should interact. Most people manage family relations in ways that conform to these norms. The size of their own family has less impact.

Where the typical family is large and has many young children it is crucial for behavior to be predictable. This requires high levels of social control from above. Emphasizing obedience to authority, conformity to norms, and fulfilling role obligations unquestioningly is functional. If family members view themselves as inseparable parts of a family collectivity and identify with its interests, even large families can run smoothly. These family practices and norms help build cultural embeddedness and hierarchy in the society. Large families are incompatible with cultural autonomy and egalitarianism. The demands of coordination in large families prevent treating each member as a unique individual with equal rights. They discourage permitting each family member to make decisions autonomously and to pursue his or her own ideas, interests, and desires.

The preceding explains the causal influence of family size on cultural value orientations. The influence of cultural values on family size also contributes to the strong correlations. Autonomy values encourage having few children so that each can develop his or her unique abilities and interests. Autonomy and egalitarianism values encourage and justify women's pursuit of meaningful non-family roles. This too reduces the number of children. Embeddedness values promote commitment to the in-group. They sanctify group continuity and, hence, having many children to promote it. Autonomy values sanctify individual choice. They justify weighing children against alternative ways to achieve personal meaning in life, such as careers.

The above analyses demonstrate that all three cultural dimensions contribute uniquely to the explanation of important social phenomena. Though their contributions are unique, autonomy/embeddedness and egalitarianism/hierarchy showed a similar pattern of positive or negative betas in relation to each of the variables examined. This reflects the positions of their component orientations, as adjacent or opposed, in the circular structure of cultural orientations (Figure 1). The harmony/mastery dimension exhibited a different pattern of betas. Sometimes it was the same as the other two dimensions (e.g., for level of law and order) and sometimes opposite (e.g., for democratization). The harmony/mastery dimension also correlated least with the Hofstede dimensions. Thus, the aspects of culture it captures may be especially distinctive.

Conclusions

Perhaps the most striking finding when comparing the outcomes of the research based on the Hofstede, Inglehart, and Schwartz cultural value dimensions is that they identify such similar cultural regions around the world. At least two of the three approaches, and usually all three, identify African, Confucian, East-Central European (ex-communist), English Speaking, Latin American, South Asian, and West European regions. This is quite amazing, considering the conceptual differences among the dimensions, the very different methods of measurement employed (work values and attitudes; beliefs, preferences, and judgments on a range of topics; abstract values), the different types of samples (IBM employees, representative national samples, teachers, students) from which they obtained their data, and the different periods in which data were gathered (from the late '60s into the 21st century). The emergence of similar regions affirms the reality of the systematic cultural value differences these approaches are tapping.

[71]

Let me suggest two important next steps in studying cultural regions. First, we need to examine the degree of cultural homogeneity within each region and the extent to which it differs from others. In my analyses, each region is quite homogeneous and distinctive on at least three or four of the seven cultural orientations. But each also shows considerable 'within' variation on one or two orientations. Whether regions can be used, as a unit of analysis is therefore a matter of which orientations are of interest. Second, we need to examine the extent to which the different approaches agree about the substance of the cultural orientations that characterize each region. This requires a deeper understanding of the cultural value dimensions themselves.

How many dimensions are needed to capture the broad cultural value differences among societies? It is too early to answer this question definitively, but as few as three or four, each comprising a pair of nearly opposing orientations, may suffice. Note that I refer only to *value* dimensions. In the introduction I argued that these are particularly significant dimensions for comparing cultures because they affect so many different aspects of life. But other dimensions of cultural difference, such as the tightness or looseness of normative systems, holistic vs. analytic styles of thought, degree of emotional expressiveness, and time perspective, are also important.

The critical value dimensions are unlikely to be orthogonal. They evolve as preferences for resolving basic issues in managing life in society. It is not logical that preferences for resolving one issue will remain independent of those for other issues. Cultures that encourage autonomy in individual/group relations are unlikely to prefer hierarchy for managing human interdependence. Though not opposites, autonomy and hierarchy rarely appear together because they presume conflicting views of human nature. Of course, we can derive orthogonal dimensions from data. But in doing so we miss the pull toward coherence in national cultures.

[72]

Analyses of empirical and conceptual relations among the various cultural value dimensions and orientations suggests that it is useful to discriminate at least the following:

1. A dimension dealing with the desirable degree of independence of the person from in-groups vs. embeddedness in these groups: This includes my autonomy/embeddedness, Hofstede's individualism without the component of whose goals — own or group — should take precedence, and elements of both the Inglehart dimensions.[13]
2. A dimension dealing with the desirability of equal vs. hierarchical allocation of resources, roles, rights, and obligations among persons and groups: This includes my egalitarianism/hierarchy, elements of Hofstede's power distance, and the materialism aspect of Inglehart's survival pole.
3. A dimension concerned with the relative desirability of assertively using or changing the social and natural environment in the active pursuit of goals vs. maintaining harmony in relations to this environment: This includes my mastery/harmony, Hofstede's masculinity, and elements captured by Inglehart's secular-rational pole.

These three combined dimensions were evident in a multidimensional scaling analysis of the seven Schwartz cultural orientations, four Hofstede dimensions, and two Inglehart dimensions. The first two dimensions correlate substantially with economic development, while the third does not — making it especially interesting to pursue further.

To sum up: This chapter has described a relatively new set of cultural value orientations. It has illustrated their importance by locating them in the skein of reciprocal causal relations among social structural, institutional, and demographic factors that deeply affect life. These cultural value orientations may sometimes influence significant aspects of life even more than socioeconomic factors do. These orientations order national cultures in ways somewhat different from previous dimensions. Moreover, the observed orderings

---

[13] Inglehart's descriptions of the dimensions reveal shared elements that are relevant to autonomy/embeddedness. Survival and tradition both stress conformity to the in-group, submission to authority, limits on individual expression, intolerance toward out-groups, and rejection of change. Secular-rational and self-expression both stress the opposite. The empirical analysis of items yields orthogonal dimensions, but the concepts are not independent. This raises questions about the fit between data and interpretation.

of nations relate meaningfully to such characteristics of nations as socioeconomic development, political institutions, and population features. Much remains to be done to determine how much these cultural value orientations add to the insights into individual and social phenomena that other theories of cultural dimensions provide.

[73]

The current approach to cultural dimensions differs from others in several ways. (a) It derived the cultural orientations from a priori theorizing rather than post hoc examination of data. (b) It designated a priori the value items that serve as markers for each orientation. (c) It used as measures only items tested for cross-cultural equivalence of meaning. (d) It included a set of items demonstrated to cover the range of values recognized cross-culturally, a step toward ensuring relative comprehensiveness of cultural value dimensions. (e) It specified how the cultural orientations are organized into a coherent system of related dimensions and verified this organization, rather than assuming that orthogonal dimensions best capture cultural reality. (f) It brought empirical evidence that the order of national cultures on each of the orientations is robust across different types of samples from each of a large number of nations around the world. These distinctive features increase the promise of this approach for future research.

CHAPTER FOUR

Individualism, autonomy, self-expression

The human development syndrome

RONALD INGLEHART AND DAPHNA OYSERMAN

Basic cultural orientations such as Individualism and Collectivism are not static attributes of given societies, but reflect socioeconomic change. Economic development facilitates a shift toward some of the cultural syndromes associated with individualism and away from some of the cultural syndromes associated with collectivism, resulting in increased emphasis on individual freedom-focused values and reduced focus on traditional hierarchies; these cultural shifts are conducive of the emergence and flourishing of democratic institutions.

Data from scores of countries demonstrates that Individualism and Collectivism (as measured by Hofstede and Triandis), Autonomy-Embeddness (as measured by Schwartz), and Survival/Self-expression values (as measured by Inglehart) tap a similar underlying construct which reflects the extent to which people give top priority to individual choice, over survival needs. The high correlation between these measures allows for time series analyses of societal change in cultural syndrome by focusing on change over twenty years in the Inglehart measure. Analyses show that at high levels of economic development, Survival/Self-expression values have increased across generations. We propose one important way that culture changes is under the impact of economic development. Experiencing prosperity minimizes survival concerns, making social values associated with survival less important and allowing for increased focus on social values associated with self-expression and personal choice.

Introduction

After years of neglect, culture has entered the mainstream of psychology, with the concepts of individualism and collectivism playing prominent roles, along with related concepts of Autonomy vs. Embeddedness values (Schwartz) and Traditional vs. Secular and Survival vs. Self-expression values (Inglehart). Together these constructs focus on the centrality of the individual vs. the group, group traditions vs. individual wants. Triandis (1995) claims that there is more research on Individualism-Collectivism than on any other cross-cultural dimension and Oyserman, Coon and Kemmelmeier (2002) cite hundreds of studies dealing with it. Greenfield (2000) sees Individualism/Collectivism as the "deep structure" of cultural differences, from which all other differences evolved. And evidence presented here indicates that this is one of two paramount dimensions of cross-cultural variation (the other being Traditional-religious vs. Secular-rational values, also the subject of a massive literature).

[75]

Typically, individualism is conceptualized as the opposite of collectivism especially when contrasting Western and East Asian cultures. Social scientists assume that individualism is more prevalent in industrialized Western societies than elsewhere, arguing that Protestantism and civic emancipation in Western societies resulted in social and civic structures that championed the role of individual choice, personal freedom (including the right not to follow a religion), and self-actualization (Oyserman, Coon & Kemmelmeier, 2002). Individualism is defined as focus on the individual as the basic unit of analysis, collectivism is defined as focus on the group as the basic unit of analysis, a definition similar to Schwartz conceptualization of the primacy of Autonomy vs. Embeddedness values and Inglehart's definition of Survival vs. Self-expression values as the extent people value individual choice over survival needs.

As we will demonstrate, Individualism-Collectivism taps the same dimension of cross-cultural variation as does Survival/Self-expression values (which reflect the extent to which people give top priority to individual choice, over survival needs). It has been demonstrated that Survival/Self-expression values are becoming more widespread through intergenerational changes that emerge at high levels of economic development when existential constraints on human choice recede (Inglehart, 1997; Inglehart & Baker, 2000; Welzel, Inglehart & Klingemann, 2003). Furthermore, as we will demonstrate, Schwartz' Autonomy-Embeddedness construct also taps this same dimension. Individualism-Collectivism, Autonomy-Embeddedness and Survival/Self-expression values all reflect an increasing cultural emphasis on broadening human choice. This trend is linked with economic prosperity, which reduces existential constraints on human choice and liberates people from the pressures of material scarcity; and emancipates people from cultural constraints, which are necessarily relatively restrictive under conditions of scarcity.

[76]

Current cultural psychological theorizing encompasses two contradictory visions of culture as both static and malleable. Oyserman, Kemmelmeier, and Coon (2002) suggest that static models view culture as a historically pre-determined set of between group differences based in historical, religious, philosophical, and linguistic differences while malleable models view culture as a current set of relatively pliable between group differences based in focus on the self. In the latter view, just as current average cultural differences emerged, they are dynamic and changing. Typically, psychologists making the point that cultural is malleable have turned to priming studies to show that between country differences can be modeled by changing self-focus in prim-ing studies (e.g. Haberstroh, Oyserman, Kuhnen & Schwarz, 2002).

This current chapter focuses not on individual-level malleability but on society-level malleability, arguing that a powerful force producing such mal-leability in societal-average values is socioeconomic change and that the specific form of change is channeled by the dual forces of philosophical-reli-gious orientation and political organization (especially experience under communism). We outline a model describing the process, shape and direc-tion of change. To provide supporting evidence, we first show that the widely used scales of cultural difference, Individualism and Collectivism (Hofstede, Triandis), Autonomy vs. Embeddedness (Schwartz), and the two dimensions of Traditional vs. Secular values and Survival vs. Self-expression values (Inglehart) are highly correlated, suggesting considerable overlap in the underlying dimensions captured by these labels. Then we use data from one set of measures, Survival/Self-expression values, to extrapolate a more gen-eral model of cultural change. We focus on this set because the World Values Surveys and European Values Studies[1] have measured Survival/Self-expres-sion values at multiple time points across the 20 years from 1980-2000. To foreshadow our results, we will show that cross-nationally, there is a genera-tional shift toward greater acceptance of self-expression values and lower acceptance of survival values in countries with high levels of economic development (see also Inglehart, 1997; Inglehart & Baker, 2000; Welzel, 2003; Welzel, Inglehart & Klingemann, 2003). We argue that citizens in soci-eties experiencing economic prosperity (rather than scarcity) are less likely

---

[1] These surveys cover 80 societies containing almost 85 % of the world's population, and pro-vide time series data from the earliest wave in 1981 to the most recent wave completed in 2002. In order to analyze changes, the values surveys have conducted multiple waves, with a first wave in 1981-82, a second one in 1990-1991, a third wave in 1995-1997 and a fourth in 1999-2001. For detailed information about these surveys, see the World Values Survey web sites at http://wvs.isr.umich.edu and http://www.worldvaluessurvey.org, and the European Values Study web site at http://www.europeanvalues.nl.

to focus primarily on maintaining their material existence, which emancipates people from the cultural restrictions on personal choice necessary under conditions of scarcity.

Our central thesis is that economic development facilitates a shift toward the free choice aspects of individualism and away from the traditional survival aspects of collectivism, producing increasing emphasis on individual freedom-focused values and weakening the focus on traditional hierarchies. As we will demonstrate, this cultural shift is conducive to the emergence and flourishing of democratic institutions.

[77]

Defining individualism and collectivism and related terms

Individualism and collectivism

Modern usage of the term individualism is closely connected with the work of Hofstede (1980a), who defined individualism as a focus on rights above duties, a concern for oneself and immediate family, an emphasis on personal autonomy and self-fulfillment, and basing identity on one's personal accomplishments. Although Hofstede's initial research did not measure individualism and collectivism as two separate dimensions, his framework foreshadowed the multi-dimensional issues relevant to understanding cultural difference — power distance and what he termed a culture's masculinity-femininity (Oyserman, 1993; Triandis, 1995). According to Oyserman, Coon and Kemmelmeier (2002), individualism implies that (a) creating and maintaining a positive sense of self is a basic human endeavor, (b) feeling good about oneself, personal success, and having distinctive personal attitudes are valued; and (c) abstract traits (as opposed to situational descriptors) are central to self-definition. Individualism implies that open expression and attainment of one's personal goals are important sources of well-being; and that causal inference is generally oriented toward the person rather than the situation because the self is assumed to be stable. Consequently, individualism promotes a decontextualized, as opposed to situation-specific, reasoning style. Lastly, individualism implies a somewhat ambivalent stance toward relationships. Individuals need relationships and group memberships to attain self-relevant goals, but relationships are costly to maintain. Individualists balance off relationships' costs and benefits, leaving relationships when the costs of participation exceed the benefits; consequently, relationships and group memberships are impermanent and non-intensive.

The core element of collectivism is the assumption that groups bind and mutually obligate individuals. In these societies, social units with a common fate and common goals are central; the personal is simply a component of the social, making the in-group crucial. Oyserman and her colleagues (2002)

[78]

argued that collectivism implies that (a) group membership is a central aspect of identity and (b) valued personal traits reflect the goals of collectivism, such as sacrifice for the common good. Furthermore, collectivism implies that (a) life satisfaction derives from successfully carrying out social roles and obligations and (b) restraint in emotional expression is valued to ensure in-group harmony. Cognitively, collectivism suggests that (a) social context, and social roles figure prominently in perceptions and causal reasoning and (b) meaning is contextualized. Finally, collectivism implies that (a) important group memberships are seen as fixed "facts of life" to which people must accommodate; (b) boundaries between in-groups and out-groups are stable, relatively impermeable, and important; and (c) in-group exchanges are based on equality or even generosity principles.

Traditional vs. secular values and survival vs. self-expression values
Empirically, individualism and collectivism are closely linked to two other organizing frameworks of values developed independently by Inglehart and by Schwartz. First we describe the values framework developed by Inglehart. In a factor analysis of national-level data from the 43 societies included in the 1990 World Values Survey, Inglehart (1997) found that two main dimensions accounted for over 70 percent of the cross-national variance in a pool of variables tapping basic values in a wide range of domains ranging from politics to economic life and sexual behavior. He termed these "Traditional vs. Secular-rational values" and "Survival vs. Self-expression values". Together, these axes explain most of the cross-national variance in a factor analysis of ten indicators — and each of these dimensions is strongly correlated with scores of other important orientations, reflecting a common underlying dimension focusing on human emancipation and choice (as Table 1 below illustrates).

We replicated Inglehart and Baker's factor analysis, and then identified the attitudes that are closely correlated with the Survival/Self-expression dimension. Table 1 shows the wide range of beliefs and values that are strongly correlated with this dimension. A central component involves the polarization between Materialist and Postmaterialist values. As can be seen in Table 1, the Traditional vs. Secular-rational values dimension reflects the contrast between societies for which religion is very important and those for which it is not and this distinction is correlated with other related value choices. Societies near the traditional pole emphasize the importance of parent-child ties and deference to authority, along with absolute standards and traditional family values, rejection of divorce, abortion, euthanasia, and suicide as possible personal choices. These societies have high levels of national pride, and a nationalistic outlook. Societies with secular-rational values have the opposite preferences on all of these topics.

Table 1: *Correlates of survival vs. self-expression values*

SURVIVAL VALUES emphasize the following:

Attitude:	Correlation:
*R. gives priority to economic and physical security over self expressionand quality of life [Materialist/Postmaterialist Values]	.87
Men make better political leaders than women	.86
R. is not highly satisfied with life	.84
A woman has to have children to be fulfilled.83	
R. rejects foreigners, homosexuals and people with AIDS as neighbors	.81
*R. has not and would not sign a petition	.80
*R. is not very happy	.79
R. favors more emphasis on the development of technology	.78
*Homosexuality is never justifiable	.78
R. has not recycled something to protect the environment	.76
R. has not attended a meeting or signed a petition to protect the environment	.75
A good income and safe job are more important than a feeling of accomplishment and working with people you like	.74
R. does not rate own health as very good	.73
A child needs a home with both a father and a mother in order to grow up happily	.73
When jobs are scarce, a man has more right to a job than a women	.69
A university education is more important for a boy than for a girl	.67
Government should ensure that everyone is provided for	.69
Hard work is one of the most important things to teach a child	.65
Imagination is not of the most important things to teach a child	.62
Tolerance is not of the most important things to teach a child	.62
Leisure is not very important in life	.61
Scientific discoveries will help, rather than harm, humanity	.60
Friends are not very important in life	.56
*You have to be very careful about trusting people	.56
R. has not and would not join a boycott	.56
R. is relatively favorable to state ownership of business and industry	.54

SELF-EXPRESSION VALUES take opposite position on all of above

Note: The original polarities vary; the above statements show how each item relates to this values index. The five items used in the factor analysis that generated this dimension are indicated with an asterisk. To make cross-time comparisons possible, only items that were asked in all four waves of the survey were used — hence some items that show very strong correlations with this dimension were not used to generate this factor.
Source: World Values Surveys and European Values Studies.

[80]

Similarly, societies that differ in Survival vs. Self-expression values also differ in a range of values that can be seen as Materialist vs. Post-materialist values. That is, those endorsing self-expression values also give high priority to environmental protection, tolerance of diversity (including gender equality, and tolerance of outgroups — foreigners, gays and lesbians) and value broad-based participation in decision-making in economic and political life as well as child-rearing values emphasizing teaching the child imagination and tolerance rather than hard work. Societies that rank high on survival values tend to emphasize Materialist values, show relatively low levels of subjective well-being and report relatively poor health, are relatively intolerant toward outgroups, low on interpersonal trust, and they emphasize hard work, rather than imagination or tolerance, as important things to teach a child. Societies high on self-expression values tend to have the opposite preferences on all of these topics. Environmental protection issues are also closely linked with this dimension, as well as an emphasis on gender equality and the toleration of gays and lesbians.

Those who emphasize survival values have not engaged in recycling, have not attended environmentalist meetings or supported environmental protection in other ways; but they favor more emphasis on developing technology and are confident that scientific discoveries will help, rather than hurt, humanity. Those with self-expression values tend to have the opposite characteristics. They are more aware of technological risks, more sensitive to human rights and more attentive to discrimination against underprivileged groups.

One of the most important social changes of the past few decades has been the revolution in gender roles that has transformed the lives of a majority of the population throughout advanced industrial society. Since the dawn of recorded history, women have been narrowly restricted to the roles of wife and mother, with few other options. In recent decades, this has changed dramatically. Several of the items in Table 1 involve the role of women: The survival/self-expression dimension reflects mass polarization over such questions as whether "A woman has to have children to be fulfilled"; or whether "When jobs are scarce, men have more right to a job than women"; or whether "A university education is more important for a boy than a girl". But one item taps this dimension particularly well: the question whether "Men make better political leaders than women". Responses to this question are very strongly correlated with the survival/self-expression dimension — almost as strongly correlated as is the Materialist/Postmaterialist values battery.

These dimensions of cross-cultural variation are robust. Inglehart and Baker (2000) provide full details on how these dimensions were measured, together with factor analyses at both the individual level and the national level, demonstrating that the same dimensional structure emerges at both levels.

Moreover, when the 1990-1991 World Values factor analysis was replicated with the data from the 1995-1998 World Values surveys, the same two dimensions of cross-cultural variation emerged as from the earlier surveys — even though the new analysis was based on surveys that covered 23 additional countries that were not included in the earlier surveys.   [81]

Autonomy vs. embeddedness values
In a separate empirical approach to understanding cross-national convergence and divergence of values, Schwartz and his colleagues studied values in a series of surveys of students and teachers in scores of societies. Based on the assumption that all societies must resolve basic tensions between individual and group needs in some way, Schwartz has examined a large array of value choices. Dimensional analysis reveals an Autonomy-Embeddedness construct that fits well with the basic notions of individualism and collectivism. According to Schwartz:

> "In autonomy cultures, people are viewed as autonomous, bounded entities. They cultivate and express their own preferences, feelings, ideas, and abilities, and find meaning in their own uniqueness. *Intellectual autonomy* encourages individuals to pursue their own ideas and intellectual directions independently. Important values in such cultures include broadmindedness, curiosity, and creativity. *Affective autonomy* encourages individuals to pursue affectively positive experience for themselves. Important values include pleasure, exciting life, and varied life."

> "In embeddedness cultures, meaning in life comes largely through social relationships, identifying with the group, participating in its shared way of life, and striving toward its shared goals. Embedded cultures emphasize maintaining the status quo and restraining actions that might disrupt in-group solidarity or the traditional order. Important values in such cultures are social order, respect for tradition, security, obedience, and wisdom." (Schwartz, 2003).

Individualism and collectivism are strongly linked with the values expressed in autonomy vs. embeddedness and survival vs. self-expression, traditional vs. secular values
Using the country-level measures of Individualism-collectivism provided by Hofstede (1980a, 2001) and Triandis (1989, 2001, 2003), Schwartz's (1992, 1994, 2003) country-level Autonomy country-level scores, and Inglehart's (1997, 2000) country-level Self-expression values scores, we examined overlap in these constructs. Empirically, mean national scores on these three variables show correlations that range from .62 to .70, with an average strength of .66. Factor analysis of the mean national scores, reveals that Individualism, Autonomy and Self-expression values measure a single underlying dimen-

[82]

sion; only one dimension emerges and it accounts for fully 78 percent of the cross- national variance (see Table 2). Triandis' individualism-collectivism ratings are also highly correlated, dimension (r = .88), but it makes little sense to add it to this factor analysis, since his scores are based on Hofstede's data, supplemented with estimated scores for a number of additional countries.[2] Although crude, this analysis suggests that individualism, autonomy and self-expression values all tap a common dimension of cross-cultural variation, reflecting relative emphasis on human emancipation and choice. High levels of Individualism go with high levels of Autonomy and high levels of Self-expression values. Hofstede's, Schwartz's, Triandis' and Inglehart's measures all tap cross-cultural variation in the same basic aspect of human psychology– the drive toward broader human choice. Societies that rank high on self-expression tend to emphasize individual autonomy and the quality of life, rather than economic and physical security. Their publics have relatively low levels of confidence in technology and scientific discoveries as the solution to human problems, and are relatively likely to act to protect the environment. These societies also rank relatively high on gender equality, tolerance of gays, lesbians, foreigners and other outgroups; show relatively high levels of sub-jective well-being, and interpersonal trust, and they emphasize imagination and tolerance, as important things to teach a child.

This dimension is remarkably robust. It emerges when one uses different measuring approaches, different types of samples and different time periods. Hofstede found it in the late 1960s and early 1970s, analyzing the values of a cross-national sample of IBM employees. Schwartz measured it in surveys of students and teachers carried out from 1988 to 2002; and Inglehart first found it in analysis of representative national samples of the publics of 43 societies surveyed in 1990; the same dimension emerged in representative national samples of 60 societies, interviewed in 1995; and in surveys of the publics of more than 70 societies carried out in 2000. This dimension seems to be a robust and enduring feature of cross-cultural variation — so much so that one could almost conclude that it is difficult to *avoid* finding it if one measures the basic values of a broad sample of cultures.

A dynamic perspective on cross-cultural differences: Economic prosperity as a source of cultural change

As the previous section clarified, a number of theoretical-empirical approach-es overlap in suggesting that societies differ systematically in whether the group or the individual is centralized. Although important, describing these

---

[2] Hofstede's Power Distance rankings are also strongly related to this dimension; r = -.72.

Table 2: *The individualism/autonomy/self-expression dimensions.*
      Emphasis on human choice

	Variance explained
Principal Component Analysis	78%
Inglehart Survival/Self-expression values	.91
Hofstede Individualism-Collectivism rankings	.87
Schwartz Autonomy-Embeddedness, (mean of student/teacher samples)	.87

[83]

Source: based on mean national scores for the respective measures. High scores on the respective dimensions reflect Self-expression values, Individualism and Autonomy.

differences does not provide a framework to understand the extent to which these are more or less permanent attributes of given cultures, how societies come to make value choices favoring the group or the individual, or how these choices may change over time in systematic ways. Two basic organizing themes have been suggested — concerns about survival and religious/philosophical meaning systems.

Concerns about survival

It has been suggested that societies may emphasize collective values because, in resource poor contexts, survival depends on the ability of individuals to work together in supportive groups, making survival of the group central, this initial level of scarcity may permanently set in motion a society weighted toward collectivism (Oyserman, Kemmelmeier & Coon, 2002). Following this line of reasoning, the extent survival or self-expression values (and Individualism vs. Collectivism) are centralized, reflects the extent physical survival is perceived to be secure or insecure. Throughout most of history, survival has been precarious for most people. Malnutrition and associated diseases were the leading cause of death. Under these conditions, survival values take top priority. Survival is such a fundamental goal that if it seems uncertain, one's entire life strategy is oriented by this fact.

Religious/philosophical meaning systems

Alternatively, it has been suggested that worldviews/religions/philosophies may shape emphasis on interdependence or independence of individuals — again, with historical differences becoming fixed social frameworks even when conditions change. Within the West, Protestantism and Catholicism were seen in this way, Weber (1904/1958) argued that a key difference between Protestant societies and Catholic societies was the individual focus linked with Protestantism, versus the collective focus of Catholicism. Tönnies (1887/1963) emphasized the distinction between *Gemeinschaft* and *Gesellschaft*, or community and society. Gemeinschaft reflects mutual sympathy, habit, and common beliefs that have an intrinsic value to their members; associations based on Gesellschaft are intended to be means to specific ends. More recently, Nisbett (2003) argues for differences in Eastern and Western thought based on whether figure and ground are contrasted (individual as separate) or viewed as a whole (individual as part of the group).

Fitting survival and religious/philosophical themes into a model about cultural change

While interesting, neither survival nor religion-based frameworks propose a systematic model of how cultures change. More than a century ago, Tönnies suggested that economic development tends to bring systematic changes in worldviews. We follow this line of reasoning, as reintroduced by Inglehart (1971). Inglehart (1971) proposed that, as a result of the rapid economic development and the expansion of the welfare state that followed World War II, the formative experiences of the younger birth cohorts in advanced industrial societies differed from those of older cohorts in fundamental ways that were leading them to develop different value priorities. Specifically, he argued that throughout most of history, the threat of severe economic deprivation or even starvation has been a crucial concern for most people, resulting in relatively high levels of traditional as opposed to humanistic values. The post war generation in most industrialized societies experienced an historically unprecedented degree of economic security, leading to a gradual shift from "Materialist" values (emphasizing economic and physical security above all) toward "Postmaterialist" priorities (emphasizing self-expression and the quality of life). This would mean that both Protestant-shaped and Catholic-shaped societies should be moving toward more valuation of self-expression values, though the movement would be shaped by the initial contours set by these divergent worldviews. Evidence of the proposed intergenerational value change began to be gathered by Inglehart and his colleagues cross-nationally in 1970; a long time series has now been built up, making it possible to carry out cohort analyses over a 30-year period. The results demonstrate that the predicted intergenerational value change has indeed taken place (Inglehart, 1997: 131-159).

More recent analyses indicate that this shift is only one component of a broader cultural shift, from Survival values to Self-expression values (Inglehart, 1997; Inglehart & Baker, 2000). Data from scores of societies indicates that self-expression values increase over time as economic prosperity increases. But this shift does not occur uniformly enduring religious-ideological worldviews and historical experiences shape the contour of the shift.

In recent history, a growing number of societies have attained unprecedented levels of economic development. Real per capita GNP has risen to levels far higher than were ever experienced before the 20th century — in some cases, 30 or 40 times higher. Increased societal wealth and the emergence of the welfare state have reduced the danger of starvation to a peripheral concern — opening up a much broader range of choice in people's selection of religious and political orientations, their partners, their careers, their leisure activities and lifestyles. While it is undeniable that wealth and secular, self-expression values are linked, we argue that the causal path is more strongly from increasing wealth to values shift rather than the reverse (values shift encouraging increased societal wealth).

[85]

Self-expression values: a dynamic perspective on cross-cultural differences

We borrow from regulatory focus theory to make our case for this causal reasoning. Regulatory focus theory (e.g., Förster, Higgins & Idson, 1998; Higgins, 1999) proposes that in situations that make salient threat and the need for survival, individuals become "prevention focused" seeking to avoid problems and failures even if the cost is high. Conversely, when situations focus attention on the possibility of attaining gains and successes, individuals become "promotion focused" seeking to attain goals and not miss opportunities for advancement. Because promotion focus targets chances of success, concerns about possible costs of failure pale in comparison to concerns about missing chances to fulfill one's potential. Conversely, because prevention focus targets chances of failure, concerns about possible costs of avoiding failure pale in comparison to concerns about failure itself — failing to be the person one ought to become, failing to keep one's children safe, failing to live up to standards. Even subtle shifts in situations can prompt shift in self-regulatory focus. Indeed, promotion and prevention focus seem physiologically linked to approaching (or bringing toward the self) stimuli and avoiding (or moving away from the self, pushing away) stimuli.

We extrapolate from this mostly experimental social psychological evidence to propose that when social situations involve insecurity and threats, people are more likely to be oriented toward a "prevention focus", applying survival strategies and trying to avoid harmful losses and failures. Conversely, when social situations involve secure and opportunities for advancement and achievement, people are more likely to be oriented toward a "promotion focus", striving to attain successes through initiative, creativity and self-expressive strategies. From this perspective, economic development is immensely important because it changes the social situation of whole populations on a permanent basis. When economic development removes concerns about survival, a "promotion focus" becomes an enduring part of a society's cultural outlook, as reflected in a growing dominance of self-expression values over survival values. In this way, cultural change at a societal level is parallel to individual psychological mechanisms of change.

In sum, liberation from threats to material existence reduces the centrality of survival-focused values and gives higher priority to freedom of choice. This change has immensely important societal implications, transforming orientations toward religion, politics, job motivations, leisure, sexual norms, child-rearing norms and other aspects of life. In all of these domains, with prosperity comes a growing emphasis on human choice and autonomy in the selection of their religious and political orientations, their mates, their careers and their lifestyles. This increasing emphasis on human choice brings growing public pressures that keep elites accountable and strengthen democratic institutions (Welzel, 2003).

Evidence of the postulated shift over time from the World Values Survey
Do postmaterialist values emerge among birth cohorts that grew up under conditions in which people take survival for granted and no longer feel the existential insecurity that restricts human autonomy and choice? We do indeed see an intergenerational shift from emphasis on economic and physical security, toward increasing emphasis on self-expression, subjective well-being and quality of life concerns (Inglehart, 1971, 1990, 1997). During the past 30 years, these values have become increasingly widespread throughout advanced industrial societies, but they are only one component of a much broader dimension of cultural change. Analyses of the Values Survey data shows that over time, the emergence of high levels of material prosperity and the reduction of existential threats to survival at the societal-level tends to transform human motivations and worldviews, bringing fundamental changes in various domains of human values from job motivations to gender roles, and leading to political changes that are conducive to the emergence and survival of democratic institutions (Welzel & Inglehart, forthcoming).

In keeping with this claim, Self-expression values are much more widespread among the publics of rich countries than in poor ones (Inglehart, 1997; Inglehart & Baker, 2000). Further, this framework explains the anomaly noted in Oyserman and colleagues' (2002) meta-analyses, which showed that Japanese, are no lower on individualism than Americans. Moreover, in wealthy societies we find large intergenerational differences, with younger birth cohorts being much more likely to emphasize Self-expression values than are members of the older cohorts. The intergenerational change toward

Self-expression values is based on intergenerational differences in societal prosperity. Accordingly, the Values Survey time series data show that from 1981 to 2000, most countries that experienced high levels of prosperity moved toward increasing emphasis on Self-expression values. That the effect is due to prosperity is bolstered by the fact that the effect was found only in prosperous countries and not in low-income countries.

[87]

Economic development is associated with predictable changes away from absolute norms and values, toward a syndrome of increasingly rational, tolerant, trusting, and self-expressive values that emphasize human choice. We find large and pervasive differences between the worldviews of people in rich and poor societies; their basic values and beliefs differ on scores of key variables, in a coherent pattern. Richer societies tend to be high on both self-expression and secular values, while low-income societies tend to be high in survival and traditional values. Does this mean that economic development brings predictable changes in prevailing values? The evidence suggests that it does: time series evidence from the World Values surveys shows that with economic development, societies tend to move from the values prevailing in low-income societies, toward the values prevailing in high-income societies (Inglehart & Baker, 2000). Inglehart and Baker (2000) also show that shift from traditional to secular values is linked with the transition from agrarian society to industrial society: societies with secular-rational values tend to have a low percentage of their work force in the agricultural sector (r= -.49) and a high percentage of industrial workers (r= .65). The shift from survival to self-expression values, on the other hand, is linked with the transition from industrial society to a knowledge society, showing a .72 correlation with the percentage of the labor force in the *service* sector.

The World Values Surveys and European Values Studies show that sub-stantial changes have occurred in the values and beliefs of the publics of advanced industrial societies, even during the relatively brief time span since 1981.[3] These changes are closely linked with long-term economic changes that are reflected in a society's level of prosperity. Societies that experience economic development tend to shift their emphasis from Traditional values and Survival values, toward increasing emphasis on Secular-rational values and Self-expression values.

---

[3] In order to analyze changes, the values surveys have conducted multiple waves, with a first wave in 1981-82, a second one in 1990-1991, a third wave in 1995-1997 and a fourth in 1999-2001. For detailed information about these surveys, see the World Values Survey web sites at http://wvs.isr.umich.edu and http://www.worldvaluessurvey.org, and the European Values Study web site at http://www.europeanstudies.nl.

Evidence that shift toward societal values shift moves with shift toward democracy

[88] The finding that cross-nationally, as social wealth increases, social valuation of Survival decreases (and of Self-expression increases), meshes well with a self-regulatory frame. This suggests to us that socio-cultural change is systematic and follows lines that are rooted in the architecture of the human psyche. Subjective emphasis on human choice becomes strengthened as soon as objective existential constraints on human choice recede. This has further consequences, as we will demonstrate. Mass emphasis on human choice tends to favor the political system that provides the widest room for choice: democracy. Thus, democracy is not simply a matter of institutional rationality. It is part and parcel of a broader human development syndrome that is ultimately anchored in human psychology.

Abundant human resources are conducive to Self-expression values because they diminish existential constraints on human choice. In keeping with this interpretation, we find a .84 correlation between the Individualism/Autonomy/Self-expression dimension, and the UN Human Development index (which measures the level of such human resources as incomes, education, and health).

Religious-ideological worldview and national heritage as contexts shaping the course of cultural change

In spite of these similarities across societies with increasing wealth, we also see differences — cultural change given wealth seems dependent on religious/philosophical worldview as well. The fact that a society was historically Protestant or Orthodox or Islamic or Confucian gives rise to cultural zones with distinctive value systems that persist when one controls for the effects of economic development (Inglehart & Baker, 2000). A society's culture reflects its entire historical heritage, including religious traditions, colonial ties, the experience of communist rule and its level of economic development.

Throughout history, one of the key functions of religion has been to provide a sense of security and predictability in a dangerous and unpredictable world. High levels of uncertainty about survival can bring a sense of helplessness and despair. Virtually all traditional religions have alleviated this by providing a sense that one's fate is in the hands of benevolent higher power, who will ensure that things work out for the best, provided one follows a certain set of clear, absolute and inflexible rules — the very inflexibility of which, enhances one's sense of predictability. Various religious traditions have shaped people's value systems quite apart from the extent to which they

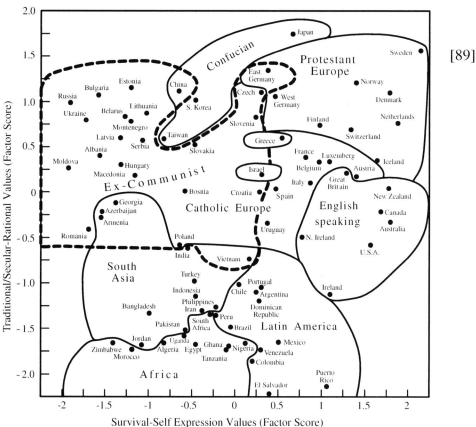

Figure 1: *Locations of 80 societies on two dimensions of cross-cultural variation*

experience high or low levels of existential security. Throughout most of recorded history, religion was the dominant response to conditions of insecurity, but in modern times such ideologies as fascism and communism provided secular forms of reassurance and predictability, claiming to provide infallible answers under the leadership of infallible rulers. The rigid, absolute rules of traditional religions provided a vitally-needed sense of security in a highly uncertain world; but they conferred it at the cost of rigid constraints on individual autonomy: the range of human choice concerning gender roles, sexual behavior and sexual orientation, and other aspects of life style were narrowly confined by absolute rules. The pressures to conform within totalitarian ideologies were different, but equally rigid. The emergence of unprecedentedly high levels of existential security, for most of the population in advanced industrial societies, has eroded the need for absolute rules and opened the way to an increasingly broad scope for human choice. However, what is meant by choice is shaped by the nature of the society's religious/philosophical traditions.

Figure 1 shows a two-dimensional cultural map on which the value systems of 80 societies are depicted. The vertical dimension represents the Traditional/Secular-rational dimension, and the horizontal dimension reflects the Survival/Self-expression values dimension. Both dimensions are strongly linked with economic development: the value systems of rich countries differ systematically from those of poor countries. Germany, France, Britain, Italy, Japan, Sweden, the U.S. and all other societies with a 1995 annual per capita GNP over $15,000 rank relatively high on both dimensions — and without exception, they are located in the upper right-hand region of Figure 1.

Conversely, all of the societies with per capita GNPs below $2,000 fall into a cluster at the lower left of the map; this economic zone cuts across the African, South Asian, ex-Communist, and Orthodox cultural zones. The remaining societies fall into two intermediate cultural-economic zones. Economic development seems to shape societies' value systems in a predictable fashion, regardless of their cultural heritage.

Nevertheless, distinctive cultural zones persist two centuries after the industrial revolution began. Different societies move on different trajectories even when they are subjected to the same forces of economic development, in part because situation-specific factors — a society's religious/philosophical or national heritage, also shape how a particular society develops. The forces of economic development channel cultural change into a relatively broad corridor that leaves considerable variation unexplained. Much of this remaining cultural variation is explained by religious traditions. Huntington (1996) has emphasized the role of religion in shaping the world's eight major civilizations or "cultural zones": Western Christianity, Orthodox, Islam, Confucian, Japanese, Hindu, African, and Latin American. These zones were shaped by religious traditions that are still powerful today, despite the forces of modernization.

All four of the Confucian-influenced societies (China, Taiwan, South Korea, and Japan) have relatively secular values, constituting a Confucian cultural zone, despite major differences in wealth. The Orthodox societies constitute another distinct cultural zone, as Huntington argued. The eleven Latin American societies show relatively similar values. And despite their wide geographic dispersion, the English-speaking countries constitute a relatively compact cultural zone. Similarly, the historically Roman Catholic societies (Italy, Portugal, Spain, France, Belgium, and Austria) display relatively traditional values when compared with Confucian or ex-Communist societies with the same proportion of industrial workers. And virtually all of the historically Protestant societies (e.g., West Germany, Denmark, Norway, Sweden, Finland, and Iceland) rank higher on both the traditional-secular rational dimension and the survival/self-expression dimension than do the historically Roman Catholic societies.

Religious traditions appear to have had an enduring impact on the contemporary value systems of the 80 societies. Another source of long-lasting ideological imprints are the institutions and ideals that formerly imperial powers have imposed on other societies. This can be seen in two distinctive groups of countries: the English-speaking countries that once have been parts of the British Empire and have been influenced by Britain's liberal tradition; and the post-communist countries that have been directly or indirectly controlled by the Soviet Union and experienced the Leninist version of state-socialism. Accordingly, communism left a clear imprint on the value systems of those who lived under it. East Germany remains culturally close to West Germany despite four decades of Communist rule, but its value system has been drawn toward the Communist zone. And although China is a member of the Confucian zone, it also falls within a broad Communist-influenced zone. Similarly, Azerbaijan, though part of the Islamic cluster, also falls within the Communist superzone that dominated it for decades. Changes in GNP and occupational structure have important influences on prevailing worldviews, but traditional philosophical/religious worldview or national heritage influences persist. Economic development shapes the corridor along which cultural change tends to move ahead. But this corridor is relatively broad: Within it there is much cultural variance that is unexplained by economic development. Most of this remaining variance reflects a society's ideological heritage, nourished by religious traditions and imperial legacies.

Not surprisingly, communist rule seems conducive to the emergence of a relatively secular-rational culture: the ex-communist countries in general, and those that were members of the Soviet Union in particular (and thus experienced communist rule for seven decades, rather then merely four decades) rank higher on secular-rational values than non-communist countries. And to an equally striking extent, ex-communist countries in general, and former Soviet countries in particular, tend to emphasize survival values far more heavily than societies that have not experienced communist rule.

Decades of communist rule had a significant impact on the values and beliefs of those who experienced it, but a given cultural heritage can partially offset or reinforce its impact. Thus, as Inglehart and Baker (2000) demonstrate with multiple regression analysis, even when we control for level of economic development and other factors, a history of communist rule does account for a

[92]

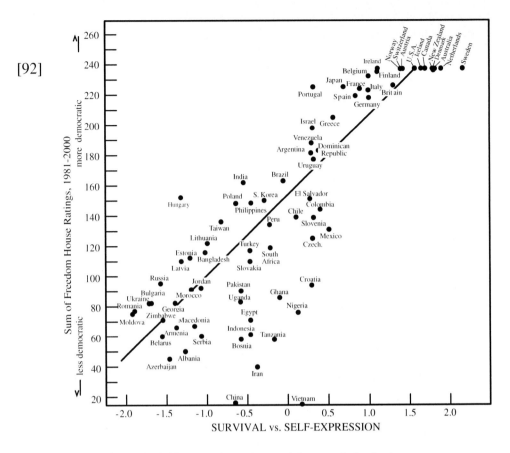

Figure 2. Self-expression values and democratic institutions.
r = .83, N=76, p < .000
Source: World Values Surveys/European Values Surveys, latest available survey.
Polarity of Freedom House rating has been reversed to make high scores
indicate high levels of democracy.

Figure 2: *Self-expression values and democracy*

significant share of the cross-cultural variance in basic values (with seven
decades of communist rule having more impact than four decades). But an
Orthodox tradition seems to reduce emphasis on Self-expression values, by
comparison with societies historically shaped by a Roman Catholic or Protestant cultural tradition. Central and East European countries have a shared experience of communist rule, but their respective religious traditions set them on
distinct trajectories that were not erased by communism. A given society's culture continues to reflect its ideological heritage today. The two major sources
of this heritage, religious traditions and imperial legacies, are still visible.

Survival/Self-expression values are linked with Democracy.

The psychological attributes that we have been discussing are not merely an interesting aspect of cross-cultural variation. They affect how societies function, sometimes with immensely important consequences. As we have argued, the dimension of cross-cultural variation tapped by Individualism-Collectivism, Autonomy/Embeddedness and Survival/Self-expression values has a common theme, emphasizing freedom of choice. Consequently, the presence and strength of this emphasis represents an emancipative social force that acts powerfully on the emergence and strengthening of democracy — a political that is explicitly designed to minimize elite domination and maximize human choice. [93]

Figure 2 illustrates the relationship between each country's score on the Survival/Self-expression dimension, and its levels of democracy as measured by the expert ratings generated by Freedom House, from 1981 to 2000. The levels of democracy in the countries analyzed here are closely linked with their scores on the Survival/Self-expression dimension. There are a few outliers. China, Vietnam and Iran have lower levels of democracy than their publics' values would predict: a determined elite, in control of the military, can repress mass aspirations — at least for a considerable time. And Hungary, India and Portugal show higher levels of democracy than their publics' values would predict: pro-democratic elites can sometimes accelerate the pace of democratization. But overall, the linkage between political culture and political institutions is remarkably strong, producing a .83 correlation.

The global trend of the past several centuries has been toward economic development. And economic development tends to give rise to growing mass emphasis on human choice and self-expression — providing social and cultural conditions under which democracy becomes increasingly likely to emerge and survive. The evidence in Figure 2 suggests that a number of societies may be closer to democracy than is generally suspected. For example, Mexico's position on the Survival/Self-expression values axis is only slightly lower than that of Argentina, Spain or Italy. Probably by no coincidence, Mexico made the transition to democracy in 2000, shortly after the Mexican survey was carried out. A number of other societies are also in this transition zone, including Turkey, the Philippines, Slovenia, South Korea, Taiwan, Poland, Peru, Chile and South Africa. Both China and Vietnam are experiencing rapid economic growth, which tends to bring a shift toward Self-expression values. The communist elites of these countries are committed to maintaining one-party rule, and as long as they retain control of the military, they should be able to remain in power. But their people show a cultural predisposition toward democracy that is inconsistent with their political institutions' very low rankings on the Freedom House ratings. In the long run, repression of a people's aspirations for self-expression is likely to exert growing costs. In the booming coastal regions of mainland China one can already observe how the emergence of a prosperous, educated, and self-confident middle-class erodes the communist party's authority and control over society.

Authoritarian rulers of some Asian societies have argued that the distinctive "Asian values" of these societies make them unsuitable for democracy. In fact, the position of most Asian countries on Figure 2 is about where their level of economic development would predict. Japan ranks with the established Western democracies on both the Self-expression values dimension, and on its level of democracy. And Taiwan and South Korea's positions on both dimensions are similar to those of other relatively new democracies such as Poland, the Philippines, Chile or Slovenia. The publics of Confucian societies may be readier for democracy than is generally believed.

All of the Islamic societies rank below the midpoint on the Survival/Self-expression dimension. But we do not find an unbridgeable chasm between Islamic societies and the rest of the world. The belief systems of these Islamic countries fall roughly where one would expect them to be on the basis of their level of economic development. The most developed of them, Turkey, is now in the transition zone along with such countries as South Africa and Slovenia; and the public of the second richest of these Islamic countries, Iran, shows a surprisingly pro-democratic political culture: in the last two national elections, overwhelming majorities of the Iranian public voted for reform-oriented governments– only to have their aspirations thwarted by a theocracy that controls the army and secret police.

Inglehart and Welzel (forthcoming) examine the syndrome of economic prosperity, changing values and democratic institutions, demonstrating *why* economic development goes with democracy: cultural change towards stronger emphasis on self-expression provides the major link between economic development and democratization. They first test the impact of self-expression values at Time 1, on subsequent levels of democracy at Time 2. They find that a society's mean score on the Survival/Self-expression dimension has by far the most powerful influence on its level of democracy. Although economic development is at the root of this causal sequence, it is important mainly in so far as it contributes to the emergence of Self-expression values.

They then test the reverse causal model: that democratic institutions cause a shift from Survival values to Self-expression values. Since these values show a .83 correlation with democracy, if one used democracy alone as a predictor of these values, it would "explain" most of the variance. But when economic development is also included in the regression, they find that democratic institutions explain only an additional 2 % of the variance in Self-expression values, beyond what was explained by economic development and religious heritage. Culture seems to shape democracy far more than democracy shapes culture.

[95]

Theoretical considerations also suggest that the strong linkage between self-expression values and democracy shown in Figure 2 reflects, at least in part, the impact of political culture on democracy. One way to explain the strong linkage we have observed between political culture and democracy, would be to assume that pro-democratic attitudes are *caused* by the presence of democracy, emerging through "habituation" or "institutional learning" from the use of democratic institutions. Confronted with the evidence in Figure 2, proponents of this view would argue that democratic institutions give rise to the self-expression values that are so closely linked with them. In other words, democracy makes people tolerant, trusting, and happy, and instills Postmaterialist values. This interpretation is appealing and suggests that we have a quick fix for most of the world's problems: adopt a democratic constitution and live happily ever after.

Unfortunately, the experience of most of the Soviet successor states does not support this interpretation. Since their dramatic move toward democracy in 1991, the people of these societies have not become more trusting, more tolerant, happier, or more Postmaterialist: for the most part, they have moved in exactly the *opposite* direction, with the sharp decline of their economy and society (Inglehart & Baker 2000). Evidence of declining support for democracy is also striking in Latin America. From 1995 to 2001, support for democracy declined among the publics of all 17 Latin American countries surveyed, with an average decline of 12 % (LatinoBarometer report, July 2001). Clearly, sheer experience with democratic institutions does not necessarily bring them growing acceptance and legitimacy.

Human Development and Cultural Change

In the nineteenth and early twentieth centuries, modernization theorists from Marx to Weber speculated about the future of industrial society, emphasizing the rise of rationality and the decline of religion. In the twentieth century, non-Western societies were expected to abandon their traditional cultures and assimilate the more advanced ways of the West. Obviously, this has not happened.

Although few people would accept the original version of modernization theory today, one of its core concepts still seems valid: the insight that economic development produces pervasive social and cultural consequences, from rising educational levels and occupational specialization, to changing gender roles and increasing emphasis on individual autonomy. The World Values Survey and European Values Studies data demonstrate that the worldviews of the people of rich societies differ systematically from those of low-income societies across a wide range of political, social, and religious norms and beliefs. And such seemingly different phenomena as economic development, self-expression values and democracy, that may appear to be completely distinct at first glance are actually systematically linked through their common focus on human choice — generating a coherent syndrome of human development.

Our findings suggest that in order to understand the functioning of human societies, social scientists have much to learn from understanding the mass psychological mechanisms that govern the formation of human values — probably more than from the abstract formal models that dominate the rational choice paradigm.

As this chapter has demonstrated, Individualism is not a static individual-level psychological attribute but is closely linked with processes of socioeconomic development. Individualism-Collectivism and Autonomy-Embeddedness tap the same dimension of cross-cultural variation as does Survival/Self-expression values; these attributes are becoming more widespread through intergenerational changes that emerge at high levels of economic development, which liberates people from the constraints of material scarcity; and from cultural constraints that tend to be narrowly restrictive under conditions of scarcity. This transformation of human motivations is conducive to the emergence and survival of democracy — the political system designed to maximize free choice.

CHAPTER FIVE

Methodological problems of value research

WOLFGANG JAGODZINSKI

Whether value research has made progress during the last decades is an open question. It might be argued that some of the most fundamental problems still are unsolved, particularly the problem of a value definition, the measurement problem or the stability problem of values. This chapter attempts to develop a more differentiated view. It will be argued that the definition problem and some other problems probably have no satisfying solution but that this is no obstacle to scientific progress in value research. In other instances like the measurement and the stability problem, scientists disagree about the solution because they apply different methodological standards. Even though a consensus between the two camps seems to be very unlikely the discussion between the groups has considerably improved our methodological knowledge in value research. And finally, there is a third class of problems which for a solution may be found in the future but so far have not been carefully addressed. Most relevant in this respect is the multi-level problem in value research.

The chapter will suggest a pragmatic solution to the definition problem in the first section. As there is a consensus on some properties of values (Van Deth & Scarbrough, 1995) these properties should be considered as necessary requirements of values. If they are met, the respective author can deliberately decide whether her or his theory should be classified as a theory of values or not. Indirectly relevant to future progress in value research is the ontological question whether values are properties of individuals, of collectives or something else. In the second section it is suggested that empirical research should focus on two concepts of values, on the value orientations of individuals and on the collective values of cultures, nations, or other collective actors. On the basis of these distinctions a sketch of a multi-level model of values is outlined in the third section. The major methodological problems in the research on value orientations are addressed in the fourth section, and the major problems of the conceptualization of collective values in the fifth section. The final section draws consequences for future value research.

[98]

The meta-concept of values

If we classify individualism, postmaterialism or tolerance as values, we talk about these specific values in a meta-language. For this reason, we call the concept of value a meta-concept. There is a long and almost endless discussion on the definition of this concept and Lautmann (1969) has counted hundreds of definition attempts. Now, an explicit definition can be formalized as an equivalence statement consisting of two parts, the definiendum and the definiens. In the well-known textbook example: "An individual is a *bachelor* if and only if the individual is an *unmarried man*", *bachelor* is the definiendum or the expression to be defined and *unmarried man* is the defining expression or the definiens. This definition can also be seen as a statement that specifies the necessary and sufficient conditions for being a bachelor. Being both, unmarried and male, is necessary and sufficient for being a bachelor.

If the necessary and sufficient conditions are stated clearly, the value definition should enable the researcher to distinguish values from related concepts like interests, ideologies, attitudes, desires or needs. Yet, no proposal has ever reached this goal. Kluckhohn's (1951) famous definition, for instance, does not discriminate between values and ideologies. An ideology can also be understood as a conception of the desirable, it can be implicit or explicit, it is distinctive of an individual, or characteristic of a group, and it affects the modes, means, and ends of action. For similar reasons it will also be difficult to distinguish between values, norms, interests, or needs (cf. Kmieciak, 1976; Scholl-Schaaf, 1975).

Whether an attitude meets the requirements of Kluckhohn's definition or not, depends exclusively on our interpretation of the term 'conception of the desirable'. If the protection of the life of an embryo is a conception of the desirable, a negative attitude towards abortion could be subsumed under definition and would be called a value. We may try to avoid this consequence by distinguishing in the tradition of Thurstone (1928) between general and specific topics. A value is a general conception, which refers to no object or very general objects. Attitudes, by contrast, are orientations towards specific objects (Kmieciak, 1976). In practice, this new criterion is difficult to apply. A value can always be related to an object like the ideal world, the ideal society, or the desirable state, so that all depends on the distinction between specific and general: When is an object specific enough to generate attitudes, when is it sufficiently general to generate values? Is an orientation towards the British Parliament an attitude, the orientation towards representative democracy a value? Is the protection of the life of an embryo an attitude towards an object, the protection of life of human beings the object of a value? We may agree that the orientation towards abortion is too specific to be classified as a value. However, we will never agree on the precise demarcation between values and attitudes. Regarding this difficulty, we suggest the following solution: If researchers can agree on the minimum level of generality, we can consider this minimum level as a necessary requirement for a value. Even if a conception passes the minimum level of generality and fulfils all other definition criteria, the researcher is free to speak of a value or not. The minimum level of generality allows us to state a necessary requirement of values, and the same holds for other criteria as well. We will not be able to identify a set of criteria, which is necessary and sufficient. We therefore should give up the search for an explicit definition of values. This idea will be elaborated in the next subsections.

[99]

Four necessary requirements of values
We cannot use the term value as we like. The concepts that are called values in empirical research share a number of common characteristics that will be considered as necessary requirements. In contrast to an explicit definition, however, the combination of these necessary conditions is not a sufficient condition for the classification as a value. If all necessary requirements are met, the concept may nevertheless be classified as an ideology, a general interest or something else.

The first condition is that values are not directly observable but have to be indirectly inferred from observations.[1] We can therefore distinguish between observed and latent classes, between directly measurable indicators and indirectly measurable latent concepts, or between observed variables and latent variables, latent dimensions, or latent constructs. Subsequently, I will most often use the term latent dimension because this seems to be the simplest way to describe values.[2]

In general, the latent value dimension can be nominal, ordinal or metric. In practice, values are usually conceptualized either as latent classes or as latent metric continuous variables. If concepts like individualism[3] and col-

---

[1] One may introduce a more restrictive requirement: Values can be indirectly derived from behavior with a fairly high degree of reliability. I will not introduce this criterion here but discuss the question of reliability in the measurement section.

[2] It will not be assumed that several latent dimensions are orthogonal to each other.

[3] Individualism is an extremely ambiguous concept (cf. Jagodzinski & Klein,1998). It is not necessary to explicate its meaning in this paper, however. Mostly the concept is used in the sense of autonomy, self-actualization and self-expression.

[100]

lectivism are introduced, it is near at hand to interpret them as two latent classes and the underlying value as a dichotomous variable. This is only one alternative, however. Individualism and collectivism can also be interpreted as the two poles or endpoints of a latent continuum. There is also a third possibility: individualism and collectivism can also be understood as two separate dimensions. The latter view is held by Triandis (1993) and his colleagues.[4] All three possibilities have to be considered. There is a further complication: concepts like individualism sometimes designate a bipolar individualism-collectivism dimension, and sometimes only a continuum, which ranges from high to low or non-existent individualism. Furthermore, individualism can refer to the latent value dimension or to the position of the individual on the latent dimensions.

Which of these interpretations is most appropriate can only be decided by a careful reading of the text. The matter becomes fairly complicated if the researcher starts with a bipolar value concept in the theoretical part and ends with two or more independent latent value dimensions in the empirical analysis. In contrast to those studies, postmaterialism theory was always very clear with regard to this aspect of value conceptualization: materialism and postmaterialism are the endpoints of a continuous latent variable. In spite of all criticism, Inglehart (1994) has never given up the assumption of uni-dimensionality. In practice, this latent continuum is mapped into variables with smaller numbers of categories because the position of the individuals on the underlying continuum cannot be determined more precisely due to the crude measurement. The standard four item postmaterialism index, for example, distinguishes three classes of respondents: postmaterialists, mixed types, and materialists. Depending on the number of rankings and the technique of index construction we may produce rank orders of four or more categories. However, all these techniques severely restrict the possibility to determine the location on the latent continuum.

The second necessary condition is that the latent value dimension is derived from or related to a special class of preferences or priorities, which we call value preferences. Preferences presuppose the perception of alternatives (cognitive aspect), the evaluation of these alternatives (evaluative aspect), and an emotional relation to the alternatives (affective aspect). Values therefore have a cognitive, an evaluative, and an affective component. Again, these three criteria are vague. We will not be able to accurately define the amount of cognitive and evaluative elaboration or of emotional involvement, which is required for values. In each case, we may however, agree on a

---

[4] It should be emphasized that Triandis considers individualism and collectivism not as values but as components of a global perspective.

minimum level. We suggest taking this minimum level as a necessary requirement for the classification of values.

Value preferences are peculiar in two respects. First, they include a normative component. If we prefer vegetarian cooking, we usually do not expect our neighbors and friends to share this preference. Our desires do not need to converge with their desires. Value preferences are completely different. Note that the reference to a value usually carries three pieces of information: (1) It is my preference, (2) it is the preference of a large group of people, and (3) it should be the preference of all group members if not of all human beings. The latter preference can be called the (general) normative preference. It seems to be an essential component of most value concepts. The value of life may serve as an illustration. The statement that the respect of life requires the abolishment of the death penalty usually includes three messages: The author is against the death penalty, a large group of people is against death penalty, and everyone should oppose the death penalty. The normative preference is usually used as a means to persuade the other participants in the discourses: because everyone should hold this preference, you should hold it too. Values therefore are not desires but conceptions of the desirable. Good measurement instruments should observe this difference and should also measure the normative preference. If sometimes a change in the relative importance of religion, the family, or the job is interpreted as an indication of value change, this particular feature of values is not adequately taken into account. The importance, which we assign to objects or domains, may be mainly determined by our desires and much less by our values.

The normative preference is general because it is assumed to be valid for all human beings or at least a large group. Value preferences are general in a second sense, however. They do not refer to specific objects in time and space but to broadly defined objects and events. General preferences in this second sense are derived either from a larger set of fairly specific preferences or from items which make use of fairly general value notions as will be shown in the next section.

As a third condition we state that the latent value dimension is relatively stable. By the use of the term "relatively" it is already indicated that the amount of stability cannot be precisely defined. Even though the stability of values is rarely demonstrated empirically, it is one of the more fundamental assumptions about values. Many so-called causal inferences about values are based on the implicit assumption that values are more stable than most other evaluations and cognitions (but see further).

A fourth necessary condition is that values affect or structure more specific attitudes and opinions, and that they have an impact on a variety of

[101]

[102]

behaviors. If we distinguish between the behavior[5] from which the position of a person on the value dimension is derived or estimated and the behaviors, which are external to the value measurement, values should also affect the latter. For example, postmaterialism is assumed to affect among other things religiosity, positions on environmental and gender issues, political participation and the choice of a profession (see also further).

The decision of the theoretician

Obviously, these four conditions are met by many sociological and psychological variables, which like extra- and introversion, anxiety or rigidity usually are not called values. Some of them may be ruled out by our second criterion because they are not derived from or related to preferences. However, many measurement instruments in value research address preferences in a very indirect way so that the second criterion remains ambiguous to some extent. Apart from that the researcher always has some freedom to expose a latent variable either as a value or as a personal trait or as some other orientation. Take the example of rigidity. If we introduce it as the polar opposite to tolerance, we will probably call it a value. If we introduce it as a feature of the cognitive system, however, we may call it a structural property of the cognitive system and not a value. Therefore, the researcher partly determines by the exposition and the name of the theory or the names and labels of the latent dimensions depending on whether his theoretical approach is classified as a theory of values or as something else.

If the latent dimensions meet the four requirements and a set of hypotheses is called theory of values or value change we should accept this classification. In practice, researchers often not only speak of a theory of value change but use value concepts with a strong evaluative undertone like postmaterialism, materialism, hedonism, rationalism or individualism with which to designate their key concepts. From a methodological point of view, the practice provokes ambivalent feelings. On the one hand, these labels help us to identify the approach as a theory of values. On the other hand, the use of value concepts calls the scientific neutrality of the researcher into question. At least the European middle class reader knows that postmaterialism is good and materialism is bad and that therefore a change from materialism to postmaterialism is a positive change. For the same reason increasing hedonism insinuates a negative development. There are no reasons given why these developments are good or bad but it is attempted to induce the reader's evaluation solely by the use of value concepts. Therefore, value concepts are

---

[5] In our case it is the response behavior.

strictly avoided by those who adhere to the principle of a value-free discourse in the tradition of Hans Albert (1979). Leaving these methodological
problems aside, we can state in any case that the classification of a theory as a
value theory is partly determined by the labels and names of the concepts.

[103]

The ontological problem: values as eternal entities, properties of objects, individuals, and collectives

In general, it is better to avoid ontological discussions because they almost
inevitably end in logical fallacies. Nevertheless it seems helpful to briefly
clarify alternative ontological conceptions of values. We can roughly distinguish four ontological positions: Values are (a) eternal entities, (b) properties
of objects, (c) orientations of individuals or (d) properties of collectives. In
some sense all values are eternal. The values of the Christian medieval age
do not end with the rise of modernity and the values of Voltaire do not end
with his death. However, this paper is not concerned with values, which only
exist in the spiritual world like the values of a former era or a deceased
philosopher. Rather, we focus on values, which still influence the behavior of
people and systems.

With regard to these still effective values social scientists can hold different positions. They can implicitly or explicitly assume that a value like justice affects the behavior of people in all societies, which is at least not very
far from the assumption that values are platonic entities. One may also
assume that some values can be conceptualized as properties of goods, states,
or even localities. By contrast, methodological individualism will insist that
values have to be conceptualized as properties of the individual or individual
actions. Finally, one may consider values as properties of organizations,
nations or cultures.

In contrast to Adler (1956) it is assumed that at least the ontological positions (b), (c), and (d) can be defended with reasonable arguments. They are
also compatible with the four necessary requirements for the values stated
above.

(a) As far as values as platonic entities are concerned some doubts may
arise. It is true; they are stable by definition because they exist from the
beginning to the end of humankind. Those who believe in the existence of
eternal values usually assume that these entities are not directly observable
but can only be recognized by special techniques of value recognition. Values therefore may be invisible to the layman but visible to the priest. As we
learn from religious scriptures and other sources these eternal values can
become manifest in a large variety of human actions. However, these text-
books do not distinguish between behaviors from which we infer the exis-

tence of the platonic entity and behaviors, which are external to the measurement. Platonic entities furthermore are not systematically related to observed behavior. Also, if we introduce measurement reliability as a further necessary requirement, platonic values will probably not meet the criterion.

(b) The assumption that some values are properties of physical objects at a first glance sounds strange but it can be defended with pragmatic arguments. It is certainly true that physical objects have no preference and therefore cannot hold values. Yet, if all persons evaluate an object in the same way, we may treat this evaluation as an attribute of the object. If all human beings consider the diamond a precious stone, why should we not call the diamond precious? This simplifies our language. Otherwise we would have to state that most human beings in society X consider the diamond as a precious stone. This is more appropriate but also much more complicated.

(c) Modern value research is less concerned with platonic entities and with values inherent in objects. Rather, the individualistic conception of values has clearly dominated the quantitative empirical research during the last decades. Values are conceptualized as dispositions, preferences or as orientations of individuals. They belong to the inner system of the individual, which is not directly observable. This is the reason why methodological individualists accept the second necessary condition stated above: Value orientations of the individual become manifest in the actions and reactions to external stimuli and have to be inferred from observable behavior.

(d) For a long time, values as properties of collectives have been widely ignored in social theories. They have always played a role in the empirical analysis, however. If group averages of values are estimated in variance or regression analysis these averages are, technically spoken, analytical properties of collectives. They are usually not perceived as distinct collective variables but rather as a tool for testing the individual-level relationships between values, their determinants and their consequences.

If group means were calculated by the researcher her- or himself, they frequently served the same purpose, i.e. for an indirect test of individual-level hypotheses. Thus, cohort analysis was mainly used for indirectly testing the stability of individual-level value orientations. Similarly, a positive relationship between a country's level of economic development and the percentage of postmaterialists can be interpreted as indirect support of the scarcity hypothesis.

Even nowadays, values of collectives are rarely explicitly introduced as distinct variables. Hofstede (2001) belongs to the few scientists who are very explicit in this respect. It often requires a careful reading to detect their traces. The remark that values are elements of a culture, for instance, gives us a hint. A culture is more persistent than an individual. Cultural values therefore must also be more persistent than the values of the individual. Another hint is a distinction between the effects of culture and the effects of values of the individual. If it is argued, for instance, that the culture of Protestantism has a much stronger effect on achievement values than the Protestant ethic of the individual, there is obviously a distinction between the moral values of the individuals and the collective values of the Protestant culture. Which values are meant in the two examples? If the culture of Protestantism is measured by the percentage of Protestants in a country and the Protestant ethic by Protestant denomination or affiliation, this will never become apparent. The variables on the micro- and on the macro-level are diffusely related to Protestantism but not to specific Protestant values and norms. We will return to this measurement problem in a later section.

[105]

A multi-level model of values

If we distinguish between the values of individuals and collectives or between macro- and micro-level values, the explanatory problems of value research can be outlined by means of Coleman's (1990) famous bathtub. In figure 1 only two out of many possible levels of analysis are displayed, the individual level and the national level. Macro-level values are called *collective values* or cultural values, and *micro-level* values are called value orientations. This model can be easily extended by various intermediary levels of analysis. For example, religious, political, or professional organizations in each country may hold specific sets of values. One could even differentiate between the values of the local, regional and central divisions of larger organizations if these differences are theoretically and empirically relevant. We could also move to a higher than the country level by specifying values of the Islamic or Christian cultures. For the present purpose, two levels are sufficient, however.

Values can affect other values, attitudes, beliefs and/or behavior. In figure 1 individual behavior has been chosen as dependent variable. The figure illustrates types of direct and indirect relationships between values and behavior. In order to illustrate the indirect relationships, other determinants of behavior have been depicted besides values. As far as these other variables are concerned, the model is very incomplete. A large number of macro-level variables (X_M in Figure 1) like the economic and technical development and formal and informal norms can affect the value orientations and behaviors of individuals in very complicated ways. Our model simplifies these relationships by depicting only direct effects of X_M on value orientations, exogenous micro-level variables X_I, and on individual behavior.

It seems unlikely that collective values have a direct causal effect on

[106]

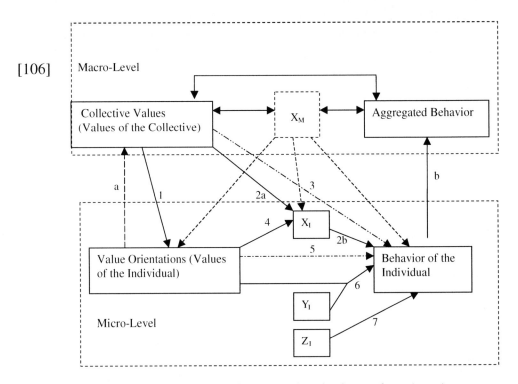

Figure 1: *Types of relationships between cultural values, value orientations and behavior*

individual level behavior. Either the individuals are aware of the collective values and take them explicitly into consideration or collective values implicitly influence the decision process. In any case, there should be one or more intervening or interacting individual-level variables between the collective value and the behavior. For this reason, arrow 3 has been depicted as a dotted line. Collective values can determine the outcome of the socialization process. If they affect all children in the same way, a direct effect like arrow 1 seems appropriate. More often, however, the effects of cultural values will be mediated by socialization agents. Middle class families, for instance may be more susceptible to the dominant cultural norms than upper and lower class families. Children of middle class families would therefore be socialized more effectively into the dominant cultural norms. If such a hypothesis were true, we had to specify an interaction effect between the cultural norms and the relevant properties of the socialization agents.

One can also imagine that collective values impose conformity pressure on the individual. This relationship is depicted as an indirect effect: the collective value has a direct effect (arrow 2a) on the perceived cultural norm (X_1), which in turn has an impact on the behavior (arrow 2b). Actually, the relationship is more complicated because collective values most likely interact with perceptions, personal traits, and other individual level variables if they affect individual level behavior at all.

[107]

As in the case of collective values, a direct impact of value orientations on behavior or the behavioral intention will rarely occur. It is most plausible in the case of value-rational actions where the action is more or less exclusively motivated by values (arrow 5)[6]. Value orientations may shape more specific attitudes and perceptions (X_1), which in turn can affect the behavior (arrow 4 in combination with arrow 2). Value orientations can also interact with variables Y_1 (arrow 6). This would be case, for instance, if only the voting behavior of postmaterialists would be affected by environmental issues Y_1. Finally, there often are exogenous variables Z_1, which affect the behavior besides value orientations and collective values.

Collective values may not only have an impact on value orientations (arrow 1) they may themselves be analytically derived from value orientations. This is the case, for instance, if the values of a country are calculated as modes or averages of the value orientations of all country members. This analytical relationship is indicated in Figure 1 by a vertical dashed arrow from the value orientation to the collective value (arrow a). A similar analytical relationship is depicted between individual level and aggregate level behavior (arrow b). Divorce and suicide rates, GNP per capita, or average church attendance are examples of macro-level variables, which are analytically derived from individual-level behavior and might appear on the right side of the model. A basic and essential assumption of the multi-level model in figure 1 is that these dependent macro-level variables are never directly influenced by collective values, particularly not by collective or cultural values. Therefore, it is not sufficient to analyze macro-level relationships if we want to empirically establish a causal effect of, for instance, cultural individualism on suicide or alcohol consumption. Rather, we have to demonstrate an effect of the cultural value on the individual and its behavior. The double-headed arrow between the collective values and the aggregated behavior indicates that there is no direct causal relationship at the macro-level. A satisfying explanatory model always has to consider the multi-level relationships.

If we confine ourselves to only one level of relationships and make inferences for the other level, we run the well-known risk of committing cross-level fallacies. This is the case, for instance, if we postulate in the tradition of

---

[6] More precisely the action aims at the fulfillment of norms, which are derived from value orientations.

[108]

Durkheim an individual-level relationship between individualism and suicide[7] but confine ourselves to the analysis of aggregate-level data. Figure 1 already indicates that this strategy may results in all kinds of spurious relationships. Even worse: a negative micro-level correlation is compatible with a positive macro-level correlation. Suppose that individualism has a negative impact on suicide and only collectivists commit suicide. Due to feelings of isolation, however, their suicidal tendency is higher in individualistic than in collectivistic societies so that a strong positive correlation with the proportion of individualists in a country and the suicide rate emerges. Without additional micro analysis this result easily leads to the ecological fallacy that individualists are more likely to commit suicide.

It is one of the shortcomings of modern value research that these multi-level relationships are rarely analyzed adequately. Researchers focus on the macro-level or on the micro-level, or they analyze both levels separately. From a methodological point of view, this is inadequate. This shortcoming can easily be overcome because modern statistical programs permit the analysis of multi-level relationships. Subsequently, we will discuss the core problems of value research separately for value orientations and collective values.

Value orientations

The measurement problem

(a) Value measurement probably is the core problem of value research. This chapter will focus on value measurement in survey research by means of standardized questions. As values are general preferences there are actually two dominant measurement strategies. One may confront the respondents with very general statements and hope that all the respondents will understand them in the same way. Or one may try to infer values from fairly specific attitudes or preferences. A famous example of the first way is Rokeach's (1973) measurement of terminal and instrumental values where the respondents have to rank general value concepts like freedom, equality, peace or love. An example of the second strategy is the attempt to measure individualism by questions on dressing and hairstyle (cf. Triandis & Gelfard, 1998 for similar items).

The objection to the first strategy is that the general concepts will not be fully understood by many respondents and therefore produce an erratic response behavior of those who are less familiar with general concepts. Accordingly, one can expect the measurement error to decline with the level

---

[7] Hofstede (2001) analyzes this and many other forms of aggregated behavior like alcohol and coffee consumption or diseases.

of education. The major objection to the second strategy is that specific preferences may be affected by situational factors, which cannot be controlled for in the interview. For example, how one dresses is dependent on the income of the person and on the existence of dress regulations at the working-place, etc. If these factors are not taken into account, and they rarely are, the responses will not tell us much about individualism. [109]

Most authors have conceptualized measurement instruments between these extremes on a middle level of generality. The postmaterialism items may serve as an illustration. Political goals like maintaining order, fighting rising prices or political participation and freedom of speech are relatively clear and fairly general because they do not refer to specific political measures and a particular point in time. Rather, a fairly large time frame of ten years is established in the introductory remark. Nevertheless even these items can be affected by actual short-term forces, particularly by the inflation rate as we have learned in the seventies and eighties (Böltken & Jagodzinski, 1985; Clarke & Dutt, 1991; Inglehart, 1990 with further references). An increase in the inflation rate results in a higher priority of fighting rising prices, which in turn produces a shift towards materialism. The ideal measurement instrument which is neither affected by short-term period effects nor dependent on the cognitive competence of the respondent so far has not been developed.

(b) Closely related to this problem is the issue of overgeneralization. Let us call a set of indicators which refer to a particular domain like politics, the economy, the family, or the working place domain-specific. The fewer domains are covered by the measurement model, the more domain-specific is the measurement and the larger the gap between the claim of the theory and the observed relationships tend to become. The size of the gap depends on the conceptualization of the value orientations. If the theory postulates a broad and general value orientation like individualism, the gap may be large. If the theory already distinguishes domain-specific modes of individualism, however, the gap may be small or non-existent. The size of the gap can be easily determined by carefully comparing the hypotheses of the measurement model with the theoretical statements.

Hofstede (2001) derives individualism from three items on the style of leadership and therefore measures a domain-specific mode of individualism, which might be called working-place individualism. He does not explicitly mention that his empirical findings refer to this domain-specific individualism. This is sometimes criticized as an overgeneralization of the empirical findings. It is fairly obvious that the empirical analysis is based on working-place individualism and not on individualism in general. The reader knows very well that a test of the general hypothesis requires a broader measurement of individualism. Therefore, the overgeneralization of empirical findings seems to be a minor problem. Triandis and Gelfard (1998) present a somewhat broader set of indicators but it is still not broad enough. So we still wait for a model, which includes individualism in the private and in the public life, in the family and at the working place, in the economy, in politics, law or religion.

If no suitable measurement model can be found, we have to give up the concept of a broadly defined overarching individualism and introduce concepts of domain-specific individualism instead. Whether these concepts are positively intercorrelated has to be tested empirically. If they are correlated we can also try to establish general individualism as a higher order factor.[8]

(c) If a theoretical concept has a broader meaning then its operationalization, one also speaks of a surplus meaning. The traditional vs. bureaucratic-rational dimension of Inglehart (1999; Inglehart & Baker, 2000) in this sense has a surplus meaning. The indicators cover a traditional orientation, which is characterized by a traditional monotheistic religiosity and the corresponding family morality, furthermore by the emphasis on strong leadership, authority and the nation. The bipolar labeling seems to be inadequate because no indicator really refers to a bureaucratic-rational orientation.[9] Regarding this, two solutions seem to be possible. One should either replace the bi-polar label of the value dimension by a single label like traditional or traditional-hierarchical orientation, or one has to add indicators, which really measure bureaucratic rationality. The later strategy is much more appealing because the emergence of a new rationality seems to be indeed an important feature of the industrialized society. The belief in a calculable and controllable world may be the essential feature of this new rationality (cf. Jagodzinski & Dobbelaere, 1995 with further references) and we may try to develop indicators along this line.

(d) If value orientations are conceptualized as broad and overarching

---

[8] Triandis (1993; see also this volume) conceptualization of individualism may ultimately lead to a higher order factor model too. In his model, individualism and collectivism do not only affect our value orientations but also our cognitions, the attribution of success and failure, and many other things. The model assumes that specific orientations are always influenced by both, by the individualistic and the collectivistic component. The weight of both components may vary from one domain to the other and from one time point to the next. These general considerations suggest the specification of individualism and collectivism as second or higher order factors in a covariance structure model. Unfortunately, an adequate measurement model so far has not been presented.

[9] Not only theologians but also most sociologists of religion would deny that a bureaucratic rational orientation could be equated to the absence of church religiosity and traditional family orientations.

dimensions and operationalized by a large set of heterogeneous indicators from different domains one usually obtains fairly low factor loadings and reliability coefficients at the individual level.[10] This at least is the experience of a large number of factor analyses on postmaterialism (cf. Inglehart 1977; 1990) or on similar value orientations (cf. Klages & Herbert 1983). A large number of factor loadings range between .3 and .6., and only a few are above that level. The reader will easily identify a larger number of other value studies, which report standardized factor loadings of similar magnitude.[11] If a factor loading amounts to .3, only nine percent (=.3^2 *100) of the observed variance is explained by the latent value orientation. If the loading is .6, exactly 36 percent of the observed variance is explained. These figures are not impressive at all. Methodologists may therefore argue that these factor loadings are too low and that systematic measurement error can heavily distort the effects of unreliably measured latent variables (cf. Jagodzinski, 1984a). Value researchers will object that we cannot expect stronger effects because broad and general value orientations are only loosely and often indirectly related to response behavior. Even though value measurement will probably never reach the rigorous standards of methodologists, these have stimulated the research for better measurement instruments.

[111]

(e) One can always increase the explained variance by increasing the number of latent value orientations. In exploratory factor analysis the decision on the number of factors is often based on the eigenvalues or the scree tests. These are soft criteria, and therefore theoretical considerations and other criteria are observed too. Some authors, who initially had postulated a single bi-polar dimension like individualism versus collectivism, may be persuaded by the scree test to choose a two-dimensional solution and consider individualism and collectivism as two separate dimensions. Others may stick to their theoretically postulated solution even though the explained variance is fairly small. As a consequence, discussions on the dimensionality of value orientations are rarely definitely settled. Flanagan (1982a; 1982b; 1987), Herz (1979; 1980) and others, for instance, have argued that materialism and postmaterialism actually are two separate dimensions. Inglehart has always

---

[10] This is true for the individual level of analysis. We usually obtain fairly high factor loadings if we analyze mean scores at the macro-level. Many examples can be found in Hofstede (2001).

[11] Inglehart's (1997) new value dimensions are based on items which display somewhat higher inter-correlations and factor loadings, particularly the indicators of sexual and life morality and of religiosity. In this sense, this study can be seen as an exception from the rule. There may be other exceptions. For instance, in a politically polarized society religious, moral and political attitudes may highly correlate and therefore produce high factor loadings and high reliability coefficients.

rejected this position. The discussion remains unsatisfactory because value researchers do not even agree on the statistical criteria, which should be used for deciding the question of dimensionality.

[112]

The dimensionality question is also affected by technical decisions. Postmaterialism is usually measured by forced-choice items. Individuals are forced to rank political priorities and cannot treat different priorities as equally important. Whether this ranking is superior to rating seems to be almost a metaphysical question. At least, considerable efforts are necessary to demonstrate the superiority of one or the other method. If we assume that people really consider two alternatives as equally important, rating scales should be more adequate.[12] If forced choice items stimulate the respondents to think about the priorities more carefully and to find at least small differences, this type of item is better suited. In any case, the use of rating scales seems to be favorable to two-dimensional solutions (Van Deth, 1983; Bean & Papadikis, 1994a and b; Inglehart, 1994) while forced choice frequently result in one-dimensional solutions (see also Alwin & Krosnick, 1985; Krosnick & Alwin, 1988).

(f) Estimations in measurement models are also dependent on the error assumptions. The standard model postulates random error, which has an expected value of zero and is uncorrelated with the underlying value dimension. Random error can explain, for instance, why the correlation between a value orientation and other dependent and independent variables remains low as long as no adequate correction of the measurement error (correction for attenuation) is performed. Is the measurement error random? Let us take the example of the four item postmaterialism index, one of the most widely discussed measurement indices. It has already been mentioned that this index is sensitive to a change of inflation rates because it includes fighting rising prices as one of the four political goals. If the socialization hypothesis is true, changing inflation rates should not alter materialist and postmaterialist value orientations but should in the first place produce measurement error. Suppose that we have carried out a panel analysis with the first wave in 1970 and a second in 1976, and that we have calculated a simple additive postmaterialism index. In 1970 the inflation rate was low and in 1976 it was high. The expected value of the postmaterialism index is calculated as the overall average from both waves. The expected values for 1970 and 1976 will systematically deviate from the overall average due to the changing inflation rate. This systematic deviation is not caused by value change in adulthood but reflects measure-

---

[12] Klein and Arzheimer (1999) have recently published a study in which postmaterialism is measured twice, by ranking and by rating. They present evidence for a response bias: Those who rate the political goals as equally important tend to select the first two items from the forced choice items as most important.

ment error. Thus, the expected value of the measurement error is different from zero at both points in time. The systematic measurement error will leave the correlations of a linear-additive postmaterialism index unaffected. If materialism and postmaterialism are calculated in the usual way, however, the lagged correlations can be distorted.[13] Thus, we may have to specify more complicated measurement models in future research.

[113]

(g) The measurement instrument should not only be reliable but also valid. Davis and Davenport (1999) have recently analyzed the construct validity of postmaterialism by investigating the causes and effects of post-materialism in the United States. The results are mixed. In general, they find weak or even insignificant effects. A few effects have the wrong sign. In his reply as well as in many other publications Inglehart (1977; 1990; see also Inglehart & Abramson 1999) has presented results, which confirm his theoretical expectations. In general, the construct validity of value orientations should be examined more systematically.

(h) A further problem of value research can be loosely related to the concept of discriminant validity. So far, we find an abundant number of value orientations in the literature. The value orientations of different authors are similar to each other but not identical. For instance, stimulation and self-direction (Schwartz, 1994; Schwartz & Bardi, 2001) are related to individualism (Hofstede, 2001; Triandis, 1993), and to postmaterialism and self-expression (Inglehart, 1997). Identical or similar indicators are used for measuring different value orientations. The situation is far from the perfect world where each indicator has one and only one factor loading above .6 on a latent value dimension and zero loadings elsewhere. The ideal indicators therefore discriminate between different value orientations. Furthermore, this ideal and parsimonious world consists of only a few overarching higher order orientations and a larger number of first order value orientations, which are sub-dimensions of these higher order value orientations. A new value dimension or sub-dimension is only admitted, if its measurement model sufficiently discriminates between the new and the old sub-dimensions. It would be easy for the scholars to learn these sub-dimensions as well as their causes and effects by heart. Unfortunately, we will probably never arrive in this world. It is true;

---

[13] It has recently been suggested to replace the inflation item in the four-item index by fighting unemployment. Clarke et al. (1999) have shown that this replacement results in an impressive increase of the percentage of materialists (see also Inglehart, 1999). With regard to the measurement problem the unemployment item is not better than the inflation rate item. The responses to both items are affected by short-term period effects, in one case by the inflation rate and in the other by the unemployment rate. If the socialization hypothesis is true, the short-term effects produce systematic measurement error.

one can try to reduce the number of value dimensions by factor analyzing the value indicators of a large number of (original) value orientations or by using smallest space analysis for that purpose (Schwartz, 1992). Schwartz identifies ten sub-dimensions. However, these ten sub-dimensions cannot replace the original value orientations because the former will not display the same correlations with the causes and effects of the latter. This alone will be a sufficient reason to reject them. Furthermore, most value researchers will have difficulties accepting new labels for their value orientations. Therefore, the somewhat chaotic situation in value research will most likely persist.

The stability problem
Stability is essential to the concept of value orientations. The latter are only useful for a parsimonious explanation and prediction of attitudes and behavior if they do not change over night. Otherwise, they could be substituted by dispositions and characteristics of individuals, which can be easily measured. Actually, there are two strategies to demonstrate the stability of values: cohort analysis and panel analysis. Cohort analysis is usually based on a sequence of cross-sectional data and can at best test a necessary condition of individual-level stability. If value orientations in adulthood are perfectly stable, the percentages of materialists, individualists, or persons with other value orientations should remain constant in cohorts or generations. Stable value orientations imply stable percentages in cohorts but not vice versa. If 1000 coins are flipped at time point t_0 we will obtain about 50 percent heads and tails. If we repeat the experiment at a later point in time we will probably receive a similar percentage even though only about half of the coins will display the same result in the first and second experiment. Let us call a coin, which in all experiments has displayed the same result, a stable coin and the complementary coin a switcher. If we repeat the experiment again and again, the percentage of stable coins will steadily decline but in each experiment we will receive about 50 percent heads. If heads have a probability of .8 and tails of .2, it takes a little bit longer before the switchers outweigh the stable coins but after five experiments it is already the case. Thus, even a constant percentage of 80 or more may be the result of considerable individual-level change or switching.

The longest sequence of cross-sectional data can probably constructed for postmaterialist value orientations from the Eurobarometers. It is therefore not astonishing that postmaterialist values have been more often analyzed by means of cohort analysis than other value orientations. These empirical analyses lead to two major conclusions: first, the percentage difference between postmaterialists and materialists within cohorts is not stable at all but heavily affected by the actual inflation rate. Inglehart (1990) explains this fluctuation by period effects, which are predicted by the scarcity hypothesis. Second, the differences between cohorts are stable in the sense that younger cohorts always display higher percentage differences of postmaterialists and materialists than older ones. Inglehart explains these differences between cohorts as cohort effects which are predicted by the socialization hypothesis. Differences between cohorts, however, can also be due to age effects and it is common knowledge with cohort analysis that age-period models and cohort-period models often fit the data equally well. Indeed, Jagodzinski (1996) can demonstrate in this particular case that a cohort-period model and an age-period model both explain more than 90 percent of the variance at the aggregate level. Both models have very different interpretations. If the observed fluctuation is attributed to measurement error, the first model postulates stable values and measurement error. By contrast, the age-period model assumes life-cycle change and short-term change. Both models are compatible with the data and it is not possible to reject one of them.

[115]

One might hope to gain conclusive evidence about the relative strength of age and cohort effects from three dimensional age-period-cohort models. This is only possible, however, if there would be one and only one theoretically admissible way to impose the identifying restrictions on the cohort, age, or period effects. In practice, it is always possible to defend different identifying restrictions with acceptable theoretical arguments. Now, by choosing different but equally plausible restrictions one can manipulate the size of the age and cohort effects (cf. Jagodzinski, 1983, for an empirical example). Different minimally restricted cohort models can be rotated into each other (Jagodzinski, 1984b).

In the end, the question of stability and change of value orientations cannot be definitely settled by means of cohort analyses. Surprisingly enough, it is also extremely difficult to demonstrate the stability of value orientations by means of panel data. Whatever measurement model we apply, we will observe a large fluctuation in response behavior. This fluctuation can either be attributed to measurement error or to instability of the underlying value orientations. By the choice of estimation techniques and by the modification of the model assumptions we can influence the decomposition of the observed fluctuation into measurement error and value instability. If the observed intra-wave correlations of value indicators are similar in magnitude to the inter-wave correlations and if we postulate random measurement error, ML-estimation techniques in covariance structure models will usually result in high stability coefficients (Jagodzinski, 1984a).[14]

---

[14] Perfect stability in these models means that the relative positions of the individuals to each other do not change. Thus, linear life-cycle change would result in perfect stability. The concept of latent stability to some extent deviates from the common sense understanding of the term.

[116]

As long as panel data show a large fluctuation of the value indicators, the stability issue will remain unsettled. Some value researchers will believe in the stability of values and some methodologists will not. The discussion has increased our knowledge about value measurement.

The causality problem

The concept of probabilistic causality has been intensively discussed in recent years. Suppes (1970) has elaborated the idea of statistical qualitative and quantitative causality. Steyer (1992) has further elaborated the latter concept for linear models. Causality is defined for systems of variables. Roughly spoken, it requires (1) an effect of an independent on a dependent variable in the system, (2) temporal succession, and (3) the assumption that variables outside the system do not alter the effects of the independent variables. According to the principle of temporal succession the change in the independent variable must occur before the change in the dependent variable. This principle is rarely tested empirically and one can doubt whether it is testable at all if only internal or mental variables like value orientations, attitudes, beliefs, or ideologies are included in the statistical model. In this case, even the degree of stability is of little help. If value X is more stable than attitude Y, a causal effect of Y on X is less likely but not logically excluded. Accordingly, the causal ordering of variables is more or less deliberately determined by the author and at best based on plausibility considerations.

In general it can be expected that a theory on value X will conceptualize X as the key determinant of behavior and also of attitudes and other values. Thus a theory on individualism or postmaterialism will probably consider individualism not only as a determinant of social and political behavior, but also of political attitudes, achievement values, or religion. Vice versa, a theory on religiosity and religious values will not only specify a causal effect of religiosity on religious behavior but also on collectivism, postmaterialism, solidarity, altruism, sexual morality, achievement values and political orientations. As a consequence of these strategies, we will sooner or later arrive at an inconsistent causal order. A first researcher estimates the effect of value orientation X on value orientation Y and the second the effect of Y on X. Why don't both estimate reciprocal causal relationships? The answer is very simple: first, these reciprocal structures are only identified if we find suitable instrumental variables for X and Y which is not easy at all. Second, the reciprocal effects are heavily dependent on the predictive power of the instrumental variables. Regarding this, the (internal) causal structure of the mind will remain a black box. Particularly, the causal relations among different value orientations will remain unexplored.

Value Orientations and Behavior

The relationship between value orientations and behavior has been investigated in many studies. The typical model specifies (1) either reported behavior like volunteering (participation in protest actions, the behavioral intentions as dependent variable (cf. Inglehart, 1977; 1990), or the results of a decision like membership in voluntary organizations (Schofer & Fourcade-Gourinchas, 2001) and (2) value orientations like postmaterialism besides demographic variables or attitudes as independent variables. The direct effects are estimated by means of regression analysis or logit analysis. This procedure remains unsatisfactory because no attempt is made to integrate value orientations into elaborated theories of action. If we take a well-known version of these theories (cf. Coleman, 1990) the choice of action is in the first place determined by the outcomes of the alternative actions. Two aspects of these outcomes are relevant to the choice, their probability and their utility. If the person has no doubts at all that the outcome o will be realized if action i is taken, the subjective probability of o is 1. If there are doubts, she or he will assign a lower subjective probability to the respective outcome o. The actor also tries to determine the utility of outcomes. The highest utilities are assigned to those outcomes, which are most desirable, and the lowest to those, which are least desirable. The choice of an action is determined by the expected utility of the action, which is calculated as the weighted sum of the utilities of all outcomes. Weights are the subjective probability of the outcomes. It is assumed that the actor will choose the action with the highest expected utilities.

Values can be incorporated in such a theory of action in two ways. First, they will almost certainly affect the utilities of the outcome. A postmaterialist, for example, will presumably assign a higher utility to measures of environmental protection than a materialist. In this way, value orientations will indirectly affect the choice. Value orientations can have a more direct effect on the expected utility of action, however, if they are logically or empirically related to norms. If environmentalists derive from their internalized value orientations the norm that we have to protest against animal experiments, the observance of this norm is a desirable outcome to them. An actor realizes the desirable outcome with probability 1 if he or she participates in a protest action because the norm then is observed. Thus, the utility of norm observance can directly enter into the calculation of the expected utilities.

One objection to the subjective expected utility theory is that it is much too restrictive and that utilities so far have not been measured adequately. We may therefore prefer an alternative theory of action like the prospect theory (cf. Kahneman, 2000) or the theory of planned behavior (Ajzen & Fishbein, 1980). They all are based on the idea that aspects of the outcome of action

[117]

largely determine the choice or the behavioral intention. Whatever theoretical approach we choose, we should not abandon the idea that the choice of action is determined by aspects of its outcomes. The direct and indirect impact of value orientations on the choice of action or the behavioral intentions can only be seriously tested if value orientations are integrated into these theories.

[118]

Collective or cultural values

In contrast to individual-level theories the theories of collective values are only rudimentarily developed. It must therefore be sufficient to list a number of questions, which have to be answered by future research.

(a) How do we conceptualize cultural values? While we have fairly clear ideas about the conceptualization of value orientations the properties of collective values are more diffuse. We may suggest, for instance, that a value orientation which becomes manifest in the actions of a smaller or larger group of people is a cultural value. One consequence is that we will find myriads of cultural values in each society. The values of a poet remain cultural values as long as his poems are read and somehow influence the behavior of individuals. The values of a small religious community would not only be collective values of this community but also values of the society or the culture. Different collective values may partly complement, partly contradict and partly overlap each other. In order to reduce their number we may focus on those collective values, which are most relevant to the society. This immediately leads to the second question:

(b) How do we determine the relevance of a collective value? Obviously, the answer depends on the goals of our research. If we want to identify those values, which influence the response behavior of the majority of people, it may be quite appropriate to look for the modal value or to calculate means and averages. If we want to identify those collective values, however, which have the largest impact on the change of a system or subsystem the values of the majority may not be the most relevant ones. Suppose that the large majority of the citizens favors a more egalitarian income distribution but that the employers and managers believe in the motivating forces of income inequality. Even in a democracy the latter group may be more successful in realizing their goal than the egalitarian majority. Consequently, the inequality in the society may increase and not decrease. This suggests that we focus on those groups, which are most powerful and have the largest influence in the respective domain. In the European monarchies the values of the queens, kings, popes and their advisors probably have been most influential in the field of politics. In an oligarchy we would have to study the values of the elite. To be sure, we can easily rule out the relevance problem by deciding that cultural values always are the values of the majority. We then risk, however, that we focus on collective values with little or no impact on the dynamics of our societies. The relevance problem can only be solved if we can answer the next question:

[119]

(c) How is the micro- and macro-level behavior affected by collective values? It has already been stated in a previous section that the there is no direct effect of the collective values on macro-level behavior. Collective values can only indirectly influence individual level behavior and the channels of causality are fairly complex. If we have identified the causal structure of the value-behavior relationship we will already have found an answer to the next question:

(d) How do different collective values affect behavior and attitudes? So far, the interplay of different collective values is rarely investigated. Typically, a society is characterized by its position on the collective value dimension and it is stated, for instance, that the spiritual religiosity is higher in postmaterialist societies (cf. Inglehart, 1990; 1997) or that risk avoiding societies register fewer heart attacks (cf. Hofstede, 2001). Occasionally, the interaction of two value dimensions is considered (cf. Jackson, 2001). Quite often, however, the distribution of collective values will determine the outcome. Inglehart (1977), for instance, has explained the political protest of the seventies in the Western societies by value conflict between the old, still materialist political elites and the younger, highly educated postmaterialist generations. If this hypothesis is true it is less important whether a society is more or less postmaterialistic. Rather, the positions of materialists and postmaterialists in the social structure are important.

The so-called economic theory of religion (Iannaccone, 1991; Iannaccone et al., 1997; Stark & Iannaccone, 1994; Stark, 1999) emphasizes the importance of religious competition on religious participation. In general, the value commitment of a person may be positively affected by the degree and intensity of competition in a society. In order to determine the degree of competition we have to identify the groups, which hold different religious values and beliefs. Again it is not sufficient to focus on a single percentage, the average or the mode.

A number of interesting hypotheses can be stated if we consider more than one value dimension. Taking up the distinction between religious monopolies and religiously mixed societies (Martin 1978) we may raise the question whether the family values of Catholics in a Protestant or Catholic monopoly or in religiously mixed societies are the same. Or we may ask in the tradition of the Protestant ethic (Weber, 1958) whether the achievement values of Catholics in these three types of societies differ. If Catholics adapt to the dominant culture their achievement values should be higher in Protestant than in Catholic monopolies. If religious minorities are particularly resistant to the influence of the dominant culture we should find no difference or even the reverse effect. In any case, multi-level value research should pay much more attention to these composition effects in pluralizing societies.

(e) After all these problems are solved the measurement problem of collective values can be addressed. No doubt, Hofstede's (2001) highly sophisticated measurement procedures are much more appealing than using country dummy variables as a proxy for collective values or economic indicators as an indirect measure of secular values or occidental rationality (cf. Jagodzinski & Dobbelaere, 1995; Dobbelaere & Jagodzinski, 1995).[15] However, whether an aggregate level factor analysis of means and other aggregate measures is superior to the averaging of individual level factor scores can only be decided after the preceding questions are answered. In particular, we have to clarify the causal structure of the multi-level model in Figure 1 for each collective value.

Conclusion

Value research has made important progress during the last decades, particularly on the individual level of analysis. In those instances where a consensus was not reached, the discussions have increased our methodological and substantial knowledge considerably. This is true for the measurement issues and the stability problem as well. What still remains to be desired at the individual level is the connection to the existing theories of action.

Research on the macro-level has been largely stimulated by Hofstede. His research has considerably improved our knowledge about other societies. Many other researchers have followed his model and nowadays present statistical and, above all, graphical macro-level analyses along with micro-level results. What seems to be the most important task for the next years is to bridge the gap between the macro- and the micro-level. This requires in the first place to extend micro-level models with macro-level variables and to use multi-level estimation techniques. If this is not done the risk of ecological fallacies is large particularly with regard to minority behavior like suicide or violent crime. If we conclude from a positive macro-level effect of individualism on suicide rates that the individualists are endangered we may develop psychological programs for the wrong subpop-

---

[15] Authors who use these indirect indicators almost always apologize for not having better and more direct measures.

ulation. Consequently, we have to improve our knowledge about the causal impact of collective values. If we want to change society by piecemeal engineering, this knowledge is indispensable. Collective values, however, can only influence micro-level behavior via or in interaction with other micro-level variables.

A theory of collective values should not only state a set of causal hypotheses, it must clarify the epistemological status of collective values, to conceptualize the interplay between different values, and to elaborate the relationship between collective value conflicts and social structure. Furthermore, it has to be supplemented by a measurement model for collective values. Thus, there remains an ample field for future research.

[121]

CHAPTER SIX

The structural roots of values

An anthropological interpretation of Hofstede's value dimensions

HANS-PETER MÜLLER AND PATRICK ZILTENER

This chapter explores the relation between Hofstede's value dimensions und traditional social organization in 11 Asian countries. It demonstrates that the value configuration of these countries depends on the level of traditional structural complexity and — related to that — on the degree of cultural homogeneity. More complexity and more homogeneity means higher uncertainty avoidance and lower power distance. The negative correlation between uncertainty avoidance and power distance distinguishes Asia from the Western world, where these values correlate positively.

Introduction

However radically or rapidly cultural change and social transformation take place, new ways of life, at least partially, reflect the older patterns in which they are rooted. Modern development never marks a complete break with the past, but is an evolutionary process, both continuing and transforming what has been there before. If we want to understand differences in development, we should know more about differences in the local and national preconditions.

Even though this view might be undisputed, it nevertheless opens up many areas of controversy and debate. Of the many questions that immediately arise, we mention those that will play a crucial role in the following pages: How strong is the influence of the past on the process of modernization or 'development'? What is the relationship between values and social structures in the process of change? And how much cultural leveling and homogenization may reasonably be expected from future globalization?

In the following, we explore these questions by referring to previous research of ours. We begin with the culture-structure relationship. One of the merits of Hofstede's (2001) study is to have shown that even in such a modern and transnational 'place' as the IBM enterprise, there can be detected deeply rooted national cultural differences. At least this is how Hofstede interprets his 'work related attitudes': as differences in the collective programming of the mind "that have very old historical roots (some, for example, going back as far as the Roman Empire)" (Hofstede, 2001: 11). Some of the values are able to explain normative preferences and individual behavior, but they need further exploration. Values are not suspended like clouds over some types of social landscapes, but are better compared to captive balloons: flexible, but secured to the ground.

[123]

In this chapter we present an exploratory analysis of the connection between traditional social structures and values. The data we use stem from a new research instrument, the culture indicators of the *Atlas of Pre-Colonial Societies[1]* (Müller et al., 1999, in the following pages shortened to ATLAS). Based on field research from the first half of the 20th century, past conditions are recorded, namely the forms of social organization of some 2000 ethnic groups in Africa and Asia. From this, data for 87 countries were obtained by aggregating population-weighted ethnological data. These are the ethnological indicators that can be linked to quantitative value analyses. Unfortunately, both of these data sets overlap only partially, which makes the interpretation of empirical results somewhat challenging. Further, the data differs in that the ethnographic data have not measured individuals' opinions, as in most value studies, but the institutional arrangements of ethnic societies before the start of modern development. The aggregated ethnological indicators then were correlated with Hofstede's value dimensions, which mirror the mental profiles of the IBM personnel in each country. While the individuals' answers always represent the time of the survey (around 1970), the ethnological information stems from the first half of the 20th century and, thus, predominantly describes pre-colonial conditions.

We would like to emphasize that the concept of *development* points here to two different fields of significance: on the one hand, to the long-term historical and cultural development of, say, the last 10,000 years (social evolution) and on the other hand, to modern developments such as industrialization, economic growth and the improvement in the living conditions of national populations.[2] The concept is introduced in the next section, together

---

[1] German title: *"Atlas vorkolonialer Gesellschaften: Kulturelles Erbe und Sozialstrukturen der Staaten Afrikas, Asiens und Melanesiens"*.

[2] In modern development, economic progress and social progress are not necessarily in accordance, as is shown in the *Human Development Index (HDI)* of the *United Nations Development Programme (UNDP)*. For empirical research, see especially Firebaugh and Beck (1994) and Easterly (1997).

with the second core concept of this analysis: cultural homogeneity. After this follows a summary of our findings about the connection of traditional societal organization and modern socio-economic development in the *non-Western world*[3]. Based on this, the non-western countries of the Hofstede study will be characterized with the help of structural (ethno-sociological) criteria, and conclusions will be reached according to their representative characteristics. Those variables that proved to be predictors of modern development are related to Hofstede's value dimensions. From this, it becomes clear that the value structures in Asian countries are closely connected with their historic-evolutionary positions. In the third section we will return to the complete sample of Hofstede's study and show that a structurally geared approach can contribute to the interpretation of the interrelations of value configurations.

Structural dimensions in the non-Western world

Socio-political differentiation and cultural homogeneity
The ATLAS contains a variety of coded traits of traditional social structure. The category central to our question is structural complexity. It is measured as development level in three areas: intensity of agricultural production (agriculture with plow or horticulture); the population size of ethnic groups; the level of socio-political differentiation. The *Index for socio-political differentiation (SPD)* measures the levels of political centralization and social stratification, the mean size of local communities and the existence of a written language.[4] Social evolution, i.e. the increase of structural complexity, is characterized by the iterative development of these indicator variables.

Structural complexity not only includes endogenous characteristics, but also encompasses the power potential of societies in their intersocietal competition for resources. The greater the structural complexity, the greater the

---

[3] The sample includes countries where elements of European population were not partly or totally predominant during colonial rule. This excludes, besides Europe and Russia, the European settler colonies (in North America, Australia and New Zealand). In Central and South America the population element from Europe was not in all cases the dominant one, but western thinking and behavior patterns were. The sample covers 87 countries of Africa, Asia and Melanesia.

[4] The SPD index is the sum of four ranked variables: *mean size of local communities*; *jurisdictional hierarchy beyond local community*; *class stratification*; *written language* (Murdock, 1967; Müller et al., 1999). Besides this the ATLAS offers a vast amount of information in other fields such as types of kinship organization (mainly rules of descent, of inheritance, of marriage), sexual division of labor, household composition, etc. The data set and details regarding the index construction can be found at www.ethno.unizh.ch/cultural-indicators.

chance of winning against competing units and of grasping an increasing share of foreign resources (and vice versa). Along with the level of structural complexity, the *forms* of the elementary societal institutions (regarding production, distribution, securing subsistence, socialization etc.) and of individual life-worlds also change.

[125]

As a second concept we introduced the cultural homogeneity of the countries examined. *Cultural homogeneity* (or heterogeneity, with a negative sign) refers to internal cleavages of a society, such as different ethno-linguistic units or religions coexisting within a country. Ethnic homogeneity has been defined in various ways (e.g. Rae & Taylor, 1970; Morrison & Stevenson, 1972; Lijphart & Crepaz, 1991). In our research project, homogeneity is measured with respect to ethnic, linguistic and religious cleavages. All three indicators are measured directly at national level, following the same logic; they measure the proportion (percentage) of people representing (i) the largest spoken language group, (ii) the largest religious group (not sects) and (iii) the largest ethnic group.[5]

In the existing literature, cultural homogeneity (or, negatively, *fractionalization*) appears mostly as a predictor in econometric growth models (cf. Alesina et *al.*, 2002). [6] In this connection we are mainly interested in the historical reasons for the substantial differences in homogeneity in the world of states of today. Basically, we can say that the structural complexity and population size of ethnic units have risen in parallel during social evolution. The centers (kingdoms) that have developed in the historical process have been superimposed on, and have then integrated, the local societies. In the long term this led to ethno-linguistic homogeneity, along with social differentiation of ethnic societies. Therefore we expect that homogeneity has increased with growing differentiation. Figure 1 confirms the view that the past has an impact on the present.

Even the sometimes absurd colonial borders have not been able to really alter this correlation of socio-political differentiation (SPD) and cultural homogeneity (HOMO), which is highly significant ($r = .72$, $p < 1\%$) and becomes clear even within the sub-Saharan context ($r = .39$, $p < 1\%$). Most African and

---

[5] 'Largest ethnic group' is identical with the variable 'size of population' mentioned above.

[6] Our index of cultural homogeneity correlates highly (negatively) with the indicators for fractionalization developed by others. Taylor and Hudson's (1972) index of ethno-linguistic fractionalization (ELF), constructed with data for 1960, correlates with the combined ethnic and linguistic dimensions of our index $r = -.94$. Our three-dimensional index correlates with a combination of the three fractionalization dimensions provided by Alesina et *al.* (2002) with data for the 1980/90s $r = -.84$. Differences in coding are mainly found in the Melanesian countries.

[126]

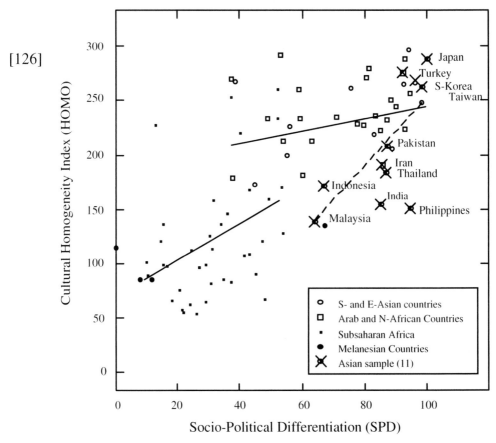

Figure 1: *Cultural homogeneity of present-day nation states as a function of the socio-political differentiation of traditional societies: The case of the non-Western world*

Melanesian countries are found in the lower half of the scale, for SPD as well as for homogeneity. Exceptions are countries like Rwanda, Burundi, Swaziland and Lesotho. They link an extensive homogeneity with a medium structural complexity. At the opposite extreme to the African world, we can find countries from North Africa, from West Asia and from South and East Asia. They are mostly found in the upper half of both scales. While the Arabian world seems culturally more homogeneous, the South and East Asian world is structurally more complex.

Here we would like to point out that structural complexity and cultural homogeneity were especially significant in explaining the different development performances of non-Western countries in our findings: The higher

SPD and homogeneity were, the more favorable the conditions for catching up. This is consistent with another observation from Figure 1. If we examine the countries of the IBM study for their cultural homogeneity and traditional structural complexity, a remarkable bias is found. IBM investments are situated without exception in the uppermost third of traditional structural complexity scale and in the upper half of the homogeneity scale (where we would find the city states of Hong Kong and Singapore as well, although they were not considered in our study). Given the significant correlation between structural complexity, homogeneity and economic development, this distribution does not come as a surprise. [127]

In conclusion, we can say that the ethno-linguistic and religious homogeneity of the non-Western countries of today is determined by the structural differentiation of pre-national societies. This explains why the conditions in different regions of the world differ greatly. The specially highlighted countries are those that figure in both, our sample of the non-Western world, as well as in Hofstede's study. These 11 Asian countries are the focus of our analysis in the third section.[7]

Structural complexity, cultural homogeneity, and development

As mentioned before, our concept of development is not only concerned with the long-term evolution of societies, but also with the modern process of economic growth and the improvement of living conditions. As early as 1984, Lenski and Nolan demonstrated empirically in an influential article that there is a close connection between the historic-evolutionary position and modern socio-economic development of non-European countries. According to their ecological-evolutionary theory, environmental conditions determine the type of traditional subsistence economy (agri- vs. horticulture) and these in turn determine the social structures and, thus, the chances of development in the post-colonial period (in the 1960 and '70s).[8] Using a number of socio-economic variables, they demonstrated that horticulture has an adverse effect on development.

We can confirm Lenski and Nolan's finding inasmuch as in our study, with a longer period of observation (1965-95), more valid indicators, and more rigid statistical controls, the *subsistence economy* in fact has an influ-

---

[7] Not included are the three regions (Middle East, East Africa, West Africa) from Hofstede (2001) that cannot be specifically allocated to a country, as well as South Africa as a historic special case. For our study we could not ethnographically code and classify Israel, Hong Kong and Singapore, because of their immigration history.

[8] Compare Lenski (1984), Nolan and Lenski (1996), Crenshaw (1992, 1993).

[128]

ence on modern socio-economic development: The more dominant plow cultivation and other indicators of agro-technical efficiency, the higher the rate of economic development (Müller, 1996; Ziltener & Müller, 2003). However, it can be ascertained empirically that traditional *structural complexity* is an even more important factor for economic development in the post-colonial phase: Countries with a complex social organization were able to raise their per capita income significantly faster than others between 1965 and 1995. These results proved to be completely robust in different model specifications controlled for a wide range of other factors (e.g. ecologicy, oil exports, trade, aid dependency, political regimes etc.). Both the immediate economic aspect and the social side of the developmental process are influenced by this historical-cultural inheritance. For instance, life expectancy in countries of the non-Western world depends positively on the pre-colonial level of structural complexity in the 60s as well as in the 90s of the past century.

How to account for these findings? It appears that traditional structural complexity is advantageous in two ways, regarding (macro-social) development dynamics of *societal institutions* and (micro-social) *moral-mental discipline*. When the institutions of the pre-colonial societies had already developed the principles of *state* organization — government, bureaucracy, taxation, a regular army, territorial infrastructure, culture of the written word etc. — then the prerequisites for *nation building*, for creating institutional frameworks and for economic growth were more favorable than in those cases where the central institutions rested upon kinship systems and differences of gender and generations. If pre-colonial mechanisms of governance and legitimating already existed, then they only needed to be modernized in the course of the nation building process.

The increase in political hierarchy as well as the intensification of agriculture resulted in an augmentation of the level of *discipline*. Cross-cultural research shows that the general prolongation of work time for productive and reproductive activity forced men into involving themselves more in agricultural work (Minge-Klevana, 1980; Boserup, 1982). Parallel to this an extensive transformation of the individual's social world took place. Key characteristics of this are the integration of women into patriarchal social structures, the subordination of the population majority (women *and* men) to aristocratic classes in expanding tributary societies, introducing a more authoritarian child education, and the establishment of a moral order of deferred (even post-mortal) gratification pattern (Levinson, 1980; 1990).[9]

---

[9] Compare Putterman (2000: 6ff), who examined the influence of 'pre-modern level of development' on economic development in a comparable period for 48 developing countries: "One way those legacies may have affected growth is through their impact on conceptions and prac-

Besides high traditional structural complexity, cultural homogeneity is an advantage for development. Per capita income as well as life expectancy in countries of the non-Western world depend (positively) on their cultural homogeneity. This goes for the 1960s as well as the 1990s; in fact, the significance of this seems to increase over this period (Müller et al., 2002), a finding confirmed by econometric research. Easterly and Levine (1997) have shown in their influential study that a higher degree of ethno-linguistic fractionalization results in lower economic growth (cf. Sachs & Warner, 1997; Brock & Durlauf, 2001: 44ff). Usually cultural homogeneity is connected to a higher level of internal conflicts, but also to an institutional development deficiency. Mauro (1995) established a negative correlation between the efficiency of institutions and ethnic heterogeneity. La Porta et al. (1999) found that ethnic-linguistic fractionalization was, apart from other factors, a (negative) determinant for the quality of government. In sum, the results of empirical-quantitative research point unequivocally to a positive effect of cultural homogeneity and traditional structural complexity on modern socio-economic development.

[129]

Ethnic culture, value configuration in corporations and national culture

Firstly, we can state that Hofstede makes a methodological assumption that is also made in a similar way by ethnologists. Hofstede interprets the different attitudes that were found within the IBM staff of different countries as expressions of different national cultures. Because the IBM personnel are actually recruited in different geographic surroundings, it is reasonable to assume that the various interview answers mirror different social surroundings. This is similar to the ethnological research reports: Although only a few people living at a small place were observed and interviewed, the results are interpreted as characteristics of a much larger ethnic group, i.e., representativeness is claimed. The presumption is that the observance at the local point of examination mirrors characteristics of a not clearly specified ethnic environment.

An important difference, however, should not be overlooked. In cross-

---

tices of productive activity. (...) The peoples of agrarian societies that had adapted to the drudgery of intensive farming may have become more conditioned to (and, in the language of economics, more willing to supply) long, arduous hours of work than would less intensive farmers or pastoralists. They may have more sharply distinguished between work and leisure time, their values and expectations may have become better adapted to specialized and hierarchical economic interactions, and they may have perceptually separated their economic and non-economic social interactions in ways more closely resembling those of people in industrial societies".

cultural analysis the scale of findings of any dimension is surely much greater than in cross-national comparison of the IBM staff or of Schwartz's (1995) surveys in different national settings. With the personnel of singularly operating corporate groups or of educational institutes, one can only find what is compatible with the goals of these organizations. There will hardly be any values present that are incompatible with the competitive constraints or the institutional goals of different organizations. So, because the forms of societal adaptation in the natural and social environment are more varied and broader than those in a multi-national corporate group in the capitalist world system (or members within educational institutions which are, worldwide, very similar), value dimensions will basically be very different in varying institutional frame works and are likely to show very different results. Clearly, normative and cognitive patterns — comparable to the pre-state (tribal) societies — are difficult to find in a multinational or at a university campus.

Relating Hofstede's value dimensions to structural complexity

Knowing the limits of a small study of only 11 countries — those included in both our sample and Hofstede's — we would like to emphasize the exploratory character of the following paragraphs, considering the lack of previous research on the connection between evolutionary structure and values. Therefore, in the first step, bivariate correlations are presented, connecting the two explanatory concepts of our analysis (traditional structural complexity and cultural homogeneity) with the four value dimensions of Hofstede. The results are presented in Table 1 for 11 Asian countries.

This bivariate analysis shows significant correlations with two of the four value dimensions of Hofstede, power distance (PDI) and uncertainty avoidance (UAI). No correlation is found with the indices for individualism and masculinity. UAI, on the other hand, reveals the strongest connections with our structural variables, so this shall be discussed first, followed by PDI. After this, the third section leads us back to the complete sample of the Hofstede study, showing that a structurally geared approach can contribute to interpreting the interrelation of value dimensions.

First dimension: uncertainty avoidance (UAI)

Structural complexity and Uncertainty Avoidance
The indicators for structural complexity deal with societies which existed long before capitalist companies became rooted in what developed into post-colonial nation states, and so they are the truly independent variables in any

Table 1: *The correlations between Hofstede's values dimensions (4), indicators of traditional structural complexity (3) and cultural homogeneity*

	PDI	UAV	IND	MAS	Plow	SPD	Size	Homo
PDI	1.00							
UAI	-0.80**	1.00						
IND	0.03	0.00	1.00					
MAS	-0.02	0.27	0.66*	1.00				
Plow	-0.42	0.73*	-0.25	0.13	1.00			
SPD	-0.61*	0.67*	0.25	0.26	0.62*	1.00		
Size	-0.61*	0.88*	0.14	0.16	0.71*	0.63*	1.00	
Homo	-0.75**	0.95**	0.02	0.23	0.65*	0.67*	0.96	1.00

[131]

** p =< 1%; * p =<5%; N = 11.

PDI   = Power Distance Index (Hofstede, 2001)
UAI   = Uncertainty Avoidance Index (Hofstede, 2001)
IND   = Individualism (Hofstede, 2001)
MAS   = Masculinity (Hofstede, 2001)
Plow   = Traditional agriculture with plow (Müller et *al*., 1999)
SPD   = Socio-political differentiation (Müller et *al*., 1999)
Size   = Size of the largest ethnic unit, % of total population (Müller et *al*., 1999)
HOMO   = Ethnic, linguistic, and religious homogeneity (Müller et *al*., 1999)

model explaining the normative preferences of IBM staff in the 1970s. Therefore, high correlations of SPD and UAI are interpreted in causal terms, reflecting historically earlier social conditions. These can continue to exist for large proportions of the population when, for example, subsistence still has to be provided within family solidarity because state-run social insurance is missing, or when the state does not exert a monopoly of power and disputes are therefore still solved within and between families. Since such value systems maintain their functionality in the large informal sectors of developing countries and provide a sense of cultural difference and identity, they shape the interactions in formal institutions as well (Etounga-Manguelle, 2000). They can continue even under widely established modern conditions, provided they are compatible with the functional demands of a nation state, a monetarized economy and an urban social structure. Therefore, IBM personnel can express values rooted in traditional and informal social structures, even though, personally, they work in a highly formalized social context.

In Table 1 above the concept of traditional structural complexity is represented by three groups of indicators: (i) the traditional pattern of agriculture that is based on plow and draught animal; (ii) the SPD index that measures social and political differentiation of earlier local societies, and (iii) the estimated population size of the ethnic societies in 1960. All three indicators correlate highly with the UAI.

[132]

Our findings — that IBM personnel (1970) more strongly accentuate uncertainty avoidance the more pronounced the structural complexity of traditional local societies has been — might be surprising at first. The UAI index measures "[t]he extent to which the members of a culture feel threatened by uncertain or unknown situations" (Hofstede, 2001: 161), or "the extent to which a culture programs and its members feel either uncomfortable or comfortable in unstructured situations" (ibid. S. xix).[10] This stronger aversion to open situations in societies with greater structural complexity in the past is understood when one examines the evolutionary context. The intensification of agriculture, social hierarchy and political centralization increased in the course of social evolution parallel to the growing population density, to longer hours of work and stronger behavior controls within authoritarian political norms (Sheils, 1972; Minge-Klevana, 1980; Chick, 1997). The great agrarian religions of Asia were able to assert their claim in the course of political centralization and expansion against shamanistic and other local religions. They established systems of meaning, which through religion legitimized and stabilized the growing strain and social disparity. When trying to grasp the psychological quality of these symbolic worlds, the agrarian religions (Hinduism, Buddhism, Shintoism, etc.) rightly demand our attention. We suspect that the higher uncertainty avoidance in societies with a traditionally higher structural complexity can be ascribed to the growing workload [11] under increasingly hierarchic conditions and a growing density of regulation. Under these conditions the ritualization of social communication and daily actions gains prevalence, regardless of the specific denomination of the written religions. The seeming paradox is that the fear of unstructured situations seems greatest when the chance to ever be in such a situation is the smallest: in culturally homogeneous societies. The opposite applies to societies with high cultural differentiation on local level.

Uncertainty avoidance also correlates with geographic lattitudes, but Hofstede (2001: 179) maintains "latitude cannot be considered a fundamental cause". In fact, latitudes just point to ecological factors such as tropical forests, tsetse flies, etc., which are directly relevant for the traditional subsistence technology, in particular the possibility of plow-based agriculture.

---

[10] An abstraction from three dominant factor variables: (i) the need of employment stability; (ii) high rule orientation; and (iii) high nervous tension at work (Hofstede, 2001: 150).

[11] Only in the course of industrialization and with the use of abiotic energy is it possible to combine growing production of goods with decreasing hours of work. Value adjustments quickly arise, or even race ahead of the economic growth rate process via diffusion.

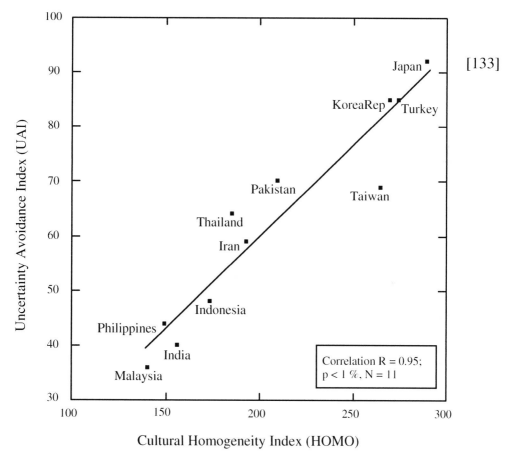

Figure 2: *Uncertainty avoidance as a function of cultural homogeneity and, indirectly, of traditional structural complexity*

This, and not latitudes as such, explains why high structural complexity was more difficult to establish in tropical woodlands than in more moderate latitudes.[12]

---

[12] The argument gets additional support from Hofstede's finding that "[s]tronger uncertainty avoidance is negatively related to geographic latitude, like PDI, but only for the wealthier countries; the poorer countries show a positive relationship" (2001: 179). Since ours is a poor country sample, higher PDI and UAI values are more frequent in higher latitudes, i.e. in the subtropical areas more than in the inner tropics. This is consistent with our view that plow agriculture and structural complexity are proxi-determinants of PDI and UAI.

Cultural homogeneity and Uncertainty Avoidance

The homogeneity index is composed of indicators of ethnic, linguistic and religious homogeneity. The correlation of uncertainty avoidance and cultural homogeneity is, with r = .95, the highest (Table 1). We would like to point out that, unlike structural complexity, these variables characterize nation states of today and not pre-colonial societies. The time of this survey corresponds to 1960 and the value dimension to around 1970.

[134]

The causal connection behind this correlation is difficult to interpret, but two channels of impact are feasible. Firstly, a high grade of cultural heterogeneity can impede the development of a, or erode an existing, culture of uncertainty avoidance. A great store of cultural mutuality is essential for sophisticated regulations of social situations, for which Japan is a telling example. Furthermore, uncertainty avoidance and cultural homogeneity mutually stabilize each other. Societies that favor uncertainty avoidance are more likely to reject immigration (Hofstede, 2001: 180), especially from cultures that seem 'different'. Societies with heavily increasing cultural heterogeneity are challenged to reduce their preference for highly structured situations. These are *modern* processes that are accentuated with the influence of globalization. Here we are especially interested in the structural roots of values. As has been shown, today cultural homogeneity is closely interwoven with the evolutionary position regarding structural complexity (Figure 1) and therefore an interpretation within a larger historical frame comes to mind, as already pointed out. According to this, the correlation of cultural homogeneity and uncertainty avoidance indicates trajectories of increasing complexity, in the past as well as in the present.[13]

Second dimension: Power Distance (PDI)

The second value dimension correlating with our structural variables is power distance. Hofstede (2001: xix) defines power distance as "the extent to which the less powerful members of organizations and institutions accept

---

[13] Unfortunately, variations of lower homogeneity (high heterogeneity) are not ascertainable with our indicator. Whereas high values are unambiguous, lower values can indicate two different situations: (i) a complex cultural composition in the local context as in certain parts of the former Ottoman empire or under modern urban conditions, or (ii) the fractionalization of a country in traditionally clearly separated cultural regions, e.g. Vietnam. High uncertainty avoidance at the individual level could be expected in countries with relatively low cultural homogeneity *if* the different ethno-linguistic and religious elements live in relatively discrete groups. However, the high correlation between cultural homogeneity and uncertainty avoidance shows that the imprecise quality of the indicator in the Asian countries examined carries little weight and has not to be considered further.

and expect that power is distributed unequally". The index does not refer to societal disparities, for example the legitimacy of class differences, but refers to inter*personal* power relations. One is reminded of Max Weber's famous differentiation of charismatic and bureaucratic power: While PDI calls forth the expectation and respect of personal authority (actually the legitimacy of 'charismatic' use of power), UAI represents an attitude of what we think of as a cultural adaptation to institutionalized hierarchy (actually legitimacy of 'rational' use of power).

[135]

In the light of this interpretation, both value dimensions, UAI and PDI, are complementary and should correlate negatively. In the course of history, the more the personal use of power is replaced, or at least disguised, by an institutionalized use of power — the more the kings and monasteries have marginalized the local chiefs and shamans — the weaker should power distance be today and the more strongly formed should uncertainty avoidance be. Because the cultural homogeneity of the nation states of today depends on how far this evolutionary process could proceed in the pre-colonial societies, we can also expect a negative correlation of PDI and homogeneity. As seen in Table 1, this is indeed the case for the examined countries of Asia. UAI and PDI stand in an inverse relationship to all structural variables and are very significantly associated with each other ($r = -.80$; $p > 1\%$).

Here the question arises, how far such an interpretation can be generalized. Until now our argument has been very general and without impeding ancillary conditions and should therefore be applicable to all societies. In the following section, we will reopen the examination and check if it is possible to interpret the data according to the 'Asian paradigm'.

PDI and UAI in the Western and non-Western World

First, we will compare the pattern common to the Asian countries to Hofstede's complete sample. Our starting point is Hofstede (2001: 150ff), who found in his total sample only a weak significant relation between uncertainty avoidance and power distance, whereas in his subsample of European countries he found a very significant positive correlation. In his total sample the connection is not significant because of a few Asian and African countries which occupy the 'PDI high and UAI low' quadrant.

These findings can easily be replicated and confirmed. However, it seems that value configurations in the Western and non-Western world differ much more radically than a reading of Hofstede might suggest. The crucial point here is not a few anomalous cases in Asia, which push down the positive correlation in the European subsample, but rather that the Asian countries show — when compared to Europe and the Western countries in

[136]

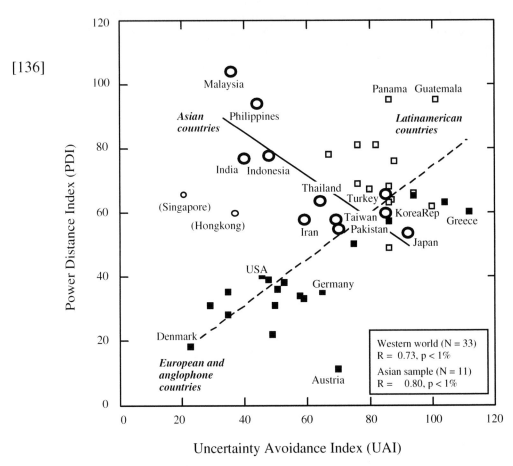

Figure 3: *Power distance and uncertainty avoidance in Asia and the Western world*

general — a contrary pattern (Figure 3). The negative correlation among the 11 Asian countries (r = .80) is not less striking than the positive correlation among the 17 European countries (r = .78) or the 33 Western countries (r = .73). Both major regions stretch over a wide range of the UAI scale, but they differ fundamentally on power distance. A few (Latin) European countries overlap with a few Asian countries in the medium PDI area. For the rest, the Asian countries are found in the upper and the European countries in the lower PDI area, when compared with values of uncertainty avoidance.

Finally, it is notable that the Latin American countries, with their high values of PDI *and* UAI, form their own cluster. Admittedly, this group of countries could be counted as part of the European complex, especially when compared with the values here discussed. The Latin European countries, such as Italy, Spain, Portugal and France are exactly between the Anglo-Germanic and the Latin American countries and at the intersection of the Asian and Western group of countries. Further evidence for the common value sphere can be seen when Latin America is included in the European subsample, after which the correlation of PDI-UAI decreases only minimally, but increases in significance. For this reason, in the following we differentiate only between a general Western pattern with a positive correlation and an Asian pattern with a negative correlation of UAI and PDI. [137]

What can be said of such a dichotomy of the world (excluding Africa)? We assume that in the different value configurations of the examined countries, especially in both inverse correlations, two fundamentally different types of logic are manifested. Both have the reduction of PDI in the course of development in common. But while in Asian countries decreasing PDI is associated with higher uncertainty avoidance, in Western countries decreasing PDI values are connected with decreasing uncertainty avoidance. In the latter, this dynamic is — unlike the Asian paradigm — to be interpreted as caused by increasing cultural heterogeneity in the course of the social and economic development of Western countries. The regression line, reaching from Panama and Guatemala at the upper end, via the Latin countries of Europe to the Northwestern European and Scandinavian countries (including the USA) at the lower end,[14] corresponds with a development gradient, but also with a process of increasing mobility, urbanization and differentiation of social roles. The heterogeneity of societies and individuals' lifeworlds has contributed substantially to increasing the ability to process cognitive dissonances in the course of development. What people with high uncertainty avoidance can experience as a terrifying loss of security, can, with reduced uncertainty avoidance, be experienced as cultural enrichment and urbane quality of life.

The difference between a long-term evolutionary and a modern phase of development seems to be crucial for the interpretation of the Asian and Western paradigms. Earlier, we argued that when the principle of kinship-based societal organization is pushed aside by the state principle, there is a decrease of (personally defined) power distance, while uncertainty avoidance starts to suffuse an increasingly hierarchically structured daily life. This process reaches its limit with large agrarian societies, whose aristocratic power is legitimized and stabilized by one of the great literal religions. In the course of

---

[14] Correlation of the human development index with PDI is $r = -.60$ ($p < 1\%$) and $r = -.45$ ($p = 1\%$) with UAI.

[138]

modern, European-influenced development, there seems to be a change of value configurations. While de-legitimatization of personal power continues (further reduction of PDI), the dislike of ambiguous situations decreases (reduction of UAI). Both these value displacements are caused by structural changes in modern societies.

How the future development of value changes will look cannot be answered coherently within our analysis. Regarding PDI, the data used leads us to surmise that the personal (charismatic) form of power relation continues to lose acceptance with people in societies with higher structural complexity as well as with increasing modern development. With UAI, meanwhile, there are two theses that oppose each other.

The first thesis construes today's difference between the Asian and the Western world as an expression of non-simultaneity in evolutionary development. According to this thesis of *convergence,* all countries should drift towards the direction of the lower left quadrant. With today's conditions of globalization, we can expect countries like Malaysia or the Philippines to steer directly to a configuration with low PDI and low UAI from the positions they have today. In doing this, they would leave the historic trajectory of the Asian countries.

The thesis opposed to this construes the differences of today as an expression of deeply rooted world views which are unlikely to be eroded by increasing income, new designs of society or normative preferences. According to this, every cultural region may keep their value preferences in the course of economic development. In Figure 3, for example, Japan is not expected to drift towards the European paradigm, but to keep its high UAI value, even at a further reduction of power distance. As long as countries with corresponding traditions keep on operating economically successfully, institutions that show higher uncertainty avoidance should keep their role model in the Asian area. This would corroborate the thesis of the development of a non-Western Asian modernity (Tu, 1996). In the same vein, a country like Greece would always define itself as European, based on its history and identity, and in this way follow the cultural models of successful Western European states. Though by doing so, it would be confronted with an especially intense cultural change.

Conclusion

Our aim was to provide an exploratory analysis of the interrelation of value dimensions and traditional social structures. Based on a new set of data, we demonstrated for 11 Asian countries that two of four value dimensions from Hofstede's IBM study depend heavily on the structural complexity of traditional societies and, as a consequence, the cultural homogeneity of the modern nation state. Structural complexity is operationalized in terms of traditional socio-political differentiation, intensity of traditional agriculture, and size of the pre-colonial cultural groups. The larger the traditional cultural units of a country, and the larger the proportion of people stemming from societies with pre-colonial state organization and plow cultivation, the more is uncertainty avoidance (UAI) supported and power distance (PDI) rejected by the IBM-staff in these countries — regardless of the level of economic development. This can be explained by the long-term co-evolution of structural complexity, cultural homogeneity and normative orientations.

[139]

These findings shed new light on the correlations between PDI and UAI. Hofstede (2001: 63), controlling for income level, finds that the correlations are positive in the wealthier subgroup and non-existent in the poorer subgroup. In contrast, we detected an Asian and a Western pattern, with rich Asian countries overlapping the Western group and poor Western countries overlapping the Asian group. It appears that higher levels of structural development in the Asia paradigm not only are connected with decreasing PDI (as in the West), but also with increasing UAI. In Asia, development tends toward 'national cultures' (Hofstede 2001: 13-14) that *strengthen* ritualized and extrinsic mechanisms and methods, on institutional and individual level, regulating social behavior.

The Western world follows another logic. Although we do not possess data for the traditional structural complexity of these societies (on our scale they would probably figure very high in general), Figure 3 showed a significant modernization-induced combined reduction of power distance *and* uncertainty avoidance. This specific Western pattern has been interpreted not only in terms of rising levels of income per-capita,[15] but even more so of increasing cultural heterogeneity in the range of everyday life. In order to confirm or falsify the thesis of a value convergence, further and comparatively structured analysis is needed. The benefit, even the necessity, of a differentiated analysis according to world regions, as pioneered by Hofstede, has been made more evident by our analysis.

Our statistical analysis serves mainly to make clear the plausibility of a structural and historical approach to the interpretation of 'national cultures'.

---

[15] Increasing income influences 'individualism', another of Hofstede's values. Individualism probably shows the least historic depth and depends the most directly on the level of consumption. In Asia there seems to be no connection or interrelation between individualism and traditional structural complexity. The positive correlation of individualism and income (Hofstede, 2001: 252) is interpreted as an adaptation of values to the more urban and more open conditions of life in richer countries, independent of cultural regions.

[140] The eurocentric certainty that the world should coalesce with the Western lifestyle is put into perspective through the possible development of a multi-linear and a more open evolution — which is a paradigm that could help give Africa more leeway. Our findings indicate why non-Western value configurations can be compatible in modern societies with companies operating worldwide; the loss of legitimacy of personal (charismatic) power is, in Asia, not accompanied by a parallel reduction of uncertainty avoidance. High values in this second dimension may seem to be a sign of traditionalism and therefore of backwardness, but high uncertainty avoidance can also affirm an order that disencumbers individuals of the collective pressure to individualize.

CHAPTER SEVEN

Cultural nationalism in Japan

A starting point for comparing cultures

KAZUFUMI MANABE, HENK VINKEN, AND JOSEPH SOETERS

A survey of the literature on nationalism reveals that the concept has been used most frequently in the context of politics. For example, Mattei Dogan says as follows:

> *Nationalism is still the most significant basic political value in the contemporary world, but not in Western Europe, and not in Japan either* (Dogan 1992).

Despite this observation, we can still see tendencies of what we might call 'cultural nationalism' occurring in several places around the globe. In Japan, the focus of this chapter, there is for instance an established genre of Japanese popular culture variously called *Nihon bunkaron*, *Nihon shakairon*, and *Nihonjinron*. *Nihon* is Japan. *Ron* refers to theory, idea, hypothesis, model, etc. *Bunka* and *shakai* refer respectively to "culture" and "society". *Jin* refers to "person". Thus, these three terms denote roughly the "theory" of Japanese culture, society, and character (or personality) respectively. As *Nihon bunkaron*, *Nihon shakairon* and *Nihonjinron* are used loosely and interchangeably rather than as distinct genres or separate fields, we will simply use the term *Nihonjinron*.

Nihonjinron is a body of discourse that purports to demonstrate Japan's cultural differences from other cultures and Japan's cultural uniqueness in the world and thus tries to establish Japan's cultural identity. It may be seen as a reflection of Japan's history as an insular society, which kept itself isolated from the rest of the world for centuries. *Nihonjinron* is said to be the worldview of the middle class and the ideology of Everyman. It also risks forming a justification for narrow-minded cultural nationalism, its extreme form being (right-wing) ethnocentrism, emphasizing the superiority of the Japanese people. In general one might regard it as a testimony of the uniqueness and purity of an unchanging "Japanese culture", a culture that has hardly undergone major change since prehistoric times, presupposes the Japanese

[142]

are radically different from all other people on the globe, and that regards the Japanese as willingly nationalistic including a display of hostility towards any issue that might not derive from Japanese sources (see Dale, 1986; Atkins, 2000).

Some *Nihonjinron* is serious academic discourse. Classic are philosophies and theories insisting that Japanese people do not have the same concept of nature as Western people (see e.g., Watanabe, 1995). Most Japanese, it is said, do not draw a clear boundary between humans and nature, while Westerners discuss nature in the context of its relationship to humans.[1] Loving nature, as the argument goes, is more inherent to traditional Japanese culture than to Western culture. This is one of the reasons that science class in Japanese schools is not only for teaching natural science, but also for teaching a background philosophy of loving nature. Therefore it is understandable that an environmental way of thinking in Japan blends smoothly with traditional elements of Japanese culture (Aoyagi-Usui et al., 2003).

This way of thinking, stressing Japan's (or sometimes Asian's) uniqueness, is highly influential among both academics and the general population in the country. A great bulk of *Nihonjinron* is communicated in a more popular fashion — in newspapers, television, radio, magazines and popular books. It is this popular version of *Nihonjinron* that we wish to examine here. Hence, the focus of this chapter will be on the way the Japanese adhere to this particular form of cultural nationalism. Prior to giving research data on the subject, we will try to develop some ideas on comparing cultures from the perspective of nationalism. This will help us to set an agenda for future studies on this topic as will be shown at the end of this chapter.

Nationalism and cultural values

Cultural nationalism is a phenomenon that is closely knit with concepts of national character, national identity, and national culture. Within the framework of this book it is interesting to focus on relationships of cultural nationalism with the cultural dimensions of the key scholars in this field: Hofstede, Triandis, Schwartz, and Inglehart.

Hofstede (2001: 175-176) explicitly links his dimension of *uncertainty avoidance* to nationalism. *Uncertainty avoidance* refers to the way people deal with ambiguities in life and uncertainties about the future. In *uncertain-*

---

[1] This of course relates to the harmony with nature orientation dominant in Schwartz' value concepts (Schwartz, 1994; see also chapter three in this volume). See also Gudykunst and Ting-Toomey (1988) on the subject and see Aoyagi-Usui et al., 2003 on a comparison of — amongst others — Schwartz' harmony values between Japan and the Netherlands.

ty avoiding cultures people tend to develop many and elaborated rules and regulations, which is a formal way of coping with ambiguity-related issues; in families they transfer rigid norms about virtues and moral behavior to their children. Deviance from these rules and norms are not likely to be tolerated. This generally leads to relatively high levels of stress, anxiety and feelings of unease among the population, especially when people are confronted with unfamiliar events. These emotions are connected to a general dislike of the unexpected and a resistance to change among the people in *uncertainty avoiding* societies. From this perspective it may come as no surprise that for- eigners are seen as strange and sometimes they are even regarded as hostile. Japan is among the countries where this cultural dimension is most strongly developed, as are, for instance, Turkey and Greece (Hofstede, 2001). Not surprisingly, in all these three countries a strong sense of collective identity, based on a prestigious history that underlines the country's uniqueness, is believed to be cherished. It is no exaggeration to say that nationalism is a clear element of these countries' cultures. Conversely, it is not an exaggera- tion to note that authors tend to overstate the 'uniqueness' of Japanese *Nihon- jinron* literature, says Atkins (2000: 36): "Japanese are not alone in proclaim- ing their singularity and purity".

[143]

An obvious relationship seems to be found with the dimension of *indi- vidualism* versus *collectivism,* or in the concepts used by Triandis (1995: 52- 57): *looseness* versus *tightness* of cultures. This dimension refers to the extent to which people are integrated in groups. In more collectivistic — tight — societies, such as Japan, people are integrated into strong, cohesive groups (families, organizations), which throughout people's lifetime contin- ue to protect them in exchange for unquestioning loyalty. In individualistic — loose — societies, such as the US and many Western European countries, people are expected to look after themselves and their immediate family; other loyalties are far less developed or non-existant. As De Mooij (2003) has convincingly shown, people in collectivist societies have a tendency to think their culture, values and customs are unique, which in fact reflects a particularistic worldview. With this view people focus on differences rather than on similarities, thinking that their culture is so unique that no foreigner will understand its basics. In contrast, people in individualistic societies tend to think the opposite; they think their rules, values and customs apply all over the world. This reflects a universalistic worldview, believing that one's own values are valid for all other parts of the world and should be shared by all, of course, leading to numerous conflicts and mistakes, both in international pol- itics (for instance the emphasis on 'human rights') and in international adver- tising (e.g. the use of US-origin image styles; see De Mooij, 2003).

One might expect a positive relationship between cultural nationalism and the *conservatism* or embeddedness concept of Schwartz (1994; see his chapter in this volume). Conservatism relates to values emphasizing the status quo and de-emphasizing actions that might disturb the existing order. As Schwartz states, the conservatism dimension is closest to the individualism-collectivism dichotomy presented above. The conservatism dimension does build on individual-level value syndromes in which *tradition* is a basic feature. Tradition in turn taps respect for, commitment to, and acceptance of the customs and ideas that traditional culture or religion imposes on the self. Cultural nationalism found in *Nihonjinron* might be seen as the specific translation of these types of values. It can be regarded as a very explicit form of expressing the traditions of a specific in-group, a form that in turn, re-enforces the beliefs of uniqueness of this in-group.

Also, Inglehart's two-fold dimensions of survival versus well-being or self-expression, and traditional versus secular-rational authority values might be related to cultural nationalism in general or *Nihonjinron* in particular. The well-being value pole, and especially its dominant component of postmaterialism, relates positively with the level of tolerance towards out-groups in a society (Inglehart, 1990). Traditional authority values are related to societies in which social and political life is dominated by religious and hierarchical institutions, where male dominance and parental authority is defended and where authoritarian attitudes prevail. Individual freedom, rejection of traditional power institutions, and an incessant challenge of, if not a constant discontent with authority institutions in society, are characteristic for societies emphasizing secular-rational authority values. Respect for the authority of traditional culture and acceptance of collective forms of identity and control over one's destiny are unthinkable among people of these secular-rational authority cultures who strongly believe in their individual competence, their unique self, and their own particular walk of life. All in all, one would expect cultural nationalism phenomena like *Nihonjinron* to be most vividly present in survival and traditional authority cultures and least supported in well-being and secular-rational authority cultures. Yet, Japan ranks highest among a large number of countries in secular-rational authority value support (see also Figure 1 in the chapter by Inglehart and Oyserman in this volume) and relatively high in well-being value adherence. This finding, of course, makes a strong case to thoroughly investigate the contemporary popularity of *Nihonjinron* as a phenomenon of cultural nationalism.

This brief digression clearly shows that the issue of cultural nationalism might be connected to larger cultural dimensions in society. This is an important observation for future studies, as we will argue at the end of this chapter. First, we want to focus on Japan's cultural nationalism.

Popularity of *Nihonjinron*

The popularity of this *Nihonjinron* is reflected in the large number of books that are published in this genre. The Nomura Research Institute's compilation of *Nihonjinron*-related books, published between 1945 and 1978, for example, lists some 700 titles (Nomura Sôgô Kenkyûjo, 1978). By now, the total has reached at least 1,000 titles in this category. These books deal with a wide range of social phenomena (from 'race', social structure and language, to ecology, economy, psychology, and even international relations), but all these phenomena are treated under a common denominator. This varied and complex discourse treats Japanese culture as a unique and unparalleled product of racial, historical, and climatic elements that underlies the essence of current social phenomena.

[145]

One of the problems of *Nihonjinron* is that except for a very few studies, such as the so-called "national character surveys" (Kokuminsei Chôsa 1, 2, 3, 4 and 5), *Nihonjinron* arguments lack quantitative substantiation. That is, *Nihonjinron* arguments are continuously offered without any idea about how many Japanese in fact endorse the tenets of *Nihonjinron*. Does the whole population support the Nihonjinron beliefs or does only a very limited number of the Japanese adhere to these thoughts? And if only some of them support the ideas of *Nihonjinron*, what kind of people are they and what percentage of the total population do they represent?

To fill the gap of empirical studies, Harumi Befu and Kazufumi Manabe conducted a questionnaire survey in the summer of 1987 to determine the extent to which *Nihonjinron* tenets are supported by the Japanese and to identify the characteristics of those who do and those who do not uphold these tenets. The questionnaire was distributed to a random sample of 2,400 adults in the city of Nishinomiya, which lies nestled between Osaka and Kobe in the southeastern section of the Hyogo Prefecture. In total, 944 people completed the questionnaire, which equals 39% of the original sample. For the first time in the history of the study of *Nihonjinron*, it became possible to establish the extent of its popularity.

Eighty-two per cent of those who responded said they were indeed interested in the subject and read about it in newspapers, while others found television, radio, magazines and books useful in this regard (Figure 1).

From this figure some general conclusions can be drawn:
1. With regard to the level of interest in *Nihonjinron*, over half of the respondents expressed interest in *Nihonjinron* in magazines and books, and with respect to newspapers and television the interest level neared 80%.
2. With respect to the perceived desirability of the increase in *Nihonjinron* in

[146]

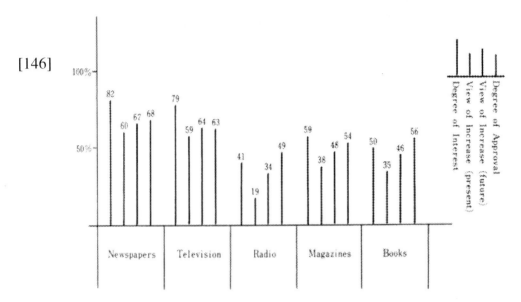

Figure 1: *Degree of interest in, view of increase in, and degree of approval of increase in nihonjinron*

the various media, respondents expressing their approval of this trend numbered roughly 50% with regards to radio, over 50% with respect to magazines and books, and nearly 70% with respect to television and newspapers. It can be conjectured that this high level of interest in and approval of *Nihonjinron* is what supports the *Nihonjinron*-boom phenomenon.

3. In all five media, we see that respondents feel that *Nihonjinron* will increase even more in the future than it has up until now. Especially with respect to television (over 60%) and newspapers (nearly 70%), respondents predict that *Nihonjinron* will increase even more in the future.

Nihonjinron has been popular in Japan since long ago, but, especially since the 1960s, it has enjoyed a long-term boom in popularity that continues to this day. One of the main features of *Nihonjinron* for the past twenty years or so, however, has been the abundance of a foreigner-based *Nihonjinron* literature; that is, literature written by foreigners describing Japanese people, Japanese society and Japanese culture.

In the survey, the researchers chose 21 *Nihonjinron* books that are currently in circulation and that have gone through a comparatively high number of printings. The respondents were asked 1. whether they have heard of the

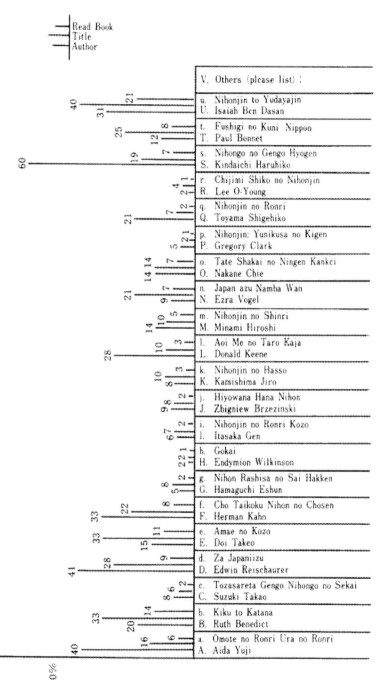

Figure 2: *Familiarity and contact with nihonjinron authors and books*

author, 2. whether they have heard of the book, and 3. whether they have read the book. The results of the responses are shown in Figure 2.

[148]   The following observations can be inferred from Figure 2:
1. the names of ten authors of the books that had been mentioned in the questionnaire were known by at least 20% (going up to 70 %) of the respondents; among them were a number of non-Japanese names such as Ruth Benedict, Donald Keen, Paul Bonnet and Edwin Reischauer.
2. the titles of 12 books mentioned in the questionnaire were familiar to 10 to 40% of the respondents (which is almost two thirds of the total); almost half of the respondents knew one single title, a book drafted by the non-Japanese author Isaiah Ben Dasan.
3. 11 books (which is roughly half of the books mentioned) were read by at least 5% of all respondents (going up to 30% of the respondents who had been reading one particular book); again the book drafted by Ben Dasan was the most popular in this respect. If we were to extrapolate this percentage to the whole of Japan's population, we would arrive at a figure of more than five million people. Of course, it is possible that these figures reflect the peculiarity of Nishinomiya city, the area in which the survey was conducted, and which is a "bedroom" community feeding mostly middle class office workers to nearby big cities of Osaka and Kobe. Even so, it is difficult to deny that awareness of and contact with *Nihonjinron* is high.

Tenets of *Nihonjinron* and the percentage of *Nihonjinron* believers

On the basis of a content analysis of the body of *Nihonjinron* literature various tenets of *Nihonjinron* were distinguished, and these tenets have been included in the questionnaire. The tenets were grouped into four major categories:
1. the idea of homogeneity: this relates to whether or not the Japanese are a homogeneous people, living in a homogeneous society and experiencing a unique culture.
2. the idea of whether or not Japanese "blood" is essential for mutual communication, mutual understanding, understanding of the culture, and physical appearance as Japanese.
3. the idea of cultural competence: this issue refers to whether or not foreigners are capable of fully understanding Japanese culture and mastering the Japanese language.
4. the idea of social participation by foreigners: here the question is whether or not the sociocultural territoriality of Japan should be defended and whether or not foreigners should be excluded in the areas of marriage, employment, teaching, and political and artistic leadership.

The following tables (Tables 1 to 4) indicate the percentages of those who agree or disagree with specific *Nihonjinron* propositions in these categories.

Table 1: *Japan's homogeneity*   [149]

%	Agree	Disagree	Can't say / DK
Are Japanese a homogeneous people (*tan'itsu minzoku*)?	38	23	39
Is Japanese society homogeneous (*dôshitsu*)?	36	6	58
Is Japanese culture unique?	49	9	42

As to the level of agreement with these three propositions, the table shows that more than one third to almost half of the respondents agrees with the various statements. In the eyes of many respondents the "world" of the Japanese indeed has its own homogeneous character, and accordingly its culture is something unique. More interestingly perhaps is the fact that the number of respondents that do not agree with these propositions is rather low (less than 10% with respect to two statements). Many Japanese respondents, however, clearly prefer not to answer to these questions about Japan's homogeneity, instead of disagreeing with them. Around four to six out of ten people respond not to be able to say anything useful on the subject; a major indication that *Nihonjinron*, at least as regards the beliefs in homogeneity and uniqueness of Japan, is very modest.

The idea that the Japanese share the same "blood," and that this sharing constitutes the basis of the exclusivity of Japanese is generally submerged in the semi-consciousness of the Japanese people. However, from time to time it is brought to the surface of consciousness. In Table 2 the responses to the question of the importance of blood are reported. The influence of shared blood is acknowledged most frequently with regards to physical appearance (which is understandable), followed by its perceived role in communication, and finally, its role in social and linguistic competencies. At least one out of every five respondents believes that a person would need to have Japanese "blood" in his or her veins to master the Japanese language.

Again, high proportions of Japanese do not have substantive answer to the importance of sharing Japanese blood. In almost all cases, the proportion of people who indicate they cannot say of do not know whether or not to agree with these statements is higher than the proportion of those who agree or disagree (exceptions refer to the obvious item of 'only those with Japanese blood have the Japanese appearance' and the last item 'only those with

Table 2: *Importance of "Blood" for the Japanese*

%	Agree	Disagree	Can't say / DK
For physical appearance as Japanese	52	17	31
For mutual understanding	29	18	53
For becoming part of the society	26	30	44
For understanding Japanese culture	24	34	42
For speaking Japanese	20	41	39

[150]

Japanese blood can speak Japanese', a statement with which the highest proportion of respondents disagree!).

Another proposition of *Nihonjinron* to date is a deliberate emphasis on how foreigners differ from Japanese. This hypothesis involves the previously mentioned particularistic way of looking at Japanese culture (as opposed to a universalistic way of thinking). In order to investigate this hypothesis, five statements were included in the survey.

Table 3: *Foreigners' cultural competency*

%	Agree	Disagree	Can't say / DK
Japanese culture can't be understood completely in foreign languages	63	17	20
Cannot understand Japanese culture completely	63	17	20
Cannot totally assimilate into Japanese society	41	32	27
Cannot master Japanese	36	43	21
Cannot achieve total mutual understanding with Japanese	30	40	30

As for foreigners' cultural competence, as Table 3 shows, 63% of the respondents said foreigners are incapable of completely understanding Japanese culture. As for assimilation into Japanese culture, mastering the Japanese language, and achieving mutual understanding with Japanese, again, about three to four out of ten respondents thought foreigners lack these cultural competencies. From these results at first sight we are tempted to conclude that in modern Japan particularistic ways of thinking are still rather strong. However, this conclusion is much too strong. It is striking that the proportions of people who do not have a substantive answer is relatively low, at least as regards the two first items: understanding Japanese cultures in a foreign language and understanding Japanese culture in general. Regarding assimilation into Japanese society, mastering the Japanese language and mutual understanding between foreigners and Japanese people, this is much less so. What is left from the analyses is a general idea that understanding Japan is difficult and requires specific competences. The proof that the Japanese can be typified by a full-scale *particularistic* belief when addressing attitudes towards foreigners is way too weak.

[151]

The results are more or less similar as far as the social participation of foreigners in Japanese society is concerned. As can be inferred from Table 4, the domain in which acceptance of foreigners is highest is education (with the highest level of acceptance at the college level, followed by high school, then junior high and elementary school). Next, one can observe a fairly large support for foreigners being employed by private companies, followed by acceptance of the principle of foreigners living in Japan permanently and foreigners taking on Japanese citizenship. More than 50% of respondents expressed approval of foreigners taking on this type of functional (status-) roles. This result shows that the Japanese are not xenophobic, and that they really want to learn from foreigners if and when they think this may be advantageous to them. Historical proof of this disposition is quite robust (e.g. Hofstede & Soeters, 2002). When it comes to the domains of government and politics or the private domain of marriage, the degree of approval drops rather impressively. Still, again, the proportions of Japanese who argue they cannot say or do not know an answer specifically in these realms are also rather impressive. For instance, while every two out of ten Japanese who oppose a foreigner to be employed by the Japanese government, around four out of ten are in favor and another four out of ten refrain from a substantive answer. All in all, this is additional of proof that the Japanese cannot be regarded as full-range *Nihonjinron* believers.

Table 4: *Social participation of foreigners*

%	Agree	Disagree	Can't say / DK
Have a regular appointment at a public college	74	4	22
Regular teacher at a high school	71	5	24
Regular teacher at elementary or middle school	62	11	27
Live permanently in Japan	58	4	38
Employment in Japanese company	57	6	37
Gain Japanese citizenship	53	7	40
Employment in government	39	21	40
Marriage with a Japanese	35	9	56
Leadership in traditional arts/crafts	33	23	44
Political leadership	8	62	30

The believers and the non-believers

[152]

Thus, when we refer to those who endorse the tenets of *Nihonjinron*, we should be well aware that we are not speaking about the entire population of Japan, but only of a segment of the population, whose size varies depending on the question at hand. The results of our study have demonstrated this unequivocally.

Now, obviously some Japanese support the tenets of *Nihonjinron* more than others, some less than others. Who are the believers and who are the non-believers? In order to answer these questions, we calculated Pearson's Correlation Coefficients for each of the *Nihonjinron* proposition items with demographic items and foreign experience items (Table 5).

Table 5: *Correlations of* Nihonjinron *proposition items with background items*

(Low-High)	Sex (Female-Male)	Age (Young-Old)	Education (Low-High)	Liv'g stand (Low-High)	Trav'l abroad (No-Yes)	Foreign friend (No-Yes)
Homogeneity Japanese are a homogeneous people	–.0197	.1415	–.0779	.1630	.0078	–.0158
Japanese society is a homogeneous society	.0743	.0883	.1101	.1086	.0487	.0696
Japanese culture is a unique culture	.0244	.1222	–.0118	.0129	–.0409	.0258
Blood	.0821	.4117	–.1852	.0310	–.0524	–.0944
Social participation	.0512	–.1078	.1737	.0509	.1972	.1842
Cultural competence	.0354	.1873	–.0313	.0384	–.0244	–.0627

What we see here most prominently is a consistent correlation of age with *Nihonjinron* tenets: the older the respondent, the more likely he or she believes in *Nihonjinron*. In terms of gender, men tend to believe in the efficacy of "Japanese blood", whereas women do not; for the other variables, too, there is a positive correlation with sex, although the significance level is not very high. Education is negatively correlated with endorsing the *Nihonjinron* tenets: the more a respondent is educated, the less likely he or she is to believe in *Nihonjinron*. These correlations are related to the positive correlation with age, since the younger generations are receiving more education, especially college education, than the older generations.

Those reporting a higher standard of living tend to agree with the homogeneity and "blood" theses of *Nihonjinron*. This may seem curious in view of the fact that, generally speaking, education and living standard are positively correlated. However, education and age are slightly negatively correlated. This implies that the older Japanese are somewhat less educated than younger people. Because of the seniority rule in Japan's industry, however, older persons tend to earn higher wages, allowing a higher standard of living. This seniority rule is loosing some of its dominance nowadays, but at the time the data were collected (1987) this rule was still very much prevailing in Japanese corporate governance (Aoki, 2002). Thus the positive correlation between "blood" and living standard in this study is probably a reflection of the age factor.

[153]

Travel experience abroad and having foreign friends seem to have a certain impact on belief in *Nihonjinron*. Those who have traveled in a foreign country and those who have foreigners as friends tend to believe less in the tenets of *Nihonjinron* than those without foreign experience or foreign friends. Befu (1983) has once suggested that the trauma of having to adjust to foreign customs and to negotiate in a foreign language would have the effect of convincing Japanese to believe in *Nihonjinron*. The data shown here demonstrate this hypothesis does not hold.

We were also interested in the general outlook of respondents toward other aspects of *Nihonjinron*. We found, for example, that those believing in *Nihonjinron* tenets tend to:

1. be interested in the media coverage of *Nihonjinron* (which is hardly surprising);
2. believe that *Nihonjinron* discussion has been on the increase and will continue to increase — perhaps an expression of wishful thinking;
3. think that media coverage of *Nihonjinron* is a good thing rather than a bad thing;
4. believe that in comparison with the rest of the world Japan has a higher level of technological, artistic and economic achievement;
5. think that *Nihonjinron* performs a positive function for them, to the extent that it helps them to know themselves, to satisfy their self-pride and their pride as Japanese, to satisfy their intellectual curiosity, to reflect on Japan's role in the world, etc.

In conclusion, then, *Nihonjinron* is the world view of the older male with a higher standard of living. It is the world view of those in the mainstream and

[154] those in power. These older men with higher incomes tend to be upbeat about the tenets of *Nihonjinron* and the role it plays. They are also upbeat about their *Nihonjinron*-based self-identity. *Nihonjinron* is thus the world view and the ideology of the establishment. It may be believed in by less than a majority in a numerical sense, but those who support the tenets of *Nihonjinron* clearly belong to the political and economical power elite.

Developments

The data of the survey suggest a weakening of *Nihonjinron* in Japan. First, younger generations have doubts about *Nihonjinron*. As they grow older, there is a possibility that the hold of *Nihonjinron* on the Japanese population will weaken, at least when the adherence to *Nihonjinron* depends on generation effects with a young Japanese generation taking their rejection of *Nihonjinron* with them in their later phases of life. Second, belief in *Nihonjinron* is negatively correlated with education, traveling abroad and having foreign friends. All of these three factors are likely to increase over time. Given the great concern of the Japanese with education, the general level of education in Japan cannot but rise. Also, given the strong global economic position of Japan, more and more Japanese, with increased income, are likely to travel abroad in connection with academic or business assignments. As this happens, the Japanese will encounter more and more foreigners. The data show that all these developments will have the tendency to weaken the hold of *Nihonjinron* on the general populace of Japan.

In general, the effects of globalization have a considerable impact on Japan's habits, customs and culture. Globalization is shown to have impacted Japan's eating habits and clothing styles, as well as the opinions of Japan's intellectual elite and the marketing and human resource strategies of Japanese firms (Aoki, 2002). Youngsters in particular are affected by these developments, as they are getting more dissatisfied with Japan's living conditions and are yearning more for a good life based on a "post-material" orientation (Castells, 1998: 235-236). In addition, the position of Japanese women is changing as can be seen from their participation in the labor force, the increasing marriage age as well as the rising divorce rates. These developments may (have) impact(ed) the support of *Nihonjinron* throughout Japanese society.

On the other hand, changes are still slow and cultures are fairly stable (Hofstede and Soeters, 2002). Divorce rates in Japan, although on the rise, are still way below those in other wealthy countries, to give just one example (Castells, 1998: 227). In general, there seem to be two opposing tendencies as far as the support of *Nihonjinron* is concerned. In contrast to the possible weakening significance of *Nihonjinron,* one can also argue that as a person gets older he or she tends to become more conservative. Thus, the younger generation in years to come will tend to behave more and more like the older generation. The reason for this conservative tendency is that the conservative values of the society are not just accidentally associated with the establishment. Rather they exist, because they buttress the existing economic and political institutions. These institutions change slowly. As they persist, the value system supporting them, — amongst others reflected in governmental policies –, also is likely to persist. Under the direction of the Ministry of Education emphasis in Japanese schools is still placed on traditional culture, a complex examination system and strict discipline (Castells, 1998: 228; see also: Kawamura, 1994). On the basis of these internalized traditional values, young Japanese are likely to become more conservative in outlook once they have joined the established economic and political institutions. Following this line of argument, they will consequently adhere to more conservative values; in short, they will support the tenets of *Nihonjinron.*

[155]

Which of these two sets of opposing forces will dominate in the future is, of course, unclear. One scenario would have Japan become more internationalized and less oriented toward *Nihonjinron.* The other would forecast a more conservative Japan increasingly favorably oriented toward *Nihonjinron.* Still a third scenario would see both trends continue, with increasingly divergent and polarized public opinion, where conservatives in the establishment upholding tenets of *Nihonjinron* will continue to guard the establishment while the liberals, disenchanted with *Nihonjinron,* will gain in numerical force without being able to capture political power. As can be seen elsewhere in our globalizing world, de-traditionalization and re-traditionalization may very well co-exist (Heelas et *al.,* 1996: 2-3).

Comparative perspective

In the beginning of the chapter we argued that neither *Nihonjinron* in Japan nor cultural nationalism in general are isolated social phenomena. We are of course not claiming that specific contents of *Nihonjinron,* which are inevitably unique to Japan, are shared by other cultures. Obviously they are not. However, there are likely to be general patterns in the various manifestations of cultural nationalism worldwide. What we would suggest to find out is whether or not claims of ethnic uniqueness based on such factors as "blood," language, history, religion, race, geography can be found in other parts of the world. In this perspective a comparison between Japan and Turkey would be particularly appealing, since it has been shown previously that both societies show some remarkable similarities in culture-related val-

[156]

ues and practices (Wasti, 1998). In both countries one can find clear expressions of cultural nationalism as well. But the comparisons could go further than that and entail an additional country-comparison. An empirical investigation of Quebecois nationalism, German identity, American worldview and Chinese worldview — to name but a few examples — might be an interesting topic for future studies. In particular, it would be fascinating to compare societies that are high on the combination of *uncertainty avoidance* and *collectivism* (the *tight* societies), such as Japan and Turkey, with societies that show a contrasting profile in this respect (the *loose* societies), such as the Netherlands and the UK. This would prove to be especially useful considering the divergent relationship of forms of cultural nationalism such as *Nihonjinron* with the different sets of basic cultural dimensions. In some cases, support for cultural nationalism was predicted by 'dimensionalist' cross-cultural theory (e.g. as being related to *uncertainty avoidance* and *collectivism*). Results in this chapter show that despite Japan having an uncertainty intolerant and collectivist (or tight) culture, the phenomenon of *Nihonjinron* was not very wide-spread. The rejection of cultural nationalism was foreseen in one of the theoretical perspectives (e.g. concerning the rise in *self-expression* and *secular-rational authority* values). Relatively speaking, Japan is secular-rational and self-expression oriented, orientations that do not fit well with cultural nationalism such as *Nihonjinron*. Also from a theoretical perspective therefore, it is high time to organize a large-scale cross-cultural study on cultural nationalism — perhaps also taking into account more forms of expression in popular culture, e.g. in music, visual arts, and the like (see Craig, 2000) — and address the relationship with dimensions of national culture and cultures that supersede national boundaries. If this chapter will contribute to set up such studies, it will have fulfilled its objective.

CHAPTER EIGHT

Dimensions of culture in intra-cultural comparisons

Individualism/collectivism and family-related values in three generations[1]

GISELA TROMMSDORFF, BORIS MAYER, AND ISABELLE ALBERT

The goal of the present study is to supplement inter-cultural comparison of values as a cultural dimension by intra-cultural comparisons, and to go beyond comparisons of single values representing cultural dimensions by studying value patterns on the individual level. Therefore, relationships among general (individualism, collectivism) and domain-specific (family- and child-related) values and the transmission of values in three generations of one family were analyzed. The sample consisted of 100 complete triads of three generations (grandmothers, mothers, and adolescents). The results showed that the individual value orientations of these three generations differed in the expected direction. Individualistic values were more supported by the younger and less by the older generation. While individualism did not show significant relations to other specific values, collectivism was the most powerful dimension to predict family- and child-related values. Individualism and collectivism clearly turned out as separate dimensions with different functions for the individual value system. The value structure of grandmothers as compared to the younger generations showed more internal consistency. A relative transmission of values was obvious for the adjacent generations. The results are discussed from the perspective of cultural change and stability, and the relation among cultural dimensions and individual value orientations.

[1] This research was supported by a grant from the Deutsche Forschungsgemeinschaft (TR 169/9-2) to the first author and is part of the study "Value of Children and Intergenerational Relations in Six Cultures" (principal investigators: Gisela Trommsdorff, University of Konstanz and Bernhard Nauck, Technical University of Chemnitz).

The study of values in social sciences and psychology: an overview

[158]

The study of values has since long been an important topic in social sciences. In contrast, in psychology, the study of values which goes back to the work of Lewin (1936) has for a long time lost much of its previous relevance. Studies on attitudes, intentions, goal setting, or future orientation do not explicitly deal with values; also they usually ignore Lewin's culture-psychological implications. Only recently, the concept of value has gained new interest due to the studies by Hofstede, Triandis, Schwartz, and Inglehart (see this volume). These studies are explicitly based on cross-cultural comparisons and suggest perceiving values as part of cultural dimensions. These studies underline that values such as individualism and collectivism represent *cultural dimensions*. The question, however, is what the function of these cultural values is for social and psychological phenomena on the *individual* level.

The concept of values can be used to describe and compare cultures, nations, social groups, and individual persons. Values can also be analyzed as relevant factors explaining social and psychological phenomena, e.g., social change and individual behavior. Values as *explanatory variables* have contributed to sociological and psychological research. An example from sociology is the explanation of the late, but rapid, and successful industrialization of Japan by referring to traditional Confucian values reactivated during the Meiji revolution (and sometimes regarded as functional equivalent to the Protestant ethics and its impact on the early industrialization in Germany) (Bendix, 1965/66). Another example from psychology is the motivation theory by McClelland (1985) explaining differences in the economic success and productivity of various nations on the basis of achievement motivation and related individual values (McClelland, Atkinson, Clark, & Lowell, 1953). The study of values as *explanandum* is the focus of Inglehart's theory (1997) who links economic development to changes in values.

Values can also be studied as *modifying* and *moderating* variables. An example is the 'Value of Children (VOC)' study in the 70's (Arnold et *al.*, 1975; Fawcett, 1974, 1976). This study was initiated by demographers and economists who attempted to explain the overpopulation in various countries, and more specifically, to explain differences in fertility on the basis of economic conditions. This approach was followed by a more differentiated model focusing on family-related values, especially the value of children, as mediating links between economic conditions and fertility. Results from this study have shown, e.g., that *low economic* development is related to *high* socio-economic and *low* emotional *value of children* and this in turn predicts high fertility and furthermore, preference of obedience as a child-rearing goal (e.g., Kağitçibâşi, 1982; Hoffman & Hoffman, 1973).

The present study is based on a larger cross-cultural project attempting a partial replication and substantial modification of the original VOC study (Value of Children and Intergenerational Relationships, VOC/IGR) (Nauck, 2001; Trommsdorff, 2001, 2003; Trommsdorff & Nauck, 2001; Trommsdorff, Zheng & Tardif, 2002) which is based on an eco-cultural framework explaining individual behavior on the basis of eco-cultural conditions (e.g., Berry, Poortinga, Segall & Dasen, 2002; Trommsdorff & Dasen, 2001). The starting point of this study (VOC/IGR) was the observation of dramatic demographic changes (partly due to longevity and decreasing fertility) all over the world; one question was whether related changes on the macro- and micro-level of societies are related to value changes on the individual level. The present study deals with individualism/collectivism as a basic *individual value orientation.* We attempt to expand the study of values as a *cultural* dimension and as an *individual* phenomenon by intra-cultural comparisons of generations from the same family, thus attempting to supplement cross-cultural studies by intra-cultural comparisons. [159]

The goal of the present study is to understand the social and psychological processes which link culture and individual behavior. We will first present a theoretical framework for the study of general values of individualism and collectivism and their respective (and possible different) relations to more specific individual values which are seen as especially relevant for questions of socio-cultural, demographic, and value change: values of family, children and child-rearing. In the second part, we will present empirical data from the ongoing VOC/IGR study.

Theoretical framework for the study of individual values in different generations of one culture

First, we will discuss similarities and differences of individual value orientations among different generations. Second, our focus is on the internal structure of the individual value system. Third, the question of cultural stability and change will be dealt with by studying the transmission of values.

Values as a cultural dimension and as an individual orientation:
a developmental culture-psychological approach
Hofstede, Triandis, Schwartz, and Inglehart (this volume) have stimulated a rich body of value research which has its roots in systematic cross-cultural and cross-national comparisons fostering an interdisciplinary perspective. Hofstede's work suggests that certain values are closely connected to cultures and nations as a whole thus representing a cultural dimension. This idea may have contributed to the recent rise of cross-cultural studies in psycholo-

gy. Descriptions of cultures in terms of value dimensions refer to psychologically relevant variables. The explanation of differences and similarities of behavior among various cultures is certainly not easy since the complex construct of culture has to be dealt with theoretically. Moreover, reference to cultural values is necessary when selecting culturally appropriate measurements or when interpreting the results. However, this does not mean that cultures can be reduced to value dimensions.

Instead, cultural and individual values have to be regarded as *conceptually and methodologically different*. Thus, the unit of analyses is different: cultural values comprise *aggregate* data; individual values are based on *individual* data. Usually, values are measured on the individual level and then aggregated for social groups, nations, or cultures. 'Cultural values' are conceptually not the same as values held by the individual person. Cultural values are part of a complex system of ecological, demographic, and economic conditions and related social institutions. Even though overlapping with certain values of social groups and individual persons from the specific culture, cultural values function on a different level than individual values.

Starting from a conceptual differentiation, the question is what the *relation between cultural and individual values* is like. In line with the ecological model by Bronfenbrenner (1977), one may assume that the three levels, the macro-level, the level of sub-cultures, and the individual level are interconnected. The cultural values constitute the conditions under which individual and also social development takes place. Individual values and behavior set the conditions for cultural change and continuity mediated by intergenerational relations. From a psychological perspective, the interesting question is how cultural values are linked to individual value orientations.

Here, we follow a developmental-psychological perspective and more specifically, a motivation-theoretical approach. *Individual values* are conceptualized here as part of the self-concept and identity of the person, including individual beliefs, wishes, expectations, and goal setting, and guiding the person's decision making, planning, and goal-directed behavior. This conceptualization assumes that values are dynamic systems, structured in certain ways and influenced by individual experience during individual development in a socio-cultural context. The relation between cultural and individual values is regarded here to be based on life-long development and social interaction processes.

Cultural values are conceived of as part of the developmental niche (Super & Harkness, 1997) in which social interactions and individual development takes place; cultural values affect the child's socialization conditions by, e.g., shaping the caretakers' subjective theories, child-rearing goals and behavior (Schwarz, Schäfermeier & Trommsdorff, in press; Trommsdorff &

Friedlmeier, in press). It is assumed here that individual values develop in interaction with the person's environment, and thus are a product of bi-directional processes, not only being influenced by others but also affecting the social interaction partners and the wider socio-cultural context (Trommsdorff & Kornadt, 2003).

The expected close relations among cultural values and individual values may vary according to the cultural context and the prevailing norms and values. Thus, the study of values should allow a better understanding of the interplay between culture and the individual person. However, an interdisciplinary perspective is needed when dealing with values on the cultural and individual level.

Individualism and collectivism as a cultural dimension and as an individual value orientation in culture-informed research
The concept of a cultural dimension describes cultures and at the same time introduces a psychologically valid reason for comparing psychological phenomena in different cultures (Hofstede, 1980a, 2001, in press; Triandis, 1995; Triandis, McCusker & Hui, 1990). Hofstede has studied values of large samples (of experts) in various nations in order to describe cultures on a global level. He focused on whole cultural entities representing specific economic, religious, social characteristics which can empirically be assessed on the basis of five cultural dimensions. The concept of individualism/collectivism is only one — but the most prominent — of the five cultural dimensions originally conceptualized by Hofstede. Shalom Schwartz' (Schwartz, 1992; Schwartz & Bilsky, 1990) universalistic approach to cultural differences in values demonstrates a multidimensional structure of a 'universal' value system consisting of seven (mutually adjacent and contrasting) dimensions; this was replicated in numerous cross-cultural studies. Cross-cultural studies show that socio-structural conditions are related to the preference of specific dimensions, e.g., individualism is linked to economic well-being, and availability of higher education. Here, similarities to Inglehart's (1997) theory of economic well-being and the preference of 'postmaterialist' values become obvious.

While the concept of individualism and collectivism has stimulated much research in cross-cultural psychology, it also met much criticism which, however, partly is based on a misinterpretation of Hofstede's work and the neglect to distinguish between the *cultural and individual level of values*. Several studies view individualism/collectivism as a cultural dimension and at the same time as an individual orientation assuming that 'individualistic' values represent 'modern' or 'western' values while 'collectivistic' values represent more 'traditional' and also Asian values. However, ignoring intra-cultural and inter-individual differences, and equating the cultural and individual dimension of values is misleading. Another problem is that cross-cultural studies using the concept of individualism/collectivism often fail to empirically investigate whether their choice of cultures really is valid to represent this cultural dimension; often it is simply assumed that the Western and the Eastern world, and industrialized and modern versus agrarian and traditional societies differ on this cultural dimension.

In order to separately assess the cultural and the individual level of values Triandis (1995) has suggested measuring the individual values of individualism and collectivism on the basis of the concepts of 'idiocentrism' and 'allocentrism'. This conceptual bridge between the global 'cultural' and the 'individual' approach has proved useful to assess cross-cultural and intra-cultural differences (e.g., Hui, 1988; Hui & Triandis, 1985). This also allows testing hypotheses on the universal relationships between the specific value orientations and other psychological phenomena by disregarding formal cultural membership (Trommsdorff & Friedlmeier, in press). Individual values differing on cultural dimensions have also been related to the self-concept (or self-other relation) as described by the concept of *independence* versus *interdependence* (Markus & Kitayama, 1991, 1994). Some authors explicitly refrain from differentiating between individualism / independence and collectivism / interdependence (cf. Greenfield, 1994) assuming that both concepts imply similar patterns of psychological phenomena. These seem to represent opposite poles of one dimension (the Western and non-Western mind). However, the meaning of these values can vary in different cultures. Thus, a conceptualization of individualism/collectivism as representing a bipolarity of values has been widely criticized (e.g., Kâgitçibâsi, 1996). In an attempt to take into account culture-specificities, Triandis (1995) has differentiated between horizontal and vertical individualism/collectivism.

Individualism usually refers to an individualistic orientation with preference of own independence, autonomy, self-actualization, rationality, and abstract rules. In contrast, collectivism usually refers to a social orientation, especially relatedness to the family and in-group, acceptance of duties, context-related rules, and obligations for the group (see Triandis, 1995; Kim, Triandis, Kâgitçibâsi, Choi & Yoon, 1994). In line with most of the literature we understand individualism as the preference for independence and self-determination; in reference to Schwartz's analyses of values, we understand collectivism as a preference for more conservative and traditional values. Our goal is to get a better understanding of the possible relations between individualism and collectivism and their respective relation to other more specific values, beliefs, and goals. Do people either hold individualistic or collectivistic values, and is their value system structured in a dichotomous way? Or can both value orientations co-exist on the individual level? Empirical studies on this question are inconsistent. Watson and Morris (2002) have shown for a North-American sample of men and women that individualistic and collectivistic values are compatible and positively correlated. Other studies on Chinese and American samples have shown negative correlations between individualistic and collectivistic values (Chan, 1994). These results underline the necessity to study whether individualism and collectivism constitute two separate dimensions with different functions, and whether individual differences have to be taken into account. [163]

The present study will therefore deal with the questions a) in how far the person can identify with both, individualistic and collectivistic values, and b) what the relative importance of these values in the individual value system is like.

Intra-cultural differences in values related to individualism and collectivism
Comparisons of whole cultures have to be supplemented by comparisons of relevant sub-groups with respect to their value preferences. Intra-cultural studies are needed to deal with the problem of wrongly assumed homogeneity of cultures. In western industrialized societies, homogeneity of values does not exist, while more homogeneity of values can be assumed for traditional cultures characterized by collectivistic values. Heterogeneity of values may be a consequence and a precondition of social change which affects different social groups in different ways. For studies on social change the question is which social groups should best be selected for the assessment of their values.

Social class has traditionally been focused upon for studies on values (cf. Kohn, 1969); other approaches are *cohort studies* (Inglehart, 1990, 1997), or studies on *regional differences* taking into account economic conditions, as e. g., the study on value differences in *urban* and *rural* samples in Turkey as part of the 'Value of Children Study' (Kağitçibâşi, 1982, 1996): in rural areas the economic value of the child (child is expected to support aged parents) and fertility was higher than in urban areas. Studies on acculturating groups may be very useful to analyze how social and value change are dealt with and how values are transmitted. As an example for social and value change after the German unification some studies have shown that value differences between East and West Germany partly decreased especially in the younger generation giving rise to more 'individualistic' values in the East German population (e.g., Trommsdorff, 1996; Hormuth, Heinz, Kornadt, Sydow & Trommsdorff, 1996; Meulemann, 1998) while at the same time some continuity of 'conservative' values such as family orientation occurred (Trommsdorff & Chakkarath, 1996).

Even though more complicated processes in East Germany (e.g., break-down of the life-long secure employment; acculturation effects) have to be taken into account, some of these value changes seem to be in line with Ingle-hart's (1990, 1997) theory on changes to post-materialistic values in Western industrialized societies due to economic development. This theory explains changes towards post-materialism (rationality, tolerance, trust, participation) in Western industrialized societies on the basis of increasing economic development and related socialization of the young generation (scarcity and socialization thesis). The younger as compared to the older generation has been brought up in economic security (lack of scarcity). The related prefer-ence of post-materialistic and individualistic values is expected to stimulate an overall change (a 'silent revolution') towards post-modern values.

The predicted value changes towards postmaterialism, e.g., less authori-tarian and less religious orientation, and declining closeness of parent-child relationships, were only partly supported by empirical studies. Hellevik (2002) reports a preoccupation with material possessions and consumption patterns rather than post-materialist values for Norwegian samples. Inglehart (1997) reports on several changes in the expected direction while the expect-ed decline of the parent-child relationship could not be shown. Primary bonds of family members seem not to loose their importance in spite of the ongoing changes in the family structure. This is in line with results on the presently still relatively high importance of family values in East Germany beside otherwise significant changes towards individualism (Mayer & Trommsdorff, 2003). This is also in line with other studies in family sociolo-gy which empirically demonstrate a stable pattern of family solidarity in spite of changing family structures (cf. Bengtson, 2001).

The present study thus will deal with the question whether the younger and the older generation can be differentiated according to their preference of individualistic and collectivistic values with more individualistic and less traditional values held by the younger generation and vice versa for the older generation.

On the basis of the above-mentioned theoretical and empirical studies, we will test the following hypotheses: (1) Individualism is expected to be more preferred by the younger than by the older cohorts, and vice versa for collectivism/traditionalism. (2) In line with results from the original VOC study we expect differences in individualism and collectivism to be related to specific values such as an emotional versus socio-economic value of the child, and child-rearing goals of independence versus obedience. (3) In line with findings on the stability of family values it is expected that the different cohorts do not differ with respect to family-related values.

*Multidimensionality of value orientations: individualism and collectivism
as part of a broader value system*
The above stated questions and hypotheses underline the necessity to go
beyond the study of single values and rather look for patterns of values. A
major criticism on former studies on individualism and collectivism has been
that these concepts suggest opposite poles of one dimension (e.g.,
Kâgitçibâsi, 1996). Cross-cultural studies investigating the diverse functions
(and combinations) of individualism and collectivism and its related values
such as autonomy (individualism) and relatedness (collectivism) point out to
the culture-specific meaning of such values in the specific cultural contexts
(Rothbaum & Trommsdorff, 2003). In the same line of reasoning, Tripathi
and Leviathan (2003) have warned against focusing primarily on universal
attributes of individualism/collectivism. Specific cultural processes give a
specific meaning to these concepts and, moreover, to the related respective
values. [165]

To give an example, 'independence' and 'autonomy' can be highly preferred parental values in an individualistic and a collectivistic cultural context. These constructs are an abstract description of a certain cultural model
including a complex of values and beliefs. Values which are presented on a
general, abstract level allow for a wide variety of interpretations which are
consistent with the respondent's preferences and the specific cultural model.
The general cultural model is organized around general belief patterns and
stereotypes shared in the respective culture and social group. Thus, depending on the cultural context and the membership of a certain group, the meaning of global values is different. In a collectivist context, children are expected to pursue collective duties 'independently'; they are expected to fulfill
their obligations properly starting early in their development. On the other
hand, children can expect to be taken care of by their in-group. Thus, children's obedience to social norms is at the same time compensated by parental
warmth and acceptance (e.g., Rothbaum & Trommsdorff, 2003; Trommsdorff & Kornadt, 2003). Empirical results from cross-cultural studies are in
line with these notions (e.g., Leyendecker, Harwood, Lamb, &
Schoelmerich, 2002; Schwarz, Schäfermeier, & Trommsdorff, in press;
Trommsdorff, 1995). To summarize, the meaning of values has to be studied
in the broader cultural context and with respect to the individual value system focusing especially on the relation among general and specific values.

Therefore we attempt here to focus on the differen functions of individualism and collectivism as global value orientations for more domain-specific
values, in order to analyze the internal structure of individual value orientations in different social groups. E.g., that certain global values may serve different goals for the individual person: e.g., family values can be in line as

well with an individualistic as with a collectivistic value orientation. This approach would allow specifying the quality of inter-individual differences in values, the structure of values and the function of values for psychological phenomena.

These notions underline that not only *heterogeneity of cultures* (differences between sub-groups and inter-individual differences) but also *multidimensionality of values* should be taken into account for the study of individualism/collectivism. Here we expect that general individualistic and collectivistic-traditional values (which may be endorsed to a different extent by different cohorts) are differentially related to more specific values. In line with the 'cultural model' of a progressive industrialized society, individualism is assumed to constitute the dominant value orientation in Germany. Accordingly, endorsement of this value is not necessarily based on an individual commitment and therefore may not allow gaining insight in the specific individual value structure of a person. In contrast, endorsement of the non-dominant collectivistic-traditional value orientation would allow predicting individual differences in values.

More specifically, it is expected that in all cohorts, general collectivistic values are positively related to family and child-related values as well as to conservative child rearing goals (e.g., obedience). Furthermore, probably partly due to their different developmental age, we expect a clearer pattern of the value structure in older than in the younger cohort. Adolescents, who are in a developmental stage of establishing an identity, might well have a less clear value structure as compared to older age groups.

Continuity and change of values: the perspective of transmission of values
While the 'dimensionalists' of cultural studies search for a systemic whole and a meaningful set of values to explain the variety of beliefs, life styles, and actual behavior by disregarding the active role of the individual person in the construction and change of culture (see Vinken, Soeters, & Ester, Chapter 1, this volume), the present study starts from the assumption that individual persons construct culture by transmitting cultural and individual values through processes of social interactions.

Cohort studies can differentiate among various age groups of a society with respect to value preferences. Many of those studies and one-shot survey studies in particular, however, give only limited information on social change even though they imply a diachronic perspective. In that case it remains difficult to discern cohort from age and period effects. As an alternative it is fruitful to compare cohorts as *generations belonging to the same family* in order to study whether and in how far value preferences are transmitted from one generation to the next. The extent of such transmission is an interesting indicator of the stability or change in a culture's value system. We recognize that using time series data and combining genealogical and socio-logical generation perspectives — i.e., surveying generational issues within same families and across cohorts that express ideas of sharing similar forma-tive experiences — might give a more definite clue about stability or change (see, e.g., Diepstraten et *al.*, 1999b; see also Vierzigmann & Kreher, 1998). [167]

The previous discussion on the cultural and individual level of values, the possible changes on both levels, and the multidimensionality of values all are related to the question whether and how cultural values are transformed into individual values, and how individual values are transmitted from one generation to the next. Transmission of values can be conceived of as a nec-essary condition for the continuity of a society and a cultural system. This question has been especially prominent in acculturation research in order to predict the value orientation of the younger generation and their integration into the new culture. So far, only relatively few studies have been carried out on this topic (e.g., Schönpflug, 2001; Boehnke et *al.*, 2002).

The transmission of values will be examined here with respect to individ-ualism/collectivism and other family related value orientations. Our study will focus on three different generations of the same family who all have been socialized in a cultural context where the cultural value of individual-ism is very dominant. Therefore, we expect the transmission of individualis-tic values to be most visible, while we also expect considerable transmission of other values from one generation to the next.

Summary of research questions
First, it is attempted to study individual differences among value orientations and individual goals of three generations, starting from the assumption that developmental age and related experience throughout the life span affect the individual's value and belief systems. Partly in line with Inglehart (1990, 1997) it is assumed that the older differ from younger age cohorts preferring less individualistic and more conservative values.

Differences and similarities of single values, however, do not give a clear picture of the subjective (or cultural) meaning of these values since each val-ue is a part in a complex belief system consisting of several levels and ele-ments. The more abstract values may have a different meaning depending on the more concrete values, and vice versa. Thus, the meaning of items repre-senting 'individualism' and 'collectivism' may differ.

Second, it is therefore attempted to describe the pattern (internal structure) of individual value orientations, focusing on relations among abstract and more concrete values and goals with a focus on individualism/collectivism, and on family-, and child-related values. It is assumed that individualism and collectivism each have a different relationship with more specific values.

[168]   Third, with respect to the general question of cultural stability and change, it is asked whether a transmission of values can be observed in the different generations of the same family. Thus, the present study goes beyond the study of intra-cultural similarities and differences of values.

Empirical study: value orientations of three generations

Background of the study
The present study is part of the modified and extended cross-cultural study on 'Value of Children and Intergenerational Relations (VOC-IGR)'. This study attempts to test whether individual behavior and intergenerational relations can be predicted on the basis of socio-structural data, cultural, and individual values, and how the macro-, meso- and individual level are related. The cultural dimensions were identified on the national level, taking into account beside ecological, economic and socio-structural characteristics the general cultural values of individualism and collectivism. Altogether, six cultures were included (Germany, Israel, Turkey, Republic of Korea, People's Republic of China, and Indonesia). A specific design of multi-generation samples from one family is needed to empirically test questions on intergenerational relations and transmission processes and effects. This is the methodological starting point of the present study.

Method
Sample. The present study focuses on three-generation triads (N = 100 in each cohort) from the same families: grandmothers, mothers, and their adolescent sons and daughters. Data derive from families in the German cities of Konstanz, Chemnitz, and Essen in 2002.

Instruments. A standardized questionnaire was used where all items had to be rated on five-point scales (1 = 'not important at all' to 5 = 'very important'). *Individualism/Collectivism* was assessed through the short version of the Schwartz & Bilsky (1990) instrument developed by Chan (1994) as part of the COLINDEX; it consisted of 7 items to measure individualism [e.g. 'an exciting life (stimulating experiences)'] and 6 items to measure collectivism [e.g. 'honor of your parents and elders (showing respect)']. *Family values* were assessed through 6 items selected from the Georgas' (1991) Family Values Scale measuring responsibilities of parents and children toward each other and the family in general (e.g. 'One should maintain good relationships with one's relatives'). *Values of children* were assessed through a selection of original items from the VOC study of the 70's (e.g. Arnold et al., 1975) as well as newly developed items and some items from the Family and Fertility Survey (FFS). In all three samples exploratory factor analyses showed that items related to the emotional benefits of children loaded on one factor and that items concerning the practical, economic, and social benefits loaded on a second factor. Confirmatory factor analyses to confirm the factorial structure showed that two items regarding old-age security ('Because people with children are less likely to be lonely in old age' and 'Your children can help when you're old') should be treated as a separate factor. The final models showed satisfying fit criteria in all three samples. Three positive VOC-dimensions emerged: VOC Economic-Social, including 5 items (e.g., 'To have one more person to help your family economically'), VOC Emotional including 5 items (e.g., 'Because of the pleasure you get from watching your children grow'), and VOC Old-Age Security consisting of the two items mentioned above. In the mothers' and in the grandmothers' questionnaire additional items regarding the value of children for the benefit of the family were assessed. Exploratory and confirmatory factor analyses showed an additional VOC Family factor for both samples, comprising 4 items (e.g., 'Because any new family member makes your family more important'). Furthermore, the importance of the parenting goals *obedience*, *independence*, and *academic achievement* was assessed. Grandmothers were asked with respect to the target grandchild. Adolescents did not have to answer these questions. Reliabilities for the *Individualism/Collectivism* scales, the *Family Value* scale, and the *VOC* scales were all satisfactory.

[169]

Results

Comparisons among the three generations

Analyses of variance for dependent measures showed a significant generation effect on individualism with adolescents scoring higher on individualism than both their grandmothers and mothers (see Table 1). No difference between mothers and grandmothers occurred for individualism. All three generations scored significantly different from each other on collectivism with grandmothers being highest, adolescents lowest, and mothers taking a middle position. On family values, differences occurred between grandmothers and mothers, and between mothers and adolescents with grandmothers and adolescents scoring equally high and mothers lowest. Furthermore, t tests for dependent measures showed that for grandmothers, $T(99) = -12.13$, $p < .01$, and mothers, $T(99) = -6.04$, $p < .01$, collectivism was more important than individualism while for adolescents individualism was more important than collectivism, $T(99) = 4.92$, $p < .01$.

Table 1: *One-way ANOVAs for dependent measures in three generations: general values, family values, value of children dimensions, and parenting goals*

	Grandmothers (n = 100)		Mothers (n = 100)		Adolescents (n = 100)		F	df	Comparisons		
	M	(SD)	M	(SD)	M	(SD)			1/2	1/3	2/3
General Values											
Individualism	3.69	(.59)	3.79	(.44)	4.09	(.51)	17.78**	2/175		**	**
Collectivism	4.40	(.39)	4.09	(.46)	3.74	(.67)	43.60**	2/174	**	**	**
Family Values	4.00	(.47)	3.71	(.46)	3.99	(.47)	16.28**	2/198	**	**	**
Value of Children											
Economic-Social	2.27	(.78)	1.61	(.64)	1.86	(.64)	26.47**	2/172	**	**	**
Emotional	4.04	(.64)	4.01	(.67)	3.82	(.73)	3.07*	2/196			
Old-Age Security	3.14	(1.02)	2.80	(.95)	2.80	(.88)	4.50*	2/196	*		
Family	3.05	(.94)	2.64	(.80)	—	—	15.19**	1/99	**	—	—
Parenting Goals											
Obedience	4.13	(.75)	3.49	(.71)	—	—	46.27**	1/98	**	—	—
Independence	4.25	(.66)	4.43	(.56)	—	—	5.46*	1/98	*	—	—
Achievement	4.33	(.67)	3.89	(.68)	—	—	29.74**	1/98	**	—	—

Note. Degrees of freedom adjusted for sphericity. *p < .05. ** p < .01.

As for the value of children (VOC) dimensions, grandmothers were significantly higher on VOC Economic-Social than both mothers and adolescents. Adolescents were significantly higher on VOC Economic-Social than their mothers. Grandmothers scored higher than mothers on VOC Old-Age Security and on VOC Family. Despite significant mean differences on VOC dimensions there was a similar pattern regarding the relative importance of specific values of children in all generations: VOC Economic-Social was considered unimportant, VOC Emotional was considered important, and VOC Old-Age Security as well as VOC Family were of medium importance.

[171]

Regarding parenting goals, grandmothers scored higher on the goals of obedience and academic achievement than their adult daughters (mothers), while mothers scored higher on independence. Regardless of these differences grandmothers and mothers considered all three parenting goals as important (see Table 1).

Value Patterns in the Three Generations
Correlations. For *grandmothers*, a significantly positive correlation occurred between individualism and collectivism. Collectivism was also positively related to family values and all VOC dimensions. Family values were positively related to all VOC dimensions as well. The parenting goal of obedience was positively correlated with collectivism, family values, and all positive VOC dimensions. Independence was positively correlated only to VOC Old-Age Security, and achievement was positively correlated to collectivism, family values, VOC Emotional, VOC Old-Age Security, and VOC Family (see Table 2).

For *mothers*, individualism also correlated positively with collectivism as well as with VOC Economic-Social and VOC Emotional. Collectivism was positively related to family values and all VOC dimensions. Family values were also positively related to all VOC dimensions. Obedience was positively related to collectivism and family values. Independence was positively related only to VOC Emotional (see Table 2).

In the *adolescent* sample individualism was positively correlated with collectivism ($r = .31$, $p < .01$) and negatively with VOC Old-Age Security ($r = -.20$, $p < .05$). Collectivism was positively related to family values ($r = .30$, $p < .01$) and to VOC Emotional ($r = .25$, $p < .05$). Family values were positively related only to VOC Emotional ($r = .28$, $p < .01$).

Prediction of VOC. Hierarchical multiple regression were used to test the relative influence of general and family specific value orientations on the VOC dimensions. Respondents' demographics (age, number of children — number of siblings for adolescents —, education and socioeconomic status) were

Table 2: *Correlation analysis for grandmothers' and mothers' general values, gamily values, value of children dimensions, and parenting goals*

[172]

	1	2	3	4	5	6	7	8	9	10
1	—	.40**	.14	.20*	.23*	.18	.11	.14	.18	.06
2	.34**	—	.52**	.33**	.24*	.43**	.39**	.28**	.19	.12
3	.07	.45**	—	.37**	.21*	.47**	.32**	.32**	.08	.08
4	.08	.25*	.46**	—	.27**	.45**	.55**	.19	-.04	.00
5	.14	.51**	.43**	.36**	—	.51**	.37**	-.03	.34**	-.05
6	.02	.39**	.57**	.61**	.48**	—	.55**	.12	.09	.11
7	.14	.35**	.38**	.55**	.61**	.49**	—	.19	.14	-.07
8	.10	.38**	.53**	.46**	.37**	.41**	.37**	—	.22*	-.01
9	.17	.16	.18	.13	.19	.30**	.14	.24*	—	.01
10	.01	.39**	.35**	.17	.32**	.28**	.24*	.46**	.20*	—

Note. Grandmothers' correlations are reported in the lower left triangle, mothers' correlations in the upper right triangle. Variable labels: 1 = Individualism, 2 = Collectivism, 3 = Family Values, 4 = VOC Economic-Social, 5 = VOC Emotional, 6 = VOC Old-Age Security, 7 = VOC Family, 8 = Obedience, 9 = Independence, 10 = Achievement. Both samples N = 100. *p < .05. **p < .01.

entered in the first step. The general values individualism and collectivism were entered in the second, and the more specific family values were entered in the third step.

For the *grandmothers'* sample, the full regression equation with control variables, general values, and family values was significant on all four dependent variables: VOC Economic-Social, F(7, 85) = 5.42, p < .01; VOC Emotional, F(7, 85) = 6.46, p < .01; VOC Old-Age Security, F(7, 85) = 7.54, p < .01; and VOC Family , F(7, 85) = 4.46, p < .01. The full model explained a rather large amount of variance: 31%, 35%, 38%, and 27%, respectively. The results identified two variables as predictors for all four VOC scales in the grandmothers' sample: collectivism and family values . Both were significantly positively related to all positive VOC scales. Individualism had no predictive value for any of the scales. When family values were entered into the equation in the third step, collectivism was no longer significant for VOC Economic-Social (β = .05, ns). This suggests a mediating effect of family values between grandmothers' collectivistic values and their economic-social VOC. The same was found for the dependent variable VOC Old-Age Security where collectivism was no longer significant when family values were entered in the third step (β = .18, ns). Regarding demographic control variables, a significant effect of age on VOC Economic-Social occurred: for older grandmothers economic and social reasons to have children were more important (see Table 3).

Table 3: *Hierarchical regressions of value of children dimensions on demographical variables, general values, and family values for three generations*

[173]

| | Value of Children | | | | | | | |
| | Economic | | Emotional | | Old-Age | | Family | |
Grandmothers (n = 93)	β	ΔR^2	β	ΔR^2	β	ΔR^2	β	ΔR^2
Step 1 Demographics		.09		.05		.06		.07
Age	.25*		-.09		.12		.13	
Number of children	.08		-.19+		-.02		-.17	
Years of schooling	-.19+		.04		-.18+		-.12	
Socioeconomic status	-.03		-.03		-.15		-.10	
Step 2 General Values		.08		.25		.16		.15
Individualism	.10		-.04		.00		.07	
Collectivism	.24*		.52**		.40**		.36**	
Step 3 Family Values	.41**	.14	.26*	.05	.46**	.16	.25*	.05

Mothers (n = 94)	β	ΔR^2	β	ΔR^2	β	ΔR^2	β	ΔR^2
Step 1 Demographics		.10		.03		.02		.07
Age	.24*		-.12		-.10		.17	
Number of children	-.07		-.05		.09		-.19+	
Years of schooling	-.20+		.07		-.01		.05	
Socioeconomic status	-.16		-.08		.00		-.10	
Step 2 General Values		.08		.10		.22		.14
Individualism	.13		.19+		.00		-.10	
Collectivism	.21+		.21+		.48**		.41**	
Step 3 Family Values	.19	.02	.15	.02	.36**	.09	.15	.01

Adolescents (n = 89)	β	ΔR^2	β	ΔR^2	β	ΔR^2		
Step 1 Demographics		.04		.07		.04		
Age	-.07		.13		.07			
Number of siblings	.02		-.15		.07			
Years of schooling	-.18		.07		-.16			
Socioeconomic status	-.06		.16		-.06			
Step 2 General Values		.00		.05		.04		
Individualism	-.07		.13		-.20+			
Collectivism	.02		.14		.10			
Step 3 Family Values	.21+	.04	.26*	.06	.04	.00		

Note. +p < .10. *p < .05. **p < .01. N < 100 due to missing data in the demographic variables.

For the *mothers'* sample as well, the full regression equation was significant on all four dependent variables: VOC Economic-Social, $F(7, 86) = 3.16$, $p < .01$; VOC Emotional, $F(7, 86) = 2.14$, $p < .05$; VOC Old-Age Security, $F(7, 86) = 5.96$, $p < .001$; and VOC Family, $F(7, 86) = 3.49$, $p < .01$. The full model explained considerable variance in these variables: 20%, 15%, 33%, and 22%, respectively. For VOC Economic-Social only the demographic control variable age was significant (see Table 3). Similar to grandmothers, the older mothers valued economic and social reasons for having a child more. Regarding VOC Emotional, none of the predictor variables was significant. For VOC Old-Age Security, collectivism and family values emerged as significant positive predictors. With regard to VOC Family, only collectivism was significantly related to this variable. The more collectivistic values mothers preferred the more they valued family-related reasons for having children.

For the *adolescent* sample, the full regression equation was significant only for VOC Emotional, $F(7, 81) = 2.49$, $p < .05$. Explained variance was 18% and family values were the only significant positive predictor of VOC Emotional (see Table 3).

Prediction of parenting goals. In the next step, the relative influence of general values, family values, and the VOC dimensions on the parenting goals of obedience, independence, and achievement was tested through hierarchical multiple regression analyses in the grandmothers' and mothers' samples.

For the *grandmothers'* sample, the full regression equation with demographic control variables, general values, family values, and VOC dimensions was significant on the parenting goals of obedience, $F(11, 81) = 4.60$, $p < .01$; and achievement, $F(11, 81) = 2.82$, $p < .01$. The full model explained 38% of the variance of obedience and 28% of the variance of achievement. Collectivism and family values were significant predictors of obedience. The higher grandmothers' collectivism and family-related values the more they valued obedience. When family values were entered in the analysis, collectivism was no longer significant ($\beta = .17$, ns). Thus, family values mediated the effect of collectivism on obedience. Collectivism and family values emerged as significant positive predictors for achievement goals (as for obedience) (see Table 4).

For the *mothers'* sample, the full regression equation was only significant for obedience, $F(11, 82) = 2.02$, $p < .05$; and independence, $F(11, 82) = 2.01$, $p < .05$. The full model explained 21% of the variance of obedience as well as of independence. For obedience, collectivism was the only significant predictor (see Table 4). The more collectivistic mothers' values were, the more they

Table 4: *Hierarchical regressions of parenting goals on demographic variables, general values, family values, and value of children dimensions for grandmothers and mothers*

[175]

	Obedience		Independence		Achievement	
Grandmothers (n = 93)	β	ΔR²	β	ΔR²	β	ΔR²
Step 1 Demographics		.01		.04		.08
Age	.03		-.18		-.13	
Number of children	-.03		.10		.05	
Years of schooling	-.09		.04		-.09	
Socioeconomic status	.08		-.03		-.20+	
Step 2 General Values		.15		.05		.15
Individualism	-.02		.20+		-.09	
Collectivism	.39**		.05		.42**	
Step 3 Family Values	.47**	.17	.14	.01	.23*	.04
Step 4 Value of Children		.05		.08		.01
VOC Economic-Social	.23+		-.09		-.04	
VOC Emotional	.01		-.01		.05	
VOC Old-Age Security	-.02		.38*		-.01	
VOC Family	.09		.01		.09	
Mothers (n = 94)	β	ΔR²	β	ΔR²	β	ΔR²
Step 1 Demographics		.03		.03		.03
Age	-.04		-.04		.08	
Number of children	-.16		-.16		.13	
Years of schooling	-.03		.04		-.04	
Socioeconomic status	-.05		.06		-.10	
Step 2 General Values		.09		.07		.01
Individualism	.06		.12		.02	
Collectivism	.27*		.19		.10	
Step 3 Family Values	.23+	.03	-.01	.00	-.02	.01
Step 4 Value of Children		.06		.11		.04
VOC Economic-Social	.06		-.18		.01	
VOC Emotional	-.21+		.37**		-.12	
VOC Old-Age Security	-.15		-.21		.25	
VOC Family	.19		.12		-.24	

Note. +p < .10. *p < .05. **p < .01. N < 100 due to missing data in the demographic variables.

valued obedience in their children. Also, the more mothers valued emotional reasons for having children the more important was independence as a parenting goal.

[176]

Transmission of values
In order to address the issue of transmission of values we used correlational analysis. This analysis will give a first insight in the relationships between values of the different generations in the same family. Since we expected *positive* correlations between the values held by different generations, one-tailed tests of significance were used. Regarding most values, transmission mainly occurred between adjacent generations. For individualism, transmission was significant between mothers and adolescents ($r = .23$, $p < .01$). For collectivism, transmission was significant between mothers and adolescents ($r = .16$, $p = .05$). With regard to family values, transmission was significant for all three pairs (GM — M: $r = .24$, $p < .05$; M — A: $r = .27$, $p < .01$; GM — A: $r = .17$, $p < .05$). With regard to VOC dimensions, significant transmissions mainly occurred between grandmothers and mothers: VOC Emotional ($r = .17$, $p < .05$), VOC Old-Age Security ($r = .25$, $p < .01$), and VOC Family ($r = .25$, $p < .01$). Between mothers and adolescents, only the transmission of VOC Economic-Social was significant ($r = .35$, $p < .01$), and between grandmothers and adolescents no significant transmission occurred. Additionally, there was significant transmission for all three parenting goals from grandmothers to mothers: obedience ($r = .18$, $p < .05$); independence ($r = .20$, $p < .05$); and academic achievement ($r = .28$, $p < .01$).

Discussion and outlook
The present study has analyzed whether the value orientations of three generations differ in the importance of single values and in the patterns of values. Furthermore, the question of cultural transmission of values from one generation to the next has been studied. The underlying assumption of this study was that general value orientations are related to more specific values which are transmitted to the next generation and thereby affect the cultural system either by stabilization or change. From a developmental perspective, the primary context for social interactions and for socialization of cultural values is the family. Therefore, the present study deals with the question of how abstract values like individualism and collectivism are related to more specific values and attitudes related to the family and to parenting, and how these value orientations (and their respective patterns) are represented in different generations of a family.

We *first* have dealt with the question of *cohort related value differences*. The results supported our hypothesis and showed that the older as compared to the younger generations preferred less individualistic and more collectivistic, more family oriented, and more conservative values of children and of parenting. Furthermore, grandmothers and mothers showed a higher preference of collectivistic as compared to individualistic values while for adolescents the reverse preference was found. Grandmothers were also highest in those values of children which have been preferred in more traditional samples in the previous VOC study (Hoffman, 1988; Kâgitçibâsi, 1982) such as old-age support, family and socio-economic value. Grandmothers also preferred conservative parenting goals (obedience and academic achievement) more and independence as goal less than mothers. With respect to family values, only slight differences among the generations occurred (no differences between grandmothers and adolescents).

[177]

Second, we have studied the *patterns of value orientations* in the three age groups. Our hypothesis that individualism and collectivism each are related in different ways to the more specific values was supported by the results. While individualism was not related to the specific values, collectivism was highly related to the specific values and it predicted (together with family values) the value of children on all dimensions. Family values mediated the effects of collectivism for old-age and socio-economic value of children for grandmothers. For grandmothers, the old-age security value of children, and for mothers, the emotional value of children was related to child-rearing goals of independence demonstrating different subjective meaning of independence. In general, grandmothers had a more coherent value pattern as compared to the other age groups; adolescents showed the least coherent pattern.

Third, our hypothesis that values are transmitted from one generation to the next was partly supported by our results. Not all but some values were transmitted. *Transmission* of individualism, collectivism, and family values occurred in adjacent generations.

Individualism and collectivism as bi-polar or multi-level values

The question whether individualism and collectivism constitute opposite poles of one dimension has often been debated in cross-cultural studies. Kâgitçibâsi (1996) who has criticized the assumption of bipolarity has suggested that social change can induce a transition from one value structure to another, combining and integrating aspects of independence and interdependence in a 'third' model. This thesis (which is going to be tested in our cross-cultural Value of Children Study, cf. Nauck, 2001; Trommsdorff, 2001, 2003; Trommsdorff & Nauck, 2001; Trommsdorff, Zheng & Tardif, 2002) receives some support from our present intra-cultural comparative study of an urban sample from an industrialized Western society. First, individualistic and collectivistic values are positively related in all three generations; furthermore, different from collectivistic values, no relationships among individualism and several family related values occurred. The preference of collectivistic values (which in our study mainly meant traditional and conservative values) can best explain attitudes toward having and rearing children. In all cohorts, collectivistic values are most powerful to predict domain specific values such as a preference for family values and an emotional value of children.

Thus, the pattern of thematic contents of value orientations was similar in all three generations. However, differences in value structure occurred with grandmothers showing the highest and adolescents the lowest coherence. So far, value studies did not look for developmental changes in structure. It thus has to be studied in future research whether developmental age or the preference for traditional as compared to individualistic values (or possibly both) contribute to the degree of coherence and consistency of the individual value system.

To summarize, our results have shown that individualism and collectivism do not represent opposite poles of one dimension at least on the individual level; they constitute separate dimensions, and they have different functions for the individual value system with traditional collectivistic values turning out to be the most powerful predictor for domain-specific values.

Transmission of values as linking culture and the individual person

The present study has started from the notion that individualism/collectivism as a cultural dimension and an individual value orientation are linked. From a culture-psychological perspective, the mediating link can be seen in the transmission of values which is part of the socialization process. The stability and change of cultural values depend to some degree on the transmission of individual values in the families. Cultural values are transmitted by parents' values, theories, goals and behavior, and through parent-child relationships (Albert & Trommsdorff, 2003; Goodnow & Collins, 1990; Schwarz, Schäfermeier, & Trommsdorff, in press; Trommsdorff & Friedlmeier, in press). Rothbaum, Pott, Azuma, Miyake and Weisz (2000) have shown how culture-specific pathways of individual development can be characterized. Furthermore, the transmission of values can go both ways: from the parents to the children, and from the children to the parents; these bi-directional influences differ in various cultures, and may even change in direction and impact during the life span (Trommsdorff & Kornadt, 2003).

Since parents are not the only influential factors in development, differences between the value orientations of parents and their children, partly depending on the cultural context and its changes, can arise during life-span development. Our results showed a considerable degree of relative transmission of values from one generation to the next, including individualism, collectivism, and family orientation. This indicates some stability in cultural values.

[179]

Our results on the preference for family values in all cohorts who at the same time supported individualistic values is in line with other studies referring to the importance of the family in times of social change (e.g., Bengtson, 2001; Inglehart, 1997; Mayer & Trommsdorff, 2003; Trommsdorff & Chakkarath, 1996).

While Inglehart has predicted a change to post-materialist values in Western societies as a result of economic improvement, a question for future research is whether another kind of value change will take place as a result of economic decline. Will there be a shift towards materialist and traditional values on the part of the young generation while their parents (still) prefer post-materialistic and individualistic values?

The results from our study underline the need that further research also has to deal with questions on individual and cultural values in the context of intergenerational relations and as part of the demographic and related socio-economic changes (Trommsdorff, 2003). This is even more obvious when comparing our results from the German sample with our data from three-generation families in India (unpublished data) which demonstrate an even higher value of the family, a higher economic value of the child as predicted by the eco-cultural approach of the Value of Children Study, and a higher importance of collectivistic-traditional values which are more directly transmitted from one generation to the next. This indicates cultural continuity in India but also some change towards individualistic values in the younger generation. These results from a cross-cultural study underline the importance of the cultural dimension for the explanation of individual values.

CHAPTER NINE

A cross-cultural analysis of immigrant and host values and acculturation orientations[1]

KAREN PHALET AND MARC SWYNGEDOUW

Psychological value theories have stressed the continuity, sharedness and directive force of cultural value systems as motivational structures instigating, directing or sustaining behavioral choices (Rokeach, 1973; Schwartz, 1992). On the empirical plane, *cross-cultural value studies* provide strong evidence of quasi-universal comparative dimensions of basic human values (Hofstede, 2001; Schwartz, 1992, 1994, 1996). Along these comparative dimensions, consistent cultural differences in value priorities were found. Moreover, these differences were often — though not always — found to explain significant portions of cultural diversity in human behavior. One major limitation of most value studies in cross-cultural psychology, however, is their exclusive focus on cross-national comparisons between Western and non-Western cultures (Hofstede, 2001; Triandis, 1995). Hence, the main aim of our study is to extend cross-cultural value research to the analysis of cultural diversity and change in culture contact situations. As a consequence of increased globalization and migration, there is a growing need to incorporate the impact of culture contact and culture learning into the comparative study of values. To this end, we bring together cross-cultural value studies with new developments in acculturation studies, addressing the psychological impact of culture contact. Importantly, acculturation studies have taken a dynamic approach to cultures in contact, focusing on relational orientations

[1] This study was supported by the Ministry of Brussels Capital Region. The CISB-IPSOM-ERCOMER Survey is a collaboration of VU Brussels (CISB) and KU Brussels (IPSOM) with the European Research Center on Migration and Ethnic Relations (ERCOMER) at Utrecht University. Correspondence should be addressed to Dr. Karen Phalet, ERCOMER — ICS (Interuniversity Center for Social Science Theory and Methodology), Utrecht University, P.O. box 80.140, 3508 TC Utrecht, Netherlands, e-mail: *K.Phalet@fss.uu.nl*.

and psychological adaptation or learning in acculturating cultures. In contrast, comparative studies of values are commonly undertaken from an alternative 'static' approach to cultures as deeply internalized, transmitted and shared within monocultural communities (Hong, Morris, Chiu & Benet-Martinez, 2000). Consequently, there is a relative scarcity of psychological studies on the role of values in the context of acculturation. Our study adds to the existing literature by developing a dynamic approach to value diversity and change in multicultural societies.

Specifically, we set out to answer the following research questions about values in acculturating cultures. First, to what extent do ethnic value differences between immigrant and host communities reflect national differences between the countries of origin and destination? Second, how much cultural continuity and sharedness do we find in immigrant value priorities, and what values are subject to acculturative change? And third, what is the directive force of values in acculturating cultures? What values are enhancing or impeding adaptive acculturation orientations? Whereas the first two questions refer to values as endogenous variables, which are themselves influenced by acculturation processes (cf. Feather, 1980), the last question is concerned with value priorities as explanatory variables, motivating varying acculturation orientations (cf. Schwartz, 1996).

Building on Berry's (1997, 2001, 2002) seminal acculturation research, we define *acculturation* as a process of bi-directional change following from sustained culture contact between migrant or minority groups and dominant cultural groups in multicultural societies. In his well-known bi-dimensional model, Berry (1997) distinguishes between 'maintenance' (of the minority culture) and 'contact' (with the dominant culture) as separate dimensions of acculturation. Together, both dimensions explain much of the variation in personal adaptation to culture contact situations. Another major aim of our study is to further develop and extend Berry's basic model. In particular, the domain specificity of acculturation processes, the impact of the host community, and the relational outcomes of acculturation have been rather less well researched (Berry, 2001). Therefore, until recently contextual and relational (interactive) features of the acculturation process have not received the empirical attention that they deserve (with notable exceptions such as the earlier work by Berry, Kalin and Taylor, 1977). Therefore, the present study elaborates a contextual and fully interactive acculturation model. More concretely, our analysis of culture maintenance and contact distinguishes between public and private acculturation contexts (Van de Vijver & Phalet, forthcoming) and between host and immigrant acculturation orientations (Bourhis, Moïse, Perrault & Sénécal, 1997). Finally, immigrant acculturation orientations are used to predict individual or collective mobility strategies in mostly unequal ethnic relations between immigrants and hosts. Following Moghaddam's (1988) social mobility model of acculturation, the strategies of immigrants to overcome their generally disadvantaged minority status are conceived as critical acculturation outcomes.

[183]

In sum, our study is concerned with the following research questions about acculturation and mobility: do immigrant acculturation orientations (towards maintenance and contact) differ between private and public contexts? To what extent do immigrant and host orientations converge (or diverge) in both contexts? Lastly, do immigrants prefer individual or collective mobility? And how well are distinct mobility strategies predicted by immigrant values and acculturation orientations?

In the multicultural city of Brussels where we conducted our study, the (national) majority population of Belgian hosts represents the dominant culture whereas (non-national) Turkish and Moroccan immigrants and their descendants (hereafter subsumed under the broad labels of 'immigrants' or 'minorities') constitute distinctive minority cultures. Relations between immigrant and host communities in Brussels are set against the background of a binational and multicultural city. Brussels is binational in that the national population includes a non-immigrant minority of Flemish nationals. The overarching category of 'Belgian hosts' will be used here to refer to Flemish as well as French-speaking nationals in Brussels. In addition, Brussels is exemplary as a multicultural city, with its 30% of non-national inhabitants — of which one in three are of Turkish or Moroccan origin (Van der Haegen, Juchtmans & Kesteloot, 1995). Turkish and Moroccan minorities are treated here as parallel cases, as they share roughly similar cultural backgrounds, migration histories and ethnic barriers in the host society. Thus, Turks and Moroccans have in common their migration histories as former guest workers — who were contracted by West-European governments in the seventies and mostly employed in unskilled labor. Moreover, both minorities originate mostly from rural or provincial communities with traditional or modernizing 'cultures of relatedness' in Turkey or Morocco (Kağitçibâşi, 1990, 2001). Finally, the younger generations of Turks and Moroccans growing up in Europe are both facing enduring social disadvantage and ethnic discrimination (Bovenkerk, Miles & Verbunt, 1991). For these reasons, we have no *a priori* expectations of ethnic differences between Moroccans and Turks.

Concepts and hypotheses

Acculturation orientations
One important objective of our analysis is to develop and document an interactive and contextual acculturation model. Following the public recognition

of cultural diversity in the US and in Europe, bi-dimensional models of acculturation have replaced older uni-dimensional models. In a uni-dimensional approach, 'deculturation' or the gradual loss of the heritage culture, is the necessary complement of 'acculturation' or the acquisition of the host culture. In contrast, Berry's (1997) widely used bi-dimensional model distinguishes between attitudes towards 'maintenance' of the ethnic minority culture and towards 'contact' with the dominant culture in the host society. In the remainder, the latter dimension will be labeled 'adaptation' rather than 'contact', since we are interested primarily in the cultural adaptation of immigrants to values, norms and customs in the dominant society. Across cultures, most immigrant or minority groups combine positive attitudes towards maintenance and adaptation in a so-called 'integration' orientation. Compared with alternative assimilation (i.e. adaptation without maintenance), separation (i.e. maintenance without adaptation), and marginalization orientations (i.e. neither maintenance nor adaptation), the integration orientation is not only most popular, but also most adaptive in terms of psychological adjustment and competence (Berry, 2002; Ward, Bochner & Furnham, 2001). At the same time, younger generations and immigrants with higher education are often less attached to the heritage culture, and more open to the dominant culture (Berry, Kalin & Taylor, 1977). While the bi-dimensional model of acculturation orientations has been widely replicated (Ryder, Alden & Paulhus, 2000), the issues of interactivity and context sensitivity have received less research attention.

Host and immigrant acculturation orientations. Research in various host societies suggests that the (perceived) acceptance by the host community of the immigrant cultures enhances immigrant integration (Berry, 2001; Horenczyck, 1996; Lalonde & Cameron, 1993; Piontkowski, Florack, Hölker & Obdrzalek, 2000). Accordingly, the interactive acculturation model (Bourhis et al., 1997) takes into account host acculturation orientations. Host communities differ in how accepting they are on the maintenance dimension of acculturation; and in how demanding they are on the adaptation dimension. Hence, in parallel with immigrant acculturation orientations, host orientations fall into Berry's four categories of integration, assimilation, separation or marginality — in Bourhis' (et al., 1997) terminology integrationism, assimilationism, segregation, and exclusionism. From an interactive approach, convergence between host and immigrant acculturation orientations yields harmonious relational outcomes; divergence leads to conflict. Relational outcomes refer to the friendly or hostile, inclusive of exclusive nature of ethnic attitudes and practices. As a consequence of pervasive ethnocentric bias in ethnic relations, there are built-in ethnic tensions between immigrant and host acculturation orientations. In line with social identity theory, both sides will be inclined to favor the in-group culture over the culture of an out-group (Tajfel & Turner, 1986). In addition, ethnic relations between immigrants and hosts are most often unequal. In view of their dominant group position, the host community will demand some degree of adaptation from immigrant minorities, while their acceptance of culture maintenance will vary, depending on whether they perceive the minority culture as a threat to group dominance (Bobo & Hutchings, 1996; Montreuil & Bourhis, 2002). Conversely, the minority status of immigrants is associated with heightened ethnic self-identification, thus reinforcing culture maintenance. At the same time, immigrant attitudes towards cultural adaptation will vary, depending on whether they perceive the dominant culture as a threat to group survival (Berry et *al.*, 1977). On both sides of the ethnic divide, ethnocentrism or perceived threat will decline with increasing levels of education (Scheepers, Verberck & Coenders, 2001). Hence, more harmonious relational outcomes are expected between immigrants and hosts with higher levels of education.

[185]

Acculturation contexts. The importance and impact of minority and dominant cultures depend crucially on the acculturation context. Thus, multi-item acculturation scales covering various behavioral domains (e.g., language, food, family values) brought out the domain-specificity of immigrant acculturation attitudes (Berry, 2002; Van de Vijver & Phalet, forthcoming). Likewise, cultural priming effects in experiments with 'biculturals' document 'cultural frame switching' in response to situational cues (Hong et *al.*, 2000; Lafromboise, Coleman & Gerton, 1993). In particular, acculturation contexts differ along a major perceived dividing line between public and private life in modern societies. In a study of minority school adjustment and achievement, Phalet and Andriessen (forthcoming) found that the maintenance dimension of acculturation was most important in the family context (private), while the adaptation dimension was crucial for adaptive learning in the classroom (public). By alternating between public and private contexts, immigrants negotiate contending in-group pressures from co-ethnics and dominant-group pressures from the host society. While the cultural norms of the dominant group are most salient and most influential in public contexts, family and community contexts are more often co-ethnic. Hence, ethnic cultural norms are most salient and most easily enforced in private life. It follows that an optimal person-environment fit requires the alternation between public contexts and private contexts of immigrant orientations towards adaptation and maintenance.

Hypotheses. Taken together, interactive and contextual features of acculturation invite the following hypotheses. *(H1a) In line with Berry's bi-dimensional model, Turkish and Moroccan immigrants will combine culture main-*

tenance and adaptation in a most preferred integration orientation; but the younger and those with more education will stress maintenance less and adaptation more. (H1b) As suggested by group processes in the interactive model, Belgian hosts will stress adaptation more, and maintenance less than immigrants, with the most conflictual relational outcomes among immigrants and hosts with lower levels of education. (H1c) In accordance with optimal person-environment fit in the contextual model, there will be more emphasis on adaptation, and less on maintenance, in public than in private contexts.

Mobility strategies

A related objective of this study is to explore the associations between acculturation processes and expected outcomes of group processes in ethnic relations between immigrants and hosts. Social identity theory discerns three ideal-typical reactions to minority status, varying from acceptance of the inferior status as a baseline (the typical minority reaction), through individual mobility, to collective action (Tajfel & Turner, 1986). More concretely, Moghaddam's (1988) social-mobility approach connects immigrant acculturation attitudes with individual or collective strategies for status improvement as distinct acculturation outcomes. Immigrants, who adopt an individual strategy, hope to be accepted by dominant group members on the basis of personal merit. Alternatively, immigrants who invest in family- or community-based networks and resources rely on collective strategies to get ahead in the host country. But individual and collective strategy choices are not mutually exclusive. In the presence of disadvantage and discrimination in the host society, we expect that immigrants will most often prefer combinations of individual and collective strategies. Further, not only immigrants but also (lower class) hosts may rely on collective strategies — rather than individual competition — in order to overcome disadvantage. To disentangle social and cultural differences in strategy preferences, we will compare the mobility strategies of immigrants with those of (lower class) Belgian hosts.

Immigrant and host mobility strategies. In line with the stage model of mobility strategies (Taylor & McKirnan, 1984), collective action was found to replace regular individual strategies when individual mobility is perceived as blocked. The shift towards collective action has been related to low perceived ability and to perceptions of stability and impermeability in unequal group relations (Boen & Van Beselaere, 2000; Wright, Taylor & Moghaddam, 1990). In view of their disadvantaged minority status, we expect that Turkish and Moroccan immigrants will more readily adopt collective mobility strategies than Belgian hosts. For similar reasons of limited opportunities and/or resources, immigrants and hosts with little education, and older generations of immigrants, will depend more on collective strategies. In addition, cultural collectivism and group identification also play a role (Ellemers, Spears & Doosje, 1997; Hinkle & Brown, 1990). Since collectivism reinforces group identities, collective strategies are more often the norm in minority groups with a collectivist heritage culture. Therefore, also immigrants, who are successful in their personal careers, often invest in ethnic forms of solidarity (Moghaddam, 1988).

[187]

Acculturation orientations and mobility strategies. In Moghaddam's (1988) mobility model of integration, the same group processes that support individual or collective mobility in immigrant groups are also at the basis of their acculturation orientations. Thus, in-group identification together with group competition are thought to enhance collective mobility and culture maintenance, while impeding individual mobility and adaptation across cultures. In contrast, weak in-group identification and individual competition with dominant group members would impede collective mobility and culture maintenance, while promoting individual mobility and adaptation. In support of our expectations, immigrants who engage in culture contact more often are more successful in their professional careers (Ward, Bochner & Furnham, 2001). Conversely, immigrants who are most attached to the heritage culture, also prefer collective strategies most (Moghaddam, 1988). Finally, group identity and inter-group comparison are separate dimensions of group processes (Hinkle & Brown, 1990). Therefore, immigrants with a most adaptive integration orientation may simultaneously combine culture maintenance with adaptation, and collective with individual mobility.

Hypotheses. In summary, we expect the following effects of cultural group and acculturation orientation on mobility strategies. *(H2a) Turks, Moroccans and (lower class) Belgian hosts alike are expected to prefer combinations of individual and collective strategies to get ahead. (H2b) As a consequence of their minority status and cultural collectivism, Turkish and Moroccan immigrants will prefer collective mobility more, and individual mobility less, than Belgian hosts do; also, in view of more limited resources and opportunities, immigrants and hosts with less education, and the earlier generations of immigrants, will prefer collective mobility more, and individual mobility less. (H2c) Finally, on the basis of the common group processes underlying acculturation and mobility preferences, we expect that immigrants with a separation orientation will prefer collective mobility most and individual mobility least; those with an assimilation orientation will prefer individual mobility most and collective mobility least; and those with an integration orientation may combine individual and collective mobility strategies.*

Value profiles

Another major objective of the present study is to analyze ethnic value differences between immigrant and host cultures, as well as value acculturation in immigrant cultures. We derive our expectations with regard to immigrant and host value profiles from (a) cultural differences in cross-national studies of values, (b) findings of value acculturation in immigrants, and (c) cross-cultural findings associating value profiles with education and gender.

Cultures differ in the relative importance attached to different values as a normative basis for understanding and regulating social life. Extending the findings from cross-national studies of values to multicultural societies, we can predict ethnic differences between immigrant and host value profiles (Coon & Kemmelmeier, 2001; Gaines, Marelich, Bledsoe et al., 1999). Over the last decade cross-cultural research has centered on an alleged individualism-collectivism divide between 'the West and the rest'. While authors disagree on the precise meaning and measures of the concept, individualism generally refers to the primacy of the individual as a social and moral entity, whereas collectivism stresses the embeddedness of individuals within primary groups (Hofstede, 2001; Triandis, 1995). But the individualism–collectivism divide can be broken down into distinct value types that are not necessarily in conflict, as in Schwartz' (1992, 1994, 1996) seminal cross-cultural value study. The study has uncovered a circular value structure, which is seen to reflect motivational conflicts and compatibilities along near-universal value dimensions. One dimension is akin to the well-known individualism-collectivism divide. It is labeled Openness to Change vs. Conservation, and opposes (among others) self-direction values to conformity, security and tradition values. The latter value types have in common their emphasis on in-group cohesion and continuity with the past, while the former stress individual separateness and openness to change. Another major value dimension opposes (among others) Self-Enhancing achievement values to Self-Transcending pro-social value types. On the first value dimension, West European cultures are sooner on the individualism or openness side; Turkish and Moroccan cultures on the collectivism or conservation side of the great divide (Hofstede, 2001; Kağitçibâşi, 1990; Schwartz, 1992). Hence, the value profiles of Turkish and Moroccan minorities and Belgian hosts are expected to differ accordingly. In line with this expectation, minority groups in the US and in Europe with a collectivist heritage culture were found to maintain or reinforce core collectivism values (Coon & Kemmelmeier, 2001; Gaines et al., 1997). At the same time, there is recent evidence of the co-existence of individualism and collectivism in modern(izing) collectivist cultures (Verma, 2001). Similarly, individualism in Western multicultural societies is not 'owned by' the dominant group, but minority groups were found to balance collectivist with individualistic value priorities (Coon & Kemmelmeier, 2001; Gaines et *al.*, 1997). Whereas cross-ethnic studies have focused mostly on the individualism-collectivism dimension, cross-cultural research on achievement values in modern(izing) and [189] acculturating collectivist cultures shows generally high aspiration levels in spite of unequal or limited opportunities (Phalet & Claeys, 1993; Phalet & Lens, 1995). In all, we are lead to expect enduring ethnic differences in collectivism or conservation values, in line with national value differences between Turkey, Morocco and Belgium. At the same time, we may expect some degree of individualism, along with core collectivism among Turkish and Moroccan immigrants, in accordance with recent evidence of balanced individualism-collectivism in modern(izing) or acculturating cultures of relatedness. Finally, in view of a well-documented collectivist type of achievement orientation, we do not expect immigrant-host differences in achievement or self-enhancing values.

Typically, the experience of cross-cultural contact in immigrant groups entails some degree of value acculturation in the direction of dominant values in the host society. But acculturative shifts in immigrant values are most often selective and uneven (Feather, 1980; Triandis, Kashima, Shimoda & Villareal, 1986). In line with previous findings, we expect that educational differences and generational change in immigrant value profiles reflect varying degrees of value acculturation. On the whole, second-generation immigrants and those with higher education are less committed to group norms and traditions, and more open to change (Georgas, Berry & Shaw, 1996; Lesthaege, 2000; Phalet & Claeys, 1993; Phalet & Hagendoorn, 1996; Phinney & Flores, 2002). In addition, some studies suggest complex moderator effects of gender on value acculturation (Gaines et *al.*, 1997; Phinney & Flores, 2002). On a cautionary note, acculturative change within immigrant communities cannot be wholly separated out from intra-cultural diversity that is unrelated to acculturation.

Across cultures then, similar intra-cultural value differences have emerged (Prince-Gibson & Schwartz, 1998; Schwartz, Melech, Lehmann et *al.*, 2001). While gender differences in value priorities are generally weak and culture-specific, educational differences are very robust and general. In line with Schwartz' value theory, educational experience promotes the intellectual flexibility and breadth of perspective essential for openness values. Likewise, education stimulates a critical attitude towards the group norms and traditions that sustain conservation values. There is no consistent cross-cultural evidence of educational differences in achievement values. Finally, cross-cultural age differences in conservation vs. openness to change may contribute to generational trends in immigrant value profiles, with older generations being sooner on the conservation side of the cross-cultural value space.

[190]   *Hypotheses.* Cross-cultural studies of values lead to the following hypotheses about immigrant and host value priorities. *(H3a) In line with cross-national value differences, Turkish and Moroccan immigrants will find conformity, security and tradition values more important than Belgian hosts; we have no a priori expectations of ethnic differences in self-direction and achievement values; (H3b) As a consequence of value acculturation, confor-mity-security-tradition values will be least important, and self-direction values most important to second generation immigrants or to those with higher education; (H3c) In accordance with findings from cross-cultural value studies, the younger generations and those with more education will be less oriented towards conservation values, and more towards openness values; we have no a priori expectations of intra-cultural differences in achievement values.*

The impact of values

In a last step, our focus is on the motivational force of value priorities in acculturating cultures. In particular, we will examine immigrant value pro-files as predictors of their ethnic relations with the host community. While there is a significant social-psychological research tradition on values and group relations (Schwartz, Struch & Bilsky, 1990), few studies have system-atically related values and acculturation orientations (Phalet & Hagendoorn, 1996; Roccas, Horenczyck & Schwartz, 2000). This study builds on Schwartz' (1996) motivational theory of human values to predict accultura-tion orientations among immigrants. As conformity-security-tradition values share a common goal orientation towards in-group cohesion or conservation, they are expected to motivate ethnic culture maintenance (i.e. separation or integration). Conversely, self-direction values would enhance adaptation to the dominant culture (i.e. integration or assimilation) as part of an overarch-ing goal orientation towards openness and change. Moreover, cross-cultural research on group relations leads to the following expectations with regard to social mobility strategies. We know that cultural collectivism facilitates a cognitive shift from individual to group-level identification and status attri-bution, which is associated with collective mobilization (Hinkle & Brown, 1990; Taylor & McKirnan, 1984). Hence, conformity-security-tradition val-ues are expected to support collective strategies, whereas self-direction val-ues would rather promote individual mobility. Finally, self-enhancing achievement values may serve either individual or collective ways of self-improvement.

Hypotheses. Following on from Schwartz' theory of values and cross-cultural studies of group relations, it is hypothesized that *(H4a) immigrants with a separation or integration orientation will find conformity-security-tradition values more important, and self-direction values less important, than those with an assimilation orientation. In parallel, (H4b) immigrants who prefer individual mobility, will attach more importance to self-direction values, and less to conformity-security-tradition values, than those who don't; conversely, immigrants who prefer family mobility or ethnic mobility, will find self-direction less, and conformity-security-tradition more important.* [191]

Comparative design, measures and analyses

Participants
The data are drawn from the 1999 CISB-Ipsom-Ercomer Survey.[2] The comparative design includes random samples of (n=587) Turkish and (n=391) Moroccan men and women aged 18 and above. Turks and Moroccans are sampled on the basis of formal nationality, which corresponds closely to ethnic self-identification (*in casu* 95% overlap; Phalet & Swyngedouw, 2002). Post-stratification is based on the age by gender association structure in the respective populations (Swyngedouw, Phalet & Deschouwer, 1999). Most immigrants have little or no education: 80% of the Turkish and 72% of the Moroccan sample have completed no more than secondary school in Belgium or primary school in Turkey or Morocco. The immigrant samples consist of four migration generations, which refer to combined age generations and migration waves: the *pioneer generation* makes up 30% of the Turks and 30% of the Moroccans; the *first generation* 30% of the Turks and 27% of the Moroccans; the *second generation* 24% of the Turks and 29% of the Moroccans; and the *newcomers* 16% of the Turks and 15% of the Moroccans.[3] Turkish and Moroccan participants were approached by trained multilingual Turkish and Moroccan interviewers for face-to-face structured interviews in the language of their choice. The language universe of the 1999 Survey comprises the main minority languages (Turkish and Moroccan-Arabic) and both

---

[2] Non-response rates are 19.8% (8.5% refusals) for Turks, 26.4% (9.2% refusals) for Moroccans, and 31.4% (19% refusals) for Belgians.

[3] 'Pioneers' are born in Turkey or Morocco, above 40 years of age and more than 15 years in Belgium; the 'first generation' are born in Turkey or Morocco, above 30 and 20 years or less in Belgium, above 40 and 15 years or less in Belgium; the 'second generation' are 30 years or younger and more than 20 years in Belgium, above 30 and born in Belgium; the 'newcomers' are 30 years or younger and 20 years or less in Belgium (Lesthaege, 2000).

[192]

national languages (French and Dutch). All questions and rating scales have been translated, backtranslated, and decentered if necessary. Apart from questions about their social background and migration history, participants were asked about their acculturation attitudes in private and public contexts, preferred mobility strategies, and value orientations. In line with an interactive approach to acculturation, similar questions have also been presented to a matched comparison group of (n=402) Belgian nationals with similarly low levels of education, who are sampled from the same, mostly disadvantaged neighborhoods in Brussels. To optimize the cross-cultural comparability of immigrant and host samples, post-stratification of the Belgian comparison sample is based on the pooled age by gender by education structure in both immigrant populations (Swyngedouw et al., 1999). Hence, the Belgian comparison group is not representative of the Belgian population at large.

Measures
Culture maintenance and adaptation. The assessment of acculturation attitudes among Turkish and Moroccan minorities is based on a modified immigrant acculturation scale with symmetrical maintenance and adaptation questions: '*Is it considered of value to maintain the Turkish or Moroccan culture?*' and '*Is it of considered of value to adapt to the Belgian host culture?*' This last question elicits lower rates of endorsement than Berry's original question about the desirability of culture contact in the host society (Sayegh & Lasry, 1993). Participants indicate their attitudes on rating scales from (3) maintain completely, over (2) in part, to (1) not at all, and from (3) adapt completely, over (2) in part, to (1) not at all. Both questions are first rated in the private context ('*home and family life*') and next in the public context ('*school and work*'). Our parallel measure of acculturation attitudes in the Belgian comparison group refers to host expectations from immigrants in private and public contexts: '*Are they expected to maintain the Turkish or Moroccan minority culture?*' and '*to adapt to the Belgian host culture?*' Combining both questions, immigrants and hosts are classified into Berry's (1997) fourfold typology of acculturation orientations (i.e. assimilation, separation, integration, and marginalization). Each participant is categorized twice: once in private life and once in public life.[4]

Individual and collective strategies. To measure mobility strategies, all participants are given a social-psychological task, which amounts to the par-

---

[4] 'Assimilation' is complete adaptation to the dominant culture, and little or no maintenance of the minority culture; 'separation' is little or no adaptation and complete maintenance; 'integration' is maintenance and adaptation to the same degree; and 'marginalization' is neither maintenance, nor adaptation.

adigmatic social dilemma between 'sticking together' and 'falling apart' in the face of disadvantage or discrimination (Ellemers et al., 1997). As distinct from most mobility studies in social psychology, this study compares minority and dominant strategies; it allows for combinations of individual and collective mobility; and it adds a distinction between ethnic or community-based types and more narrow family-based types of collective mobility (in view of the instrumental function of immigrant family ties; Nauck, 2001). Concretely, participants may choose individual mobility (*'rely on personal efforts and capabilities'*), family mobility and ethnic mobility strategies (*'give mutual help and support within the family'* and *'within the minority/ host community'*). Preference for each *'way to get ahead'* in the host society is rated separately from *(4) most preferred option* to *(1) not an option*.

Value priorities. Participants are asked how much importance they attach to a shortlist of values. The list is adapted from Rokeach's (1973) and Schwartz's (1994) well-researched value wordings and ratings scales for use in face-to-face interviews with semi-literate immigrant populations. It samples core values with a stable placement in the self-direction, achievement, or conformity-security-tradition segments of the cross-cultural value space.[5] Participants rate the importance of each value *'as a guiding principle in their lives'* on a scale from *(1) against my principles* and *(2) not important at all* up to *(9) extremely important*. The list contains six self-direction and achievement values: *'creativity', 'independence', and 'choose one's own goals'*, and *'competence', 'success', and 'ambition'* and six conformity-security-tradition values: *'politeness', 'social order', 'national security', 'obedience', 'respect for tradition', and 'honor parents and elders'*.

Analyses

To test *Hypotheses 1a, 1b, and 1c, and 2a and 2b* about acculturation orientations and mobility strategies, we inspect the classification of immigrant and host samples into distinct acculturation types and mobility preferences. Next, we test differences in acculturation orientations (i.e. maintenance and adaptation) between contexts (as a within-subject factor) and between cultures, levels of education, generations and gender (as between-subject factors) in repeated-measures analyses of variance. We use a [Context by Cultural Group by Education by Gender] design for immigrants and hosts, and a [Cultural Group by Migration Generation by Education by Gender] design

---

[5] Due to time constraints, other value types, such as hedonism or spiritual values, which seem less directly relevant to ethnic relations between immigrants and hosts, are not included in the survey.

for immigrants only. Similarly, we test differences in mobility strategies (i.e. individual, family and ethnic mobility) by way of [Cultural Group by Education by Gender] analyses of variance with immigrants and hosts, and [Cultural Group by Generation by Education by Gender] analyses of variance with immigrants only. Only significant effects at $p<.01$ or less are discussed.

To test *Hypothesis 2c* on associations of immigrant acculturation orientations with mobility strategies as acculturation outcomes, preferences for individual, family and ethnic mobility are entered as dependent variables in analyses of variance with acculturation orientations (i.e. separation, integration, assimilation and marginalization) as an independent variable. Bonferroni's correction is used in post-hoc comparisons of means $(p<.05)$. To explore culture-specific acculturation effects, we also test interactions with cultural group (Van de Vijver & Leung, 1997).

To test *Hypotheses 3a, 3b, and 3c* common value dimensions are identified as a basis for cross-cultural comparison. To this end, Turkish, Moroccan and Belgian value structures are validated across cultural groups by way of pooled-within exploratory factor analysis (i.e. principal component analysis with varimax rotation, after double centering around individual and group means; Leung & Bond, 1988). Next, we analyze cultural differences and intra-cultural variation in value profiles by way of [Cultural Group by Education by Gender / Response Tendency] analyses of covariance with immigrants and hosts, and [Cultural Group by Generation by Education by Gender / Response Tendency] analyses of covariance with immigrants only.[6] Only significant effects at the .01-level or less are discussed.

Finally, to test *Hypotheses 4a and 4b* about the impact of values on acculturation orientations and mobility outcomes, we analyze immigrant value priorities as a function of their acculturation orientations in private and public contexts, and their preferences for individual, family and ethnic types of mobility. Again, Bonferroni's correction is applied to post-hoc comparisons of means $(p<.05)$. And we add interactions with cultural group to explore the limits of cross-cultural generalisability.

Results

Immigrant and host acculturation orientations
Table 1 shows the proportions of Turks, Moroccans and (lower class) Belgians falling into Berry's (1997) four acculturation orientations in private

---

[6] Specifically, the overall individual means across value types are used as the covariate, so that mean differences in the importance of distinct value types are adjusted for ethnic differences in global response style (Fontaine, 1999; Schwartz, 1992).

Table 1: *Immigrant and host acculturation orientations: proportions of Turks,
Moroccans and Belgians in public and private contexts*

Acculturation Orientations	Separation	Integration	Assimilation	Marginalization
Turkish Immigrants				
Public	18.2 %	61.5%	10.5%	9.8%
Private	40.5%	50.8%	6.4%	2.3%
Moroccan Immigrants				
Public	31.1%	47.4%	17.1%	4.4%
Private	53.7%	40.1%	4.7%	1.5%
Belgian Hosts				
Public	3.1%	43.0%	44.0%	9.9%
Private	25.8%	43.3%	27.7%	3.4%

Note: Significant effects in repeated-measures analyses of variance with culture
maintenance and contact dimensions as dependent variables:
– main effects of acculturation contexts on culture maintenance ($F(1)=248.55$; $p<.0001$)
  and adaptation ($F(1)=20.52$; $p<.0001$),
– main effects of immigrant or host culture on maintenance ($F(2)=60.09$; $p<.0001$) and
  adaptation ($F(2)=21.28$; $p<.0001$),
– context by culture interaction effects on maintenance ($F(2)=6.94$; $p<.001$) and adaptation
  ($F(2)=12.94$; $p<.0001$), and
– a culture by education interaction effects on maintenance ($F(2)=6.88$; $p<.001$) and
  adaptation ($F(2)=5.80$; $p<.01$) and a culture by gender interaction effect on adaptation
  ($F(2)=7.79$; $p<.0001$).

and public contexts. In line with Berry's (1997) basic model (see *Hypothesis
1a*), in public contexts both immigrant groups prefer integration most, followed by separation and assimilation in decreasing order of preference. But
integration seems somewhat more popular among Turks, while Moroccans
are more often divided between opposite separation and assimilation
options. Overall preference for integration should be qualified, however, in
private contexts. In their family lives, immigrants are almost equally divided
between integration and separation, although Moroccans favor separation,
Turks integration. Very few immigrants opt for assimilation in private life.
Finally, Belgian hosts and immigrants make similar distinctions between
public and private acculturation contexts, but their orientations do not fully
match. In line with expectations from an interactive approach, (lower class)
Belgians are roughly equally divided between assimilation and integration

orientations in public life. In private life, they prefer integration most, with assimilation and separation as distant second choices.

[196]

In a next step, *Hypotheses 1b and 1c* about differences between immigrants and hosts and between public and private contexts of acculturation are tested (see Table Note under Table 1). Multivariate analyses mostly confirm the expected contextual and cultural differences in acculturation orientations. In accordance with *Hypothesis 1c* about acculturation contexts and optimal person-environment fit, we find that immigrant and host communities both draw a line between public and private acculturation contexts. Across cultures, maintenance of the ethnic culture is less important, and adaptation to the dominant culture more important, in public than in private life. Yet, context differences between public and private maintenance are smaller for immigrants than for hosts; and context differences between public and private adaptation do not reach significance for Turkish immigrants. Across contexts, and in line with *Hypothesis 1b* about acculturation and group processes in ethnic relations, immigrant and host orientations also differ. Specifically, (lower class) Belgian hosts attach less importance to culture maintenance than both immigrant groups. Conversely, Belgians find adaptation more important than Turks and Moroccans. There is an additional ethnic difference, so that Moroccans value maintenance (even) more than Turks. Lastly, the analyses support the expected impact of education on immigrant and host acculturation orientations (see also *Hypothesis 1 b*). Thus, relational outcomes are more conflictual between immigrants and hosts with lower levels of education. Across contexts, immigrants with lower levels of education value culture maintenance more, whereas hosts with lower levels of education accept less maintenance from immigrants. And they also expect more adaptation to the dominant culture. In addition, gender plays a role too. Specifically, Moroccan immigrant women are more open to the dominant culture than men.

Immigrant and host mobility strategies
Table 2 shows the relative preferences (i.e. first and second choices) of Turks, Moroccans and Belgians for individual and collective mobility strategies. Thus, Turks prefer ethnic mobility most, followed by family mobility and individual mobility in decreasing order of preference. Conversely, Moroccans and Belgians prefer individual mobility most, family mobility somewhat less, and ethnic mobility least. Across cultures, the pattern of preferences confirms *Hypothesis 2a* about mixed individual and collective strategy choices. As expected, both immigrants and (lower class) hosts combine individual mobility with collective strategies to overcome social disadvantage.

To test *Hypothesis 2b* about the role of cultural collectivism and social disadvantage, we analyze ethnic, educational and generational variation in strategy choices (see Note under Table 2). In line with predictions from cultural difference and ethnic inequality, immigrant and host mobility choices [197] differ. Thus, Belgians prefer individual strategies most, Moroccan immigrants somewhat less, and Turkish immigrants least. Conversely, immigrants prefer ethnic strategies more than hosts, and Turks even more than Moroccans. Interestingly however, Belgians select family strategies even more (not less!) often than immigrants. This unexpected finding invites a closer look at different variants or degrees of collectivism within the Western world (Hofstede, 2001). Across cultures, we find the expected differences in strategy choices between more advantaged or disadvantaged segments of immigrant and host communities. Thus, collective (family and ethnic) strategies

Table 2: *Individual and collective mobility strategies among immigrants and hosts: Proportions of first and second choices for Turks, Moroccans and Belgians*

Mobility Strategies	Individual Mobility	Family Mobility	Ethnic Mobility
Turkish Immigrants			
First	17.8%	14.1%	17.5%
Second	10.2%	19.7%	19.5%
Moroccan Immigrants			
First	35.8%	15.5%	9.9%
Second	12.5%	18.5%	18.7%
Belgian Hosts			
First	38.5%	16.8%	3.4%
Second	17.7%	28.9%	7.4%

Note: Significant effects in analyses of variance with strategy preferences as dependent variables:
– main effects of cultural group on individual ($F(2)=29.19$; $p<.0001$), family ($F(2)=12.81$; $p<.0001$) and ethnic mobility ($F(2)=28.55$; $p<.0001$),
– main effects of education on family ($F(1)=6.52$; $p<.01$) and ethnic mobility ($F(1)=9.58$; $p<.01$),
– main effects of migration generation on individual ($F(3)=5$; $p<.01$) and family mobility ($F(3)=5$; $p<.01$) in immigrant groups, and
– a main effect of gender ($F(1)=12.78$; $p<.001$) and a generation by gender interaction effect ($F(3)=4.63$; $p<.001$) on family mobility.

become less attractive with higher levels of education. And the second generation of immigrants opts more often for individual mobility, and less often for family mobility, than older generations and newcomers do. In addition, immigrant women appear to value family solidarity more than men, especially the older generations of women.

[198]

In a final step, we put to a test *Hypothesis 2c* about common group processes underlying acculturation and mobility strategies (see Note under Table 3). In the absence of significant acculturation by culture interactions, both immigrant groups were pooled. Post hoc comparison of means revealed the expected trends (see Table 3). Immigrants with a public assimilation orientation select individual mobility most often; and those with a marginalization orientation least often. Conversely, immigrants with a private separation orientation prefer family mobility more than those with an integration orienta-

Table 3: *Immigrant mobility strategies as a function of acculturation orientations: Mean levels of preference across minority cultures*

Mobility Strategies	Individual Mobility	Family Mobility	Ethnic Mobility
Acculturation Orientations: Public			
Separation	1.19	*1.38*	.94
Integration	.99	.76	*1.01*
Assimilation	*1.32*	.81	.68
Marginalisation	.88	1.06	1.05
Acculturation Orientations: Private			
Separation	1.16	*1.11*	.96
Integration	.98	.78	1.01
Assimilation	.96	.89	.60
Marginalisation*	–	–	–
Overall Means	1.07	.93	.95

Note: Significant effects in analyses of variance among immigrants with mobility preferences as dependent variables:
– main effects of public acculturation orientations on individual ($F(3)=3.04$; $p<.05$) and ethnic mobility ($F(3)=2.72$; $p<.05$), and
– main effects of private ($F(3)=15.35$; $p<.0001$) and public acculturation orientations ($F(3)=6.35$; $p<.0001$) on family mobility.
* Cell means for scarce cells (bottom line: n < 20) are not included in the analysis for reasons of unreliability. Italic values differ significantly from each or make a significant trend.

tion. Similarly in public life, immigrants with a separation orientation prefer family mobility more than those with integration or assimilation orientations. Finally, ethnic mobility is more attractive to immigrants with a public integration orientation than to those with an assimilation orientation. Overall, culture maintenance (in separation or integration orientations) and adaptation (in integration or assimilation orientations) successfully predict collective and individual mobility strategies respectively.

[199]

Immigrant and host value profiles
Pooled-within exploratory factor analysis of immigrant and host values closely replicates Schwartz' (1992) cross-cultural value structure. The common three-factor solution explains 45% of the total variance: the first bipolar factor opposes conformity and security values (hereafter labeled Conformity as shorthand for the composite term) to autonomy or self-direction values; the second factor groups Achievement values; and the third factor consists of Tradition values.[7] Distinct self-direction and achievement values confirm previous findings with different measurement methods (Phalet & Claeys, 1993; Schwartz et al., 2001). While self-direction values stress individual separateness and openness to change, achievement values are primarily self-enhancing. An additional distinction between conformity and tradition values in our study overlaps only in part with cross-cultural value types (Schwartz, 1996). It seems to reflect complementary concerns with social cohesion (conformity-security) and cultural continuity (tradition) as distinct aspects of conservation values.

Table 4 shows the adjusted mean levels of importance (after taking out response style) for self-direction, achievement, conformity and tradition values in Turkish, Moroccan and (lower class) Belgian comparison groups — ranging from 5 = rather important to 9 = extremely important at the positive end of the rating scale. Largely similar mean value profiles qualify *Hypothesis 3a*, which extends cross-national value differences to ethnic diversity in

---

[7] Factors are labelled on the basis of core values (rule of thumb: core values have loadings >.40 and cross-loadings <.40). Thus, Conformity refers to 'politeness', 'social order' and 'national security' (reliabilities α =.73 for Turks; .71 for Moroccans; .61 for Belgians); Self-direction consists of 'independence' and 'choose one's own goals' (α =.55 for Turks; .54 for Moroccans; .45 for Belgians); Achievement includes 'ambition', 'competence' and 'success' (α = .61 for Turks; .75 for Moroccans; .68 for Belgians); Tradition consists of 'respect for tradition' and 'honour parents and elders' (α = .61 for Turks; .32 for Moroccans; .43 for Belgians). The values 'creativity' and 'obedience' are not included because they lack cross-cultural equivalence. Specifically, 'creativity' is dissociated from all other values and 'obedience' is associated with achievement in immigrant groups only.

multicultural settings. Across cultures, mean value profiles of immigrants and hosts combine individualistic with collectivist value priorities. Moreover, cultural differences between immigrants and hosts are small and gradual in nature, after taking into account differential response tendencies (see Footnote 6). In Moroccan value profiles, tradition values are most important, followed closely by conformity and achievement values; self-direction values are least important. In Turkish value profiles, tradition and conformity values are also most important; achievement and self-direction are rather less important. Among Belgian hosts, all four-value types are roughly equally important. Note that Turks show the most positive overall response style; Belgians the least positive.

[200]

Table 4: *Immigrant and host value profiles: Adjusted mean levels (controlling for response tendency) of importance for Moroccans, Turks and Belgians*

Value Profiles	Selfdirection Values	Achievement Values	Conformity-Security	Tradition Values	(Response Tendencies)
Moroccan Immigrants	5.9	6.9	7.4	7.8	6.9
Turkish Immigrants	6.7	6.5	7.2	7.5	7.4
Belgian Hosts	6.8	6.9	7	6.7	6.5

Note: Significant effects in analyses of covariance with value priorities as dependent variables (and with overall response tendency as a covariate):
– main effects of culture on conformity ($F(2)=25.79$; $p<.0001$), tradition ($F(2)=72.18$; $p<.0001$), self-direction ($F(2)=35.85$; $p<.0001$) and achievement values ($F(2)=12.98$; $p<.0001$),
– main effects of education on conformity ($F(1)=39.76$; $p<.0001$), tradition ($F(1)=74.96$; $p<.0001$), self-direction ($F(1)=18.28$; $p<.0001$) and achievement ($F(1)=8.48$; $p<.01$),
– main effects of gender on conformity ($F(1)=15.78$; $p<.0001$) and achievement ($F(1)=7.37$; $p<.01$).
– a cultural group by gender interaction effect on conformity ($F(2)=14.72$; $p<.0001$), education by gender effects on tradition ($F(1)=19.13$; $p<.0001$) and self-direction ($F(1)=12.40$; $p<.0001$), and a cultural group by education by gender interaction effect on tradition ($F(2)=4.99$; $p<.01$),
– main effects of migration generation on conformity ($F(3)=5.72$; $p<.001$), tradition ($F(3)=6.16$; $p<.0001$) and achievement values ($F(3)=10.46$; $p<.0001$), and
– generation by gender interaction effects on tradition ($F(3)=5.72$; $p<.001$) and self-direction values ($F(3)=6.74$; $p<.0001$) for immigrants only.

Cultural differences. To test whether the cultural differences predicted by *Hypothesis 3a* are significant, analyses of covariance are conducted (with response style as a covariate; see Note under Table 4).[8] As expected, Belgian hosts attach significantly less importance to collectivism values than immigrants. Thus, conformity and tradition values are most important to Moroccans, less important to Turks, and least important to Belgians. Conversely, immigrants also value individualism less than their hosts: self-direction values are most important to Belgians, less important to Turks, and least to Moroccans. The latter finding replicates the global individualism-collectivism divide and goes against recent evidence of consensual individualism in modern multicultural societies (Coon & Kemmelmeier, 2001). Overall, after controlling for response style, Turks seem to hold a middle ground between Moroccans on the collectivistic side and Belgians on the individualistic side of the global divide. Interestingly, Moroccans in Brussels are not only most collectivist, but also most achievement oriented, thus exemplifying a well-documented collectivist type of achievement motivation (Phalet & Lens, 1995).

[201]

Intra-cultural variation. The same analyses are used to test *Hypothesis 3c* about intra-cultural differences within immigrant and host communities (see Note under Table 4). The hypothesis predicts a cross-cultural shift from conservation to openness values with higher levels of education. Accordingly, immigrants and hosts with more education are less oriented towards conformity and tradition, and more towards self-direction and achievement values, than those with less education. In addition, educational differences in tradition and self-direction values are larger for women than for men; and the educational difference in tradition values is largest for immigrant women in particular. Although we have no *a priori* expectations of cross-cultural gender differences, women tend to value conformity more, and achievement somewhat less than men. But only Moroccan women are significantly more conforming than men.

Value acculturation. As predicted by *Hypothesis 3b* about acculturative change, the analyses reveal significant generational change among immigrants only. Thus, the younger generations of Turkish and Moroccan immigrants attach less importance to conformity and tradition values; and they are more achievement oriented than the older generations. But generational

---

[8] There is a very significant effect of cultural group on response style (F(2)=121.61; p<.0001) and a weak but significant culture by education interaction (F(2)=10.36; p<.001). On average, immigrants rate all values as more important than Belgians, and Turks do so even more than Moroccans do. Moreover, cultural differences in response style are most outspoken between immigrants and hosts with little education.

[202]

change is uneven across gender. In particular, a generational decline in tradition values is limited to immigrant women; and only second-generation immigrant women, not men, are also more autonomy oriented. Note that generation effects confound the acculturative impact of migration with culture-general value differences between age generations.

The impact of values

Table 5 shows immigrant value profiles (after centering) as a function of acculturation orientations and mobility strategies. Since we find significant acculturation by culture interactions (with some associations being significantly stronger in the Moroccan than in the Turkish sample), the analyses are controlled for main and interaction effects of culture.

In support of *Hypothesis 4a* about associations of acculturation with immigrant value profiles, immigrants with different value profiles also differ in their acculturation orientations (see Note under Table 5). More concretely, immigrants who prefer private or public separation, value tradition more than those who prefer integration or assimilation. Conversely, immigrants who prefer public assimilation, attach more value to self-direction than those who prefer either separation or marginalization (especially Moroccans). Lastly, immigrants who favor private assimilation or integration are somewhat more achievement-oriented than those who favor separation.

With regard to mobility strategies (see Table 5), the analyses support *Hypothesis 4b* about associations of individual and collective mobility with immigrant value profiles. In all, cross-cultural value differences predict the mobility preferences of immigrants reasonably well. But some value differences are more outspoken in the Moroccan group than in the Turkish group. Firstly, immigrants who prefer individual mobility more, are less conformity oriented and more oriented towards self-direction (especially Moroccans); and they are also somewhat more achievement oriented. Secondly, immigrants who prefer family mobility more, attach more value to tradition and conformity (especially Moroccans), and less value to self-direction. Finally, immigrants who favor ethnic mobility, also value tradition more, and self-direction less (especially Moroccans).

Conclusion

As a consequence of increased globalization and migration, there is a growing need to incorporate culture contact and social mobility into cross-cultural studies of values. Our study among Turkish and Moroccan immigrants and Belgian hosts in Brussels (N=1380) had a double aim: to elaborate contextual

Table 5: *Immigrant value profiles as a function of acculturation orientations and mobility strategies: Mean levels of importance (after centering) across minority cultures*

[203]

Value Profiles	Self-direction	Achievement	Conformity-Security	Tradition
Acculturation Orientations: Public				
Separation	-.85	-.28	.35	.95
Integration	-.58	-.24	.30	.48
Assimilation	-.25	-.20	.26	.28
Marginalisation	-.94	-.34	.25	.62
Acculturation Orientations: Private				
Separation	-.68	-.33	.33	.78
Integration	-.56	-.19	.27	.46
Assimilation	-.68	*-.11*	.42	.23
Individual Mobility				
Low	*-.73*	*-.32*	.34	.52
High	*-.41*	*-.14*	.21	.66
Family Mobility				
Low	-.57	-.22	.23	.46
High	-.77	-.27	.42	*.81*
Ethnic Mobility				
Low	*-.59*	-.19	.27	.50
High	*-.74*	-.40	.34	.72
Overall Means	-.62	-.26	.30	.57

Note: Significant effects in analyses of covariance with value priorities as dependent variables (and with overall response tendency as a covariate):
– main effects of acculturation orientations on tradition (private: $F(3)=11.41$; $p<.0001$; public: $F(3)=11.37$; $p<.0001$), self-direction (public: $F(3)=5.04$; $p<.01$), and achievement values (private: $F(3)=3.52$; $p<.05$), and
– an acculturation by culture interaction effect on self-direction (public: $F(3)=5.43$; $p<.001$),
– main effects of individual mobility on conformity ($F(1)=6.35$; $p<.01$), self-direction ($F(1)=28.88$; $p<.0001$) and achievement values ($F(1)=5.26$; $p<.05$); of family mobility on tradition ($F(1)=28.38$; $p<.0001$), conformity ($F(1)=11.24$; $p<.001$) and self-direction values ($F(1)=4.19$; $p<.05$); and of ethnic mobility on tradition ($F(1)=5.22$; $p<.05$) and self-direction values ($F(1)=6.42$; $p<.01$), and
– interaction effects of individual mobility by culture on self-direction ($F(1)=25.80$; $p<.0001$); of family mobility by culture on tradition ($F(1)=6.55$; $p<.01$) and conformity ($F(1)=10.15$; $p<.001$); and of ethnic mobility by culture on self-direction ($F(1)=8.71$; $p<.01$).
* Italic values differ significantly from each other or make a significant trend.

and relational features of Berry's acculturation model; and to relate cross-cultural studies of values to recent developments in acculturation research. Building on Berry's acculturation model, we documented how acculturation processes in public and private contexts shape more or less conflicted ethnic relations between immigrants and hosts. Moreover, we successfully predicted distinct individual or collective mobility strategies of immigrants in mostly unequal ethnic relations. Next, extending Schwartz' cross-cultural value studies to issues of ethnic diversity, we elaborated a dynamic approach to values and acculturation. Although ethnic value differences between immigrant and host cultures are generally small, they reflect a global divide between conservation and openness values. Within acculturating cultures, values also differ between migration generations and levels of education; and gender is revealed as a key moderator of acculturative change. To conclude, our final analyses show how immigrant value profiles coordinate distinct acculturation and mobility orientations. While conservation values were found to support ethnic culture maintenance and collective mobility, openness and achievement values motivate culture contact and individual mobility. Below, we discuss more at length the conceptual implications of these findings.

Towards a dynamic approach of values
The first major aim of this study was to extend cross-national research on values to the study of ethnic differences and value acculturation in multicultural societies. In a preliminary step, we have validated our value measure, which was adapted for survey research in acculturating groups with generally low levels of education. In support of the cross-cultural validity of our measure, distinct self-direction, achievement, conformity-security and tradition values emerged across cultural groups, which closely replicate Schwartz' (1992, 1994, 1996) well-established cross-cultural value types.

After taking out differences in response style, we find that ethnic cultural differences between immigrant and host value profiles are generally small and gradual in nature. In line with existing cross-ethnic comparisons (Coon & Kemmelmeier, 2001), host and immigrant value profiles typically balance conservation (or collectivism) values with openness to change (or individualism). Looking beyond these striking commonalities, ethnic differences between immigrant and host value profiles are roughly in line with a global individualism-collectivism divide. Accordingly, Turkish and Moroccan immigrants are more attached to collectivism or conservation, and less to individualism values, than Belgian hosts. To conclude, our findings support the relevance of a cross-cultural individualism-collectivism or openness-conservation dimension for the assessment of cultural distances between immigrants and hosts.

In acculturating cultures more than in dominant cultures, the assumed sharedness and continuity of cultural value systems is limited by internal diversity and acculturative change. In line with existing evidence of value acculturation among immigrants, the younger generations of Turks and [205] Moroccans, and those with more education, are less attached to conservation values, and also more open to change and more aspiring, than the older generations and the less educated. The impact of education in our study convincingly demonstrates the crucial role of education as an institutional instrument to incorporate immigrants from diverse cultural backgrounds. Across cultures, increased exposure to formal education promotes openness, and questions conservation values. Hence, immigrant and host value profiles tend to converge with higher levels of education.

Moreover, gender is revealed as an important moderator of the process of value acculturation (Phinney & Flores, 2002). Indeed, acculturative shifts in values — away from conservation and towards increased openness — are most outspoken for immigrant women. In particular, Turkish and Moroccan women of the second generation, and women with longer and higher education, are most open to change. The moderating role of gender suggests that immigrant women from more traditional cultures of relatedness — with a low intra-familial status for women — may act as pioneers in building bridges between cultures in plural societies. One obvious reason for the pioneering role of immigrant women is that they may have less to loose and more to gain from culture change than their male counterparts.

Lastly, ethnic differences between Turkish and Moroccan communities also came to the fore, with Moroccan immigrants being (even) more attached to conservation or collectivism — along with achievement values — than Turkish immigrants. This ethnic difference was found in spite of the fact that most Turkish and Moroccan families in Brussels come from modernizing cultures of relatedness. Further research, comparing immigrant communities in various host societies with non-immigrant communities in the home countries, would be needed to throw light on these subtle value differences. Possibly, pre-migration differences between Moroccan and (more advanced) Turkish modernization and nation building play a role. But Turkish research attests to the continuing value of relatedness in modern Turkish society (Kağitçibâşi, 1990). Possibly also, differences between Turkish and Moroccan migration and community building play a role, with a less conflicted and more cohesive 'lagged' acculturation pattern in the Turkish community (Phalet & Schönpflug, 2001). In the latter case, increased Moroccan commitment to collectivism is due (at least in part) to ethnic affirmation, accentuating their distinctiveness from the host culture (Triandis et al., 1986).

In all, ethnic, educational, generational and gender differences in value profiles highlight the uneven character of value acculturation, which calls for a dynamic approach of value diversity and change in multicultural societies.

[206] *Ethnic relations, acculturation and mobility*
Our second major research aim was to further develop and document contextual and relational features of Berry's (1997, 2001, 2002) acculturation model. The overall pattern of findings provides convincing evidence of the hypothesized contextual and interactive characteristics of the acculturation process.

As predicted on the basis of converging evidence from cross-cultural acculturation studies (Berry, 2002), both Turks and Moroccans opt primarily for integration in the public contexts of school or work. Thus, they combine enduring attachments to their heritage cultures with simultaneous adaptation to the dominant culture in the host society. But the expected preference for integration receives rather mixed support in the private context of family life. Within immigrant families, separation is at least as much preferred as integration. The latter finding suggests a greater emphasis on culture maintenance, rather than adaptation, in mostly co-ethnic private contexts, in line with optimal person-environment fit in the contextual model.

Comparing immigrant and host orientations, the findings confirm the expected asymmetry on the basis of social identity and group dominance theories. Thus, Belgian hosts attach less importance to culture maintenance and expect more adaptation to the dominant culture than immigrants do. In parallel with immigrants themselves however, Belgian hosts accept much more culture maintenance in the private life of immigrants than in public life; and they expect more adaptation from immigrants in public than in private situations. Furthermore, in accordance with educational differences in ethnocentrism or perceived ethnic threat, acculturation orientations are most divergent, and ethnic relations most conflictual, between the less educated segments of immigrant and host communities. Interestingly, gender also makes a difference, in line with earlier evidence of enhanced cultural openness and adaptation among immigrant women (Kağitçibâşi, 1990, 2001; Phalet & Schönpflug, 2001; Phinney & Flores, 2002). Clearly, more research is needed into the gendered nature of acculturation processes.

To conclude, Bourhis' (et *al.*, 1997) interactive model states that divergence between immigrant and host acculturation orientations leads to conflictual relational outcomes, whereas convergence increases relational harmony. Combining interactive and contextual features of acculturation, relational outcomes seem more conflictual in public than in private contexts. In particular, the presence of minority cultures in public contexts is a potential source of ethnic conflict. Although immigrant and host orientations converge around the value of culture maintenance in the private domain, they diverge in the public domain. Many Belgian hosts, as opposed to most immigrants, do not accept cultural diversity in the public domain. In the private domain, a potential source of ethnic tension is the resistance to dominant norms and values within immigrant families. Although most immigrants and hosts agree that cultural adaptation is required in the public domain, Belgian hosts, as opposed to many immigrants, also expect some adaptation to the dominant culture in private family life. [207]

Not only does an interactive approach improve our understanding of ethnic conflict or coordination across acculturation contexts, it is also successful in predicting immigrant mobility strategies. In accordance with Moghaddam's (1988) social mobility model, most immigrants simultaneously invest in individual and collective strategies of status improvement. As cultural collectivism and ethnic minority status facilitate a cognitive shift towards collective action (Taylor & McKirnan, 1984), immigrants are expected and found to prefer individual mobility less, and ethnic mobility more, than Belgian hosts. But collective mobility is not limited to ethnic minorities or collectivist cultures. Across cultures, individual mobility is less attractive, and collective strategies become more instrumental with increasing social disadvantage.

Most importantly, immigrant acculturation orientations successfully predict distinct mobility strategies. As expected on the basis of group identification and comparison in mostly unequal ethnic relations, assimilation is associated more often with individual mobility, separation and integration with collective mobility. Furthermore, family mobility is best predicted by private separation, ethnic mobility by public integration. To conclude, family and ethnic types of collective mobility are both tied up with ethnic culture maintenance, but some measure of culture contact and adaptation may well be required for ethnic community building.

In light of the latter finding, marked ethnic differences between Turkish and Moroccan mobility choices are worth noting. Typically, Turks show a culture specific mobility pattern, which gives precedence to collective over individual mobility. Moreover, their preferred collective strategies are community based rather than narrowly family based. Overall, the preferred Turkish pattern of ethnic solidarity and public integration differs from Moroccan preferences for more narrow family solidarity and private separation. Once again, ethnic differences seem to reflect a less conflicted and more cohesive 'lagged' acculturation mode in closely knit Turkish immigrant communities (Lesthaege, 2000; Nauck, 2001; Phalet & Schönpflug, 2001).

From immigrant values to acculturation and mobility

Bringing together values and acculturation, one final aim of our study is to connect immigrant value profiles with their acculturation orientations. Building on Schwartz' (1996) value theory, immigrant value priorities appear to predict varying acculturation orientations and mobility outcomes reasonably well. Overall, the cross-cultural analyses support the motivational force of individualism-collectivism related values, which are at the origin of alternative collectivist and individualistic paths towards status improvement in unequal ethnic relations between immigrants and hosts. Thus, collective mobility and culture maintenance are anchored in common conservation values, which reinforce conformity with group norms and cultural traditions. In parallel, individual mobility and culture contact are driven by complementary self-direction and achievement values, stressing self-enhancement and openness to change. To varying degrees, the value profiles of immigrants and hosts alike combine core conservation with openness and achievement values. In light of the functional relations between values, acculturation and mobility in our study, this balancing of individualism and collectivism should enable the coordination of ethnic *and* host cultures, solidarity *and* individual mobility. As the data have shown however, successful integration depends crucially on the more or less harmonious or conflictual character of ethnic relations between immigrants and hosts. On a positive note, the impact of education and gender on values and acculturation strongly suggests that educational opportunities and women's rights are powerful tools to improve cross-cultural understanding in multicultural societies.

CHAPTER TEN

Making maternity care

The consequences of culture for health care systems

RAYMOND DE VRIES, SIRPA WREDE,
EDWIN VAN TEIJLINGEN, CECILIA BENOIT AND
EUGENE DECLERCQ

A man collapses on a golf course outside of Paris; a woman jogging in London experiences shortness of breath and sharp pains in her chest. Both are rushed to local hospitals, diagnosed with heart failure, and wheeled into surgical suites for emergency by-pass operations. Watching these two teams of surgeons at work — one in France, the other in the United Kingdom (UK) — you would be tempted to conclude that cardiology is pretty much the same the world around. The stunning successes of medicine and the speed with which these successes are shared in international medical journals and professional meetings lead us to presume that the science, organization and delivery of health care is essentially identical everywhere in the industrialized world. But — despite the similarities in these two situations — this is decidedly not the case. Payer (1990) has shown that the provision and use of health care services vary markedly between countries with equally sophisticated health care systems. She locates the source of this variation in cultural differences: fascinated with machines that go 'ping', Americans are inclined to rely on technology when ill; true to the romantic tradition of their past, Germans pay undue attention to the heart, blaming a whole assortment of conditions on 'heart insufficiency;' the fine aesthetic tastes of the French lead them to respond to breast cancer with lumpectomies rather than mastectomies; and the British have an odd preoccupation with the bowels.

Our study of the maternity care systems of several countries in Western Europe and North America (see De Vries et al., 2001) convinced us that Payer is right. In fact, obstetric care might be the *best* place to begin analysis of the country-to-country variation in health services, because, unlike cardiology, there *is* great variation in the way different countries organize care at birth:
– in the Netherlands over 30% of births occur at home and midwives attend

the majority of those home births,
- in Finland and the UK midwives attend the majority of births and almost all occur in clinical settings,

[210]
- in the US (United States) nearly all births occur in hospitals under supervision of an obstetrical specialist.

When we began our work together, our natural inclination as sociologists was to look for structural explanations for the variation we discovered — the tradition in the field of medical sociology is to use differences in social structures to explain varied health care delivery systems. But we soon realized that structural explanations were insufficient: they simply push the question back one level. For example, our research uncovered important differences in the power of professional groups to influence health care policy — differences that had significant influence on how maternity care was delivered. Fine and good. But should we stop there? The next question is begging to be asked: Why is it that professional groups in some societies are more powerful? What does this say about a society's ideas about expertise, science, gender, and education? Cultural ideas play a substantial role in the way maternity care gets delivered by setting the stage for health-policy decisions and — in our case — by coloring individual perceptions of a 'proper' birth.

Social scientists have given surprisingly little attention to the influence of culture on health care systems. When sociologists look at the role of culture in health care, they limit their gaze to the place of culture in the encounters between patients and caregivers; only rarely do they look at the consequences of cultural ideas for the structural design of services. This lack of attention to culture is the result of a certain uneasiness with the concept of 'national culture,' a notion that has been misused in the past. Social scientists fear that to posit the existence of national culture oversimplifies complex and competing systems of meaning in a society and ignores the emergent, negotiable, and varied aspects of culture. But to discard the idea of national culture completely diminishes the study of human interaction.

Hofstede (2001) offers an avenue for the exploration of the influence of culture on organizations and social structures. In his study of IBM employees in different nations he demonstrates that the organization of work within the same corporation varies greatly from country to country. In the following pages we build on Hofstede's work, showing the important ways culture shapes the delivery of care at birth. This study, and others like it, are the beginning of a process that will change how health policy analysts think about the way health care systems are created and respond to change, both planned and unplanned.

Diversity in birth practices

To set the stage for our analysis of the role of culture in structuring of maternity care, we begin with a statistical summary of the birth systems of the [211] Netherlands, Finland, the UK and the US — four countries that represent the range of responses to pregnancy and childbirth made by modern health systems. Table 1 and Figure 1 offer a snapshot of maternity care in these countries. We are well aware of the difficulties of comparing statistics on the birth practices of different countries — Declercq and colleagues (2001) point to the problems of equivalence, aggregation and context that attend such comparisons — but the differences represented by these numbers are sufficiently large to affirm substantial variation in the way maternity care is delivered. The Netherlands stands out for its high percentage of home births and low percentage of caesarean section (C-section). The number of C-sections is trending upward in all four countries, but there is great variation in the rates

Table 1: *Comparative maternity related data Finland, the Netherlands, UK, US*

Country	Total Births (000)	IMR (per 1,000 live births)	% Hospital Births	Attendant % Physician	Midwife	Overall Cesarean %
Finland (2001)	56	3.8	99.9	24.5†	75.5†	16.5
Netherlands (1999)	207	5.1	69.2	65.5	34.5	12.9**
United Kingdom (2000)	700*	5.6	97.3	31	69	21.5
United States (2000)	3,935	6.9	99.1	92.3	7.7	24.5***

Note: *1999 ** 2000 ***2001; †The Finnish Birth Register does not collect data that specifies the professional position of the birth attendant. These figures are cautious estimates, in which only normal vaginal births were assumed to be cared by midwives, whereas all other births, including those for which information is missing, were counted for physicians.
Sources: OECD Health Data, 2002 and: Finland: Finnish Birth Register 2002. Netherlands: Roumen, F. & Bouckart, P. (2002) Primaire keizersnede bij stuitligging (Dutch: Primary CS by breech presentation), Medisch Contact 57: 743-56; UK: Thomas, J., Paranjothy, S. (2001) RCOG Clinical Effectiveness Support Unit, National Sentinel Caesarean Section Audit Report, London: RCOG Press; US: Martin J.A., B.E. Hamilton, S.J. Ventura, F. Menacker and M.M. Park. 2002. *Births: Final data for 2000. National Vital Statistics Reports; vol 50 no. 5.* Hyattsville, Maryland: National Center for Health Statistics. Martin J.A. Park M.M., Sutton PD. 2002b *Births: Preliminary data for 2001. National Vital Statistics Reports*; vol 50 no 10. Hyattsville, MD: National Center for Health Statistics.

[212]

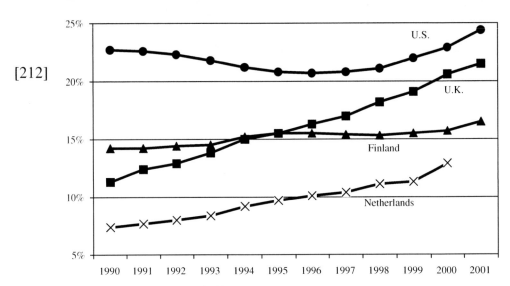

Source: OECD Health Data, 2002
* 2001 rates provisional in each country

Figure 1: *Caesarian section rates in Finland, the Netherlands, U.S., UK,*
1990-2001

themselves and the speed with which they are increasing — in one country, the US the rates actually fell, but then accelerated quickly in the late 1990s. In Finland and the UK midwives attend the overwhelming majority of births, while in the US midwives attend less than ten percent of births. Note too, the differences in infant mortality rates, with the rate in the US nearly double that of the rate in Finland.

When we look at these statistics we are seeing the *end* of the story, the outcomes of systems designed to deliver care to women before, during and after birth. The beginning of the story lies in culture, in the values that generate and support maternity care systems. Health care systems embody a society's values; it is in the structuring of health care delivery that a society moves from ideas to practice. Once created, these structures include the kind and extent of health care made available to citizens. Consider the case at hand: although caregivers in each of these countries have access to the same technologies of birth — tools for monitoring and for aiding in the delivery — the structure of maternity care determines how often and in what ways these technologies are used. Our goal is to illustrate the very real ways cultural values shape the organization of health care systems. Hofstede (2001) and Inglehart et al. (1998) have shown that values vary between societies and that these value differences have important effects on communication patterns and management styles. Our work goes a step further, showing how values get built into social structures — in this case the system of maternity care.

In order to illustrate the role of culture in the structuring of maternity care, [213] we begin with a few words about the way each of these countries organize care at birth. After briefly describing the societal structures that support these different 'ways of birth,' we move on to examine the cultural values that provide the foundation upon which these structures are built. Unlike others who compare cultural ways of working, we do *not* score our countries on a common list of values or 'dimensions;' instead we identify certain *core values* that exert a defining influence on the way maternity care is organized and delivered.

Finland

Maternity care is available under the umbrella of the public health system to all women who are permanently residing in the country. The birth system is a conglomerate of two separate systems: local health centers provide prenatal care and health education while hospitals focus on providing care at birth and prenatal care for women deemed to be at risk.

Three features are central to the organization of maternity care in Finland. First, prenatal care is given a great deal of emphasis in health policy. Care for mothers during pregnancy and the postpartum period is organized together with preventive health care for infants. Located at the local health center, these services are accessible, non-stigmatizing and low-tech, providing a continuum of care for all women during normal pregnancy. The second characteristic draws from another dynamic of Finnish health policy: nearly all Finnish women give birth in hospitals, all of which have access to the latest high-technology equipment. The third characteristic has to do with the screening of pathology during pregnancy. The health centers have the responsibility to screen pregnant women for (potential) pathologies and refer them to hospital-based services. At present, nearly all women are in contact with specialized services during pregnancy, and a growing proportion receives care at hospital outpatient clinics. This trend is shifting the emphasis of maternity care from social support to medical surveillance, from the local health center to the hospital (Hemminki et *al.*, 1990).

Finnish maternity hospitals are not simply centers of high-tech obstetric care, however. Midwives are responsible for providing care during normal birth and take part in all deliveries. They are also involved in prenatal care for women who are referred to the hospital outpatient clinic for monitoring (Viisainen, 2000b). The independent roles of midwives in the clinic are based on the fact that midwives in Finland are traditionally trained to practice without supervision from doctors. Instead, midwives and obstetricians are expected to have a division of labor according to which midwives care for normal pregnancy and birth and refer women with pathological conditions to obstetricians. Midwives receive four-and-a-half years of education in polytechnics, including training for independent practice both in prenatal care and birth care. However, since the 1960s, midwives are trained to deliver babies only in hospital settings, as that has been the official policy for birth care.

In the 1980s, as a result of criticism of hospital birth practices, many 'alternative' practices have been integrated, to some degree, in hospital care. At times, these activities have gained a high profile thanks to the involvement of central figures in the Finnish Federation of Midwives (Marander-Eklund, 2000: 60-71). At the same time, some gynecologists have voiced public criticism of what they label women's search for making their deliveries 'experience travel,' that is, valuing the *experience* of birth over the *safety* of the mother and child (e.g., Ekblad 1998).

The provision of maternity care in Finland must be seen as part of what some call "a universalist welfare state of the Nordic type." Maternity care is one of the core services that the public sector offers (mainly) free of charge to the users. Women pay a fixed daily fee for care at a maternity hospital (currently 26 Euros). Visits to outpatient maternity clinics at hospitals are subject to a fee that patients pay out of pocket (currently 22 Euros). Women can also use the services of a private gynecologist during pregnancy and recover part of the cost through the National Sickness Insurance.

Apart from providing very affordable care for families, the state also provides income-related compensation for work missed due to childcare. *Maternity leave* amounts to 105 workdays, after which a couple can take 158 workdays of *parental leave*. The only condition is that both parents cannot have parental leave at the same time. Fathers are also provided with a leave of 18 workdays, which can be taken simultaneously with the mother's maternity or parental leave. In 1999, six out of ten fathers applied for fatherhood leave, on average for 15 days (National Pensions Office, 2000).

The Netherlands
When a woman in the Netherlands suspects she is pregnant she will make an appointment with either a midwife or her general practitioner (*huisarts,* plural *huisartsen*) for a pregnancy test. The *huisarts* is the hub of the health care system of the Netherlands: nearly everyone in the country is registered with a *huisarts* in their neighborhood who serves as a family doctor and a 'gatekeeper' to other medical services.[1] Only in the most exceptional cases would

---

[1] For more information about the role of the *huisarts* in the Dutch medical system see Van der Velden, 1999 and De Melker, 1997.

a Dutch woman who believes she is pregnant go directly to a gynecologist, and in nearly all of those cases she would do this on the advice of her midwife or *huisarts.*

Dutch social policy directs women expecting a healthy birth into the "first line," or primary care, system. In the first line either a midwife or a *huisarts* will provide all prenatal care and will accompany a woman at birth. Women under the care of the first line are free to choose to have their baby at home or in the hospital. If they prefer a hospital birth, they will have what is known as polyclinic birth — that is, a short stay (less than 24 hours) hospital birth — under the supervision of their primary caregiver.

If complications arise during pregnancy or birth, the primary caregiver will refer a woman to the "second line," or specialist, care. After assessing the complication, the specialist — in this case a gynecologist — may send the woman back to the first line or may keep the woman under his or her care for the duration of her prenatal care and for birth. All births supervised by a gynecologist take place in a hospital; some of these will require complete clinical care, others will take place in the polyclinic and, if all goes well, mother and baby will return home within 24 hours.

Seventy percent of Dutch women begin their prenatal care in the first line (Wiegers, 1997: 26). As a result of referrals made to the second line during the course of prenatal care and labor, midwives care for just under 50% of women at the time of birth, *huisartsen* an additional 10%, and gynecologists just over 40%. Of the women remaining in the care of the first line, about 60% give birth at home, resulting in a home birth rate of just over 30%.

After a birth at home or in the polyclinic, a woman receives postpartum care at home from a specially trained caregiver known as a *kraamverzorgende. Kraamverzorgenden* do everything from household chores, to marketing, to cooking, to watching the condition of mother and baby, to offering instruction in baby care and feeding (see Van Teijlingen, 1990).

Dutch midwives are renowned for the high degree of autonomy they possess. In many other countries the scope of midwifery practice is limited by statute: midwives must work under the direct supervision of a physician. Midwives in the Netherlands are primary caregivers who work independently; they are defined by statute as "medical" — not "paramedical" — practitioners. Midwives are free to diagnose and treat their clients and to decide when a referral to a specialist is necessary. The autonomy of Dutch midwives rests on two things: 1) an extensive and well-regarded education program; and 2) a set of guidelines known as the "Obstetric Indications List."

Dutch midwives are among the best-educated midwives in the world. Interestingly, midwifery education in the Netherlands is not university-based. Would-be midwives complete five years of secondary schooling and then apply to one of the three schools of midwifery, which are part of the Dutch polytechnic education system (similar to Finland). Because the number of applicants far exceeds the number of places available, the schools use a modified 'lottery' system to select those to be admitted: candidates are screened and those who are approved are put into a pool from which names are drawn. The educational program is four years long and includes training in antenatal and postnatal care, normal low-risk deliveries — both at home and in the polyclinic setting, the identification of high-risk situations in the antepartum, intrapartum and postpartum periods, and techniques of scientific research (Benoit et *al.*, 2001).

The autonomy of midwives is further protected by the mandated cooperation that is built into the Dutch system. The "Obstetric Indications List" defines the conditions that require midwives and general practitioners to refer their clients to specialists, creating boundaries around practices that allow midwives and physicians to stake out areas that are uniquely theirs.[2]
New mothers in the Netherlands are entitled to maternity leave of 16 weeks (80 days) with full pay. This leave may begin between six to four weeks before the expected date of birth.

United Kingdom
The tax-funded National Health Service (NHS), established in 1948, provides all UK residents with a comprehensive health service covering nearly every branch of medicine and allied activity, including maternity care, free of charge. The NHS employs most obstetricians, general practitioners and midwives in the UK. Midwives experience long-term occupational security. The overwhelming majority of births are attended by midwives (69% in the late 1990s). In the UK midwives are the professionals most experienced in managing normal childbirth (Jewell et *al.*,1990: 5). Midwives were traditionally trained as nurses first before specializing in midwifery. Today, training takes place at 'midwifery colleges' that became integrated into the British university system in the mid-1990s (Benoit et *al.*, 2001: 155). The move to university-based education has opened up opportunities for 'direct-entry' midwifery, that is, entry into the profession without first completing nursing training.

Antenatal care in the UK is provided separately by midwives, GPs and/or obstetricians or in a "shared care" arrangement between midwives and obstetricians. Midwives mainly deliver antenatal education. Recent policy recommendations regarding antenatal education now include a general health / preventative role (SIGN, 2002). Some British women also attend and pay for antenatal classes organized by a non-statutory (i.e. voluntary) organization,

---

[2] See Riteco and Hingstman (1991) for a complete history of the Obstetric Indications List.

the National Childbirth Trust (NCT). The latter is generally seen as an organization catering to middle-class and more educated women (Kent, 2000: 27), while some obstetricians (and midwives) regard it as breeding ground for demanding patients.

[217]

Although the UK once had a policy of striving towards 100% hospital births in the 1970s and 1980s, currently about 2.6% of all births take place at home. However, some localities have much higher home birth rates. At the same time C-section rates are on the rise in the UK: the National Sentinel Caesarean Section Audit Report, published by the Royal Academy of Obstetricians and Gynecologists, found C-section rates of 24.2% in London and Wales and 24.8% on the Channel Islands and an overall rate is 21.5% (RCOG Clinical Effectiveness Unit, 2001).

Most women stay in hospital for a relatively short period after giving birth. In England in 1981 the average stay in hospital was over five days, in 1991 hospital stay had dropped to just over three days and by 1999 women stayed on average just over two days after giving birth (Office for National Statistics, 2001). In general, if the birth takes place without complications, most women will be home with their newborn baby within 36 to 48 hours. Postpartum care consists of a number of 'short' home visits for up to eight days after the delivery from a community midwife, who checks the baby's cord, advises on breast-feeding, and the like. Usually around the 10th day the midwife conducts a final check and the mother is transferred to the care of the health visitor. However, unlike in the Netherlands, no practical help is provided to the British woman at home. Instead, she is dependent on her partner, friends and family (Price, 1990). The NCT has some 500 breast-feeding counselors; these volunteers have received an eighteen-month training course in their spare time (Van Teijlingen, 1994: 129).

The minimum legal period of maternity leave in the UK as of April 2003 has been set at 26 weeks paid maternity leave (6 weeks at 90% of salary and 20 weeks at €160 per week). Fathers now have the right to two weeks' paid paternity leave at the rate of €160 per week. Currently, many organizations and companies separately offer 18 weeks maternity leave at full pay.

United States

The term 'maternity care system' is a misnomer in the US since the fragmented, privatized set of services that characterizes its maternity care belies any sense of national organization. The 'system' is in reality a specialist-dominated process that places great emphasis on medical intervention and reliance on technology. The result is that the US is the best country in the world in which to give birth to an infant with compromised health, because medical services are structured to save lives in extreme cases. Unfortunately, this resource intensive approach comes at a cost — a lack of attention to basic primary care for women and by far the highest infant mortality among the countries studied here (Table 1).

[218]

The nature of maternity care a mother receives in the US is primarily dictated by local hospital and provider policy. To a lesser extent state governments — through their regulatory processes, publicly funded insurance for the poor (Medicaid) programs and, occasionally, Departments of Public Health — also play a role, but typically defer to specialist providers on matters of practice. From time to time funders, primarily large private insurers, try to shape practice, as do national organizations and professional associations (ACOG, 2000). The court system, through malpractice suits, also influences practice. There are some limited consumer movements but they tend not to focus on maternity care; instead, their focus is chiefly on reproductive health policy, primarily related to abortion.

As this description suggests, no one person, agency or organization is in charge of the delivery of maternity care in the US. The dominance at the local private level is manifested through formal actions, most notably the granting or denial of practice privileges at local hospitals, and informal behaviors such as the failure to provide referrals or backup to uncooperative colleagues.

The lack of universal health care coverage in the US has a variety if implications for maternity care. A patchwork system of payment leaves multiple gaps in services resulting in unusually large numbers of women receiving little or no prenatal care. For example, in 2001 16.6% of mothers began prenatal care after the first trimester and 3.8% received no care or began in the third trimester (Martin et al., 2002); the infant mortality rate for births to mothers who received no prenatal care was five times the national average. (Mathews et al., 2002).

Since the government, through its Medicaid system, pays for a substantial proportion of all births in the US, it should presumably be able to influence practice; however, the Medicaid system rarely focuses on maternity care issues. In theory, private insurers can shape practice, but after a failed attempt to discourage the growth of C-sections in the early 1990s — through payment practices such as equalizing payments to obstetricians for vaginal and caesarean births and encouraging the use of vaginal birth after caesareans (VBACs) — their efforts have turned to potential savings in other "cost centers."

Obstetricians dominate maternity care in the US. How did they come to such control? In part because of a commitment they made to mothers in the past wherein they provided not only continuity of care, a common feature in European systems, but continuity of caregiver as well. The result was tremendous loyalty from mothers to those doctors who would guarantee they'd be there for a birth at any time of day or night. As that system has evolved to group practices to allow more freedom to obstetrician's personal lives, that loyalty has waned. This decline of loyalty, an almost nonexistent regulatory system, and the lack of universal coverage combine to encourage malpractice suits. These lawsuits can result in awards in the millions of dollars (in part because those resources may be necessary to pay for a lifetime of care for a disabled child) encouraging obstetricians to practice in a more interventionist fashion (Collins, 2000).

[219]

Why don't women rebel against a system so ready to intervene during birth? By most accounts they don't because they are satisfied with the care they are currently receiving. Many women believe that this more interventionist style of birth can not only scientifically free them from childbirth pain, but also represents the highest quality care, typified by the rise in popularity of epidurals, used in an estimated 63% of births in the US, (Declercq, 2002). This technology provides mothers with an apparent magic bullet that can allow them to be 'awake and aware' during labor and birth, but not have to experience highly anticipated pain. Childbirth education, once the source of a movement to change birth, has been largely co-opted by institutions with virtually all classes now taught in hospitals and doctors' offices. Finally, interest group efforts to change maternity care in the US are severely hampered by the fragmentation described above. Simply put, it is hard to lobby for change when there is no place to lobby. The result is a system that reinforces it specialist domination, while providing interventionist maternity care attuned to the needs of women generally satisfied with the care they receive.

The US provides no guaranteed system of paid maternity or paternity leave, though such leave is a common benefit for those privately employed by large firms.

Sources of variation in maternity care

These descriptions show that the differences in the management and outcomes of birth are no accident. They are generated by maternity care systems that are organized in very different ways. Given that the materials of obstetrics are essentially identical in these countries, why are they deployed so differently? The first place sociologists look to explain cross-national differences is *not* culture, but social structures. Sociologists are trained to do their explaining by using the structural features of society — economic, political, occupational, educational structures and the like. These structures are undeniably important, but our research forces us to push the question further: why have different countries created the different structures that sustain these greatly varied ways of delivering maternity care? Following Hofstede's (2001) lead, we look to culture for an answer to that question. After a brief consideration of the social structures relevant to maternity care, we examine the cultural sources of structural differences.

[220]

Social structures
Structural explanations of social phenomena typically revolve around *social* structures, but on occasion sociologists also pay attention to geography, to the *physical* structure of a country. In our case, geography is particularly important. Often the persistence of home birth in the Netherlands and its disappearance elsewhere is explained with reference to its unique geography: a small, flat, densely populated country — with over 16 million inhabitants. This feature distinguishes the Netherlands from our other examples — Finland, the US and the UK — all of which occupy a much larger geographical space made up of dense urban centers and vast, scarcely-populated areas. Long distances between residents in these latter countries create obstacles for organizing accessible services, obstacles that are not present in the Netherlands.

Political structures also play a role in the forming of maternity care systems.[3] In Finland, the Netherlands, and the UK maternity care is part of a polity that sees health care as a governmental responsibility. This not only enhances the accessibility of care, it also creates more rational policy. For example, these three countries, like many countries in Europe, have far greater numbers of midwives than gynecologist/obstetricians — a policy decision based on the premise that the majority of births proceed normally and do not require specialist care. The situation in the US is the opposite: obstetricians outnumber midwives by a ratio of nearly six to one. In the US the government provides almost no oversight of the health care system, giving professional groups, managed care companies, and hospital conglomerates a good deal of control. Furthermore, the two-party system in the US, together with few restrictions on lobbying, gives the more powerful professions and corporations great influence over the regulations that *do* exist.

Educational systems, and the consequent structure of the professions, also play a part in the way maternity systems operate. The *way* future caregivers are trained and the relative *number*s of caregivers trained have impor-

---

[3] Political differences are also reflected in the very different kinds of political party and electoral systems. See Swank (2002) and Olsen (2002) for recent research demonstrating the cross-national differences.

tant implications for care at birth. As noted above, in most European countries the ratio of midwives to obstetricians/obstetricians favors midwives — it is not unusual to have four midwives for every gynecologist. In the US the ratio is reversed; obstetricians outnumber midwives six to one and physician attended births outnumber midwife-attended births nine to one. The content of professional training also has an important effect on care systems. Gynecologists in Finland, the Netherlands and the UK are taught to work in a partnership with midwives. In most states in the U.S., nurse-midwives, who account for 95% of the midwife attended births (Martin et *al.*, 2002), must work under the supervision of an obstetrician. [221]

Most sociologists would end their explanation of the differences in birth systems here, satisfied that the observed variation is best understood as the result of differences in health systems, geography, political structure and educational programs. But there is something unsatisfactory about stopping with structural explanations — a thorough social scientist is forced to ask: why have these societies created these different structures? The only way to answer this question is to look to culture, to the values that support the structures of society.

Culture

Although some social scientists, especially anthropologists, are wary of the notion of national culture, Hofstede (2001) demonstrated that there are real and significant differences between the behavior of citizens of different nations. Our study shows that the varied forms of maternity care are the result of these same cultural differences; cultural differences explain the variation in birth care *and* the societal structures that sustain this variation. In Hofstede's (2001: 1-5) terms we examine how the "mental programming" of a nation's citizens shape maternity care systems, which in turn reinforce and extend that same mental programming.

We begin our analysis with a look at the way cultural ideas influence the way maternity care is conceived and organized and then move on to look at the way culture supports the larger social structures that are implicated in care at birth. In our analysis we do not measure how these four societies differ in the extent to which they subscribe to a certain common set of values; rather we identify core values in each society, commonly shared values that are built into maternity care systems.

Values that support maternity policy

The Netherlands[4]

Of the four countries we are considering, the Netherlands has the most peculiar birth system. While Finland, the UK and the Netherlands all give midwives a significant role in pregnancy and birth, the Dutch are alone in their continued support for birth at home. What caused the Dutch to preserve this distinct option in birth care that most other countries labeled 'old-fashioned' or dangerous over half a century ago?

Dutch views of the 'family' and of the role of women in the family are distinctive. The Dutch were the first among modern nations to experience the 'nuclearization' of the family — according to van Daalen (1993, 1988) the Dutch family nuclearized in the late 17th and early 18th centuries, earlier than the other nations of continental Europe. This peculiarity of Dutch family history is confirmed in their language. Dutch is the only Germanic language with a unique word for the nuclear family: *gezin*. Furthermore, as the wives of farmers, fishers and traders — the primary occupations in the Netherlands — Dutch women have been tied, both economically and ideologically, to home and family. The strong identification of femininity with home and with the *gezin* is reflected in their historically high fertility rates and their low rates of participation in paid labor (Pott-Buter, 1993).

These unique features of Dutch family life create and maintain a preference for home birth. Van Daalen (1988) explains how the early nuclearization of the family hindered the hospitalization of birth. She points out that in other European countries the nuclearization of the family occurred simultaneously with industrialization and was marked by the increasing use of professional help for events once attended by family members: birth, sickness and death. Having nuclearized earlier, the Dutch family resisted the institutionalization of birth and death (Van Daalen, 1988: 432):

Institutional birth [which was becoming popular in the early nineteenth century] did not fit well in Dutch society... in 1826, the Rotterdam city council declared the 'national character' to be in opposition to the establishment of maternity clinics.

... Dutch family life was organized in a way we call 'modern,' far before the emergence of professional groups and institutions that, in the last 100 years, have become closely involved with the cares and concerns of the modern family and that...have undermined the autonomy of these families. Could it

---

[4] See DeVries, 2004 for an extended discussion of the cultural and structural supports for maternity care policy in the Netherlands.

be that the Dutch have developed a family culture that offers more possibilities to resist such professional interference?

Many other observers have commented on how the distinctive ideas about the family found in the Netherlands — have shaped the character of Dutch society and its social policies (e.g., Goudsblom, 1967: 128-139). Van Daalen (1988: 433-434) claims that this tradition is responsible for the slow movement of married women into the paid labor force and limited use to professional childcare and for the less-than-generous policies for parental leave.

[223]

Domestic confinements also fit well with Dutch ideas about home. According to Rybcinski (1986), the Dutch are responsible for our current notions of 'home' as a place of retreat for the nuclear family. The Dutch were the first to develop single-family residences — small, tidy, well-lit homes — ideally suited for the *gezin*. The importance of the nuclear family, coupled with the domestic role of women and the tidiness of their homes, made home the logical place for birth. When you ask Dutch women and men why they prefer birth at home to birth in the hospital they will often reply that home birth is more *gezellig*. *Gezelligheid* is often translated as 'coziness,' but in fact there is no single English word that captures the full meaning of the term. Cozy comes close, but *gezellig* also implies warmth, affection, contentment, enjoyment, happiness, sociability, snugness and security. For the Dutch, birth at home is *gezellig* in a way birth in the hospital can never be. Over 50 years ago a Dutch gynecologist summarized the link between birth care in the Netherlands and Dutch ideas about home and family. Writing in the journal of the association of Dutch midwives, Rottinghuis (1947) noted: "Birth is a family event (*gezinsgebeuren*) and, given the high value placed on the family (*gezin*) in the Netherlands, it must occur in that context" (quoted in van Daalen, 1988: 432-433).

Home birth is further supported by Dutch ideas about medicine, science and Dutch notions of 'thriftiness." The Dutch are not quick to seek medical solutions to bodily problems, a fact evidenced by their low use of medications (see van Andel and Brinkman, 1997: 152). There is some evidence to suggest that the Dutch have a more stoic approach to pain — until recently Dutch dentists were unlikely to offer anesthetics for the filling of teeth and the Dutch Red Cross does not offer local anesthetics before drawing blood for donations. This attitude toward pain is evident at birth. A comparative study of women giving birth in the hospital in Iowa (US) and Nijmegen (the Netherlands) found national differences in expectations of labor pain:

Iowa women, in general, expected labor to be more painful than did Dutch patients, and further anticipated that they would receive medication for labor pain. In virtually the same proportion, Iowa women did receive pain medication. By contrast, women in Nijmegen did not expect labor to be as painful, tended not to anticipate receiving analgesia, and usually did not receive any (Senden et *al.,* 1988: 542).

Dutch public policy is characterized by very rationalist ideas about the use of science in the formation of public policy, leading to the avoidance of moral-istic stances and to an institutionalized willingness to experiment with new approaches, testing their efficacy and efficiency. This frame of mind shapes Dutch policy on soft drugs, prostitution, euthanasia and the location of births. The government has funded many studies to examine the safety, cost, and desirability of home births and has made policy decisions based on those studies (see, for example, Eskes, 1989; Wiegers, 1997). The most recent of these studies openly acknowledges that the study was initiated because of a concern that "the steadily decreasing number of home births...threatened to diminish the home birth rate to a level where home birth would no longer be a viable option [and that] the increasing number of hospital births would lead to unnecessary medicalization of pregnancy and childbirth...." (Wiegers, 1997: 1). Visible in these concerns is another feature of Dutch culture, *zuinigheid* or thriftiness, which inclines the Dutch to preserve home birth as a less expensive option in maternity care.

Dutch ideas about heroes also seep into maternity care policies. The Dutch are disinclined to celebrate the heroic, a fact that is evidenced by the absence of large monuments in Dutch cities. Dutch children are still reminded, "*Doe maar gewoon, dan doe je gek genoeg*" ("Just behave normally, that is crazy enough"), and "*Kom niet boven het maaiveld*" ("Don't stick out above the mown field," implying that if you do, you might get your head cut off). Gyne-cology reflects this Dutch tendency to downplay the heroic. In marked contrast to obstetricians in the US — who are *inclined* to heroic interventions, rescuing a laboring woman from protracted pain and life-threatening complications with surgery (episiotomies, forceps, and C-sections) or medications — gyne-cologists in the Netherlands shun the role of hero. During interviews several Dutch gynecologists went out of their way to mention that they do not take a heroic approach to birth. The following is typical (from De Vries, 2004):

Why is the Dutch maternity system so different?

> I think maybe it has a lot to do with the history of our country. We always have been very individual, self-assured, emancipated people; a little bit mistrusting anyone...including doctors. I always say hospitals are dangerous...

> And maybe it has to do with the character of the people, that the doctors think with a little bit of relativity about their own duties and possibilities. We are not so much heroes, we do our best. That's the difference...

[When you play the hero] you don't let [your patients] grow. [You should] just play your role in a very simple way...You're there, like a tiger sleeping in the sun, I sometimes say. With just one eye open to do the correct thing in the right time. Just a moment, and then you sleep again.

[225]

Finland

Health policy in Finland reflects a long tradition of solving perceived social problems through public policy. The process of hospitalizing birth reflects this strategy. When in the 1930s, maternal and infant mortality became defined as indicators of social problems, many policymakers, including women politicians in the Parliament, saw hospitalization of birth as a solution to these problems (Wrede et *al.*, 2001). Rapid implementation of the policy resulted in the near total hospitalization of birth in the mid-1960s. However, parallel to the building of hospital maternity units, the Government also invested in a comprehensive system of community-based centers for prenatal care and children's health care (Wrede, 2001).

At present, the comprehensive maternal health services still have a solid basis in the local primary health centers and in public hospitals, even though private services do exist. Since the 1960s, a central aim of Finnish health policy in general has been to strengthen primary care (Lehto & Blomster, 1999). This has not resulted in a change of policy concerning hospital birth. There remains — in maternity care and elsewhere — a strong belief in technical solutions. This is reflected in what has been called the "norm of universal hospital birth care" (Viisainen, 2000a). Home birth is considered to create a risk for both health care providers and parents. The norm of hospital birth is enforced by the national health insurance board that refuses compensation for private midwifery care at home because of the risks associated with home birth (Viisainen, 2000a: 795-796).

Maternity policy is part of a Finnish welfare state that emphasizes equality and support for the family. Since the 1960s, the rhetoric of public policy has emphasized the need to make the roles of women and men in childrearing more equal (Vuori, 2001). In the Finnish context, the equality-driven emphasis on the shared responsibility of parents for their children appears to have suppressed the rhetoric of woman-centeredness found in maternity care policies elsewhere in Western countries (Wrede, 2001). This is in line with the strategy of the Finnish women's movement to seek cooperation and avoid confrontations that may lead to the undermining of issues that only concern women (Bergman, 2002).

Equality between men and women is one of the central values shaping Finnish welfare- state policies. This value must be understood in terms of a larger political culture that seeks to avoid conflict and instead favors the accommodation of diverse, even somewhat conflicting, demands in public policies. The emphasis on equality is often related to the fact that Finnish women have long been a part of the paid labor force. Nowadays women participate in paid work equally often as men. In the post-World War II period, the dual-earner family has become established as the dominant family in Finnish society.

The emphasis on equality has not eliminated the cultural expectation that women should carry the primary responsibility for providing for the health and well-being of the child, a norm institutionalized in health services. The services provided by maternity and child health centers have been characterized as work "for the benefit of children, among women" (Kuronen, 1994). Most health care providers in this type of service, and the majority of doctors, are women. It also points to another important feature of dual-earner families in Finnish welfare society: parenting, and especially mothering, takes place within an institutional matrix of the welfare services that structure the everyday life of families. Central constituents of this institutional matrix are health services, day-care and other social services.

Further evidence of the influence of the value of equality on the Finnish birth system is found in one of the central transformations in birth care: the inclusion of fathers at birth. In the 1970s men were not admitted to the delivery room in many maternity hospitals, but by the 1990s the system began (more or less) to *expect* that men take part and even make themselves useful. Allowing men into the delivery room has been a part of a movement toward a more 'human' birth: most hospitals now offer — and advertise — family rooms, rooming-in, and various alternative birthing practices.

The humanization of birth has not, however, replaced the use of technologies; rather there is an effort to merge elements from both ways of thinking into one practice. Hospital policies tend to give primacy to technologies, especially if the use of technology is associated with avoiding perceived medical risks (Viisainen, 2000b). Using technology in the best interest of the child appears to have a high legitimacy across Finnish society. There is a readiness among both clients and professionals to rely on technologies to manage birth. A recent trend in Finland is the demand, voiced by some women in the media, to be allowed to choose a Caesarean section even when there was no medical reason to do so. It is difficult to say whether this trend will actually increase C-section rates in the future. At present the proportion of planned procedures appears to be holding steady (Stakes, 2002). If compared with the 1-2 % increase in C-sections during the 1990s, the near doubling of vacuum extractions during the 1990s (from 3.2 % to 5.6 % in 2002) appears to be a more worrisome trend (Stakes, 2001, 2002).

An unparalleled use of technology at birth has occurred in connection to pain relief. Even though alternative pain relief practices have become integrated in midwifery care in many hospitals, often on the initiative of midwives, technology seems to offer a favored solution (Viisainen, 2000b). Women activists of many different backgrounds have demanded the right to be freed from labor pain. The central goal for such campaigns has been to guarantee birthing women access to epidural analgesia at hospitals at all times. At present, epidurals are nearly always available on demand. In 2000, they were given to 38.5 % of all women giving birth. Three out four women use some form of medical technology to relieve the pain. The use of nitrous oxide has remained at the same level as in the early 1990s, but the use of epidural and paracervical anesthesia has become increasingly common so that 58.1% of women use one of these methods (Stakes, 2001).

[227]

United Kingdom
Maternity care is an integral part of health care provision in the UK, which is in itself part of the wider government policy-making. Thus if the British government decides to buy more war ships or increase police officers' salaries, less money will be available expenditure on health (unless taxation is increased). It this sense maternity care is always part of a political process. This situation gives rise to pressure groups and stakeholders trying to influence the political agenda. Although, as noted above, midwives are the lead health care practitioners at the majority of births in the UK, local selection criteria for, for example home birth or water births, have traditionally been established by committees dominated by hospital-based obstetricians. One pressure group highlighted this anomaly:

> "Most deliveries in this country are conducted by midwives. Yet maternity care policies have been dominated by obstetricians ... midwives have had to follow clinical policies laid down by the medical staff, even when they felt this was not in the interest of the woman they were caring for" (House of Commons, 1992: xv).

Recent changes in the tone of official reports in Britain (House of Commons 1992; Department of Health, 1993) away from total hospitalization have been influenced by consumer organizations and maternity pressure groups, as well as by the already mentioned changes in national health policies. The types of evidence and the kind of witnesses interviewed differ as between the Short Report (Social Services Committee, 1980) which recommended a 100 per cent hospital delivery rate and the 1992 Winterton Report (House of Commons, 1992). The latter has focused much more on the organizations and individuals critical of the prevalent obstetrical practice. The resulting report touches on far more aspects of the social model, compared to the previous two Parliamentary reports in the 1970s and 1980s (Declercq, 1998).

One of the cultural images of the British from abroad is their apparent necessity of keeping a stiff upper lip. This accounts for the generally stoical conduct of British patients. One is expected to take the treatment without complaining. As Payer (1990: 112) says, "British society appears to have little tolerance for individuals who fail to maintain their self-control." There seems to be a paradox in the relatively high use of pain relief in childbirth "in a country where the people would seem to be stoical about their bodies" (Payer, 1990: 115). The explanation for this phenomenon, according to Payer (1990: 115) is that "the high status of pain relief may not reflect that the British fear pain, but rather that they fear the loss of control that may come with pain. Porter (1990: 192) certainly noted in her study that working-class women seemed to prefer a more technological-assisted/pain-free childbirth.

Keeping a stiff upper lip may also partly explain why maternity services tend to be highly rated in patient satisfaction surveys (see Garcia et al., 1998; Hundley et al., 2000). One further explanation for high satisfaction levels is that in a publicly-funded service, service users might be reluctant to express critical comments about their care (Fitzpatrick & Hopkins, 1983), what Øvretveit (1992) referred to as 'gratitude bias'.

United States
The hospital-based, technologically driven system of birth care found in the US reflects the generally shared values of that country. In the US home birth began to disappear in the 1920s and was nearly eliminated by the 1960s; the move away from home and toward the hospital was driven by:

- the rise of hospitals as centers of scientific care;
- new technologies for birth available only in the hospital including the advent of 'twilight sleep,' which promised freedom from the pain of childbirth;
- the elimination of midwifery (see Declercq et al., 2001).

These factors reflect several features of American culture. American attitudes about home, for example, prevent it from being seen as the appropriate place for birth. In the early to mid-1900s the 'modern' woman sought out physician care in the hospital as the clean, technologically sophisticated, modern way to give birth; only 'ignorant' and 'dirty' immigrant women chose to give birth at home. As this attitude became more prevalent, immigrant women also aspired to hospital birth, in their case as a mark of their assimilation into American culture (see Borst, 1995). In modern, mobile America homes are not so much the center of family life as they were stepping stones to a better life, symbols of one's attainments, and investments for the future (see Veblen, 1953).

There is also a certain amount of xenophobia in the effort to eliminate midwives, who were often associated with the 'backward ways' of immigrant groups — true Americans were called on to leave the ways of the 'old country' behind and to adopt the modern ways of the 'new world.' An important value in this world was faith in technology. As a society born in the midst of the industrial revolution, Americans are fascinated with technology, to the point that they tend to see the body as a machine. Payer (1990) attributes the popularity of this metaphor to the American fascination with the automobile, and indeed, she cites how-to books that suggest that in order to care for their health Americans must not 'drive to fast,' and should use the correct 'fuel.'

[229]

America is a society that celebrates the heroic and favors aggressive approaches to its problems, values often linked to its frontier past, where aggressiveness and heroism were necessary for survival. Payer (1990) sees these values and the American celebration of technology as underlying causes for the widespread use of episiotomy at birth and for the extremely high rates of C-section.

The highly medicalized birth that is typical in the US does seem contrary to another American value — the admiration of simple, rational approaches to problems and policies. Seen in this light the American way of birth seems at odds with its own values: there are billions of dollars to be saved by reducing the many technological interventions in birth — interventions that seem completely unnecessary when looked at in comparison to other countries. In this case, however, the value on rational policy is trumped by America's extreme emphasis on individuality, as noted by sociologists since the De Tocqueville's *Democracy in America* (published in 1830). How does this value pertain to birth? First, Americans dislike the idea of a government mandated policy on birth; most American women would be uncomfortable with the Dutch limits on access to specialist care for women expecting a low-risk birth. Second, as both de Tocqueville and Riesman (1952) pointed out, extreme individualism allows for easy manipulation of the citizenry. Cut free from traditions, left on their own, Americans are susceptible to advertising and authority; in Riesman's terms, Americans are 'other-directed,' they look to each other when deciding what is the best thing to do. In the absence of a countervailing tradition, women must rely on the expert advice of physicians, advice that is clouded by professional interests and socialization.

Values that sustain political arrangements

[230]

The link between cultural ideas and health systems is mediated by the political structure of each country. Here too we can explore the cultural values that support existing structures. The most striking difference between the US and the countries of Europe is a higher level of solidarity in the democracies of Europe. The health policies of Finland, the UK and the Netherlands — all of which include a guaranteed basic package of benefits, controls on the price/cost of services, and limited access to certain services — give evidence of a cultural notion of 'solidarity' where all members of society feel a responsibility for the care of all others. Health policy in the US is more individualistic and market-driven. The political culture in Finland is dominated by negotiations and often complex compromises rather than confrontations. Negotiating has also been a strategy for the Finnish women's movement, reflected in creation of what has sometimes been termed 'state feminism'. Dutch solidarity is often linked to the 'polder model' of economic and social organization — a model that takes its name from the kind of cooperation needed to keep the polders from flooding. The polder model — sometimes referred to as the *overlegeconomie* (the consultation economy) — is characterized by ongoing and constructive dialogue between employers, unions and the government and is credited for reducing government debt, lowering the overall tax burden, and strengthening the market economy. In the US, there is not even a forum of decision-makers where one could go to negotiate and consult in the manner found in the Netherlands, Finland or the UK.

An attitude of solidarity allows citizens to see their own health care in the context of the larger system ("if I demand specialist care for my normal birth it will drive the cost of health care up and reduce access for others") and promotes cooperation between different caregivers in the health care (and maternity care) system — attitudes that are noticeably absent in the US.

Conclusion

Having identified cultural ideas that lie behind the organization of maternity care, it is fair to ask how much explaining we can we ask these ideas to do. At least one caveat is in order: this portrayal of the role of culture in the shaping care at birth does not necessarily imply that all women in each of these societies share identical views of family, home, medicine and the like. Indeed, all four societies are increasingly multicultural, and, as Hofstede (2001: 6) notes, "most people simultaneously hold several conflicting values." In each of these countries, however, the majority of policy-makers are steeped in the traditional ideas of the national culture and the organization of maternity care bears the marks of that culture.

The differences we discovered between maternity care systems — and our explanation of those differences — fit well with the Hofstede's (2001) evidence on the dimensions of national culture. It is no surprise that Finland and the Netherlands score much lower on the 'masculinity index'[5] and lower on the 'individualism index' than the United States and the United Kingdom. Indeed, with regard to the former index, Hofstede (2001: 280) links cultural ideas about masculinity and femininity to the distribution of gender roles at birth:

[231]

> "Men must be more concerned with economic and other achievements and women must be more concerned with taking care of people in general and children in particular. It is not difficult to see how this pattern fits the biological sex roles: Women first bear children and then breast-feed them, so they must stay with them.

Our work has important implications for health policy makers, who often proceed as if structural features are all that matter. Health care reformers believe that with enough tinkering they will find the perfect balance of incentives and disincentives to create and affordable and just way of delivering health care. As we have shown, health care reform must attend to the cultural ideas that sustain health systems.

What would culturally informed health care reform look like? Social scientists of all stripes will agree that, although culture changes, it is extremely difficult, if not impossible, to engineer that change. Thus, the challenge of employing cultural ideas in health policy work is to 1) identify the relevant cultural assumptions of the society in which a reform is proposed and 2) to find a way to link the proposed reform to some commonly held value. Analysis of any society will uncover a plethora of values, many of which contradict others. Bringing these contradictions to the surface is much preferred to ignoring them and allowing a vague uneasiness and confusion to be exploited by the well-placed advertising of vested interests. Culturally informed health reformers must look for models of successful reform both at home and abroad and must attempt to understand how these reforms fit with the values of the host culture.

Admittedly, culture is not *the* explanatory variable: it is shaped by the structures of society even as it shapes those structures. The difficulty of measuring culture and parsing out its influence, however, should not stop us from examining the important ways it shapes health care systems. Health reform will not succeed until cultural analysis becomes a routine part of health policy work.

---

[5] In his Masculinity Index for fifty countries and three regions Great Britain has a shared 9th/10th place, the US is 15th, and at "the extreme feminine pole are the four Nordic countries and the Netherlands" (Hofstede, 2001: 285).

CHAPTER ELEVEN

The cultural relativity of employee empowerment

A comparative study in the European hotel industry

ANTONIOS K. KLIDAS

Several decades after the publication of Culture's Consequences and as the authors in this book show, the message of cultural diversity is today not as revolutionary as it was then. Despite the strong converging forces of globalization there is increasing consensus that cultures shape societies and organizations. Social sciences need to re-address the question of the universality of management theories and practices. This chapter looks into employee empowerment, for long an alleged panacea for organizations, yet only sporadically considered from a cross-cultural perspective. Considering Hofstede's work on cultures and the findings of a comparative study[1] in the hotels of a major American international company in seven European countries, it is argued that the empowerment doctrine is the cultural product of American culture and its propositions are not necessarily embraced in different cultural contexts.

Introduction

Since the 1980s industry and academia have shown growing interest in the notion of employee empowerment. Empowerment is generally seen in the management literature as the process of delegating or decentralizing decision-making power (Conger & Kanungo, 1988). The concept has become

[1] The study was conducted following funding from the European Commission in the context of the Training and Mobility of Researchers program, which is part of the Marie Curie Fellowships. For this I would like to express my grateful thanks to the European Commission and to the Department of Leisure Studies at Tilburg University in the Netherlands, which hosted the research project. I am also grateful to Prof. Theo Beckers and Dr. Greg Richards who have supervised the research.

especially important for industries, such as services and hospitality, where 'frontline' employees need the authority to respond promptly to the individual needs of the increasingly demanding consumer and to unpredictable service situations (Hartline & Ferrell, 1999).

Despite growing internationalization of business the vast majority of published literature on empowerment maintains an Anglo-Saxon cultural perspective and has barely addressed the implications of applying the concept in an international and multicultural context. As a result, advocates of empowerment propose radical changes in the form of organization (e.g. hierarchical structure) and in the management style and make arbitrary assertions that employees will invariably embrace empowerment. However, according to Hofstede's (1991) work on national cultures the form of management style and organization and even what constitutes a supreme motivator for workers are to a significant degree specific to the cultural context of each country. A handful of authors who have addressed the notion of empowerment from a cross-cultural perspective clearly challenge the universal validity of the propositions of the empowerment doctrine (Hoppe, 1990; Durcan & Kirkbride, 1994).

In this chapter I address the problem of the cultural relativity of employee empowerment on the basis of the work of Hofstede on national cultures. Hofstede's "monumental research on work values" is generally considered among "the most influential", which "has provided one of the few empirically and conceptually based sets of cultural dimensions on which contemporary cultures or nations can be arrayed" (Schwartz, 1994: 86). It is, however, the implications of these cultural dimensions for management and organizations that make it an ideal, as much as a valid framework, for the examination of empowerment from a cross-cultural perspective.

Then, I present the findings of a cross-cultural comparative research, which was conducted in the European hotel industry in order to examine whether the industry reality confirmed the theoretical considerations. Lastly, I report the main conclusions of this study and draw some implications for management. But first it is important to define employee empowerment in the context of services and hospitality.

Empowerment defined

Despite the conceptual ambiguities accompanying employee empowerment in the management literature (Wilkinson, 2001), there seems to be some unanimity regarding the underlying notions of the concept in services and hospitality. There, most of the accounts of empowerment interpret the term as delegation of decision-making authority and responsibility (e.g., Maxwell,

1997) and focus predominantly on customer-contact or frontline employees and the employee-guest encounter (e.g., Bowen & Lawler, 1992). The common goal in all these accounts is the control and enhancement of service quality and customer satisfaction at the point of production of service, as employees are able to meet and respond promptly to unpredictable service situations according to their judgment, without reference to an interminable hierarchy (Baum, 1995). Empowerment is therefore defined here as *"the notion of devolving decision-making authority and responsibility to frontline employees for control and enhancement of service quality and customer satisfaction during service delivery"* (Klidas, 2001: 34-35).[2] It is the 'cultural relativity' of empowerment as specifically defined above that I address in the remaining of this chapter.

The theory of Hofstede on national cultures

Before proceeding to the main issues of concern of this chapter it is necessary to clarify the meaning of the term 'culture'. In social anthropology it is more or less agreed that the core of culture is formed by deeply embedded values, which are shared by the members of large (sub-) populations (Drenth & Groenendijk, 1998). Values are instilled in individuals implicitly and unconsciously in early childhood and are therefore very difficult to change in the course of one's life (Hofstede, 1991). In an analogy of the way computers are programmed, values are instilled in individuals in a similar way that software is installed on computers (ibid.). Extending this analogy with the programming of computers, Hofstede (1991: 5) defines culture as "the collective programming of the mind which distinguishes the members of one group or category of people from another". Therefore, the question posed here is whether distinct patterns or dimensions of this collective programming of the mind may influence employee empowerment across different categories of people.

The theory of Hofstede on national cultures resulted from an internation-

---

[2] I do want to emphasize, however, that this definition represents a restrictive conceptualization of the term 'empowerment' and is not entirely consistent with its etymological properties. There is, for example, no justification stemming from the etymology of the term 'empowerment' that the transfer of power should exclusively aspire to the control or enhancement of product or service quality, as is predominantly the case in the management literature. I maintain, however, my focus on this 'restrictive' conceptualization of empowerment for reasons of consistency with the overwhelming majority of literature on empowerment in services. (For an extensive review and analysis regarding the meaning of empowerment see Klidas, 2001.)

al survey conducted between 1967 and 1973 among the employees in the subsidiaries of IBM in 72 countries (Hofstede, 1998). The research resulted in the identification of four dimensions of national cultures, which "point to four basic problems every society has to solve in its own way: inequality, togetherness, gender roles, and dealing with the unknown" (Hofstede, 1998: 28). He has named respectively these dimensions power distance, individualism-collectivism, masculinity-femininity, and uncertainty avoidance. Of interest for the present study are the dimensions of power distance and uncertainty avoidance[3], which Hofstede has identified as the dimensions that shape organizations. Indeed, Drenth and Groenendijk (1998) in their review of comparative studies on organizations across countries have concluded that organizations are "repeatedly" found to differ on these two dimensions.

Power distance is defined as "the extent to which the less powerful members of institutions and organizations within a country expect and accept that power is distributed unequally" (Hofstede, 1991: 28). Power distance reflects, among others, the degree to which individuals in various cultures prefer to be managed in a directive or a participative style. Uncertainty avoidance is defined as "the extent to which the members of a culture feel threatened by uncertain or unknown situations" (Hofstede, 1991: 113) and reflects individuals' emotional need for rules and formal structure.

The cultural relativity of the empowerment doctrine

The cultural relativity of empowerment becomes evident if one considers the specific propositions of the "empowerment doctrine" from a cultural perspective. These propositions echo culturally specific beliefs about the "ideal" leadership style and the effective form of organization and appeal to culture-specific motivational patterns of employee behavior. In what follows, the specific propositions of the empowerment doctrine about leadership, organization and motivation and their cultural relativity on the basis of Hofstede's dimensions of power distance and uncertainty avoidance are elaborated (Table 1).

[235]

---

[3] The dimensions of masculinity-femininity and individualism-collectivism also raise implications for the implementation of empowerment across cultures — although to my view not to a clear direction — and should be considered in the future. Obviously, the examination of the cultural relativity of empowerment does not need to be confined to the theory of Hofstede and could consider as well other frameworks proposed for the study of cultures (e.g., Inglehart, 1997; Schwartz, 1994).

Table 1: *The cultural relativity of the empowerment doctrine*

	Propositions	Cultural Opportunities	Cultural Barriers
Organization	Flat structure	Small PD	Large PD
	Low centralization	Small PD	Large PD
	Low formalization	Weak UA	Strong UA
Leadership	Employees demand participation	Small PD	Large PD
	Employees wilfully accept responsibility	Small PD/ Weak UA	Large PD/ Strong UA
	Employees independent in thinking and acting	Weak UA	Strong UA
	Leaders share power	Small PD	Large PD
	Leaders delegate	Small PD/ Weak UA	Large PD/ Strong UA
Motivation	Self-actualization as top motivator	Weak UA	Strong UA
	Satisfaction from increased autonomy, responsibility and self-direction	Weak UA	Strong UA
Empowered behaviour	Creativity and innovative behaviour	Weak UA	Strong UA
	Risk taking (decision-making, initiative)	Weak UA	Strong UA
	Rule-breaking	Weak UA	Strong UA

Leadership

The central proposition in the notion of empowerment is that decision-making authority should be delegated to frontline employees at the lower level of organizational hierarchy, so as to enable them to respond immediately to customer requests, problems and needs. What appears to be at first glance merely a different approach of managing the service encounter, in essence represents a drastic change in the work roles of both managers and subordinates. The former are required to shift from commanding and controlling to delegating and trusting and the latter from following instructions and rules to making their own decisions and even breaking the rules if this is necessary. In short, the empowerment doctrine promotes a shift in the leadership style and in particular the abandonment of traditional autocratic and directive leadership in favor of democratic and participative leadership (Jones, Taylor & Nickson, 1997; Lashley, 1997).

The proposed leadership style carries undoubtedly the typical characteristics of the leadership phenomenon as perceived in the United States, "with its cultural emphasis on individualism, action rather than contemplation, pragmatism, and egalitarianism" (Bass, 1990: 769). Just like in most leadership theories developed in the U.S., the proposed leadership style advocates participation of subordinates in the decision-making process following the initiative of the manager (Hofstede, 1980b). However, in countries with smaller power distance than the United States (i.e. Sweden, Norway, Germany, Israel), "there is considerable sympathy for models of management in which even the initiatives are taken by the subordinates (forms of industrial democracy) and with which there's little sympathy in the United States" (Hofstede, 1980b: 57). Accordingly, there may be little sympathy for participative or democratic leadership styles in less egalitarian cultures than the United States.

[237]

In particular, the proposed shift in the leadership philosophy may not be possible in large power distance cultures, where "superiors and subordinates consider each other as existentially unequal" (Hofstede, 1991: 35). This 'existential inequality' is expressed in analogous inequalities in power between managers and subordinates, which in turn result in a clear distinction of roles. Employees will expect to be told what to do and "will be less inclined to question authority, demand to be consulted or act independently from their superiors" (Hoppe, 1990: 205). The empowerment proposition for such independent thinking and acting would place a demand on them "to, at least, suspend their beliefs about the 'sanctity' of chain of command and authority" (ibid: 206). In such cultures "the ideal boss, in the subordinates eyes, is a benevolent autocrat or 'good father'" (Hofstede, 1991: 35). Managers are, hence, expected to lead in a directive way and "it would not be acceptable within such a culture for the leader to share or delegate the burden of decision-making to his followers" (Durcan & Kirkbride, 1994: 38). Employees would tend to lose respect for managers who do not have precise answers to their questions and seek their input in the decision-making process (Hoppe, 1990). Most importantly, failure to meet this demand for leadership and direction on behalf of the manager may even be considered as "negation of leadership rather than a positive step towards empowerment" (Durcan & Kirkbride, 1994: 38).

The shift to more participative leadership styles would not be feasible in large power distance cultures, even if superiors would eventually embrace it. The values and behavior of subordinates in such cultures would make the proposed leadership style ineffective and indeed "considerable evidence points to the greater effectiveness of autocratic leadership behavior in authoritarian cultures and of democratic leadership behavior in democratic cultures (Bass, 1990: 803). A recent study (conducted in the context of the GLOBE project[4]) on the leadership prototypes in the cross-cultural context of Europe provides further support for the belief that different leadership attributes and behaviors are valued in different cultural contexts. In particular, in the countries of South/East Europe (large power distance) the following characteristics were positively endorsed as contributing to 'outstanding leadership': "Administrative competence, autocratic, conflict inducer, diplomatic, face saver, non-participative, procedural, self-centered, and status consciousness" (Koopman, Den Hartog, Konrad et al., 1999: 512-3). In the countries of North/West Europe (small power distance) characteristics such as 'inspirational' and 'integrity' emerged as more important aspects of effective leadership (ibid.).

In conclusion, the most principal proposition of the empowerment theory is likely to be realized mainly in small power distance cultures. Neither managers, who have been long accustomed to lead in a directive and non-participative way, would embrace it, nor subordinates, who have been "acculturated" to await direction and orders, would welcome it. But even in the occasion that employees would welcome such radical change in their work-roles, in practice it would take considerable time and effort before they engaged in independent thinking and acting, which "in their experience typically results in failure and reprimands for breaking the rules or rocking the boat" (Hoppe, 1990: 206).

Organization
The empowerment theory also proposes radical changes regarding organizational structure and the centralization of power and formalization of processes. In particular, empowerment demands a flattened or delayered hierarchical structure with few intermediate management and supervisory layers in order to allow organizations to become flexible and adaptive to rapidly changing environmental conditions and consumer demands (Maxwell, 1997). Such flattening of the organizational pyramid further connotes — or results in — decentralization of power and the dispersion of decision-making authority throughout out the organization and specifically to the lower levels of organizational hierarchy. The empowerment doctrine supports also an

---

[4] GLOBE (Global Leadership and Organizational Behavior Effectiveness) is a research program examining the inter-relationships between societal culture, organizational culture and organizational leadership in over 60 nations (Koopman, Den Hartog, Konrad et al., 1999).

environment of low formalization with less policy manuals or detailed procedures and rules, so as to allow employees the latitude and flexibility to
exercise discretion and initiative.

The flexible, horizontal organization systems proposed by the empower-   [239]
ment doctrine are not necessarily suitable for large power distance and strong
uncertainty avoidance countries. In large power distance cultures the hierarchical structure is based on the 'existential inequality' between superiors and
subordinates, which can only be reflected in tall hierarchies with many intermediate layers of supervision (Hofstede, 1991). Furthermore, decentralization of power requires both superiors and subordinates to suspend their
deeply embedded values of their existential inequality and their distinct
roles. In practical terms, decentralization of power represents an equally
'giant' leap for both superiors and subordinates, which would further result
in presumably undesirable changes for both stakeholders. Superiors, on the
one hand, would need to give up — along with power — the status and privileges attached to it (e.g. the right to conform to different laws and rules),
which they have patiently acquired through the years (i.e. progression
through seniority). On the other hand, subordinates would be required to dis-
regard their strong dependence on their superiors and function independently, with the commensurate degree of risk and uncertainty that this engenders.
The latter would certainly be a highly undesirable development in strong
uncertainty avoiding cultures, where uncertainty and ambiguity are the very
situations that individuals strive to avoid (Hofstede, 1991).

Uncertainty avoidance further prescribes the ideal degree of formalization within an organization. The proposition of the empowerment theory to
replace rigorous control of employee behavior through instructions, policies
and orders with trust (Goldsmith et al., 1997) is unlikely to be fulfilled univer-
sally. Primarily, because in strong uncertainty avoiding countries the existence of many formal and informal laws and rules controlling the work
process satisfies an emotional need of people for structure and order (Hofstede, 1991). Employees in such cultures feel comfortable in structured environments, whose establishment is, in fact, an attempt to prevent uncertainty
and ambiguity in the conduct of people (ibid.). Managers are expected to issue
clear instructions and subordinates are expected to follow these instructions
and to adhere to the formal and informal rules of the organization. Therefore,
imposing a culture of low formalization in fulfillment of the demands of
empowerment would introduce an environment of high uncertainty and ambiguity, in which neither managers nor subordinates would be willing or able to
function. Secondly, because cultures "vary in their willingness to trust others"
(Bass, 1990: 791), it is doubtful whether imbuing individuals with trust can
merely occur upon demand of the empowerment doctrine.

In conclusion, the proposition of the empowerment doctrine concerning the degree of centralization and formalization in organizations is likely to be realized mainly in small power distance and weak uncertainty avoiding cultures.

[240]

Motivation

Probably the strongest evidence of the inherent cultural bias of the empowerment doctrine is the explicitly stated common belief that employees will invariably embrace the notion "in the prospect of increased personal autonomy, development and job satisfaction" (Maxwell, 1997: 54). Lashley (1996: 342), for example, claims that empowerment can "tap into the enthusiasm and intrinsic sources of job satisfaction" and should lead therefore to improved morale and performance (Lewis, 1995). Such outcomes derive from increased variety and responsibility introduced in the job content (Hope & Mühlemann, 1998) and greater feelings of involvement and importance (Go, Monachello & Baum, 1996). The alleged virtuous circle is completed with greater employee commitment, resulting in reduced labor turnover (Goldsmith et al., 1997) and with improved customer service (Jones, Taylor & Nickson, 1997).

Evident in the above claims are the individualist values prevailing in the American and Anglo-Saxon cultures, which, according to Hofstede, promote the fulfillment of 'self-interest' as the ultimate motivator of human behavior. Clearly the allure of the empowerment doctrine is based on this fundamental assumption, which has been expressed in the most popular theories of motivation developed in the United States. Empowerment, in fact, is argued to build on the higher needs for self-actualization and achievement, which are the top motivators in Maslow's Hierarchy of Needs and in Herzberg's Two-Factor Theory (Ripley & Ripley, 1992).

Hofstede argues that in strong uncertainty avoiding cultures the need for safety or security prevails over the need for achievement and, hence, individuals are not likely to find any satisfaction in — and to be motivated by — the increased opportunity for self-development and challenge offered by empowerment. In addition, the inner need for structure in such cultures and the unwillingness to take unfamiliar risks is likely to deprive individuals of any satisfaction that 'empowered' jobs can offer in terms of personal autonomy, responsibility and self-direction. On the contrary, empowerment is likely to appeal to individuals in weak uncertainty avoidance cultures, where individuals are motivated by the prospect of self-development and growth. Also, feeling comfortable with uncertainty and less structure, they are likely to enjoy and make use of the opportunities that empowerment offers for responsibility, autonomy and the exercise of discretion (Durcan & Kirkbride, 1994).

In sum, the empowerment doctrine is likely to be more appealing to indi-

viduals in weak uncertainty avoiding cultures and less so to individuals from
cultures at the opposite pole.

[241]

The hotel study

The validity of the above substantiated considerations about the 'cultural relativity' of empowerment was examined through a study conducted among
the employees and managers of 16 upscale and luxury hotels of a *single* well-
known American multinational hotel-company (see Klidas, 2001). The
selection of a single company was deliberate, in order to create well-matched
and functionally equivalent samples by holding constant other salient characteristics, such as industrial and organizational culture, occupations and so
on (Tayeb, 1994). The study was conducted in seven European countries,
namely England, Sweden, the Netherlands, Italy, Greece, Portugal and Belgium. Data were collected in the period September 1999 to March 2000 by
means of both qualitative and quantitative methods (Table 2).

Qualitative methods involved 45 semi-structured interviews with managers of
the hotels, usually with the Human Resources Manager, the Front Office Manager and the Food and Beverage Manager and one interview at the company
Head Office in Brussels. The interviews aimed at generating information
regarding the human resources policy of the hotels including employee empowerment and the company in general and were in most cases recorded on tape.

Quantitative methods involved a survey-questionnaire targeting at all
customer-contact employees, working in the Front Office and Food and Beverage departments. A total of 533 questionnaires were collected, of which
106 were considered 'non-usable' either due to missing data or because they
were completed by individuals in supervisory or managerial positions. Com-
pletion and collection of questionnaires took place mainly (72 percent) on

Table 2: *Field research: Database (usable data)*

Country	n hotels	Collected Questionnaires	Interviews
England	5	81	15
Sweden	1	20	3
Netherlands	2	38	5
Italy	4	192	13
Greece	1	13	2
Portugal	1	30	2
Belgium	2	53	5+1
Total:	16	427	46

site — usually in the training room — during special sessions, which were specifically set up for this purpose. This is indeed consistent with the recommendation of Ronen and Shenkar (1985: 453) to researchers in cross-cultural studies for the administration of questionnaires "in a similar, in-company setting". During these meetings employees were also given by the author information about the research and guidelines for completing the questionnaire. The rest of the questionnaires were collected in by the Personnel or Training Managers of the hotels, and returned by post.

The questionnaire used in the employee survey included three sections. The first measured employees' perceptions on a range of management practices (e.g. training, rewards, information, communication) and management style, all interventions considered relevant in the empowerment process. Employees' self-reported 'empowered' behavior during service delivery was also measured in this section. Due to the lack of existing measures applicable to the field of hospitality management new measures were constructed. The items selected were based on a review of the research literature (Klidas, 2001). In formulating the items, the guidelines of Brislin (1986) were followed for the design of 'translatable' items required for cross-cultural research. The items were all modified for use in the context of the hotel industry with a focus on the interactions of employees with guests. To avoid confusion, all the scales used a five-point Likert-type format with answer categories ranging from 1 (strongly disagree) to 5 (strongly agree).

The second section measured the dimensions of 'power distance' and 'uncertainty avoidance', which were measured by the respective indexes adapted from the Value Survey Module 1994 (Hofstede, 1994). Finally, the third section measured a number of socio-demographic variables, namely, employees' gender, age, nationality, educational level, position in the hotel, tenure and type of employment.

The original version of the questionnaire was produced in English. For use in the various countries — except Sweden, where the English version of the questionnaire was used — the questionnaire was translated into Greek, Dutch, French, Italian, and Portuguese. The methodology for the translation followed the 'back-translation' procedure (see Ronen & Shenkar, 1985; Brislin, 1986), with one native speaker translating from English to the target language, and a second native speaker back-translating from the target language to English. All the translators were researchers and members of the academic staff of Tilburg University (The Netherlands), and were fluent in English. In addition, the translated and back-translated items were discussed with the author, resulting in the final translations.

As the measures were used for the first time a pilot-study was conducted prior to the main part of the research. A translated (into Greek) version of the

Table 3: *Measures (scales) and alpha coefficients*

Measure/variable	Description	No. of items	Alpha coefficient
Empowered behavior	Extent to which employees make independent decisions and take initiatives enhancing service quality and customer satisfaction	7	.66
Sharing of information	Extent to which management shares information with employees	5	.84
Openness of communication	Extent to which communication from and towards every part of the organization is free	4	.71
Empowerment training	Extent to which employees have been trained to master independently routine and non-routine service situations	5	.77
Performance-related rewards	Extent to which rewards depend on individual performance	3	.73
Delegation of authority	Extent of employees' authority to function independently in their job	4	.81
Empowering management style	Extent to which superiors' management style is conducive to employee empowered behavior	12	.86

original questionnaire was administered to 70 customer-contact employees of four large hotels run by a Greek company. The scales used and their respective alpha coefficients are presented in Table 3.

Quantitative data were analyzed by means of multiple regression analysis. Due to the low samples collected in several countries, it was not considered meaningful to conduct analyses at the country level as was initially intended. Instead, the sample was divided in two cultural clusters on the basis of theories on taxonomy of cultures (e.g. Ronen & Shenkar, 1985), namely a south European cluster, including Italy, Greece, Portugal and Belgium and a north European cluster, including England, Sweden and the Netherlands. Examination of the influence of culture occurred by comparing the two clusters.[5]

---

[5] The inevitable consequence of this decision was that the indexes of power distance and uncertainty avoidance could not be used in the analyses in any meaningful way.

Findings

The findings of both the qualitative and the quantitative research uncovered a clear difference in the empowerment process between hotels in north and south Europe (Table 4). The evidence from the employee survey revealed that employees in hotels in the north are more inclined to demonstrate extra-role 'empowered' behavior during service delivery (e.g. creative rule-breaking to please customers, 'complaint ownership', 'going out of their way' to please customers). The information provided from the interviews supports this finding, as managers in the north generally reported that frontline employees in their hotels consistently engage in 'empowered behavior' and usually would not resort immediately to management assistance when dealing with non-routine service situations. On the contrary, in the south, managers generally reported that employees do not engage in behaviors outside the boundaries of their role and would usually seek management involvement when faced with non-routine situations. Especially clear was the discrepancy between north and south when it comes to making financial concessions to customers. While in the north managers generally stated that employees would often make financial concessions even without consulting first with a manager, in the south managers were in most cases very clear that making financial concessions is not part of the job of employees, who in those situations seek the involvement of a manager.

Table 4: *Main findings from qualitative research: Empowerment in South vs. North Europe*

Southern Europe	Northern Europe
Employees do not as a rule demonstrate "empowered behavior"	Higher levels of "empowered behavior"
Delegation of authority to frontline employees sporadic and limited	Delegation of authority to frontline employees more systematic and extensive
Low intensity of training mostly on the job	More extensive, intensive and formal training
Less open communication climate (communication occurring mostly informally)	More open communication (many formal processes for upward communication)
Less willingness to share information	Systematically sharing information
Imposed equal compensation according to seniority and rank	Merit pay allowed, but restricted to small incentives
Generally no differences uncovered in management style	

In addition, the survey showed that employees in the south perceive they have a lower degree of authority to function independently in their job than their colleagues in the north. This finding is reinforced by the information provided by the managers themselves regarding the extent to which they delegate authority to frontline employees. Especially in Italy, which comprises the largest proportion of the sample in southern Europe and to a slightly lesser degree in Belgium, managers made a clear distinction between the extent of authority and responsibility that should be — and eventually is — allocated to the managerial, supervisory and line level. In Italy, it was frequently stated that this distinction between the roles of managers and subordinates and their commensurate level of authority is prescribed by union agreements, which means that this absence of delegation is also institutionalized. On the contrary, in the north, managers in most cases reported delegating an increased degree of authority to employees and readily identified employees' 'expertise' in detecting customer needs and problems and in selecting the appropriate means to ensure customer satisfaction.

[245]

Furthermore, the evidence from the employee survey showed that employees in the south perceive they have been trained less to independently master routine and non-routine service situations compared to employees in the north. This discrepancy was also evidenced in the qualitative data, as managers in the north described a very formalized, extensive, intensive and on-going training process, whilst their colleagues in the south reported that employee training occurs mainly on the job.

Clear differences between hotels in the north and south Europe were found in relation to openness of communication and sharing of information. Employees in the south perceive that communication in their working environments is less open and that management shares less information with them compared to employees in the north. The information provided by managers confirms these results. Managers in the north reported a range of formal processes facilitating especially upward communication and a variety of means for the devolution of organization-related information, including new technology (i.e. intranet). In contrast, most managers in the south did not report formal means of facilitating upward communication and expressed a general preference for an informal communication climate. Occasionally, they even expressed their reluctance to devolve sensitive information to lower level employees and obviously acknowledged the absence of formal channels to do so.

Finally, a discrepancy exists between north and south in terms of the extent to which rewards are linked to performance. The qualitative data reveal a greater availability of individual incentive schemes in the north and a greater emphasis in the south on equal compensation of employees of the same rank, position and seniority. According to managers in the south it is actually the legislative framework and union agreements that impose equal compensation. Interestingly, this discrepancy was not uncovered from the employee survey, which may point to the conclusion that employee rewards for frontline staff in the hotels studied — in the south, as well as in the north — are not *primarily* based on individual performance. In other words, even if more incentives are available in hotels in the north — foremost in England and Sweden — these do not constitute a substantial proportion of employees' total remuneration, which is presumably still based to its largest extent on a fixed salary.

Interestingly, no differences were uncovered between hotels in the two regions with respect to management style. This is in principle contrary to our earlier theoretical considerations. A possible explanation for this may lie in the work context in the two departments under study. In particular, the high amount of teamwork, which takes place during work in both Front Office and Food and Beverage outlets, presumably impacts on the nature of the relationship between superiors and subordinates. These may actually resemble more relationships between collaborators with distinct roles, as opposed to traditional boss-subordinate relationships, and as such are underlined invariably by a high element of trust, support, praise, coaching and mistake tolerance, behaviors which were considered in this research as constituting an 'empowering' management style.

Discussion

The plausibility of the cultural explanation in explaining the uncovered differences appears to be quite strong and is based on the following arguments: Primarily, the differences found are largely in line with specific a priori theoretical considerations on the basis of the work of Hofstede on national cultures and the implications for management theories and practices that he has derived from the dimensions of power distance and uncertainty avoidance. Secondly, a number of other potential influences that might account for the discrepancies found, such as industry and organizational culture, technology, hotel size, segment and market, have been indirectly controlled for. Additionally, the discrepancies revealed from the quantitative data cannot be accredited to socio-demographic differences, such as gender, age, education, job tenure and type of employment, which have also been controlled for. Therefore, the cultural explanation is offered here on the basis of a systematic effort to control for other factors that might influence the empowerment process across countries.

Finally, and most importantly, the insight offered by the managers points directly to the cultural explanation and allows us to explain cross-national differences on the basis of values pertaining mostly to power distance and to a lesser degree to uncertainty avoidance. Managers in the south generally described an overall preference of employees for managerial direction, reluctance to assume responsibility and to accept authority beyond the boundaries of their job. Such descriptions are consistent with the anticipated picture in these countries and point to a cultural context of large power distance and strong uncertainty avoidance. Conversely, in the north, managers reported that employees are inclined to demonstrate initiative and make independent decisions, which again is consistent with the anticipated behavior of individuals originating from the small power distance and weak uncertainty avoidance cultures of the north. Interestingly, when managers were specifically asked to compare the behavior of employees originating from different cultural contexts, they tended to ascribe to individuals from the south (and other large power distance cultures) an inclination to await direction, as opposed to an inclination for initiative and independent action, which they ascribed to individuals from northern countries (and other small power distance cultures).

[247]

Moreover, managers in the south not only clearly expressed their reluctance to delegate authority to frontline employees, but also justified this reluctance with arguments directly echoing power distance values. Such typical arguments used include the "need to drive people by hierarchy", the perceived "gap between a manager and a 'regular' employee" and the assertion that "answering to complaints is not the job of the waiter", which are clear traces of large power distance values. Accordingly, managers in the north also justified their willingness to delegate on the basis of cultural values, emphasizing in particular the "natural fit" of empowerment with the prevailing democratic values in these countries, in which it is generally conceded that individuals should be allowed to express their opinion and make independent decisions. Again the echoes of small power distance values are evident.

Arguments implying cultural values were also expressed regarding management's reluctance to share 'sensitive' information (e.g. financial results, etc.) with lower level employees, as managers in the south occasionally mentioned that "the mentality is not to give these kind of numbers to employees" or that such information "needs to be kept secret". In general, the available evidence from the research data point to a higher centralization of power in the hotels in the south, as opposed to a lower centralization of power in those of the north, which is precisely the anticipated picture according to the theory of Hofstede and other comparative studies (Drenth & Groenendijk, 1998). This high centralization of power in the south is evidenced in the low degree of authority delegated to line level employees, the restricted availability of and access to information and a less open communication climate. In contrast, in the north the high degree of authority delegated to employees, the systematic devolution of sensitive information throughout the organization and the more open communication climate connote more decentralized organizations. From this perspective the uncovered discrepancies regarding these interventions seem to be associated with the dimension of power distance.

Although the research evidence presented above is not sufficient to prove that the revealed discrepancies between north and south are due to the cultural effect, it does underline the plausibility of the cultural explanation. There is certainly sufficient evidence to raise the issue of the cultural relativity of the notion of empowerment and to conclude that there are indeed implications when applying it in different cultural contexts. The conceptual propositions of the empowerment doctrine appear to fit more in the cultural context of countries, like Sweden, England and the Netherlands and less so in the cultural context of countries like Italy and Belgium. A word of caution is demanded here. In particular, in the presentation of the research findings reference was broadly made to north and south Europe, however data were predominantly collected from Italy and Belgium in the south and England in the north. As reference to north and south was imposed by the fact that data was drawn from these broader regions, caution is required regarding the extent to which the research findings apply to Greece, Portugal, Sweden and the Netherlands, where limited information was generated. In general, reference to such broad regions may in fact obscure the importance of differences existing between countries clustered in the same region, which obviously should also be taken into consideration.

Contribution to the field and implications for management

The main contribution of the present study to theory is the identification through empirical research of the implications of applying empowerment in different cultural contexts. At the time the research was conducted — and with the notable exceptions of Hoppe (1990) and Durcan and Kirkbride (1994) — the issue of the cultural relativity of the propositions of the empowerment doctrine has barely been raised and addressed in a systematic manner as was attempted in this study. In the hospitality and hotel context the literature has unanimously embraced the propositions of the empowerment doctrine and the issue of the cultural relativity of the notion has only been raised by Baum (1995). Yet, the findings of the present study show that the propositions of the empowerment doctrine are clearly the cultural product of the American culture and they may not readily be embraced in other cultural contexts, namely in those where large power distance and strong uncertainty avoidance values prevail.

For management, this research raises broader implications concerning the transfer of human resource management concepts and practices across national borders in view of the globalization momentum. Indeed, one of the alleged implications of globalization for business is the emergence of "universal" human resource management (HRM) practices, which will be effective everywhere (Bae & Rowley, 2001). Although multinational corporations (MNCs) would certainly welcome such a universalizing tendency for reasons of synergy and efficiency, the findings of this research challenge the assertion that the universality of HRM practices is attainable, at least in the foreseeable future. As it was shown, considerable differences exist in the practice of empowerment, but also in a range of HRM practices, such as rewards and communication, even among the subsidiaries (hotel properties) of a major MNC in the hotel industry. It is presumed that this is merely a modest representation of industry reality, which might unveil more prominent differences had the research been conducted outside the context of MNCs, for example, among small, independent hotel properties in different countries. On the basis of my study therefore, I challenge directly the principal assertion of researchers, such as Von Glinow, Drost and Teagarden (2002), about the convergence of (international) HRM practices.

Of course, the cultural relativity of empowerment underlined by this research should not inevitably be interpreted as incompatibility of the concept with certain cultural contexts. On the contrary, it is argued that the application of empowerment should take into account and eventually adjust to the specific cultural context of each country. While in the northern countries empowerment seems to fit with a cultural demand for a democratic working environment, in which employees want the opportunity to express their opinion and to grow through assuming greater responsibilities, in the southern countries empowerment may fit with the creativity and 'sense of hospitality' inherent in these cultures. The latter was repeatedly emphasized during the interviews with managers, both in the south and in the north. Conversely, a favorable cultural context is in itself inadequate in ensuring the application of a high level of empowerment. In England, for example, the favorable cultural environment — the willingness indeed to empower and to be empowered — is to some extent 'contradicted' by the pressures imposed to the hotels from very intensive competition, limitations of the labor market and high labor turnover.

At long last, the cultural relativity of empowerment raises broader implications for the 'universal validity' of management and organizational theories, which Hofstede has long questioned. The real problem is not the mere

[250]

fact that the developed theories and concepts claim universality, but the fact that they do so while disregarding the different ways of thinking and feeling in other parts of the world. Until social and organizational sciences fully consider the universe of cultures, forms of organizations and social institutions and human behaviors, values and beliefs, we should remain wary of any theory claiming universality.

CHAPTER TWELVE

Integrating the Hofstede dimensions and twelve aspects of negotiating behavior

A six country comparison

LYNN METCALF AND ALLAN BIRD

In the more than 25 years since Hofstede's seminal work on culture first appeared, cross-cultural research has explored seemingly all aspects of behavior. With regard to cross-cultural negotiating behaviors, there is an embarrassment of riches. As data continue to accumulate, the search for a comprehensive synthesis seems not only appealing as a means of facilitating understanding, but also a necessary element of true knowledge creation.

In the following analysis, we relate Hofstede's dimensions of cultural variability to cross-cultural negotiating behavior in six countries. We propose that a careful application of Hofstede's framework to the large body of work on cross-cultural negotiating behavior is a first step in simplifying and clarifying our level of understanding.

Cultural variation has long been recognized as a key background factor in models of international negotiation (Sawyer & Guetzkow, 1965). Interestingly, a review of the country-specific negotiation literature revealed scant effort to relate dimensions of cultural variability to the large body of work that exists regarding negotiating behavior.

To test the approach, the authors undertook a systematic review of prior work on the negotiating behavior of six countries — Japan and five of its major trading partners USA, Germany, China, Mexico and Brazil. We began by reviewing the literature for negotiating styles in each of the six countries, thereby developing a comprehensive understanding of the 'typical' negotiating behavior in each country. We classified each country's behavior on twelve negotiation dimensions according to a high, medium, low scheme. Next, we ranked each of the six countries according to their index values on Hofstede's four dimensions of cultural variability: power distance, individualism, mas-

[252]

culinity and uncertainty avoidance. We propose a set of relationships between Hofstede's dimensions and each country's negotiating behaviors,[1] which are supported by the existing body of research. We then test these relationships via nonparametric measures of correlation. We found that negotiating behaviors cluster around one or more of the Hofstede dimensions.

A negotiating framework

In 1985, Weiss and Stripp (1985) proposed a framework for analyzing cross-cultural negotiations. In 1998, they proposed a refinement of the original framework (Weiss & Stripp, 1998). The framework consisted of 12 dimensions, grouped into five categories: two dimensions were categorized as relating to a general model or concept of negotiation; three dimensions referred to aspects of negotiator roles; negotiator dispositions relating to negotiation interactions encompassed three more; three other dimensions related to aspects of the negotiation process; finally, one dimension related to negotiation outcomes. Although the original framework was proposed more than fifteen years ago, to date no empirical investigations of its validity have been published. Perhaps one of the reasons the framework has not been empirically validated is that a number of the dimensions incorporated concepts that were not mutually exclusive or that could not be traced along a bipolar continuum.

By contrast, research replicating and supporting the validity of Hofstede's work-related cultural values is extensive, numbering more than 1500 published studies. Surprisingly, few of these studies have attempted to organize knowledge of cultural differences in terms of negotiating behaviors. Of the 1500, we identified two studies as specifically addressing Hofstede's dimensions: Graham, Mintu, and Rodgers, 1994; Lytle, 1995 (Hofstede, 2001). Both studies included negotiators from multiple countries; however, the simulations were set up so that both parties to the negotiation came from the same country. Simulation outcomes did vary with each country's score on the Hofstede dimensions. So, while these studies demonstrate that national culture affects negotiation outcomes when both parties to a negotiation are from the same country, we learn very little about intercultural negotiations.

---

[1] We note that each of the Hofstede dimensions, as well as each of the dimensions comprising the Weiss and Stripp framework is bi-polar. For brevity's sake, we have included only one of the two possible relationships between a particular negotiating dimension and a particular cultural value. Readers may infer that, where support was found for the hypothesis in the text, support for its inverse was also found. An example of the inverse of a hypothesis included in the text may be found in note 2.

In the following sections, we present a refinement of the Weiss and Stripp framework. Each dimension has been recast to fit a bipolar continuum. Additionally, in consultation with Weiss, we sought to ground the dimensions more firmly in the negotiation and communications literature, while remaining faithful to the aims and content of the original framework. Our intent was to identify specific aspects or dimensions of negotiation and the continua along which a range of culturally variant behaviors could be mapped. Our fundamental premise is that specific cultural values are related to specific dimensions of negotiating behavior. Working from this premise, we speculated that the Weiss and Stripp framework would specify the dimensions of negotiating behaviors and the Hofstede dimensions would specify the cultural values influencing those behaviors. [253]

Basic concept of negotiation: Distributive vs. integrative

This dimension refers to how each party views the negotiating process.

Distributive perspective. Negotiators from countries that fit this profile believe there will be a winner and a loser (Mintu-Wimsatt & Gassenheimer, 2000). Consequently, the negotiator's goal is to establish dominance (Donohue & Ramesh, 1992). Negotiators take a hard-line approach, seeking to meet only their own goals or interests, in order to maximize the benefit for their side (Li & Labig, 1996). Negotiators assume their interests directly conflict with those of the other party" (Bazerman & Neale, 1992). As a result, negotiators demonstrate a strong concern for themselves and little concern for others. Their goal is to induce the other party to change their attitudes and positions, which may be accomplished either by using promises or threats or by remaining polite and neutral (DeMente, 1987). Their aspiration levels may be high and rigid, which makes them resistant to making concessions (Chan, 1998). Alternatively, in order to exploit their position to the greatest extent, negotiators may continuously adapt their strategy based on the other party's actions (DeMente, 1987). The atmosphere may be contentious or frustrating as negotiators focus on the need for the other party to concede (Gelfand et al., 2001).

Integrative perspective. Negotiators from countries that fit this profile believe that mutually beneficial solutions can be generated. Consequently, integrative negotiators take a problem-solving approach, where the focus is on exchanging information in order to identify the underlying issues and interests of both sides and to generate outcomes that benefit both parties. Negotiators adopting integrative behaviors attempt to understand the underlying issues and their relative importance to both parties. Their goal is to capitalize on the different interests to find effective trade-offs. Negotiators concede less important issues to gain on more important ones (Bazerman & Neale, 1992). Consequently, negotiators share information about their own interests and seek information about the other party's interests. Through exchanging information, both parties react to the other's arguments and adjust their stances on the issues (Putnam & Holmer, 1992). Negotiators reach agreement by employing creative problem-solving approaches to develop solutions that expand the size of benefits available to everyone.

[254]

Negotiating behaviors and national culture. The negotiating behaviors described above correspond to behaviors observed along Hofstede's Masculinity/Femininity dimension. A masculine orientation is usually characterized by ego enhancement strategies (Hofstede, 1991) and masculine cultures emphasize assertiveness, competition, and toughness. A feminine orientation is characterized by relationship enhancement strategies (Hofstede, 1991). Feminine cultures emphasize nurturing, as well as a concern for relationships and for the living environment (Hofstede, 2001). Members of masculine cultures are driven to win and are more likely to resolve conflicts through competition. Business people from masculine cultures are aggressive, competitive, assertive, and decisive. Compromise and cooperation are not goals because a compromise entails giving up part of one's desires, which translates into a loss relative to what could have been won (Hofstede, 2001). Members of feminine cultures are more likely to resolve conflicts through problem solving. Business people from feminine cultures are cooperative, accustomed to seeking consensus, and intuitive rather than decisive (Hofstede, 2001).

> H_1: *Countries with high scores on Hofstede's Masculinity index will adopt a basic concept of negotiation that is distributive.*[2]

Most significant type of issue: Task vs. relationship-based

This dimension refers to the types of issues negotiators spend more time discussing.

Task. Negotiators from countries where task issues are more important spend most of their time discussing specific operational details of the project, as opposed to broad objectives. They tend to negotiate a contract in an item-by-item way (Victor, 1992). Negotiators feel that it is important to come

---

[2] For all hypotheses, the opposite relationship also holds. In other words, for H1, countries with low scores on Hofstede's Masculinity index will adopt a basic concept of negotiation that is integrative.

away with a clear understanding regarding the control, use, and division of resources (e.g., profits, management, ownership).

Relationship. Negotiators from countries where relationship issues are more important spend most of their time engaging in activities that build trust and friendship between the members of each team and in discussing broad objectives. They believe a good relationship must be established before task issues can be discussed and that as the social relationship develops, task issues will be resolved (Victor, 1992).

[255]

Negotiating behaviors and national culture. According to Hofstede (2001), separating the people from the issues, which is common among negotiators with a task frame view, assumes an individualist value set. In collectivist cultures, where relationships prevail over tasks, it is impossible to separate the people from the issues at hand. Hofstede (2001) also states that, in collectivist cultures, "*the personal relationship prevails over the task*...and should be established first," whereas in individualist cultures, "*the task...[is] supposed to prevail over any personal relationships*." Furthermore, collectivism implies a need for stable relationships, so that negotiations can be carried out among persons who have become quite familiar with each other. Replacing even one member on a team may seriously disturb the relationship and often means that a new relationship will have to be built (Hofstede & Usunier, 1996).

H_2: *Cultures high in Individualism will place greater emphasis on task issues during negotiations.*

Selection of negotiators: Abilities vs. status

This dimension refers to the criteria each party uses to select members of the negotiating team.

Abilities. Managers from achievement-based cultures consider job-specific skills or substantive expertise, which they believe is relevant to a particular negotiation, when selecting members of the negotiating team. Examples of relevant skills or expertise include education, technical or scientific knowledge, legal training, vocational achievement, negotiating experience, or language fluency. Negotiating teams from achievement-based cultures may consist largely of technical advisers and people that have demonstrated proficiency and are knowledgeable about the project at hand (Trompenaars, 1994).

Status. Managers from status-based cultures consider who the candidates are and whom the candidates know, when selecting members of a negotiating team. Examples of relevant characteristics include family background, influential connections, seniority, age, or gender (Trompenaars, 1994). Negotiating teams from status-based cultures may consist largely of senior, high-ranking officials, who wield considerable influence in their organizations and who may also command great respect in the community at large (Kras, 1989).

Negotiating behaviors and national culture. Hofstede (2001) proposes that Power Distance affects the importance of the status of the negotiators. According to Hofstede, low Power Distance cultures tend to minimize the importance of inherited privilege and status. Roles in the organizational hierarchy can change; a person who is someone's subordinate today may become his boss tomorrow (Hofstede, 2001). People at all levels in the organizational hierarchy earn respect on the basis of how effectively they perform their assigned tasks and how adequate their knowledge is. By contrast, in high Power Distance cultures, inequality among people is expected and desired. Superiors in the organizational hierarchy are viewed as being superior people. Respect is based on seniority and high status in the organizational hierarchy (Hofstede, 2001).

Members of low Power Distance cultures are more likely to appoint people to a particular negotiating team because they have capabilities that are relevant to the task, while members of high Power Distance cultures are more likely to select members of the negotiating team based on status-related factors.

H_3: *Cultures demonstrating high Power Distance will emphasize status over ability in the selection of negotiators.*

Influence of individual aspirations: Collectivist vs. individualist

This dimension refers to the emphasis negotiators place on the achievement of individual goals and the need for individual recognition.

Individualist. Triandis (1995) defines individualists as people who see themselves as independent of collectives. They are motivated primarily by their own preferences, needs, and rights and they give priority to their personal goals over the goals of others. Individualist negotiators are emotionally independent from the organization to which they belong. They may strive to achieve outcomes that are in their own best interests. They keep organization's interests and goals in mind because they expect personal reward and recognition for their decisions (Trompenaars, 1994).

Collectivist. Triandis (1995) defines collectivists as people who see themselves as parts of one or more collectives. They are motivated primarily by the norms of and duties imposed by the collectives to which they belong and give priority to collective goals over their own personal goals. Collectivist negotiators have a strong sense of identity with and loyalty to their organization. Consequently, they will strive to achieve outcomes that are in the organization's best interest and will do so with little expectation of personal gain. The negotiating team will assume joint responsibility and/or receive joint recognition for actions taken or decisions made (Trompenaars, 1994). [257]

Negotiating behaviors and national culture. The negotiating behaviors described above correspond to behaviors observed along Hofstede's Individualism/Collectivism dimension. Employees in individualist cultures are expected to act rationally according to their own interests. Work tasks are organized in such a way that an employee's self-interest and an employer's interests coincide. In collectivist cultures employees are expected to act in accordance with the interests of the organization, which may or may not coincide with their individual interests (Hofstede, 2001).

H_4: *Negotiators from individualist cultures will be strongly influenced by individual aspirations.*

Internal decision-making process: Independent vs. consensus

This dimension refers to the system that negotiators use to reach decisions within their teams.

Independent: Leaders or other influential individuals on the negotiating team may make decisions independently without concern for the viewpoints of others on the team. Negotiators are expected to use their own best judgment in speaking and acting on behalf of the organization (Trompenaars, 1994).

Consensus: Decision-making power is delegated to the entire team. The team leader must obtain support from team members and listen to their advice.

Negotiating behaviors and national culture. Hofstede (2001) found that cultures with high Uncertainty Avoidance scores demonstrate a preference for consultative decision processes and group decision-making. Cultures with low Uncertainty Avoidance scores tend to demonstrate a preference for independent decision processes and individual decision-making. Consequently, we propose that

H$_5$: Cultures high in Uncertainty Avoidance will adopt consultative internal decision-making processes.

[258]

Orientation toward time: Monochronic vs. polychronic

This dimension refers to the value each party places on time.

Monochronic. Negotiators with a monochronic orientation believe that time is money. They set agendas for meetings and adhere to preset schedules. They schedule negotiations in ways that create psychological pressure in having to arrive at a decision by a certain date (Hall & Hall, 1990). They believe that outstanding or contentious issues in a negotiation should be resolved effectively within an allotted time frame. Negotiators from mono-chronic cultures also tend not to mix business with pleasure.

Polychronic. Negotiators from polychronic cultures believe that time is never wasted. They feel that getting to know their counterparts and building a relationship is more important than adhering to a preset schedule. Time spent actually discussing and resolving issues is of minor importance.

Negotiating behaviors and national culture. According to Hall (1983), whereas people in monochronic cultures adhere religiously to plans, "matters in polychronic culture seem in a constant state of flux. Nothing is solid or firm...even important plans may be changed right up to the minute of execution. These monochronic and polychronic behaviors seem to correspond to behaviors observed along Hofstede's Uncertainty Avoidance value dimension. Cultures high in Uncertainty Avoidance seek clarity and structure, whereas low Uncertainty Avoidance cultures are comfortable with ambiguity and chaos.

H$_6$: Cultures high in Uncertainty Avoidance will demonstrate a preference for monochronic time.

Risk-taking propensity: Risk averse vs. risk tolerant

This dimension refers to negotiators' willingness to take risks.

Risk averse: Risk-averse negotiators take steps to avoid the failing to come to an agreement (Bazerman & Neale, 1992). They may be more likely to make concessions in order to avoid failing to reach an agreement (Ghosh, 1996), or they may accept lower rewards for a higher probability of success (Moran & Stripp, 1991).

Risk Tolerant: Risk-tolerant negotiators believe there is a level of accept-able risk any negotiation. They are interested in reducing risk, not avoiding it altogether. Risk-tolerant negotiators show greater willingness to fail to come to an agreement by making fewer concessions or demanding more (Bazerman & Neale, 1992). They may be less likely to make concessions in order to avoid failing to come to an agreement (Ghosh, 1996) or they may choose a strategy offering higher rewards but with a lower probability of success (Moran & Stripp, 1991).

[259]

Negotiating behaviors and national culture. Kahn and Sarin (1988) propose that psychological factors leading to risk aversion also lead to uncertainty avoidance. They suggest that ambiguity accentuates the effects of risk aversion. Hofstede (2001) also suggests a relationship between risk aversion and uncertainty avoidance. Cultures with lower Uncertainty Avoidance accept both familiar and unfamiliar risks, whereas cultures with high Uncertainty Avoidance scores tend to limit themselves to known risks.

H_7: *Negotiators from high Uncertainty Avoidance countries will employ risk-averse negotiating behaviors.*

Basis of trust: External to the parties vs. internal to the relationship

Trust is one party's belief that the other party will take action to honor agreements that have been reached (Wilson & Moller, 1991).

External to the parties. Negotiators trust the other party because a contract has been negotiated and agreed to, which can be litigated and enforced (Fukuyama 1995). The legal system and governmental agencies are viewed as providing an adequate, reliable, and effective underpinning for contracts. Contracts will be honored because the legal system will impose sanctions otherwise. The written word is binding; a deal is a deal. A trustworthy partner is simply one who complies with the law.

Internal to the relationship. Negotiators may trust the other party because a relationship that has been built up over time and they believe the other party is committed to it. The relationship between the parties is what matters (Victor, 1992). When trust is internal to the relationship, less emphasis is placed on detailed, written contracts. Negotiators expect that the other party will changing circumstances over time. A trustworthy partner is one who strives to maintain the relationship, possibly by modifying an existing contract to reflect new developments (Trompenaars, 1994).

Negotiating behaviors and national culture. In cultures where the legal system and governmental agencies are viewed as providing an adequate support, trust in the legal system enables parties who don't know each other well

[260]

to do business with each other (Fukuyama, 1995). Consequently, trust in the legal system reinforces behavior that is consistent with behavior in low Uncertainty Avoiding cultures — a greater willingness to take unknown risks and to enter into unknown ventures with parties that are not well known (Hofstede, 2001). In cultures where institutionalized law is views as inadequate, lack of trust in legal systems, encourages negotiators to deal with parties whom they know well (Yu, 2001) — organizations that are linked via family ties, cross shareholdings, or relationships of long duration (Fukuyama, 1995). The preference for dealing with only those whom one knows is consistent with behavior in high Uncertainty Avoiding cultures (Hofstede, 2001). This leads us to propose that

H_8: *Negotiators from high Uncertainty Avoidance countries will base trust in relationships.*

Concern with protocol: Formal vs. informal

This dimension has to do with the importance that negotiators place on the existence of and adherence to rules for acceptable self-presentation and social behavior (Weiss & Stripp, 1985).

Formal. Negotiators with a high concern for protocol will adhere to strict and detailed rules that govern personal and professional conduct, negotiating procedures, as well as the hospitality extended to negotiators from the other side. Rules governing acceptable behavior might include dress codes, use of titles, and seating arrangements (Weiss & Stripp, 1985). Negotiators on the team believe that there are few appropriate ways to respond to a particular situation and there is strong agreement on the team about what constitutes correct action. Team members must behave exactly according to the norms of the culture and suffer severe criticism for even slight deviations from norms (Triandis, 1995).

Informal. Negotiators with low concern for protocol adhere to a much smaller, more loosely defined set of rules. Compulsive attention to observing the rules is not necessary and those who deviate from norms are not necessarily criticized. Team members not only believe that there are multiple ways to respond appropriately to a particular situation but may even disagree about what is appropriate (Triandis, 1995).

Negotiating behaviors and national culture. Hofstede and Usunier (1996) propose that negotiators from uncertainty-avoiding cultures prefer highly structured, ritualistic procedures during negotiations. People in high uncertainty avoiding cultures seek structure and formalization, in an attempt to

make interactions and events transpire in a clearly interpretable and predictable manner. People in low uncertainty avoiding cultures are tolerant of
ambiguity in structures and procedures (Hofstede, 2001).

[261]

*H_9: High Uncertainty Avoidance cultures will demonstrate a high concern for
formal protocol during negotiations*

Style of communication: High context vs. low context

This dimension refers to the degree to which people rely on nonverbal cues
to convey and to interpret intentions and information in dialogue (Weiss &
Stripp, 1998).

High context. Negotiators who prefer high-context communication are
more tuned in to and reliant on non-verbal cues. They will tend to use language that is indirect, ambiguous, and understated (Trompenaars, 1994).
High context negotiators expect their partners to pick up on and to understand unarticulated intentions and feelings, subtle gestures, and other non-
verbal or environmental cues (Anderson, 2000). Negotiators will take it personally when the other party directly criticizes their work, or the proposal
they have put on the table. High context negotiators will not conclude agreements with business partners whom they do not like (Triandis, 1994).

Low context. Negotiators who prefer low context communication are less
likely to notice and understand non-verbal cues. The communicator is direct
and to the point, using language that is precise, open, and frank (Trompenaars, 1994). Low context negotiators are literal and often fail to perceive
nonverbal cues (Anderson, 2000). While low context negotiators may prefer
to do business with people whom they like, it is possible for them to conclude
agreements with people whom they do not like personally.

Negotiating behaviors and national culture. According to Gudykunst and
Ting-Toomey (1988), high context communication is used primarily in collectivist cultures, whereas low context communication is used predominantly in individualist cultures. Hofstede (2001) concurs and also notes that
things, which are self-evident in collectivist cultures, must be communicated
explicitly in individualist cultures.

*H_{10}: Negotiators from individualist cultures will employ a low context style of
communication.*

Nature of persuasion: Factual-inductive vs. affective

This dimension refers to the type of evidence negotiators use to develop persuasive arguments.

Factual-Inductive. Factual-inductive negotiators base their arguments on empirical facts and use linear logic (if-then statements) to persuade the other party (Johnstone, 1989). Proof used to support persuasive arguments includes such things as scientific evidence, professional standards, expert opinion, costs, market value, and other hard data (Fisher & Ury, 1991). Factual-inductive negotiators believe presenting their best arguments first makes the strongest case.

Affective. Affective negotiators may base their arguments on abstract theory, ideals (Glenn, Witmeyer & Stevenson, 1977), references to status and relationships, and/or appeals to sympathy (Adair & Brett, 2002). Evidence used to support persuasive arguments includes such things as moral standards, equal treatment, tradition, and reciprocity (Fisher & Ury, 1991). Affective negotiators develop their arguments indirectly. They may start with peripheral arguments and present their best arguments last, after the other party has reacted (Triandis, 1994).

Negotiating behaviors and national culture. Cultures with low Uncertainty Avoidance scores tend to favor inductive reasoning — the development of general principals from empirical facts (Hofstede, 2001). Cultures with high Uncertainty Avoidance scores tend to favor deductive reasoning — drawing conclusions about specific situations given a set of general principles. Consequently, we propose that

H_{11}: *Negotiators from countries with low Uncertainty Avoidance scores will rely on the factual-inductive form of persuasion.*

Form of agreement: Explicit contract vs. implicit agreement

This dimension refers to the preferred form of agreement between the parties.

Explicit contract. Negotiators favor and expect written, legally binding contracts (Weiss & Stripp, 1985). A written contract records the agreement and definitively specifies what each party has agreed to do (Trompenaars, 1994). Consequently, negotiators believe that written agreements provide stability and allow organizations to make investments and minimize business risk (Frankel, Whipple & Frayer, 1996).

Implicit agreement. Negotiators favor broad language in a contract because they feel that definitive contract terms are too rigid to allow a good working relationship to evolve. Particularly with new relationships, negotiators may feel that it is impossible to anticipate and document every conceivable contingency. They also believe that contracts inhibit parties from exploring unexpected opportunities for improvement and success. Negotiators view the contract as a rough guideline because the relationship, not the contract, is primary (Trompenaars, 1994). In some cases, an oral contract may suffice.

[263]

Negotiating behaviors and national culture. Uncertainty-avoiding cultures tend to shun ambiguous situations and prefer structures that enable them to clearly predict and interpret events (Hofstede, 2001). Written agreements provide a clearly specified framework for the relationship; hence, they serve as an uncertainty reduction mechanism. Consequently, we propose that

H_{12}: *Cultures high in Uncertainty Avoidance will seek forms of agreement that are explicit.*

Method

Negotiation dimensions. To test the hypotheses, the authors undertook a systematic review of prior work on the negotiating behavior of six countries — Japan and five of its major trading partners USA, Germany, China, Mexico and Brazil. For purposes of analyzing nonparametric correlations between negotiations dimensions and cultural value dimensions, we elected to treat the bi-polar continua on each dimension in terms of one end of the pole. We would then rate countries using a 'high,' 'medium', and 'low' scheme. We began by reviewing the literature for negotiating styles in each of the six countries, in the process developing a comprehensive understanding of the 'typical' negotiating behavior in each country. To do this, we first developed lists of books and scholarly articles on negotiating styles and behaviors in each country. Our research team, which consisted of the two authors and three research assistants, analyzed over one hundred books and articles relating to negotiating behaviors in these countries.[3] After reviewing the literature on a given country, each of the research team members independently classified that country's behavior on each of the twelve negotiation dimensions employing our 'high,' 'medium,' and 'low' scheme. Although interrater reliability was high, on occasion one or more raters differed in their assess-

---

[3] The complete list of books and articles reviewed is not included in this manuscript but is available from the authors on request.

ments. In these cases, we resolved discrepancies in assessment by employing a modified Delphi technique. Each rater was provided with the assessment of the other four raters and then asked to make a new assessment. In some instance, sharing of ratings was accompanied by discussion. In no case was it necessary to go beyond a single iteration of this process.

[264]

Cultural values dimensions. Because we were working with only six countries and used a restricted range in the negotiation dimension ratings, we adopted a similar approach with regard to the scoring of the cultural values dimensions. We began by obtaining the six countries' index values on Hofstede's (1991) four dimensions of power distance, individualism, masculinity, and uncertainty avoidance. Using these index scores, we collapsed the range by rank ordering the countries on each value in accordance with their scores, with 1 being highest and 6 being lowest.

Analysis of the data consisted of a nonparametric rank order correlation in which the cultural value rank was paired with the negotiation dimension score. Given the very small sample size, it was determined that a hypothesis would only be declared 'strongly supportive' if the rank order correlation was 1, i.e., the rank ordering of cultural values matched perfectly the rank ordering of the negotiation dimension. In instances where only 1 of the pairings did not fit the hypothesized relationship and the ranking was off by only one position, these hypotheses were deemed to be 'moderately supported'. In such instances, given that five of the six countries demonstrated the hypothesized relationship, this seemed a reasonable accommodation.

Analysis

The analysis found support for ten of the twelve hypothesized relations. Four of the hypotheses found strong support. These were the hypotheses relating to internal decision-making processes, orientation toward time, style of communication and the nature of persuasion. Six other hypotheses were moderately supported. These six hypotheses were most significant type of issue, influence of individual aspirations, risk-taking propensity, basis of trust, concern with protocol and form of agreement. Hypothesis 1, which focused on basic conceptions of negotiation, and Hypothesis 3, selection of negotiators, found no support. Table 1 presents a summary of the hypothesized relationships and findings.

Overall, these findings suggest strong support for the validity of the Weiss and Stripp framework as a means of identifying meaningful cultural variation across twelve dimensions of negotiating behavior. Moreover, the findings also demonstrate the utility of Hofstede's cultural values in identify-

Table 1: *Support for hypothesized relationship between cultural values and negotiating behavior dimensions*

Weiss & Stripp Dimension	Hofstede Cultural Value	Support for Hypothesis
General model		
1 Basic concept of negotiation	MAS	None
2. Most significant type of issue	IDV	Moderate
Role of the Individual		
3. Selection of negotiators	PDI	None
4. Influence of individual aspirations	IDV	Moderate
5. Internal decision-making process	UAI	Strong
Interaction: Dispositions		
6. Orientation toward time	UAI	Strong
7. Risk-taking propensity	UAI	Moderate
8. Basis of trust	UAI	Moderate
Interaction: Process		
9. Concern with protocol	UAI	Moderate
10. Style of communication	IDV	Strong
11. Nature of persuasion	UAI	Strong
Outcome		
12. Basic concept of negotiation	UAI	Moderate

ing a given culture's position on the various negotiation dimensions.

Several additional insights can be gleaned from Table 1. Of the four cultural value dimensions, Uncertainty Avoidance was hypothesized to be related to seven negotiating behavior dimensions, Individualism related to three dimensions, and Power Distance and Masculinity one each. Neither Power Distance nor Masculinity correlated with their hypothesized negotiating behaviors. However, for Uncertainty Avoidance, all sever negotiating dimensions were correlated — three at the 'strong support' level and four at the 'moderate support' level. The three Individualism hypotheses were also supported — two at the "moderate support" level and one at the "strong support" level. Perhaps of greater interest is the recognition that more than half of the hypotheses dealt with Uncertainty Avoidance. In retrospect, this may not be surprising as a negotiation, to a large extent involves attempts at reducing uncertainty and equivocality so as to reach an agreement.

One obvious question that arises in a study involving discretely identified cultural values is the extent to which more than one value may exert influence in any given situation. Indeed, more sophisticated treatments of

Table 2: *Support in the literature for relationships between cultural values and negotiating dimensions*

Hofstede Cultural Value	Weiss and Stripp Dimension											
	Concept	Issue	Select	Aspirations	Decision	Time	Risk	Trust	Protocol	Comm	Persuasion	Agree
PDI	No	No	Strong	No	Some	No	No	No	No	No	No	No
IDV	Some	Strong	Some	Strong	Some	No	No	No	No	Strong	No	No
MAS	Strong	Some	Some	No	Some	No	No	No	No	No	Some	No
UAI	No	No	No	No	Strong	Strong	Strong	Strong	Strong	Some	Strong	Strong

Key: No = no evidence found in the literature that a relationship exists between this cultural value and this negotiating dimension: Some = some support in the literature that a relationship exists between this cultural value and this negotiating dimension; Strong = the relationship between this cultural value and this negotiating dimension is most strongly supported by the literature culture (Osland & Bird, 2000) focus on the complex interactions of constellations of cultural values in any particular context. Our limited sample size and our use of a nonparametric approach precluded the possibility of a more fine-grained analysis involving multiple cultural values. Nevertheless, we felt it was possible to return to the literature in a search for additional cultural influences for each of the twelve negotiating dimensions. Table 2 provides a summary of our literature review findings. [267]

As Table 2 indicates, for roughly half of the negotiating dimensions the influence of a second cultural value may be postulated based on prior empirical findings. However, in only two instances does it appear reasonable to speculate as to the influence of a third cultural value. A word of caution is called for, as noted previously, of the more than 1500 empirical studies reported in Hofstede's (2001) second edition of *Culture's Consequences,* only a handful directly focus on aspects of negotiation. Consequently, the suggested link between cultural values and negotiating dimensions is predicated on studies that did not involve negotiation per se.

For negotiation researchers and practitioners alike, there are several positive implications. For negotiation researchers, rather than approaching the study of negotiation in a given country as though it is distinct and unique, the framework allows researchers to organize data in ways that will allow for meaningful comparisons. Given the vast body of country specific research and writing on negotiation, this framework holds forth the possibility of a comprehensive, country-by-country organization and synthesis of extant knowledge. At the same time, the framework will also allow scholars to identify inadequacies in research on specific aspects of negotiation in a particular country. For example, our review of the Brazil literature led us to conclude that the basis of trust in Brazilian negotiations is weak compared to what is available for other negotiating dimensions in that country.

For managers, the framework provides a useful tool to guide them in identifying what aspects of a cross-cultural negotiation are likely to vary. Because the framework is straightforward and can be aligned with cultural values, managers should be able to draw upon the extensive body of research replicating Hofstede's work to inform their understanding of negotiations. As it is not unusual for managers to work across multiple cultures when conducting negotiations in an international setting, the availability of data and literature on Hofstede, when combined with an understanding of the twelve negotiation dimensions should allow managers to be effective "quick studies" in comprehending and responding to cultural variation.

A study such as this, employing as it does such a small sample size has obvious limitations. Three seem worthy of comment. As we noted at the out-

[268]

set, the body of literature detailing distinctive aspects of negotiation in specific countries is vast, but uneven in its quality and comparability. This presents a particular problem for scholars interested in drawing comparisons. Across the six counties included in this study there was significant variation in the volume of literature available– ranging from extensive literature on Japan and China to significantly less on Brazil. Equally important, there was no common metric available for making comparisons. The intention of this paper was, in part, to test a framework that would allow for systematic comparison. One of the challenges in doing that was the absence of any agreed upon standards. Paradoxically, though lack of common metric is a limitation of this study, we believe that one of the contributions of this study is the initial development of some criteria upon which a metric can be established.

A second limitation of this study involves the issue of interrater reliability. Although it was not a substantive issue within this study, the variability in quantity and quality of information on negotiation across the six countries does raise an issue of whether or not a different set of raters might have evaluated the countries differently with regard to the 12 dimensions. We chose to have the same set of raters evaluate all six countries. An alternative approach might have been to organize a panel of experts for each of the six countries. Beyond the issue of inherent complexity and workload in organizing six separate panels, we were also confronted with the issue of whether or not these panels would have invoked the same criteria and weighting. We opted for inter-rater reliability, but in the process sacrificed depth of understanding of each country's negotiating behaviors. Given an approach that focused on reviewing the extant literature for negotiation in each country, raters were beset with having to compare and contrast differing vocabularies to describe what often appeared to be similar conceptions or behaviors. Our research team is addressing this issue by developing a questionnaire survey to be used with teams of expert panels in each country. The surveys will flesh out specific aspects of each of the 12 dimensions, thereby enabling a more fine-grained comparison within dimensions. Additionally, further work in this area would benefit from the collaborative efforts of multinational research teams that incorporate one or more experts on negotiation from each of the countries in the study.

A final limitation of this study was the small size of the sample. Even nonparametric statistical analysis is strained when sample sizes drop down to a single digit. As with Hofstede and the many researchers who have replicated his work, statistical analysis is made more credible with a larger sample (Hofstede, 2001). Our current research project includes Japan and its 25 largest trading partners in the sample. Though this number is still small by normal statistical standards, it represents a significant undertaking and should enhance the credibility of findings. An additional way to offset the issue of small sample size is to increase the number of respondents within each country. As noted above, our current research project addresses this issue by developing teams of expert panels.

[269]

Conclusions

This study is a first step toward approaching a vast body of information on negotiating behaviors, which lacked a clear structure, and giving it some coherence, thereby making it more accessible to managers. By linking cultural variations in twelve dimensions of negotiating behaviors to Hofstede's framework, we provide a synthesizing frame that enables more effective analysis of negotiation for scholars and more effective negotiation for practitioners. Moreover, linking the Hofstede dimensions to specific aspects of negotiating behaviors allows us to contextualize the application of cultural values dimensions, thereby avoiding the problem of sophisticated stereotyping (Osland & Bird, 2000). Finally, our findings are presented in a form that facilitates comparison of negotiating behaviors between countries, enabling managers to relate negotiating behaviors of 'new' countries to other countries with which they might be familiar.

Epi-dialogue

GEERT HOFSTEDE

Desiderius Erasmus of Rotterdam in his *Colloquia* (1522) published a collection of dialogues between imaginary persons. He wrote in Latin, the international language of his days, and his book was promoted as language exercises for young people. However, the dialogues also proved a very effective way of communicating Erasmus' critical views about the church, the education system, and the society of his days. Inspired by my great compatriot and namesake,[1] I decided to follow his example, venting my comments on the past chapters in the form of a discussion.

The discussion takes place in my study, between myself and three learned gentlemen: *Readall*, a librarian, *Thinkall*, a philosopher, and *Askall*, a sociologist of science.

Readall. You showed me this very interesting new book, *Comparing Cultures*. All the chapters are based on presentations during an IRIC conference at Tilburg University in April 2001. The occasion for the conference was the publication of another book, the second edition of Geert's scholarly volume *Culture's Consequences*. Long overdue, because the first edition was from 1980, and a lot has happened since!

Askall. *Comparing Cultures* seems to bundle contributions from several different disciplines. There are psychologists, sociologists, anthropologists, health researchers and management researchers. Isn't that unusual?

Readall. Yes it is, and to me it poses a problem. I don't know where to put it in my library. With cross-cultural psychology? Comparative sociology? Organizational anthropology? International management? International relations? You might think this is a minor issue, but the problem with academics is that they think very much in disciplines. Psychologists don't talk to sociol-

---

[1] Desiderius was Erasmus' self-chosen first name, a Latin translation of the name of his biological father Geert or Gerard, a priest.

ogists, let alone that they read each other's journals or could even consider publishing in them.

Askall. In theory everyone is in favor of interdisciplinary contacts, but if you want to make an academic career you better stick to your discipline and don't mix with the academic aliens from the next corridor.

[271]

Thinkall. You exaggerate, my friend. The application-oriented fields like business administration and health care management do draw from different social science disciplines. And most of the more than 200 academics from all over the world who attended the conference in 2001 traveled nicely on their department's budget.

Readall. So what was the common denominator that brought all these people together?

Thinkall. I believe it was a common paradigm, the *dimensions* paradigm, for looking at cultural differences. This was the main innovation in Geert's 1980 first edition of *Culture's Consequences*. A paradigm is not a theory, but a way of looking at the world: a set of implicit assumptions. Even authors who never read *Culture's Consequences* got caught in its paradigm. All authors in *Comparing Cultures* in some way use it.

Askall. What the participants shared is not a new discipline. It may be called a new field, but then in the sense of an open field in which different academics meet. It has no single Journal, but it is visited by people who read and write in journals like: Journal of Cross-Cultural Psychology, Comparative Sociology, Journal of Cross-Cultural Management, International Journal of Intercultural Relations, Cross-Cultural Research, Journal of International Business Studies.

Readall. I discovered this open field in the reference list of the 2001 second edition of *Culture's Consequences*. The number of references has grown enormously since the first edition of 1980, and more than half are to books and articles that appeared after 1980. From these, over 300 date from 1980-89, and over 500 from 1990-99.

Geert. And these were only the sources containing real information, the ones that made a difference. That was at best one fifth of what was published.

Thinkall. It would be a pity when the new field would become a separate discipline. The attraction of an open field is precisely that different disciplines can make complementary contributions to it, maintaining a view of the social world as a whole. But coming back to the dimensions paradigm, between you, Schwartz, and Inglehart you don't seem to agree on what the dimensions of culture are. Triandis agrees only partly with you. How can we identify the real dimensions?

[272]

Geert. What I tell my students is: *dimensions do not exist!* Culture does not exist either. Dimensions, and culture in general, are *constructs*, products of our minds that help us to simplify the overwhelming complexity of the real world, so as to understand and predict it. They are useful as long as they do this, and redundant when they don't. And because the real world is so complex, there is not just one way to simplify it. Different authors' minds produce different sets of dimensions.

Askall. Yes, and the dimension systems in themselves reflect the professional and national cultures to which their author belongs. A psychologist like Schwartz bases his dimensions on the personal ideals of individual respondents, a sociologist like Inglehart bases his dimensions on statements about the family and other institutions. Both Triandis and Inglehart find Individualism-Collectivism to be the most important dimension of national cultures; it happens to be the one on which their nation, the USA, stands out amidst all other countries. Nationality also affects the research methods used. Schwartz analyses his database with Smallest Space Analysis, a statistical method developed by the Israeli social scientist Louis Guttman, that I have never seen used by anybody but Israelis. It produces the pie-shaped diagrams that are typical of Schwartz' work, ordering variables or cases in a circular pattern.

Geert. I once tried Smallest Space Analysis for clustering countries from the IBM database.[2] But it is true that I never considered it for finding dimensions. I don't know how to use it, and it is not in the SPSS-package on my computer. I wonder what happens when Schwartz' data are put into a factor analysis, like Inglehart and I have been using. On the other hand, the real important distinctions between societies should be robust against method effects: they should pop up in spite of differences in statistical method. The dimension systems of Schwartz, Inglehart and myself are all significantly correlated![3]

---

[2] See *Culture's Consequences*, 2001: 76 (note 41).

[3] *Culture's Consequences*, 2001: 265-66, shows richer correlation patterns between Schwartz' and Inglehart's data and mine than they have described in their chapters.

Readall. So the national culture of the researcher influences not only his methods but also his results! It reminds me of a famous statement by Bertrand Russell about studies of animal behavior. Russell wrote as follows:

"One may say broadly that all the animals that have been carefully observed have behaved so as to confirm the philosophy in which the observer believed before his observations began. Nay, more, they have all displayed the national characteristics of the observer. Animals studied by Americans rush about frantically, with an incredible display of hustle and pep, and at last achieve the desired result by chance. Animals observed by Germans sit still and think, and at last evolve the solution out of their inner consciousness. To the plain man, such as the present writer, this situation is discouraging. I observe, however, that the type of problem which a man naturally sets to an animal depends upon his own philosophy, and that this probably accounts for the differences in the results. The animal responds to one type of problem in one way and to another in another; therefore the results obtained by different investigators, though different, are not incompatible. But it remains necessary to remember that no one investigator is to be trusted to give a survey of the whole field".[4]

Thinkall. That is exactly the point I wanted to make. In *Comparing Cultures* different 'investigators' did get together. Still we will never know whether we see 'the whole field'. Geert, you said a moment ago that constructs like dimensions are useful as long as they help to understand and predict the real world, and redundant when they don't. How helpful are your dimensions for this?

Geert. The really interesting studies to me are the ones with comparative data about real-world phenomena, to which I can try to relate my dimensions. I remember the thrill back in the 1970s when I found that the dimension of Uncertainty Avoidance that I had just detected correlated strongly with data on national anxiety levels derived from medical and related statistics by Richard Lynn:[5] data from entirely different sources converging to the same conclusion. What thrilled me most in *Comparing Cultures* was the revelation by Müller and Ziltener in Chapter 6 of an almost perfect correlation among Asian countries between uncertainty avoidance and their measure of cultural homogeneity. Then this chapter is followed by Manabe's in-depth study of intolerance of foreigners in Asia's most homogeneous nation, Japan, which illustrates the processes involved. Müller and Ziltener's analysis for me opens a new line of inquiry, to see whether other studies of cultural and eth-

---

[4] Russell, 1979[1927]: 23-24.
[5] Lynn, 1971; *Culture's Consequences*, 2001: 53-54, 188.

nic homogeneity also relate to the dimensions framework. Ethnic heterogeneity is one of the major political problems of large parts of the world, so
this is an extremely topical subject.

Readall. I know that you consider the summaries of significant correlations
of country index scores with data from other sources the most important part
of *Culture's Consequences*; you called these the 'synergy harvest' of the IBM
study.[6] The number of external data sources that statistically validate the
IBM indices jumped from 38 in 1980 to 140 in 2001. None of the other
dimension studies has so far paid much attention to external validation.

Geert. Hopefully this is still to come. A conference like this should make academics from one discipline or school aware of interesting ideas from other
disciplines and schools.

Askall. Reading other people's books has never been the strongest point of
professors. As early as 1991, Geert has reported on correlations between his
dimensions and country scores from the European Value Study[7] but until the
2001 conference the EVS and WVS publications never picked this up. The
fact that this conference was opened by the Chairman of the EVS consortium
is promising.

Readall. Although I noticed that Jagodzinski, who is a member of the EVS-
team, in his Chapter 5 about the methodological problems of value research
seems still to be unaware of the extensive treatment of that subject in *Culture's Consequences*, which was already part of the 1980 first edition.[8]

Thinkall. Among other things, Jagodzinski misses Geert's distinction
between the desirable and the desired, which plays an important role in, for
example, marketing applications.[9]

Geert. Coming back to external validation, if others publish correlations with
your own data, don't take those for granted. If you have access to their base
data, recalculate the correlations. The calculations may have been inaccu-
rate, or essential other variables may have been overlooked. A famous case is
the article by a collaborator of Boeing that the relative share of planes from a

---

[6] *Culture's Consequences*, 2001: 503-20.
[7] Hofstede, 1991: 48, 72, 102, 116, 119, 126, 127.
[8] Hofstede, 1980, pp.14-42; *Culture's Consequences*, 2001: 1-24.
[9] De Mooij, 1998, 2003.

country that crashed was correlated with my index for the country's power distance. She forgot to control for national wealth (GNP/capita), and poverty turned out to be a sufficient single explanation for the differences: poorer countries had older planes, more primitive airports, and less qualified personnel. Because they also tended to have larger power distances, there was a relationship between power distance and crashes, but it did not survive in a multiple regression including GNP/capita.[10]

[275]

Askall. Isn't there a limit to what one can learn from correlation coefficients?

Geert. Of course there is. Qualitative, insightful observations and interpretations are at least as useful, even if they don't cover enough countries to allow statistical analysis: they illustrate the way different societies address the same problem, The study of maternity care in Britain, Finland, the Netherlands and the USA by de Vries, Wrede, van Teijlingen, Benoit and Declercq in Chapter 10 is a magnificent example: it illustrates what cultural differences imply for such a key issue as how new citizens start their lives.

Thinkall. The study about maternity care is the only one that directly refers to the dimension of Masculinity versus Femininity. Indirectly one could associate it with Chapter 9, by Phalet and Swyngedouw, which describes the prominent role of women in the acculturation of immigrants. I know that Geert considers questions of masculinity and gender roles as very important components of culture studies. On the other hand, Triandis in Chapter 2 brushes masculinity under the rug of individualism. Hasn't the masculinity dimension remained a bit underexposed in *Comparing Cultures*?

Readall. People who want more about it should read the book Geert edited in 1998: *Masculinity and femininity: The taboo dimension of national cultures.* It bundles eight studies by different researchers with four review chapters by the editor. It deals with subjects that rarely appear in the mainstream cross-cultural literature, like emotional gender roles, religiosity, and sexuality.

Askall. Remember what I said about Americans considering Individualism-Collectivism the most important dimension of national cultures, while in Geert's data their country scored highest on individualism? From the ten authors in Geert's 1998 *Masculinity and Femininity* book, seven were from Holland which scored extremely feminine in Geert's data. Most of these Dutch authors did not even know each other before they contributed to the

---

[10] *Culture's Consequences*, 2001: 115 and Exhibit 3.17.

book — they were just the ones who had chosen this subject for their research. This shows again to what extent the national culture of a researcher affects her choice of subject and her results.

[276]

Thinkall. This worries me less in the case of Holland which is only a small country than in the case of the USA and other Anglo countries. Their individualist national culture strongly affects the *inter*national research agenda. In addition, these countries speak the dominant language in social science, English; they publish the *international* social science journals, and provide most of the editors and the authors. What is the effect of an individualist bias on the study of a collective characteristic like culture?

Askall. In the international Social Science Citation Index, published in the USA, all the most cited psychologists except Sigmund Freud are Americans, and all the most cited sociologists are Europeans.[11] Psychology has become an American science, sociology a European science. It is said that many Americans have no concept of society, so why study it? The comparison of maternity care between the USA and three European countries in Chapter 10 is an illustration. But without a concept of society, what becomes of the study of culture? Fortunately we should not generalize about Americans. Triandis and Inglehart certainly have a concept of society. Inglehart's World Value Survey contains solid sociological information — but it grew out of a *European* initiative!

Thinkall. A consequence of an individualist bias for the study of culture is that American research often confuses the cultural (societal) and the individual level of analysis. Like in answering the famous question whether individualism and collectivism are one or two dimensions. Researchers often do not understand that the answer depends on the level of analysis. Individualism and collectivism can be separate dimensions at the level of individuals within societies, as Trommsdorff, Mayer and Albert clearly illustrated in Chapter 8 for the case of Germany, but one bipolar dimension across societies. The same holds for masculinity and femininity.

Geert. What impressed me very much in Trommsdorff et *al.*'s chapter was their three-generation design which opens a perspective on how cultures develop over generations. I look forward to seeing the results of their extension to five other countries.

---

[11] In 2001: Foucault, Giddens, Bourdieu, Weber, Habermas, Durkheim.

Askall. Another consequence of the individualist bias is that studies of cultural individualism and collectivism often carry an implicit message that individualism is good and collectivism bad. Cultural individualism is strongly correlated with wealth (GNP/capita): individualist cultures are wealthier, so doesn't this show that they are better? Of course Geert has shown in *Culture's Consequences* that causality flows from wealth to individualism and not the other way round, but this message is not popular.

[277]

Geert. In the new edition of *Culture's Consequences* I have consistently controlled for differences in GNP/capita in all correlations with culture indices. My reasoning is that if I can explain phenomena across societies by differences in wealth, I don't need culture, like in the example of the plane crashes. In this way many of the effects attributed to individualism disappear. In *Comparing Cultures* it is obvious that Inglehart, the sociologist, pays the most attention to economic development and recognizes it as a separate influence that interacts with culture. In analyzing Schwartz' seven dimensions I found six of the seven to be significantly correlated with GNP/capita,[12] which raises questions in my mind. In Schwartz' new data the correlations with wealth have even become stronger.

Askall. A large part of the citations of your work comes from the management literature. In *Comparing Cultures* the Chapters 11 and 12 deal with management issues. How do you feel about these? I remember that you weren't always too happy to be cited as a management guru; it suggested being superficial and commercial, not a respectable scholar.

Geert. The two chapters you mention represent excellent management research. Klidas knows the field he writes about; his study of 'empowerment' in the hospitality industry is critical and methodologically thorough, and carries a clear message that management fads from one country should not automatically be expected to work elsewhere. Metcalf and Bird perform a cross-cultural secondary analysis of published studies about negotiation in six countries, a very creative approach which was new to me and very convincing. In general I favor secondary analysis; too often reports of past studies die slowly in libraries while newcomers reinvent the same wheels. Through secondary analysis a researcher gets a much better overview of a field, and moreover she is forced to be critical and use her judgment. My critical attitude about management studies is based on the large number of quick-and-dirty Ph.D.'s in this area, often by people who have never experi-

---

[12] *Culture's Consequences*, 2001: Exhibit 5.17

enced management, and by the gullibility of certain practitioners who run after every new fad. When I read a management book the song from *Porgy and Bess* often comes to my mind: "It ain't necessarily so."

[278]

Readall. Management and marketing books also often assume that country cultures are converging; they have little sense of history. The growing list of significant correlations of your country index scores with data from other sources, even very recent ones, illustrates case for case that country culture differences are extremely persistent. Comparing cultures will remain an important area of study for decades and probably centuries to come.

REFERENCES

ACOG Task Force on Cesarean Delivery 2000. *Evaluation of Cesarean Delivery.* Washington, DC: ACOG.

Adair, W.L. & J.M. Brett 2002. Culture and Negotiation Processes. In M.J. Gelfand & J.M. Brett (eds.), *Culture and Negotiation. Integrative Approaches to Theory and Research.* Palo Alto: Stanford University Press.

Adler, F. 1956. The Value Concept in Sociology. *American Journal of Sociology*, 62, 272-9.

Ajzen, I. & M. Fishbein 1980. *Understanding Attitudes and Predicting Social Behavior.* Englewood Cliffs, NJ: Prentice Hall.

Albert, H. 1979. *Werturteilsstreit.* Darmstadt: Wissenschaftliche Buchgesellschaft.

Albert, I., & G. Trommsdorff 2003. *Gegenseitige Unterstützung zwischen Müttern und Ihren Erwachsenen Töchtern im Zusammenhang mit Bindung und Beziehung: Ein Deutsch-Japanischer Vergleich.* Poster at the 16th Meeting of Developmental Psychology Mainz, Germany.

Alesina, A., A. Devleeschauwer et *al.* 2002. *Fractionalization.* "http://www.stanford.edu/~wacziarg/downloads/fractionalization.pdf".

Alwin, D.F. & J.A. Krosnick. 1985. The Measurement of Values in Surveys: A Comparison of Ratings and Rankings, *Public Opinion Quarterly*, 49, 535-552.

American College of Obstetricians & Gynecologists 1999. *Vaginal Birth after Previous Cesarean Delivery* (5). Washington, DC: American College of Obstetricians & Gynecologists.

Andersen, P. 2000. Cues of Culture. The Basis of Intercultural Differences in Nonverbal Communication. In L.A. Samovar & R.E. Porter (eds.), *Intercultural Communication. A Reader.* Belmont, CA: Wadsworth Publishing.

Aoki, T. 2002. Aspects of Globalization in Contemporary Japan. Pp. 68-88 in P.L. Berger & S.P. Huntington (eds.), *Many Globalizations. Cultural Diversity in the Contemporary World.* Oxford: Oxford University Press.

Aoyagi-Usui, M., H. Vinken & A. Kuribayashi 2003. Pro-environmental Attitudes and Behaviors. An International Comparison. *Human Ecology Review*, 10, 23-31.

Arnold, F., R.A. Bulatao, C. Buripakdi, B.J. Chung, J.T. Fawcett, T. Iritani, S.J. Lee & T.S. Wu 1975. *The Value of Children. Volume 1. Introduction and Comparative Analysis.* Honolulu, HI: East-West Population Institute.

Arts, W., L. Halman & J Hagenaars (eds.) 2003. *The Cultural Diversity of European Unity. Explanations, Findings and Reflections from the European Values Study.* Leiden & Boston: Brill.

Atkins, E.T. 2000. Can Japanese Sing the Blues? "Japanese Jazz" and the Problem of Authenticity. Pp. 27-59 in T.J. Craig (ed.), *Japan pop! Inside the World of Japanese Popular Culture.* Armond, NY, & London: M.E. Sharpe.

Aycan, Z. et al. 2000. Impact of Culture on Human Resource Management Practices. A 10-Country Comparison. *Applied Psychology. An International Review*, 49, 192-221.

[280]

Bae, J. & C. Rowley 2001. The Impact of Globalisation on HRM. The Case of South Korea. *Journal of World Business*, 36, 4, 402-428.

Bardi, A. & S.H. Schwartz 1996. Relations among Socio-political Values in Eastern Europe. Effects of the Communist Experience? *Political Psychology*, 17, 525-549.

Barkow, G., L. Cosmides & J. Tooby (eds.) 1992. *The Adapted Mind. Evolutionary Psychology and the Generation of Culture*. New York: Oxford University Press.

Bass, B.M. 1990. *Handbook of Leadership. Theory, Research and Managerial Applications*. New York: Free Press.

Baum, T. 1995. *Managing Human Resources in the European Tourism and Hospitality Industry. A Strategic Approach*. London: Chapman & Hall.

Bazerman, M.H. & M.A. Neale 1992. *Negotiating Rationally*. New York: The Free Press.

Bean, C. & E. Papadikis 1994a. Polarized Priorities or Flexible Alternatives? Dimensionality in Inglehart's Materialism-Postmaterialism-Scale. *International Journal of Public Opinion Research*, 6, 264-288.

Bean, C. & E. Papadikis. 1994b. Polarized Priorities or Flexible Alternatives. Response to Inglehart and Hellevik. *International Journal of Public Opinion Research*, 6, 295-297.

Befu, H. 1983. Internationalization of Japan 'Nihon bunkaron'. Pp. 232-266 in H. Mannari & H. Befu (eds.), *The Challenge of Japan's Internationalization. Organization and Culture*. Nishinomiya: Kwansei Gakuin University; Tokyo & New York: Kodansha International.

Befu, H. & K. Manabe 1987. An Empirical Study of 'Nihonjinron'. How Real Is the Myth? *Kwansei Gakuin University Annual Studies*, 36, 98–111.

Bendix, R. (ed.) 1965/66. Tradition and Modernity Reconsidered. *Society and History*, 9, 292-346.

Benedict, R. 1934. *Patterns of Culture*. Boston: Houghton-Mifflin.

Bengtson, V.L. 2001. Beyond the Nuclear Family. The Increasing Importance of Multigenerational Bonds. *Journal of Marriage & Family*, 63, 1-16.

Benoit, C., R. Davis-Floyd, E. van Teijlingen, J. Sandall, & J. Miller 2001. Designing Midwives. A Comparison of Educational Models. Pp. 139-165 in R. de Vries et al. (eds.), *Birth by Design. Pregnancy, Maternity care and Midwifery in North America and Europe*. New York: Routledge.

Bellah, R.N., R. Madsen, W.M. Sullivan, A. Swidler & S.M. Tipton 1986. *Habits of the Heart. Individualism and Commitment in American Life*. New York: Harper & Row.

Berger, P.L. & S.P. Huntington (eds.) 2002. *Many Globalizations. Cultural Diversity in the Contemporary World*. New York: Oxford University Press.

Bergman, S. 2002. *The Politics of Feminism. Autonomous Feminist Movements in Finland and West Germany from the 1960s to the 1980s*. Åbo: Åbo Akademi University Press.

Berry, J.W. 1979. A Cultural Ecology of Human Behavior. Pp. 177-207 in L. Berkowitz (ed.), *Advances in Experimental Social Psychology* (Volume 12). New York: Academic Press.

Berry, J.W. 1997. Immigration, Acculturation and Adaptation. *Applied Psychology. An International Review*, 46, 5-34. [281]

Berry, J.W. 2001. A Psychology of Immigration. *Journal of Social Issues*, 57, 615-631.

Berry, J.W. 2002. Conceptual Approaches to Acculturation. Pp. 17-37 in K. Chun, P. Balls-Organista & G. Marin (eds.), *Acculturation*. Washington: APA.

Berry, J.W., R. Kalin, & D.M Taylor 1977. *Multiculturalism and Ethnic Attitudes in Canada*. Ottawa: Ministry of Supply and Services.

Berry, J.W., Y.H. Poortinga, M.H. Segall & P.R.Dasen 2002. *Cross-Cultural Psychology. Research and Applications* (2nd rev. ed.). Cambridge: Cambridge University Press.

Bobo, L. & V.L. Hutchings 1987. Perceptions of Racial Group Competition. *American Sociological Review*, 61, 951-972.

Boehnke, K., A. Ittel & D. Baier 2002. Value Transmission and 'Zeitgeist'. An Underresearched Relationship. *Sociale Wetenschappen*, 45, 2, 28-43.

Boen, F. & N. Vanbeselaere 2000. Responding to Membership of a Low Status Group. The Effects of Stability, Permeability, and Individual Ability. *Group Processes and Intergroup Relations*, 3, 41-62.

Boldt, E.D. & L.W. Roberts 1979. Structural Tightness and Social Conformity. *Journal of Cross-Cultural Psychology*, 10, 221-230.

Böltken, F. & W. Jagodzinski 1985. Insecure Value Orientations in an Environment of Insecurity. Postmaterialism in the European Community, 1970 to 1980. *Comparative Political Studies*, 17, 453-484.

Bond, M.H. 1996. Chinese Values. In M.H. Bond (ed.), *Handbook of Chinese Psychology*. Hong Kong: Oxford University Press.

Borg, I. & J.C. Lingoes 1987. *Multidimensional Similarity Structure Analysis*. New York: Springer-Verlag.

Borst, C. 1995. *Catching Babies*. Cambridge, MA: Harvard University Press.

Boserup, E. 1970. *Women's Role in Economic Development*. London: George Allen and Unwin.

Bourhis, R.Y., L.C. Moïse, S. Perrault & S. Sénécal 1997. Towards an Interactive Acculturation Model. *International Journal of Psychology*, 32, 369-386.

Bovenkerk, F., R. Miles & G. Verbunt 1991. Comparative Studies of Migration and Exclusion on the Ground of Race and Ethnic Background in Western Europe. *International Migration Review*, 25, 375-391.

Bowen, D.E. and E.E. Lawler III 1992. The Empowerment of Service Workers. What, Why, How and When. *Sloan Management Review*, Spring, 31-39.

Brislin, R.W. 1986. The Wording and Translation of Research Instruments. In Lonner, W.J. & J.W. Berry (eds.), *Field Methods in Cross-Cultural Research*. London: Sage.

Brock, W.A. & S.N. Durlauf 2001. Growth Empirics and Reality. *World Bank Economic Review*, 15, 2, 229-272.

Bronfenbrenner, U. 1977. Toward an Experimental Ecology of Human Development. *American Psychologist*, 32, 513-531.

[282]   Campbell, D.T. 1965. Variation and Selective Retention in Socio-cultural Evolution. Pp. 19-49 in J.R. Barringer, G. Blanksten & R. Mack (eds.), *Social Change in Developing Areas*. Cambridge, MA: Schenkman.

Carneiro, R.L. 1970. Scale Analysis, Evolutionary Sequences, and the Ratings of Cultures. In R. Naroll & R. Cohen (eds.), *A Handbook of Method in Cultural Anthropology*. New York: Columbia University Press.

Carpenter, S. 2000. Effects of Cultural Tightness and Collectivism on Self-concept and Causal Attributions. *Cross-Cultural Research*, 34, 38-56.

Castells, M. 1998. *End of Millennium (The Information Age Vol. III)*. Malden: Blackwell.

Chan, C.W. 1998. Transfer Pricing Negotiation Outcomes and the Impact of Negotiator Mixed-motives and Culture: Empirical Evidence from the U.S. and Australia. *Management Accounting Research*, 9, 139-161.

Chan, D.K.-S. 1994. Colindex: A Refinement of Three Collectivism Measures. Pp. 200-210 in U. Kim, H.C. Triandis, Ç. Kâgitçibâsi, S.-C. Choi & G. Yoon (eds.), *Individualism and Collectivism. Theory, Method, and Applications*. Thousand Oaks, CA: Sage.

Chan, D.K.-S., M.J. Gelfand, H.C. Triandis & O. Tzeng 1996. Tighteness-Looseness Revisited. Some Preliminary Analyses in Japan and the United States. *International Journal of Psychology*, 31, 1-12.

Chick, G. 1997. Cultural Complexity. The Concept and its Measurement. *Cross-Cultural Research*, 31, 275-307.

Chiu C., C.S. Dweck, J.Y. Tong & J.H. Fu 1997. Implicit Theories and Concepts of Morality. *Journal of Personality and Social Psychology*, 73, 923-940.

Chiu, C. & Y. Hong 1999. Social Identification in a Political Transition. The Role of Implicit Beliefs. *International Journal of Intercultural Relations*, 23, 297-318.

Clarke, H.D. & N. Dutt 1991. Measuring Value Change in Western Industrialized Societies. *American Political Science Review*, 85, 905-20.

Clarke, H.D., A. Kornberg, C. McIntyre, P. Bauer-Kaase & M. Kaase 1999. The Effect of Economic Priorities on the Measurement of Value Change: New Experimental Evidence, *American Political Science Review*, 93, 637-647.

Cheung, F.M., K. Leung, J.H. Zhang, H.F. Sun, YiQ Gan, W.Z. Song & D. Xie 2001. Indigenous Chinese Personality Constructs. Is the Five-factor Model Complete? *Journal of Cross-Cultural Psychology*, 32, 407-433.

Cohen, D. 2001. Cultural Variation. Considerations and Implications. *Psychological Bulletin*, 127, 451-471.

Cohen, D., R.E. Nisbett, B.F. Bowdle & N. Schwarz 1996. Insult, Aggression, and the Southern Culture of Honor. An "Experimental Ethnography". *Journal of Personality and Social Psychology*, 70, 945-960.

Coleman, J.C. 1990. *Foundations of Social Theory*. Cambridge: The Belknap Press of Harvard University Press.

Collins, D. 2000. Why Do Patients Sue Their Obstetrician/gynecologists? *Contemporary OB/GYN*, 8, 15-28.

Conger, J.A. & R.N. Kanungo (1988). The Empowerment Process. Integrating Theory and Practice. *Academy of Management Review*, 13, 3, 471-482. [283]

Coon, H.M. & M. Kemmelmeier 2001. Cultural Orientations in the US: Reexamining Differences among Ethnic Groups. *Journal of Cross-Cultural Psychology*, 32, 348-364.

Craig, T.J. (ed.) 2000. *Japan Pop! Inside the World of Japanese Popular Culture*. Armond, NY/London: M.E. Sharpe.

Creighton, M.R. 1990. Revising Shame and Guilt Cultures: A Forty-year Pilgrimage. *Ethos*, 18, 279-307.

Crenshaw, E.M. 1992. Cross-national Determinants of Income Inequality. A Replication and Extension Using Ecological Evolutionary Theory. *Social Forces*, 71, 2, 339-363.

Crenshaw, E.M. 1993. Polity, Economy and Technoecology. Alternative Explanations for Income Inequality. *Social Forces*, 71, 3, 807-816.

Dale, P.N. 1986. *The Myth of Japanese Uniqueness*. London: Croom Helm.

Davis, D.W. & C. Davenport 1999. Assessing the Validity of the Postmaterialism Index. *American Political Science Review*, 93, 649-664.

De Graaf, N.D. 1988. *Postmaterialism and the Stratification Process. An International Comparison*. Utrecht: ISOR.

De Graaf, N.D. & P.M. de Graaf 1988. De Samenhang tussen Leeftijd en Postmaterialistische Waardenpatronen. Een Inhoudelijke Uiteenlegging in Socialisatie- en Levensloopeffecten. (The Association between Age and Postmaterialist Value Patterns. A Substantive Differentiation of Socialization and Life Course Effects). *Sociologische Gids*, 35, 6, 397-417.

De Luque, M.F.S. & S.M. Sommer 2000. The Impact of Culture on Feedback-seeking Behavior. An Integrative Model and Propositions. *Academy of Management Review*, 25, 829-849.

De Melker, R.A. 1997. The Family Doctor. Pp. 60-72 in A.J.P. Schrijvers (ed.), *Health and Health Care in the Netherlands*. Utrecht: De Tijdstroom.

De Mooij, M. 1998. *Global Marketing and Advertising. Understanding Cultural Paradoxes*. Thousand Oaks, CA: Sage.

De Mooij, M. 2003. *Consumer Behavior and Culture. Consequences for Global Marketing and Advertising*. Thousand Oaks: Sage Publications.

De Ruijter, A. 2002. *Managing Diversity in a Glocalizing World*. Keynote Address International ENIGME Workshop 'Mapping Diversity. Understanding the Dynamics of Multicultural Societies', Leuven, Belgium, May 16-17, 2002.

De Vries, R. 2004. *A Pleasing Birth*. Philadelphia: Temple University Press.

De Vries, R., C. Benoit, E. van Teijlingen & S. Wrede (2001). *Birth by Design. Pregnancy, Maternity Care and Midwifery in North America and Europe*. New York: Routledge.

Declercq, E.R. 1998. Changing Childbirth in England: Lessons for US Health Reform. *Journal of Health Politics, Policy and Law*, 23, 5, 833-859.

Declercq, E.R. 1999. Making US Maternal and Child Health Policy. From "Early Discharge" to "Drive Through Deliveries", to a National Law. *MCH Journal*, 3, 1, 5-17.

[284] Declercq, E.R. & K. Viisainen 2001. Appendix: The Politics of Numbers. The Promise and Frustration of Cross-national Analysis. Pp. 267-279 in R. de Vries et al. (eds.), *Birth by Design. Pregnancy, Maternity Care and Midwifery in North America and Europe*. London: Routledge.

Declercq, E.R., K. Viisainen, H. Salvesen, R. de Vries, & S. Wrede 2001. Where to Give Birth? Politics and the Place of Birth. In R. de Vries et al. (eds.), *Birth by Design. Pregnancy, Maternity Care and Midwifery in North America and Europe*. London: Routledge.

Dekker, P., P. Ester & H. Vinken 2003. Civil Society, Social Trust and Democratic Involvement. Pp. 217-253 in W. Arts., J. Hagenaars & L. Halman (eds.), *The Cultural Diversity of European Unity. Explanations, Findings and Reflections from the European Values Study*. Leiden & Boston: Brill

DeMente, B. 1987. *How to Do Business with the Japanese*. Lincolnwood, IL: NTC Business Books.

Diamond, J. 1999. *Guns, Germs, and Steel. The Fates of Human Societies*. New York: W.W. Norton.

Diener, E. M. Diener & C. Diener 1995. Factors Predicting the Subjective Wellbeing of Nations. *Journal of Personality and Social Psychology*, 69, 851-864.

Diener, E. & E.M. Suh 2000. *Subjective Well-being across Cultures*. Cambridge, MA: MIT Press.

Diepstraten, I., P. Ester & H. Vinken 1999a. *Mijn Generatie. Zelfbeelden, Jeugdervaringen en Lotgevallen van Generaties in de Twintigste Eeuw*. (My Generation. Ego Images, Youth Experiences, and Ventures of Generations in the Twentieth Century.) Tilburg: Syntax Publishers.

Diepstraten, I., P. Ester & H. Vinken 1999b. Talkin' 'bout My Generation. Ego and Alter Images of Generations in the Netherlands. *Netherlands' Journal of Social Sciences*, 35, 2, 91-109.

Dobbelaere, K. & W. Jagodzinski. 1995. Religious Cognitions and Beliefs. In J. van Deth & E. Scarbrough (eds.), *Beliefs in Government. The Impact of Values* (Volume 4). Oxford: Oxford University Press.

Dogan, M. 1992. The Decline of Nationalism. In *Power Shifts and Value Changes in the Post Cold War World. Proceedings of the Joint Symposium of the International Sociological Association's Research Committees*. Kibi International University, Sophia University and International Christian University.

Donohue, W.A. & C.N. Ramesh 1992. Negotiator-Opponent Relationships. In L.L. Putnam & M.E. Roloff (eds.), *Communication and Negotiation*. Newbury Park: Sage.

Drenth, P. J. D. & B. Groenendijk 1998. Organisational Psychology in a Cross-Cultural Perspective. In P.J.D. Drenth, H. Thierry & C.J. de Wolff. (eds.), *Handbook of Work and Organizational Psychology. Personnel Psychology* (Volume 4). Hove: Psychology Press.

Durcan, J. & P.S. Kirkbride 1994. Leadership in the European Context. Some

Queries. In P.S. Kirkbride (ed.), *Human Resource Management in Europe. Perspectives for the 1990s.* London: Routledge.

Durkheim, E. (1933). *The Division of Labor in Society.* New York: MacMillan (original published in French in 1887).

[285]

Easterly, W. & R. Levine 1997. Africa's Growth Tragedy. Policies and Ethnic Divisions. *The Quarterly Journal of Economics,* 112, 4.

Easterly, W. 1997. *Life During Growth* (World Bank Paper.) Washington, DC: World Bank: http://www.worldbank.org.

Edgar, A. & P. Sedgwick 2002. *Key Concepts in Cultural Theory.* London and New York: Routledge.

Ehrlich, P.R. 2000. *Human Natures. Genes, Cultures, and the Human Prospect.* Washington, DC: Island Press/Shearwater books.

Ekblad, U. 1998. "Räätälöity Synnytys" — Yasapainoilua Äidin Elämysten Ja Sikiön Hyvinvoinnin Välillä. (A "Tailormade Delivery" — Balancing between the Experiences of the Mother and the Well-being of the Fetus.) *Duodecim,* 114, 2215-7.

Ellemers, N., R. Spears & B. Doosje 1997. Sticking Together or Falling Apart. *Journal of Personality and Social Psychology,* 72, 617-626.

Erasmus, D. 2001 (1522). *Colloquia (Gesprekken).* Translated into Dutch by Jeanine de Landtsheer. Amsterdam: Athenaeum / Polak & van Gennep.

Eskes, M. 1989. *Het Wormerveer Onderzoek* (The Wormerveer Research). Amsterdam: University of Amsterdam.

Ester, P., L. Halman & R. de Moor (eds.) 1994. *The Individualizing Society. Value Change in Europe and North America.* Tilburg: Tilburg University Press.

Ester, P., L. Halman & B. Seuren 1994. Environmental Concern and Offering Willingness in Europe and North America. In P. Ester, L. Halman, & R. de Moor (eds.), *The Individualizing Society: Value Change in Europe and North America.* Tilburg: Tilburg University Press.

Ester, P. & H. Vinken 2003. Debating Civil Society. On the Fear of Civic Decline and Hope for the Internet Alternative. *International Sociology,* 18, 4, 659-680.

Etounga-Manguelle, D. 2000. Does Africa Need a Cultural Adjustment Program? Pp. 65-77 in L.E. Harrison & S.P. Huntington (eds.). *Culture Matters. How Values Shape Human Progress.* New York: Basic Books.

Etzioni, A. 1993. *The Spirit of Community. The Reinvention of American Society.* New York: Simon & Schuster.

Evans, J. & R. Laskin 1994. The Relationship Marketing Process. A Conceptualisation and Application. *Industrial Marketing Management,* 23, 5, 439-452.

Fawcett, J.T. 1974. *The Value of Children in Asia and the United States. Comparative Perspectives.* Honolulu, HI: East-West Population Institute.

Fawcett, J.T. 1976. The Value and Cost of Children. Converging Theory and Research. Pp. 91-114 in L.T. Ruzicka (ed.), *The Economic and Social Supports for High Fertility* (Volume 2). Canberra, Australia: ANU Press.

Feather, N.T. 1980. Value Systems and Social Interaction. *Journal of Applied Social Psychology,* 10, 1-19.

Featherstone, M. & S. Lash 1999. *Spaces of Culture. City, Nation, World.* London, etc.: Sage Publications Ltd.

Firebaugh, G. & F.D. Beck 1994. Does Economic Growth Benefit the Masses? Growth, Dependence, and Welfare in the Third World. *American Sociological Review*, 59, 631-653.

Fisher, R. & W. Ury 1991. *Getting to Yes. Negotiating Agreement without Giving In.* New York: Penguin.

Fiske, A.P. 1990. *Structures of Social Life. The Four Elementary Forms of Human Relations.* New York: Free Press.

Fitzpatrick R. & A. Hopkins 1983. Problems in the Conceptual Framework of Patient Satisfaction Research. *Sociology of Health and Illness*, 5, 297-311.

Flanagan, S.C. 1982a. Changing Values in Advanced Industrial Societies. Inglehart's Silent Revolution from the Perspective of Japanese Findings. *Comparative Political Studies*, 14, 403-44.

Flanagan, S.C. 1982b. Measuring Value Change in Advanced Industrial Societies. A Rejoinder to Inglehart. *Comparative Political Studies*, 15, 99-128.

Flanagan, S.C. 1987. Value Change in Industrial Societies. *American Political Science Review*, 81, 1303-1319.

Follett, M.P. 1941. The Giving of Orders. Pp. 50-70 in H.C. Metcalf & L. Urwick (eds.), *Dynamic Administration. The Collected Chapters of Mary Parker Follett.* New York: Harper.

Fontaine, J. 1999. *Culturele Vertekening in Schwartz' Waardeninstrument.* (Cultural Bias in Schwartz' Value Instrument.) (Doctoral dissertation.) KU Leuven: Department of Psychology.

Förster, J., E.T. Higgins & L.C. Idson 1998. Approach and Avoidance Strength during Goal Attainment: Regulatory Focus and the "Goal Looms Larger" Effect. *Journal of Personality and Social Psychology*, 75, 1115-1131.

Frankel, R., J. Schmitz Whipple & D.J. Frayer 1996. Formal versus Informal Contracts. Achieving Alliance Success. *International Journal of Physical Distribution & Logistics Management*, 26, 3, 47-63.

Fukuyama, F. 1995. *Trust. The Social Virtues and the Creation of Prosperity.* New York: The Free Press.

Gaines, S.O., W.D. Marelich, W.D. Bledsoe et al. 1997. Links between Race/Ethnicity and Cultural Values as Mediated by Racial/Ethnic Identity and Moderated by Gender. *Journal of Personality and Social Psychology*, 72, 1460-1476.

Garcia J., M. Redshaw, B. Fitzsimons & J. Keene 1998. *First Class Delivery. A National Survey of Women's Views of Maternity Care.* Bristol: Audit Commision and National Perinatal Epidemiology Unit.

Gastil, R.D. 1987. *Freedom in the World.* Westport: Greenwood.

Gelfand, M., L.H. Nishii, K.M. Holcombe, N. Dyer, K.-I. Ohbuchi & M. Fukuno 2001. Cultural Influences on Cognitive Representations of Conflict. Interpretations of Conflict Episodes in the United States and Japan. *Journal of Applied Psychology*, 86, 6, 1059-1074.

Gelfand, M., J. Nishii, & L. Raver (in preparation). Cultural Tightness-Looseness. A Multilevel Theory.

Georgas, J. 1991. Intrafamily Acculturation of Values in Greece. *Journal of Cross-Cultural Psychology, 22*, 445-457.

Georgas, J., J.W. Berry, A. Shaw et al. 1996. Acculturation of Greek Family Values. *Journal of Cross-Cultural Psychology*, 27, 329-338.

Georgas, J. & J.W. Berry 1995. An Ecocultural Taxonomy for Cross-Cultural Psychology. *Cross-Cultural Research*, 29, 121-157.

Gerganov, E.N., M.L. Dilova, K.G. Petkova & E.P. Paspalanova 1996. Culture-specific Approach to the Study of Individualism/Collectivism. *European Journal of Social Psychology*, 26, 277-297.

Ghosh, D. 1994. Tolerance for Ambiguity, Risk Preference, and Negotiator Effectiveness. *Decision Sciences*, 25, 2, 263-280.

Glenn, E. 1981. *Man and Mankind. Conflicts and Communication between Cultures.* Norwood, N.J.: Ablex Co.

Glenn, E.S., D. Witmeyer & K.A. Stevenson 1977. Cultural Styles of Persuasion. *International Journal of Intercultural Relations*, 1, 3, 52-66.

Go, F.M., M.L. Monachello & T. Baum 1996. *Human Resource Management in the Hospitality Industry.* New York: John Wiley.

Goldreich, Y. & A. Raveh 1993. Coplot Display Technique as an Aid to Climatic Classification. *Geographical Analysis*, 25, 337-353.

Goldsmith, A.L., D.P. Nickson, D.H. Sloan & R.C. Wood 1997. *Human Resource Management for Hospitality Services.* London: International Thomson Business Press.

Goodnow, J.J. & W.A. Collins (eds.) 1990. *Development According to Parents. The Nature, Sources, and Consequences of Parents' Ideas.* Hillsdale, NJ: Erlbaum.

Goudsblom, J. 1967. *Dutch society.* New York: Random House.

Graham, J.L., A. Mintu & W. Rogers 1994. Explorations of negotiation behaviors in 10 foreign cultures using a model developed in the United States. *Management Sciences*, 40, 72-95.

Graham, J.L. & A. Mintu-Wimsat 1997. Culture's Influence on Business Negotiations in Four Countries. *Group Decision and Negotiation*, 6, 483-502.

Greenfield, P.M. 1994. Independence and Interdependence as Developmental Scripts. Implications for Theory, Research, and Practice. Pp. 1-37 in P.M. Greenfield & R.R. Cocking (eds.), *Cross-Cultural Roots of Minority Child Development.* Hillsdale, NJ: Erlbaum.

Greenfield, P.M. 2000. Three Approaches to the Psychology of Culture. Where Do They Come From? Where Can They Go? *Asian Journal of Social Psychology*, 3, 223-240.

Grönroos, C. 1990. *Service Management and Marketing.* Lexington, MA: Lexington Books.

Gudykunst, W.B. & Y.Y. Kim 1997. *Communicating with Strangers. An Approach to Intercultural Communication* (Third Edition). New York: McGraw-Hill.

Gudykunst, W.B., Y. Matsumoto, S. Ting-Toomey, T. Nishida, K. Kim & S. Heyman 1996. The Influence of Cultural Individualism-Collectivism, Self-construals,

[287]

and Individual Values on Communication Styles across Cultures. *Human Communication Research*, 22, 510-543.

Gudykunst, W.B. & S. Ting-Toomey 1988. *Culture and Interpersonal Communication*. Newbury Park, CA: Sage.

[288]

Guttman, L. 1968. A General Nonmetric Technique for Finding the Smallest Coordinate Space for a Configuration of Points. *Psychometrica*, 33, 469-506.

Gyekye K. 1997. *Tradition and Modernity. Philosophical Reflections on the African Experience*. New York: Oxford University Press.

Haberstroh, S., D. Oyserman, N. Schwarz, U. Kuhnen & L. Ji 2002. Is the Interdependent Self more Sensitive to Question Context than the Independent Self? Self-construal and the Observation of Conversational Norms. *Journal of Experimental Social Psychology*, 38, 323-329.

Hales, C. 1994. 'Internal Marketing' as an Approach to Human Resource Management. A New Perspective or a Metaphor too Far? *Human Resource Management Journal*, 5, 1, 50-71.

Hall, E.T. 1983. *The Dance of Life. The Other Dimension of Time*. New York: Anchor Books Doubleday.

Hall, E.T. & M. Reed Hall 1990. *Understanding Cultural Differences. Germans, French, and Americans*. Yarmouth, ME: Intercultural Press, Inc.

Hannertz, U 1992. *Cultural Complexity. Studies in the Social Organization of Meaning*. New York: Columbia University Press.

Hannertz, U. 1996. *Transnational Connections. Culture, People, Places*. London and New York: Routledge.

Harkness, J.A., F.J.R. van de Vijver & P. Mohler (eds.) 2003. *Cross-Cultural Survey Methods*. Hoboken, NJ: Wiley.

Hartline, D.M. & O.C. Ferrell 1999. The Management of Customer-contact Service Employees. An Empirical Investigation. In J.E.G. Bateson & K.D. Hoffman (eds.), *Managing Services Marketing. Texts and Readings*. Orlando: Drysden Press.

Heelas, P., S. Lash & P. Morris (eds.) 1996. *Detraditionalization. Critical Reflections on Authority and Identity*. Cambridge: Blackwell.

Hemminki, E., M. Malin & H. Kojo-Austin 1990. Prenatal Care in Finland. From Primary to Tertiary Care. *International Journal of Health Services*, 20, 221-232.

Hellevik, O. 2002. Age Differences in Value Orientation. Life Cycle or Cohort Effects? *International Journal of Public Opinion Research, 14*, 286-302.

Herz, T. 1979. Der Wandel der Wertvorstellungen in Westlichen Industriegesellschaften. *Kölner Zeitschrift für Soziologie und Sozialpsychologie*, 31, 282-302.

Herz, T. 1980. Erwiderung auf die Replik von Ronald Inglehart zum Aufsatz: Der Wandel der Wertvorstellungen in Westlichen Industriegesellschaften. *Kölner Zeitschrift für Soziologie und Sozialpsychologie*, 32, 109-198.

Higgins, E.T. 1999. Promotion and prevention as a motivational duality: Implications for evaluative processes. Pp. 503-525 in S. Chaiken (Ed.), *Dual-process theories in social psychology*. New York, NY, US: The Guilford Press.

Hinkle, S. & Brown, R. 1990. Intergroup Comparisons and Social Identity. In D. Abrams & M. Hogg (eds.), *Social Identity Theory*. Hempstead: Harvester Wheatsheaf.

Hoffman, L.W. 1988. Cross-cultural Differences in Childrearing Goals. Pp. 99-122 in R.A. LeVine, P.M. Miller & M. Maxwell West (eds.), *Parental Behavior in Diverse Societies*. San Francisco: Jossey-Bass. [289]

Hoffman, L.W. & M.L. Hoffman 1973. The Value of Children to Parents. Pp. 19-76 in J.T. Fawcett (ed.), *Psychological Perspectives on Population*. New York: Basic Books.

Hofstede, G. 1980a. *Culture's Consequences. International Differences in Work-related Values*. Beverly Hills, CA: Sage.

Hofstede, G. 1980b. Motivation Leadership, and Organisation: Do American Theories Apply Abroad? *Organisational Dynamics*, 9, 1, 42-63.

Hofstede, G. 1991. *Cultures and Organizations. Software of the Mind*. London: McGraw-Hill.

Hofstede, G. 1994. *Values Survey Module 1994 Manual*. Maastricht: IRIC, Institute for Research on Intercultural Cooperation.

Hofstede, G. 1998. A Case for Comparing Apples with Oranges. International Differences in Values. *International Journal of Comparative Sociology*, 39, 1, 16-31.

Hofstede, G. 2001. *Culture's Consequences. Comparing Values, Behaviors, Institutions, and Organizations across Nations*. Beverly Hills, CA: Sage.

Hofstede, G. et al. (ed.) 1998. *Masculinity and Femininity. The Taboo Dimension of National Cultures*. Thousand Oaks, CA: Sage.

Hofstede, G. & Usunier, J.-C. 1996. Hofstede's Dimensions of Culture and Their Influence on International Business Negotiations. In P. Ghauri & J.C. Usunier (eds.), *International Business Negotiations*. Oxford: Pergamon.

Hofstede, G.H. 1983. Japanese Work-related Values in a Global Perspective. Pp. 148-169 in H. Mannari & H. Befu (eds.), *The Challenge of Japan's Internationalization. Organization and Culture*. Nishinomiya: Kwansei Gakuin University; Tokyo and New York: Kodansha International.

Hofstede, G.H. (in press). Der Kulturelle Kontext Psychologischer Prozesse. In G. Trommsdorff & H.-J. Kornadt (eds.), *Enzyklopädie der Psychologie*. (Themenbereich C Theorie und Forschung, Serie VII Kulturvergleichende Psychologie. Band 1: Theorien und Methoden in der Kulturvergleichenden und Kulturpsychologischen Forschung.) Göttingen: Hogrefe.

Hofstede, G.H. & J. Soeters 2002. Consensus Societies with Their Own Character. National Cultures in Japan and the Netherlands, *Comparative Sociology*, 1, 1-16.

Holden, N.J. 2002. *Cross-Cultural Management. A Knowledge Management Perspective*. London: Prentice Hall.

Hong, Y., G. Ip, C. Chiu, M.W. Morris & T. Menon (in press). Cultural Identity and Dynamic Construction of the Self. Collective Duties and Individual Rights in Chinese and American Cultures. *Social Cognition*.

Hong, Y.Y., M. Morris, C.Y. Chiu & V. Benet-Martinez 2000. Multicultural Minds. *American Psychologist*, 55, 709-720.

Hope, C.A. & A.P. Mühlemann 1998. Total Quality, Human Resource Management and Tourism. *Tourism Economics*. London: Prentice-Hall.

Hoppe, M.H. 1990. *A Comparative Study of Country Elites. International Differences in Work-related Values and Learning and their Implications for Management Training and Development*. (Unpublished PhD Thesis.) Chapel Hill: University of North Carolina.

Horenczyck, G. 1996. Migrant Identities in Conflict. Acculturation Attitudes and Perceived Acculturation Ideologies. Pp. 241-250 in G. Breakwell & E. Lyons (eds.), *Changing European Identities*. Oxford: Butterworth-Heinemann.

Hormuth, S.E., W.R. Heinz, H.J. Kornadt, H. Sydow & G. Trommsdorff 1996. *Berichte zum Sozialen und Politischen Wandel in Ostdeutschland*. (Berichte der Kommission für die Erforschung des Sozialen und Politischen Wandels in den Neuen Bundesländern e.V. (KSPW): Band 4. Individuelle Entwicklung, Bildung und Berufsverläufe.) Opladen: Leske + Budrich.

House of Commons 1992. *The Health Committee Second Report. Maternity Services*. (Volume XX.) London: HMSO.

Hui, C.H. 1988. Measurement of Individualism-Collectivism. *Journal of Research in Personality*, 22, 17-36.

Hui, C.H. & H.C. Triandis 1985. Measurements in Cross-Cultural Psychology. *Journal of Cross-Cultural Psychology*, 16, 131–152.

Hundley, V., A.M. Rennie, A. Fitzmaurice, W. Graham, E. van Teijlingen & G. Penney 2000. A National Survey of Women's Views of Their Maternity Care in Scotland. *Midwifery*, 16, 303-313.

Huntington, S.P. 1993. The Clash of Civilizations. *Foreign Affairs*, 72, 22-49.

Iannaccone, L.R. 1991. The Consequences of Religious Market Structure. *Rationality and Society*, 3/2.

Iannaccone, L.R., R. Finke & R. Stark 1997. Deregulating Religion: The Economics of Church and State. *Economic Inquiry*, 35/2, 350-364.

Inglehart, R. 1971. The Silent Revolution in Europe. Intergenerational Change in Post-industrial Societies. *American Political Science Review* 65, 4, 991-1017.

Inglehart, R. 1990. *Culture Shift in Advanced Industrial Society*. Princeton: Princeton University Press.

Inglehart, R. 1994. Polarized Priorities or Flexible Alternatives? Dimensionality in Inglehart's Materialism-Postmaterialism-Scale: A Comment. *International Journal of Public Opinion Research*, 6, 289-297.

Inglehart, R. 1997. *Modernization and Postmodernization: Cultural, Economic, and Political Change in 43 Societies*. Princeton, NJ: Princeton University Press.

Inglehart, R 2003. How Solid Is Mass Support for Democracy — And How Can We Measure It? *PS: Political Science and Politics*, 51-57.

Inglehart, R. & P.R. Abramson 1999. Measuring Postmaterialism. *American Political Science Review*, 93, 665-677.

Inglehart, R., & W.E. Baker 2000. Modernization, Cultural Change, and the Persistence of Traditional Values. *American Sociological Review*, 65, 19-51.

Inglehart, R., M. Basanez & A. Moreno 1998. *Human Values and Beliefs. A Cross-*

cultural Sourcebook. Ann Arbor: University of Michigan Press.

Inglehart, R. & C. Welzel (forthcoming). *Culture and Democracy. The Impact of Self-expression Values* (book manuscript under review).

Inkeles, A. 1983. *Exploring Individual Modernity*. New York: Columbia University Press. [291]

Jackson, T. 2001. Cultural Values and Management Ethics. A 10-Nation Study. *Human Relations*, 54, 1267-1302.

Jagodzinski, W. 1983. Materialism in Japan Reconsidered: Toward a Synthesis of Generational and Life-Cycle Explanations. *American Political Science Review*, 77, 887-894.

Jagodzinski, W. 1984a. Wie Transformiert Man Labile in Stabile Relationen? Zur Persistenz Postmaterialistischer Wertorientierungen, *Zeitschrift für Soziologie*, 13, 225-242.

Jagodzinski, W. 1984b. The Identification of Parameters in Cohort Models. *Sociological Methods and Research*, 12, 375-398.

Jagodzinski, W. 1996. The Metamorphosis of Life Cycle Change in Longitudinal Studies on Postmaterialism. In C. Hayashi & E.K. Scheuch (eds.), *Quantitative Social Research in Germany and Japan*. Opladen: Leske + Budrich.

Jagodzinski, W. & K. Dobbelaere. 1995. Secularization and Church Religiosity. In J. van Deth & E. Scarbrough (eds.), *The Impact of Values*. Oxford: Oxford University Press.

Jagodzinski, W. & M. Klein. 1998. Individualisierungskonzepte aus Individualistischer Perspektive. Ein erster Versuch in das Dickicht der Individualisierungskonzepte Einzudringen. In J. Friedrichs (ed.), *Die Individualisierungsthese*. Opladen: Leske + Budrich.

Javidan, M. & R.J. House 2002a. Leadership and Cultures around the World. Findings from GLOBE. An Introduction to the Special Issue. *Journal of World Business*, 37, 1-2.

Javidan, M. & R.J. House 2002b. Special issue on GLOBE-findings. *Journal of World Business*, 37, 1-89.

Jewell, D., G. Young & L. Zander 1990. *The Case for General Practice Maternity Care*. Penrith: Association for GP Maternity Care.

Johnstone, B. 1989. Linguistic Strategies and Cultural Styles for Persuasive Discourse. In S. Ting-Toomey & F. Korzenny (eds.), *Language, Communication, and Culture. Current directions*. Newbury Park, CA: Sage Publications.

Jones, C., G. Taylor & D. Nickson 1997. Whatever it Takes? Managing 'Empowered' Employees and the Service Encounter in an International Hotel Chain. *Work, Employment & Society*, 11, 3, 541-554.

Jones, J.M. 1999. Toward a Cultural Psychology of African Americans. Pp. 52-62 in W.J. Lonner, D.L. Dinnel, D.K. Forgays, & S.A. Hayes (eds.) *Merging Past, Present, and Future in Cross-Cultural Psychology*. Lisse: Swets & Zeitlinger.

Kağitçibâşi, Ç. 1982. Old-age Security Value of Children. Cross-national Socioeconomic Evidence. *Journal of Cross-Cultural Psychology*, 13, 29-42.

Kağitçibâşi, Ç. 1996. *Family and Human Development across Cultures: A View from the Other Side*. Mahwah, NJ: Erlbaum.

[292] Kağitçibâşi, Ç. 1997. Individualism and Collectivism. Pp. 1-50 in J.W. Berry, M.H. Segall, & Ç. Kağitçibâşi (eds.), *Handbook of Cross-cultural Psychology*. (Volume 3, second edition.) Boston: Allyn & Bacon.

Kağitçibâşi, Ç. 1990. Family and Socialisation in Cross-Cultural Perspective. Pp. 135-199 in J. Berman (ed.), *Nebraska Symposium on Motivation*. Lincoln: University of Nebraska Press.

Kağitçibâşi, Ç. 2001. *Development of Self and Competence in Cultural Context*. (Uhlenbeck Lecture 19.) Wassenaar: NIAS.

Kahn, B.E. & R.K. Sarin 1988. Modeling Ambiguity in Decisions under Uncertainty. *Journal of Consumer Research*, 15, 2, 265-271.

Kahneman, D. 2000. *Choices, Values, and Frames*. New York: Russell Sage Foundation.

Kaufmann, D., A. Kraay & P. Zoido-Lobatón 1999. *Aggregating Governance Indicators*. (Working Paper.) Washington, DC: The World Bank.

Kawamura, N. 1994. *Sociology and the Society of Japan*, London/New York: Kegan and Paul.

Kent, J. 2000. Social Perspectives on Pregnancy and Childbirth for Midwives, Nurses and the Caring Profession. Buckingham: Open University Press.

Kim, U., H.C. Triandis, Ç. Kâgitçibâsi, S.C. Choi & G. Yoon (eds.) 1994. *Individualism and Collectivism. Theory, Method, and Applications*. Thousand Oaks, CA: Sage Publications.

Klages, H. & W. Herbert 1983. *Wertorientierung und Staatsbezug. Untersuchungen zur Politischen Kultur in der Bundesrepublik Deutschland*. Frankfurt: Campus.

Klein, M. & K. Arzheimer. 1999. Ranking- und Rating-Verfahren zur Messung von Wertorientierungen, Untersucht am Beispiel des Inglehart-Index. *Kölner Zeitschrift für Soziologie und Sozialpsychologie*, 51/3, 550-564.

Klidas, A. 2001. *Employee Empowerment in the European Hotel Industry. Meaning, Process and Cultural Relativity*. Amsterdam: Rozenberg Publishers.

Kluckhohn, C. 1951. Values and Value-orientations in the Theory of Action. An Exploration in Definition and Classification. In T. Parsons & E.A. Shils (eds.), *Towards a General Theory of Action*. Cambridge: Harvard University Press.

Kluckhohn, K. 1954. Culture and Behavior. Pp. 921-976 in G. Lindzey (ed.), *Handbook of Social Psychology*. (Volume 2.) Cambridge, MA: Addison-Wesley.

Kluckhohn, K. & F. Strodtbeck 1961. *Variations in Value Orientations*. Evanston, IL: Row, Peterson.

Kmieciak, P. 1976. *Wertstrukturen und Wertwandel in der Bundesrepublik. Grundlagen einer Interdisziplinären Empirischen Wertforschung mit einer Sekundäranalyse von Umfragedaten*. Göttingen: Schwartz.

Kohn, M.L. 1969. *Class and Conformity. A Study in Values*. Homewood, IL: Dorsey.

Kohn, M.L. & C. Schooler 1983. *Work and Personality*. Norwood, NJ: Ablex.

Koopman, P.L., D.N. den Hartog, E. Konrad et al. 1999. National Culture and Leadership Profiles in Europe. Some Results from the GLOBE Study. *European Journal of Work and Organisational Psychology*, 8, 4, 503-520.

Kras, E.S. 1989. *Management in Two Cultures. Bridging the Gap between U.S. and Mexican Managers.* Yarmouth, ME: Intercultural Press.

Krosnick, J.A. & D.F. Alwin 1988. A Test of the Form-Resistant Correlation Hypothesis. Ratings, Rankings, and the Measurement of Values. *Public Opinion Quarterly,* 52, 526-538. [293]

Kuronen M. 1994. *Lapsen Hyväksi Naisten Kesken. Tutkimus Äitiys- ja Lastenneuvolan Toimintakäytännöistä.* (For the Benefit of the Child, among Women. A Study of the Practices of Maternity and Child Health Centers.) Helsinki: Stakes.

La Porta, R., F. Lopez-de-Silanes et al. 1999. The Quality of Government. *The Journal of Law, Economics, and Organization,* 15, 1, 222-279.

Lafromboise, T., H. Coleman & J. Gerton 1993. Psychological Impact of Biculturalism. *Psychological Bulletin,* 114, 395-412.

Lalonde, R.N. & J.E. Cameron 1993. An Intergroup Perspective on Immigrant Acculturation with a Focus on Collective Strategies. *International Journal of Psychology,* 16, 23-49.

Lashley, C. 1996. Research Issues for Employee Empowerment in Hospitality Organisations. *International Journal of Hospitality Management,* 15, 4, 333-346.

Lashley, C. 1997. *Empowering Service Excellence. Beyond the Quick Fix.* London: Cassell.

Lautmann, R. 1969. *Wert und Norm. Begriffsanalysen für die Soziologie.* Opladen: Westdeutscher Verlag.

Lehto, J. & P. Blomster 1999. 1990-Luvun Alun Lama Ja Sosiaali — Ja Terveyspolitiikan Suunta. (The Recession of the Early 1990s and the Direction of Social and Health Policy.) *Hteiskuntapolitiikka,* 64, 207-221.

Lesthaege, R. (ed.) 2000. *Communities and Generations.* Brussels: VUB Press.

Leung, K. & M. Bond 1988. On the Empirical Identification of Dimensions for Cross-cultural Comparison. *Journal of Cross-Cultural Psychology,* 20, 133-151.

Leung, K. & M.H. Bond 2003. Social Axioms. A model of Social Beliefs in Multicultural Perspective. Manuscript for *Advances in Experimental Social Psychology.*

Leung, K., M.H. Bond, S. Reimel de Carrasquel, C. Munoz, M. Hernandez, F. Murakami, S. Yamaguchi, G. Bierbrauder & T.M. Singelis 2002. Social Axioms. The Search for Universal Dimensions of General Beliefs about How the World Functions. *Journal of Cross-Cultural Psychology,* 33, 286-302.

Levine, R. 1997. *A Geography of Time.* New York: Basic Books.

Levinson, D. & M.J. Malone 1980. *Toward Explaining Human Culture.* New Haven: HRAF Press.

Levinson, D. 1990. Bibliography of Substantive Worldwide Cross-Cultural Studies. *Behavior Science Research,* 24, 105-140.

Lewin, K. 1936. *Principles of Topological Psychology.* New York: McGraw-Hill.

Lewis, B.R. 1995. Customer Care in Services. In W.J. Glynn & J.G. Barnes (eds.), *Understanding Services Management.* Chichester: John Wiley & Sons.

Leyendecker, B., R.L. Harwood, M.E. Lamb & A. Schoelmerich 2002. Mothers' Socialisation Goals and Evaluations of Desirable and Undesirable Everyday Situations in Two Diverse Cultural Groups. *International Journal of Behavioral Development*, 26, 248-258.

Li, J. & C.E. Labig Jr. 1996. Creative Relationship-focused Negotiations in International Business. *Creativity and Innovation Management*, 5, 2, 99-106.

Liebkind, K. 2001. Acculturation. In R. Brown & S.L. Gaertner (eds.), *Blackwell Handbook of Social Psychology. Intergroup Processes*. Oxford: Blackwell.

Lomax, A. & W. Berkowitz 1972. The Evolutionary Taxonomy of Culture. *Science*, 1777, 228-239.

Lynn, R. 1971. *Personality and National Character*. Oxford: Pergamon.

Lytle, A.L. 1995. The Influence of Culture in Negotiation. *A Comparitive Intracultural Study*. University Microfilms No. 95-21759

Lijphart, A. & M.L. Crepaz 1991. Corporatism and Consensus Democracy in Eighteen Countries. Conceptual and Empirical Linkages. *British Journal of Political Science*, 21, 2, 235-246.

Manabe, K. & H. Befu 1989. An Empirical Investigation of *Nihonjinron*. The Degree of Exposure of Japanese to *Nihonjinron* Propositions and the Functions these Propositions Serve (Part 1). *Kwansei Gakuin University Annual Studies*, 38, 35–62.

Manabe, K. & H. Befu 1989. An Empirical Investigation of *Nihonjinron*: The Degree of Exposure of Japanese to *Nihonjinron* Propositions and the Functions these Propositions Serve (Part 2). *Kwansei Gakuin University Annual Studies*, 39, 139–167.

Mannheim, K. 1928/1929. Das Problem der Generationen. *Kölner Vierteljahresheft für Soziologie*, 7, 157-185, 309-330.

Marander-Eklund, L. 2000. Berättelser om Barnafödande. Form, Innehåll och Betydelse i Kvinnors Muntliga Skildring av Födsel. (Narratives about Giving Birth. Form, Content and Meaning in Women's Oral Description of Birth.) Åbo: Åbo Akademi University Press.

Markus, H. & S. Kitayama 1991. Culture and Self. Implications for Cognition, Emotion, and Motivation. *Psychological Review*, 98, 224-253.

Markus, H.R. & S. Kitayama 1994. The Cultural Construction of Self and Emotion. Implications for Social Behavior. Pp. 89-130 in S. Kitayama & H.R. Markus (eds.), *Emotion and Culture. Empirical Studies of Mutual Influence*. Washington, DC: American Psychological Association.

Martin, D. 1978. *A General Theory of Secularization*. Oxford: Basil Blackwell.

Martin J.A., B.E. Hamilton, S.J. Ventura, F. Menacker & M.M. Park 2002. *Births. Final Data for 2000. National Vital Statistics Reports*. (Volume 50, nr. 5.) Hyattsville, MD: National Center for Health Statistics.

Maslow, A.H. 1954. *Motivation and Personality*. New York (etc.): Harper & Row.

Mathews T.J., F. Menacker & M.F. MacDorman 2002. Infant Mortality Statistics from the 2000 Period Linked Birth/Infant Death Data Set. *National vital statistics reports*. (Volume 50, nr. 12.) Hyattsville, MD: National Center for Health Statistics.

Mauro, P. 1995. Corruption and Growth. *The Quarterly Journal of Economics*, 110, 3, 681-712.

Maxwell, G.A. 1997. Empowerment in the UK Hospitality Industry. In M. Foley et al. (eds.), *Hospitality, Tourism and Leisure Management*. London: Cassell.

Mayer, B. & G. Trommsdorff 2003. *Child-related Value Structures of East and West German Mothers*. Paper presented at the 6th Regional Congress of the International Association of Cross-Cultural Psychology, Budapest, Hungary.

McClelland, D.C. 1961. *The Achieving Society*. Princeton, NJ: Van Nostrand.

McClelland, D.C. 1985. *Human Motivation*. Glenview, Ill.: Scott, Foresman.

McClelland, D.C., J.W. Atkinson, R.A. Clark & E.L. Lowell 1953. *The Achievement Motive*. New York: Appleton-Century-Crofts.

Meulemann, H. (ed.) 1998. *Werte und Nationale Identität im Vereinten Deutschland*. Opladen: Leske + Budrich.

Minge-Klevana, W. 1980. Does Labor Time Decrease with Industrialization? A Survey of Time-allocation Studies. *Current Anthropology*, 21, 279-287.

Mintu-Wimsatt, A. & J.B. Gassenheimer 2000. The Moderating Effects of Cultural Context in Buyer-Seller Negotiation. *The Journal of Personal Selling and Sales Management*, 20,1, 1-9.

Moghaddam, F.M. 1988. Individualistic and Collective Integration Strategies among Immigrants. Towards a Mobility Model of Cultural Integration. Pp. 114-124 in J.W. Berry & R.C. Annis (eds.), *Ethnic Psychology*. Lisse: Swets & Zeitlinger.

Möller, K. 1983. Sozialwissenschaftliche Implikationen des Humanistisch-Psychologischen Bedürfnis-begriffs bei Abraham Maslow. *Kölner Zeitschrift für Soziologie und Sozialpsychologie*, 35, 555-576.

Montreuil, A. & R.Y. Bourhis 2001. Majority Acculturation Orientations towards Valued and Devalued Immigrants. *Journal of Cross-Cultural Psychology*, 32, 698-719.

Moran, R.T. & W.G. Stripp 1991. *Dynamics of Successful International Business Negotiations*. Houston: Gulf Publishing Company.

Morrison, D.G. & H.M. Stevenson 1972. Integration and Instability. Patterns of African Political Development. *American Political Science Review*, 66, 3, 902-927.

Mosakowski, E. & P.C. Earley 2000. A Selective Review of Time Assumptions in Strategy Research. *Academy of Management Review*, 25, 796-812.

Moss Kanter, R & R. Cron 1994. Do Cultural Differences Make a Business Difference? Contextual Factors Affecting Cross-Cultural Relationship Success. *Journal of Management Development*, 13, 5-23.

Müller, H.-P. 1996. Kulturelle Gliederung der Entwicklungsländer. Pp. 81-137 in H.-P. Müller (ed.), *Weltsystem und Kulturelles Erbe. Gliederung und Dynamik der Entwicklungsländer aus Ethnologischer und Soziologischer Sicht*. Berlin: Reimer.

Müller, H.-P., C. Kock et al. 1992. *Kulturelles Erbe und Entwicklung. Indikatoren zur Bewertung des Sozio-kulturellen Entwicklungsstandes*. München.

Müller, H.-P., C. Kock et al. 1999. *Atlas Vorkolonialer Gesellschaften. Sozialstruk-*

turen und Kulturelles Erbe der Staaten Afrikas, Asiens und Melanesiens. Berlin: Reimer.

[296] Müller, H.-P., P. Ziltener et *al.* 2001. *Cultural and Political Foundations of Socio-economic Development in Africa and Asia.* Geneva/Zurich: United Nations Institute for Training and Research (UNITAR).

Naroll, R. 1973. Galton's Problem. Pp. 974-989 in R. Naroll & R. Cohen (eds.), *A Handbook of Method in Cultural Anthropology.* New York: Columbia University Press.

National Center for Health Statistics 2002. *2000 Natality Data Set.* (Series 21, Nr. 14, CD-ROM.)

National Pensions Office 2000. Statistics on Fatherhood Leave.

Nauck, B. 2001. Social Capital, Intergenerational Transmission and Intercultural Contact in Immigrant Families. *Journal of Comparative Family Studies,* 32, 465-488.

Nauck, B. 2001. Der Wert von Kindern für Ihre Eltern. "Value of Children" als Spezielle Handlungstheorie des Generativen Verhaltens und von Generationenbeziehungen im Interkulturellen Vergleich. *Kölner Zeitschrift für Soziologie und Sozialpsychologie, 53,* 407-435.

Nisbett, R.E. 2003. *The Geography of Thought.* New York: Free Press.

Nisbett, R.E. & D. Cohen 1996. *Culture of Honor. The Psychology of Violence in the South.* Boulder, CO: Westview Press.

Nisbett, R.E., K. Peng, I. Choi & A. Norensayan 2001. Culture and Systems of Thought. Holistic versus Analytic Cognition. *Psychological Review,* 108, 291-310.

Nolan, P.D. 2002. Ecological Evolutionary Theory. A Reanalysis and Reassessment of Lenski's Theory for the 21st Century. *Annual Meeting of the American Sociological Association* (ASA). Chicago, IL: ASA.

Nolan, P.D. & G. Lenski 1996. Technology, Ideology, and Societal Development. *Sociological Perspectives,* 39, 1, 23-38.

Nomura Sôgô Kenkyûjo 1978: *Nihonjinron.* Tôkyô: Nomura Sôgô Kenkyûjo (NRI Reference, 2).

Norenzayan, A., I. Choi & R.E. Nisbett 1999. Eastern and Western Perceptions of Causality for Social Behavior. Lay Theories about Personalities and Situations. Pp. 239-272 in D.A. Prentice & D.T. Miller (eds.), *Cultural Divides. Understanding and Overcoming Group Conflict.* New York: Russell Sage Foundation.

NOV 1996. *Bevallen in Nederland. Informatie over Zwangerschap en Begeleiding door de Verloskundige.* (Giving Birth in the Netherlands. Information on Pregnancy and Guidance by the Midwife.) Bilthoven: NOV.

Office for National Statistics 2001. Mean Duration of In-patient Maternity Episodes 1981-1999. Social Trends 31. London: The Stationary Office. http://www.statistics.gov.uk/StatBase/Expodata/Spreadsheets/D3523.xls

Olsen, G. 2002. *The Politics of the Welfare State. Canada, Sweden, and the United States.* Don Mills: Oxford University Press.

Osland, J.S. & A. Bird 2000. Beyond Sophisticated Stereotyping. Cultural Sense-making in Context. *Academy of Management Executive*, 14, 1, 65-79.

Øvretveit, J. 1992. *Health Service Quality*. Oxford: Blackwell Scientific Press.

Oyserman, D. 1993. The Lens of Personhood. *Journal of Personality and Social Psychology*, 65, 993-1005. [297]

Oyserman, D., H.M. Coon & M. Kemmelmeier 2002. Rethinking Individualism and Collectivism. Evaluation of Theoretical Assumptions and Meta-analysis. *Psychological Bulletin*, 128,1, 3-72.

Oyserman, D., M. Kemmelmeier & H.M. Coon 2002. Cultural Psychology. A New Look. *Psychological Bulletin*, 128,1, 110-117.

Payer, L. 1990. *Medicine & Culture. Notions of Health & Sickness in Britain, the U.S., France & West Germany*. London: Victor Gollancz Ltd.

Pelto, P.J. 1968. The Difference Between "Tight" and "Loose" Societies. *Transaction*, 37-40.

Phalet, K. & W. Claeys 1993. A Comparative Study of Turkish and Belgian Youth. *Journal of Cross-Cultural Psychology*, 24, 319-343.

Phalet, K. & L. Hagendoorn 1996. Personal Adjustment to Acculturative Transitions. *International Journal of Psychology*, 31, 131-144.

Phalet, K. & W. Lens 1995. Achievement Motivation and Group Loyalty among Turkish and Belgian Youth. Pp. 31-72 in P. Pintrich & M. Maehr (eds.), *Advances in Motivation and Achievement*. Greenwich, CT: JAI Press.

Phalet, K. & U. Schönpflug 2001. Intergenerational Transmission in Turkish Immigrant Families. *Journal of Comparative Family Studies*, 32, 489-504.

Phalet, K. & M. Swyngedouw 2002. National Identities and Representations of Citizenship. *Ethnicities*, 2, 1, 5-30.

Phinney, J.S. & J. Flores 2002. Unpackaging Acculturation. Aspects of Acculturation as Predictors of Traditional Sex Roles. *Journal of Cross-Cultural Psychology*, 33, 320-331.

Piontkowski, U., A. Florack, P. Hölker & P. Obdrzalek 2000. Predicting Acculturation Attitudes of Dominant and Non-dominant Groups. *International Journal of Intercultural Relations*, 24, 1-26.

Porter, M. 1990. Professional-client relationships and women's reproductive health care. Pp. 182-210 in S. Cunningham-Burley & N.P. McKeganey (eds.) *Readings in Medical Sociology*. London: Tavistock/Routledge.

Pott-Buter, H.A. 1993. *Fact and Fairy Tales about Female Labor, Family and Fertility. A Seven Country Comparison, 1850-1990*. Amsterdam: Amsterdam University Press.

Price, F.V. 1990. Who Helps? Pp. 131- 152 in B.J. Bottin, A.J. Macfarlane & F.V. Price (eds.), *Three, Four and More. A Study of Triplet and Higher Order Births*. London: HMSO.

Prince-Gibson, E. & S.H. Schwartz 1998. Value Priorities and Gender. *Social Psychology Quarterly*, 61, 49-67.

Pryor, F.L. 1985. The Invention of the Plow. *Sociology and History*, 27, 727-743.

Pryor, F.L. 1986. The Adoption of Agriculture. *American Anthropologist*, 88, 879-897.

Putnam, L.L. & M. Holmer 1992. Framing, Reframing, and Issue Development. Pp. 128-155 in L.L. Putnam & M.E. Roloff (eds.), *Communication and Negotiation.* Newbury Park: Sage Publications.

[298]   Putnam, R.D. 1993. *Making Democracy Work. Civic Traditions in Modern Italy.* Princeton, NJ: Princeton University Press.

Putnam, R.D. 2000. *Bowling Alone. The Collapse and Revival of American Community.* New York etc.: Simon & Schuster.

Putterman, L. 2000. Can an Evolutionary Approach to Development Predict Postwar Growth? *The Journal of Development Studies*, 36, 1-30.

Rae, D.W. & M. Taylor 1970. *The Analysis of Political Cleavages.* New Haven: Yale University Press.

RCOG Clinical Effectiveness Unit 2001. *The National Sentinel Caesarean Section Audit Report.* London: RCOG.

Riesman, D. 1952. *The Lonely Crowd. A Study of Changing American Character.* New Haven, CO: Yale University Press.

Ripley, R.E. and M.J. Ripley 1992. Empowerment, the Cornerstone of Quality. Empowering Management in Innovative Organisations in the 1990s. *Management Decision*, 30, 4, 20-43.

Riteco, J. & L. Hingstman 1991. *Evaluatie Invoering "Verloskundige Indicatielijst".* (Evaluation of the Implementation of the "Obstetric Indications List".) Utrecht: NIVEL.

Roccas, S., G. Horenczyck & S.H. Schwartz 2000. Acculturation Discrepancies and Wellbeing. The Moderating Role of Conformity. *European Journal of Social Psychology*, 30, 323-334.

Rokeach, M. 1973. *The Nature of Human Values.* New York: Free Press.

Ronen, S. & O. Shenkar 1985. Clustering Countries on Attitudinal Dimensions. A Review and Synthesis. *Academy of Management Review*, 10, 3, 435-454.

Rosaldo, R. 1993. *Culture and Truth. The Remaking of Social Analysis.* Boston: Beacon Press.

Rothbaum, F., M. Pott, H. Azuma, K. Miyake & J. Weisz 2000. The Development of Close Relationships in Japan and the United States. Paths of Symbiotic Harmony and Generative Tension. *Child Development*, 71, 1121-1142.

Rothbaum, F. & G. Trommsdorff 2003. *Tradeoffs in Autonomy. How it Fosters and Undermines Relatedness.* Paper presented at the 2003 Biennial Meeting of the Society for Research in Child Development, Tampa, Florida, USA.

Rozman, G. (ed.) 1991. *The East Asian Region. Confucian Heritage and its Modern Adaptation.* Princeton: Princeton University.

Russell, B. 1979 (1927). *An Outline of Philosophy.* London: Unwin.

Rybcinski, W. 1986. *Home.* New York: Penguin

Ryder, A.G., L.E. Alden & D.L. Paulhus 2000. Is Acculturation Unidimensional or Bidimensional? *Journal of Personality and Social Psychology*, 79, 49-65.

Sachs, J.D. & A. Warner 1997. Sources of Slow Growth in African Economies. *Journal of African Economy*, 6, 335-76.

Sagiv, L. & S.H. Schwartz 2000. National Cultures. Implications for Organizational Structure and Behavior. Pp. 417-436 in N.N. Ashkanasy, C. Wilderom & M.F. Peterson (eds.), *The Handbook of Organizational Culture and Climate.* Newbury Park, CA: Sage.

Sawyer, J. & H. Guetzkow. 1965. Bargaining Behavior in International Relations. In Herbert C. Kelman, (ed.), *International Relations: A Social-Psychological Analysis.* New York: Holt, Rinehart, & Winston.

Sayegh, L. & J.-C. Lasry 1993. Immigrants' Adaptation in Canada. *Canadian Psychology,* 34, 98-109.

Scheepers, P., G. Verberck & M. Coenders 2001. Recent Dutch Research on Ethnocentrism in an International Perspective. Pp. 59-84 in K. Phalet & A. Orkeny (eds.), *Ethnic Minorities and Inter-ethnic Relations in Context.* Aldershot: Ashgate.

Schofer, E. & M. Fourcade-Gourinchas 2001. The Structural Contexts of Civic Engagement. Voluntary Association Membership in Comparative Perspective. *American Sociological Review,* 66, 806-828.

Scholl-Schaaf, M. 1975. *Werthaltung und Wertsystem: Ein Plädoyer für die Verwendung des Wertkonzepts in der Sozialpsychology.* Bonn: Bouvier.

Schönpflug, U. 2001. Intergenerational Transmission of Values. The Role of Transmission Belts. *Journal of Cross-Cultural Psychology,* 32, 174-185.

Schmuck, P., T. Kasser & R.M. Ryan 2000. Intrinsic and Extrinsic Goals. *Social Indicators Research,* 50, 225-241.

Schwartz, S.H. 1992. Universals in the Content and Structure of Values. Theoretical Advances and Empirical Tests in 20 Countries. Pp. 1-66 in M. Zanna (ed.) *Advances in Experimental Social Psychology.* (Volume 25.) New York: Academic Press.

Schwartz, S.H. 1994a. Are there Universal Aspects in the Content and Structure of Values? *Journal of Social Issues,* 50, 19-45.

Schwartz, S.H. 1994b. Beyond Individualism/Collectivism. New Cultural Dimensions of Values. Pp. 85-119 in U. Kim, H.C. Triandis, C. Kağitçibâşi, S-C. Choi & G. Yoon (eds.), *Individualism and Collectivism. Theory, Method and Applications.* Newbury Park, CA: Sage.

Schwartz, S.H. 1996. Value Priorities and Behavior. Pp. 1-24 in C. Seligman, J.M. Olson & P. Zanna (eds.), *The Psychology of Values. The Ontario Symposium* (Volume 18.) Hillsdale, NJ: Erlbaum.

Schwartz, S.H. 1999. Cultural Value Differences. Some Implications for Work. *Applied Psychology. An International Review,* 48, 23-47.

Schwartz, S.H. 2003. Mapping and Interpreting Cultural Differences around the World. In H. Vinken, J. Soeters & P. Ester (eds.), *Comparing Cultures. Dimensions of Culture in a Comparative Perspective.* Leiden & Boston: Brill.

Schwartz, S.H. & A. Bardi 1997. Influences of Adaptation to Communist Rule on Value Priorities in Eastern Europe. *Political Psychology,* 18, 385-410.

Schwartz, S.H. & A. Bardi. 2001. Value Hierarchies Across Cultures. *Journal of Cross-Cultural Psychology,* 32, 268-290.

Schwartz, S.H., A. Bardi & G. Bianchi 2000. Value Adaptation to the Imposition and Collapse of Communist Regimes in Eastern Europe. Pp. 217-237 in S.A. Renshon & J. Duckitt (eds.), *Political Psychology. Cultural and Cross-cultural Perspectives.* London: Macmillan.

Schwartz, S.H. & W. Bilsky 1990. Toward a Theory of the Universal Content and Structure of Values. Extensions and Cross-cultural Replications. *Journal of Personality and Social Psychology*, 58, 878-891.

[300]

Schwartz, S.H., G. Melech, A. Lehmann, S. Burgess, M. Harris & V. Owens 2001. Extending the Cross-Cultural Validity of the Theory of Basic Human Values with a Different Method of Measurement. *Journal of Cross-Cultural Psychology*, 32, 519-542.

Schwartz, S.H., & M. Ros 1995. Values in the West. A Theoretical and Empirical Challenge to the Individualism-Collectivism Cultural Dimension. *World Psychology*, 1, 99-122.

Schwartz, S.H. & L. Savig 1995. Identifying Culture-specifics in the Content and Structure of Values. *Journal of Cross-Cultural Psychology*, 26, 1, 92-116.

Schwartz, S.H., N. Struch & W. Bilsky 1990. Values and Intergroup Motives. *Social Psychology Quarterly*, 53, 185-198.

Schwarz, B., E. Schäfermeier & G. Trommsdorff (in press). The Relationships between Value Orientation, Child-rearing Goals, and Child-rearing Behavior: A Comparison of Korean and German mothers. In W. Friedlmeier, P. Chakkarath & B. Schwarz (eds.), *Culture and Human Development. The Importance of Crosscultural Research to the Social Sciences.* New York: Swets & Zeitlinger.

Sen, A. 2001. *Development as Freedom.* New York: Alfred Knopf.

Senden I.P., M. van du Wetering, T.K. Eskes, P. Bierkens, D. Laube & R. Pitkin 1988. Labor Pain. A Comparison of Parturients in a Dutch and an American Teaching Hospital. *Obstetrics & Gynecology*, 71, 4, 541-4.

Sheils, D. (1972). The Importance of Agriculture from the Perspective of Neoevolutionary Theory. *Rural Sociology*, 37, 167-188.

SIGN 2002. Postnatal Depression and Puerperal Psychosis. A National Guideline. (Guideline 60.) SIGN: Edinburgh.

Soeters, J. 2000. *Cultuur en Kennis. Over de Problemen Maar Ook de Kansen van Cultuurvergelijkend Onderzoek.* (Culture and Knowledge. On the Problems But Also the Opportunities of Culture-comparative Research.) (Inaugural Address.) Tilburg: Tilburg University.

Sperber, D. 1996. *Explaining Culture. A Naturalistic Approach.* Oxford: Blackwell.

Spini, D. 2003. Structural Equivalence of Value Types across Twenty-one Countries. *Journal of Cross-Cultural Psychology,* 34, 3-23.

Stakes 2001. Statistics Feedback on the Figures Collected for the National Birth Register.

Stakes 2002. Unpublished Information from the National Birth Register.

Stark, R. 1999. Secularization, RIP. *Sociology of Religion*, 60, 249-273.

Stark, R. & L.R. Iannaccone 1994. A Supply-side Reinterpretation of the "Secularization" of Europe. *Journal for the Scientific Study of Religion*, 33, 3, 230-252.

Stephan, W.G., C.W. Stephan & M.C. de Vargas 1996. Emotional Expression in Costa Rica and United States. *Journal of Cross-Cultural Psychology*, 27, 147-160.

Steyer, R. 1992. *Theorie Kausaler Regressionsmodelle.* Stuttgart: Fischer.

Su, S.K., C. Chiu, Y. Hong, K. Leung, K. Peng & M.W. Morris 1999. Self-organiza-
tion and Social Organization. U.S. and Chinese Constructions. Pp. 193-222 in
T.R. Tyler, R.M. Kramer, & O.P. John (eds.), *The Psychology of the Social Self*.
Mahwah, NJ: Lawrence Erlbaum. [301]

Super, C.M. & S. Harkness 1997. The Cultural Structuring of Child development.
Pp. 1-39 in J.W. Berry, P.R. Dasen & T.S. Saraswathi (eds.), *Handbook of Cross-
Cultural Psychology*. (Volume 2, Basic Processes and Human Development, sec-
ond edition). Boston: Allyn & Bacon.

Suppes, P. 1970. *A Probabilistic Theory of Causality*. Amsterdam: North-Holland.

Swank, D. 2002. *Global Capital, Political Institutions, and Policy Change in Developed Welfare States*. Cambridge, New York: Cambridge University Press.

Swyngedouw, M., K. Phalet & K. Deschouwer 1999. *Minderheden in Brussel*.
(Minorities in Brussels.) Brussel: VUB Press.

Tajfel, H. & J.C. Turner 1986. The Social Identity Theory of Intergroup Behavior.
Pp. 7-24 in S. Worchel & W.G. Austin (eds.), *Psychology of Intergroup Relations*. Chicago: Nelson Hall.

Tayeb, M. 1994. Organisations and National Culture. Methodology considered.
Organisation Studies, 15, 3, 429-446.

Taylor, C.L. & M.C. Hudson (eds.) 1972. *World Handbook of Political and Social
Indicators*. New Haven, CT: Yale University Press.

Taylor, D.M. & D.J. McKirnan 1984. A Five-stage Model of Intergroup Relations.
British Journal of Social Psychology, 23, 291-300.

Thurstone, L.L. 1928. Attitudes Can Be Measured. *American Journal of Sociology*,
33, 529-54.

Tôkei Sûri Kenkyûjo Kokuminsei 1961. *Nihonjin no kokuminsei*. (A Study of Japanese National Character). Tôkyô: Shiseidô.

Tôkei Sûri Kenkyôjo Kokuminsei Chôsa Iinkai 1970: *Dai 2 Nihonjin no kokuminsei*.
(A Study of Japanese National Character. Volume 2.) Tôkyô: Shiseidô.

Tôkei Sûri Kenkyûjo Kokuminsei Chôsa Iinkai 1975: *Dai 3 Nihonjin no kokuminsei*.
(A Study of Japanese National Character. Volume 3.) Tôkyô: Shiseidô.

Tôkei Sûri Kenkyûjo Kokuminsei Chôsa Iinkai 1982: *Dai 4 Nihonjin no kokuminsei*.
(A Study of the Japanese National Character. Volume 4.) Tôkyô : Idemitsu Shoten.

Tôkei Sûri Kenkyûjo Kokuminsei Chôsa Iinkai 1992: *Dai 5 Nihonjin no kokuminsei*.
(A Study of the Japanese National Character. Volume 5.) Tôkyô: Idemitsu
Shoten.

Trafimow, D., H.C. Triandis & S. Goto 1991. Some Tests of the Distinction between
Private Self and Collective Self. *Journal of Personality and Social Psychology*,
60, 640-655.

Triandis, H.C. 1964. Cultural Influences upon Cognitive Processes. Pp. 1-48 in L.
Berkowitz (ed.), *Advances in Experimental Social Psychology*. New York: Academic Press.

Triandis, H.C. 1972. *The Analysis of Subjective Culture*. New York: Wiley.

Triandis, H.C. 1976. *Variations in Black and White Perceptions of the Social Environment*. Urbana, IL: University of Illinois Press.

Triandis, H.C. 1989. The Self and Social Behavior in Different Cultural Contexts. *Psychological Review*, 96, 269-289.

Triandis, H.C. 1993. Collectivism and Individualism as Cultural Syndromes. *Cross-Cultural Research*, 27, 155-180.

Triandis, H.C. 1994. *Culture and Social Behavior*. New York: McGraw-Hill.

Triandis, H.C. 1995. *Individualism and Collectivism*. Boulder, CO: Westview Press.

Triandis, H.C. 1996. The Psychological Measurement of Cultural Syndromes. *American Psychologist*, 51, 407-415.

Triandis, H.C. 2000. Dialectics between Cultural and Cross-cultural Psychology. *Asian Journal of Social Psychology*, 3, 185-195.

Triandis, H.C. 2001. Individualism and Collectivism. In D. Matsumoto (ed.) *Handbook of Cross-Cultural Psychology*. New York: Oxford University Press.

Triandis, H.C. & M.J. Gelfand 1998. Converging Measurement of Horizontal and Vertical Individualism and Collectivism. *Journal of Personality and Social Psychology*, 74, 118-128.

Triandis, H.C., Y. Kashima, E. Shimoda & M. Villareal 1986. Acculturation Indices as a Means of Confirming Cultural Differences. *International Journal of Psychology*, 21, 43-70.

Triandis, H.C., C. McCusker & C.H. Hui 1990. Multimethod Probes of Individualism and Collectivism. *Journal of Personality and Social Psychology*, 59, 1006-1020.

Triandis, H.C. & T.M. Singelis 1998. Training to Recognize Individual Differences in Collectivism and Individualism within Culture. *International Journal of Intercultural Relations*, 22, 35-48.

Tripathi, R. C., & U. Leviatan 2003. Individualism and Collectivism. In Search of a Product or Process? *Culture & Psychology*, 9, 79-88.

Trommsdorff, G. 1995. Parent-Adolescent Relations in Changing Societies. A Cross-cultural Study. Pp. 189-218 in P. Noack & M. Hofer (eds.), *Psychological Responses to Social Change. Human Development in Changing Environments*. Berlin: De Gruyter.

Trommsdorff, G. (ed.). 1996. *Sozialisation und Entwicklung von Kindern vor und nach der Vereinigung*. Opladen: Leske + Budrich.

Trommsdorff, G. 2001. *Value of Children and Intergenerational Relations. A Cross-Cultural Psychological Study*. Available: http://www.uni-konstanz.de/FuF/SozWiss/fg-psy/ag-entw/

Trommsdorff, G. 2003. *Parent-Child Relations in the Life Span. A Cross-cultural Perspective*. Paper presented at the ISSBD Asian Regional Workshop "Parental Beliefs, Parenting, and Child Development from Cross-Cultural Perspectives", Seoul, Korea.

Trommsdorff, G. & P. Chakkarath 1996. Kindheit im Transformationsproze·. Pp. 11-77 in S.E. Hormuth, W.R. Heinz, H.-J. Kornadt, H. Sydow & G. Trommsdorff (eds.), *Berichte zum Sozialen und Politischen Wandel in Ostdeutschland*. (Berichte der Kommission für die Erforschung des Sozialen und Politischen Wandels in den Neuen Bundesländern e.V. (KSPW): Band 4. Individuelle Entwicklung, Bildung und Berufsverläufe.) Opladen: Leske + Budrich.

Trommsdorff, G. & P.R. Dasen 2001. Cross-cultural Study of Education. Pp. 3003-

3007 in N.J. Smelser & P.B. Baltes (eds.), *International Encyclopedia of the Social and Behavioral Sciences*. Oxford: Elsevier.

Trommsdorff, G. & W. Friedlmeier (in press). Kultur und Individuum. Ein Beitrag Kulturvergleichender Psychologie zur Rolle Subjektiver Erziehungstheorien. In A. Assmann, U. Gaier & G. Trommsdorff (eds.), *Anthropologie und Literatur.* Konstanz: Universitätsverlag Konstanz.

Trommsdorff, G. & H.-J. Kornadt 2003. Parent-Child Relations in Cross-cultural Perspective. Pp. 271-306 in L. Kuczynski (ed.), *Handbook of Dynamics in Parent-Child Relations*. London: Sage.

Trommsdorff, G. & B. Nauck 2001. *Value of Children in Six Cultures. Eine Replikation und Erweiterung der ,,Value-of-Children-Studies" in Bezug auf Generatives Verhalten und Eltern-Kind-Beziehungen. Antrag an die DFG.* (Unpublished manuscript.) Konstanz: University of Konstanz.

Trommsdorff, G., G. Zheng & T. Tardif 2002. Value of Children and Intergenerational Relations in Cultural Context. Pp. 581-601 in P. Boski, F.J.R. van de Vijver & A.M. Chodynicka (eds.), *New Directions in Cross-cultural Psychology. Selected Papers from the Fifteenth International Conference of the International Association for Cross-cultural Psychology.* Warszawa: Polish Psychological Association.

Trompenaars, F. 1994. *Riding the Waves of Culture. Understanding Diversity in Global Business.* Burr Ridge, IL: Irwin Professional Publishing.

Tu, W.-M. (ed.) 1996. *Confucian Traditions in East Asian Modernity. Moral Education and Economic Culture in Japan and the Four Mini-Dragons.* Cambridge: Harvard University Press.

Turnbull, C.M. 1972. *The Mountain People.* New York: Simon & Schuster.

Van Andel, F.G. & N. Brinkman 1997. Government Policy and Cost Containment of Pharmaceuticals. Pp. 152-162 in A.J.P. Schrijvers (ed.), *Health and Health Care in the Netherlands*. Utrecht: De Tijdstroom.

Van Binsbergen, W. 1999. *Culturen Bestaan Niet. Het Onderzoek naar Interculturaliteit als een Openbreken van Vanzelfsprekendheden.* (Cultures Do Not Exist. The Research Into Interculturality as an Opening-Up of the Obvious.) (Inaugural address.) Rotterdam: Erasmus University.

Van Daalen, R. 1988. De Groei van de Ziekenhuisbevalling. Nederland en het Buitenland. (The Growth of Hospital Birth. The Netherlands and Other Countries). *Amsterdams Sociologisch Tijdschrift*, 15, 3, 414-445.

Van de Vijver, F. & K. Leung 1997. *Methods and Data Analysis for Cross-cultural Research*. London: Sage.

Van de Vijver, F. & K. Phalet (forthcoming). Assessment in Multicultural Groups. The Role of Acculturation. To appear in *Applied Psychology. An International Review.*

Van der Haegen, H., J. Juchtmans & C. Kesteloot 1995. *Multicultureel Brussel.* (Multicultural Brussels.) Brussel: Brussels Hoofdstedelijk Gewest.

Van der Velden, K. 1999. *General practice at work*. Utrecht: NIVEL.

Van Deth, J.W. 1983. Ranking the Ratings. The Case of Materialist and Postmaterialist Value Orientations. *Political Methodology*, 11, 63-79.

Van Deth, J.W. & E. Scarbrough. 1995. The Concept of Values. In J.W. van Deth &

[303]

E. Scarbrough (eds.), *Beliefs in Government. The Impact of Values.* (Volume 4.) Oxford: Oxford University Press.

Van Nimwegen, T. 2002. *Global Banking, Global Values.* Delft: Eburon.

[304] Van Teijlingen, E.R. 1990. The Profession of Maternity Home Care Assistant and Its Significance for the Dutch Midwifery Profession. *International Journal of Nursing Studies,* 27, 355-66.

Van Teijlingen, E.R. 1994. *A Social or Medical Model of Childbirth? Comparing the Arguments in Grampian (Scotland) and the Netherlands.* (Unpublished Ph.D. thesis.) Aberdeen: University of Aberdeen.

Vandello, J. & Cohen, D. 1999. Patterns of Individualism and Collectivism across the U.S. *Journal of Personality and Social Psychology,* 77, 279-292.

Veblen, T. 1953. *The Theory of the Leisure Class.* New York: The New American Library. (Original 1899.)

Verma, J. 2001. Situational Preference for Different Types of Individualism-Collectivism. *Psychology and Developing Societies,* 13, 2, 221-241.

Victor, D. 1992. *International Business Communication.* New York: Harper Collins Publishers.

Vierzigmann, G. & S. Kreher 1998. 'Zwischen den Generationen'. Familiendynamik und Familiendiskurse in biographischen Erzählungen. *Berliner Journal für Sozologie,* 8, 1, 23-37.

Viisainen, K. 2000a. The Moral Dangers of Home Birth. Parents' Perceptions of Risk in Home Birth in Finland. *Sociology of Health and Illness,* 22, 792-814.

Viisainen, K. (2000b). *Choices in Birth care — The Place of Birth.* Helsinki: Stakes.

Vinken, H. 1997. *Political Values and Youth Centrism. Theoretical and Empirical Perspectives on the Political Value Distinctiveness of Dutch Youth Centrists.* Tilburg: Tilburg University Press.

Vinken, H. 2003. Young People's Civic Engagement. The Need for New Perspectives. In G. Holm & H. Helve (eds.), *Youth Research in an International Perspective.* Aldershot: Ashgate (forthcoming).

Vinken, H., J. Soeters & P. Ester 2002. Comparing Cultures of Change. *Sociale Wetenschappen,* 45, 2, 1-8 (Special Issue).

Von Glinow, M-A., E.A. Drost & M.B. Teagarden 2002. Converging on IHRM Best Practices. Lessons Learned from a Globally Distributed Consortium on Theory and Practice. *Human Resource Management,* 41, 1, 123-140.

Vuori, J. (2001). *Äidit, Isät ja Ammattilaiset. Sukupuoli, Toisto ja Muunnelmat Asiantuntijoiden Kirjoituksissa.* (Mothers, Fathers and Professionals. Gender, Repetition and Adaptations in Texts Written by Experts.) Tampere: Tampere University Press.

Ward, C., S. Bochner & A.F. Furnham 2001. *The Psychology of Culture Shock.* London: Routledge.

Wasti, S.A. 1998. Cultural Barriers in the Transferability of Japanese and American Human Resources Practices to Developing Countries. The Turkish Case. *Journal of Human Resources Management,* 9, 608-639.

Watanabe, M. 1995. Gendai no Hihon-Jin no Shizen-kan. Seiyo tono Hikaku. (The

Japanese View of Nature in the Modern Era. A Comparison with Westerners). In Ito Shintaro (ed.), *Japanese View of Nature*. Tokyo: Kawade Publishers.

Watson, P.J. & R.J. Morris 2002. Individualist and Collectivist Values. Hypotheses Suggested by Alexis de Tocqueville. *Journal of Psychology*, 136, 263-271. [305]

Weber, M. 1958. *The Protestant Ethic and the Spirit of Capitalism*. New York: Charles Scribner's Sons. (Original 1904-1905; English translation, 1958.)

Welzel, C. 2003. Effective Democracy, Mass Culture, and the Quality of Elites. *International Journal of Comparative Sociology*, 43, 3-5, 269-298.

Welzel, C., R. Inglehart & H.-D. Klingemann 2003. The Theory of Human Development. A Cross-cultural Analysis. *European Journal of Political Research*, 42, 3, 341-379.

Welzel, C. & R. Inglehart 2003. Human Development and the Explosion of Democracy. Analyzing Regime Change across 60 Societies. *WZB-Discussion Paper FS III 01-202*.

Weiss, S.E. & W. Stripp 1985. *Negotiating with Foreign Businesspersons. An Introduction for Americans with Propositions on Six Cultures*. New York: University Graduate School of Business Administration.

Weiss, S.E. & W. Stripp 1998. Negotiating with Foreign Businesspersons. An Introduction for Americans with Propositions on Six Cultures. Pp. 51-118 in S. Niemeier, C.P. Campbell & R. Dirven (eds.), *The Cultural Context in Business Communication*. Amsterdam: John Benjamins Publishing Company.

Wiegers, T. 1997. *Home or Hospital Birth. A Prospective Study of Midwiferycare in the Netherlands*. Utrecht: NIVEL.

Wilkinson, A. 2001. Empowerment. In T. Redman & A. Wilkinson (eds.), *Contemporary Human Resource Management*. Harlow: Prentice-Hall.

Williams, J. & D. Best 1990. *Sex and Psyche. Gender and Self Viewed Cross-culturally*. Newbury Park, CA: Sage.

Williams Jr., R.M. 1968. Values. In E. Sills (ed.), *International Encyclopedia of the Social Sciences*. New York: Macmillan.

Wilson, D.T. & K.E. Kristan Moller 1991. Buyer-Seller Relationships. Alternative Conceptualizations. Pp. 87-107 in S.J. Paliwoda (ed.), *New Perspectives on International Marketing*. New York: Routledge.

Witkin, H.A. & J.W. Berry 1975. Psychological Differentiation in Cross-Cultural Perspective. *Journal of Cross-Cultural Psychology*, 6, 4-87.

Woldemikael, T.M. 1987. Assertion versus Accommodation. A Comparative Approach to Intergroup Relations. *American Behavioral Scientist*, 30, 411-428.

Women's Social Equality 1988. *Population Briefing Paper*. (Number 20.) Washington, DC: Population Crisis Committee.

Wrede, S. 2001. *Decentering Care for Mothers. The Politics of Midwifery and the Design of Finnish Maternity Services*. Åbo: Åbo Akademi University Press.

Wrede, S., C. Benoit & J. Sandall 2001. The State and Birth/The State of Birth. Maternal Health Policy in Three Countries. Pp. 28-50 in R. de Vries et al. (eds.), *Birth by Design. Pregnancy, Maternity Care and Midwifery in North America and Europe*. New York: Routledge.

Wright, S.C., D.M. Taylor & F.M. Moghaddam 1990. Responding to Membership in a Disadvantaged Group. *Journal of Personality and Social Psychology*, 58, 994-1003.

[306]   Yu, T.F.-L. (2001). The Chinese family business as a strategic system: An evolutionary perspective. *International Journal of Entrepreneurial Behaviour & Research*, 7, 1, 22-40.

Zeithaml, V. & L. Berry (1990). *Delivering Quality Service*, New York: Free Press.

Zemke, R. & D. Schaaf (1989) *The Service Edge: 101 Companies that Profit from Customer Care*. New York: New American Library.

Ziltener, P. & H.-P. Müller (2003). The Weight of the Past — Traditional Agriculture and Socio-political Differentiation in African and Asian Societies: A Quantitative Assessment of the Impact on Modern Socio-economic Development (under review).

AUTHORS INDEX

[313]

SUBJECT INDEX